Culture
in
Process

Culture
in
Process

THIRD EDITION

ALAN R. BEALS

University of California, Riverside

Holt, Rinehart and Winston

New York   Chicago   San Francisco   Dallas
Montreal   Toronto   London   Sydney

Acknowledgment is gratefully made to the following copyright holders for permission to reprint excerpts from the works indicated. The Beacon Press for *We, the Tikopia: A Sociological Study of Kinship in Primitive Polynesia*, by Raymond Firth, 1963. (First published in 1936 by George Allen & Unwin Ltd.). Harper & Row, Publishers, Inc., for pp. 291–292 of "A Reformer of His People," by David G. Mandelbaum, in *In the Company of Man*, ed. Joseph. B. Casagrande. By permission of Harper & Row, Publishers, Inc. Kroeber Anthropological Society, for "Deviancy and Social Control: What Makes Biboi Run," by Robert Murphy, *Kroeber Anthropological Society Papers*, 24: 55–61. Martinus Nijhoff, for *Ngaju Religion: The Conception of God among a South Borneo People*, by Hans Schärer, 1963, trans. Rodney Needham. Oxford University Press, for *The Religion of an Indian Tribe*, by Verrier Elwin, 1955. University of Minnesota Press, for *The People of Alor: A Social-Psychological Study* of an *East Indian Island*, by Cora DuBois, University of Minnesota Press, Minneapolis: © 1944 by the University of Minnesota.

Cover photograph courtesy of Fred Bruemmer

Library of Congress Cataloging in Publication Data

Beals, Alan R
  Culture in process.

  Bibliography: p. 365.
  Includes index.
  1. Ethnology. 2. Culture. I. Title.
GN320.B44 1979 301.2 78-27459
ISBN 0-03-042806-8

Printed in the United States of America

9 0 1 090 9 8 7 6 5 4 3 2 1

PREFACE

Culture in Process focuses upon questions, not answers. It deals much of the time with bewilderment rather than certainty. In part, the emphasis upon questions is a matter of educational philosophy; that is, students should find things out in an active way rather than passively absorb the knowledge handed down from on high. In part, questions are emphasized because cultural anthropology has few answers of an authoritative kind.

A hundred years ago there was no organized discipline of anthropology. Even today, cultural anthropology consists mainly of questions. The bulk of its territory has yet to be explored, let alone mapped and organized. Accordingly, the study of cultural anthropology, as of any other new and therefore lively science, is the study of the jungle trails and uncharted seas of data in which so many of our brave explorers have been lost. Make no mistake. Cultural anthropologists have learned a great deal about human beings, perhaps more than anyone else. The trouble is that what we have learned most is what human beings are *not* like and the ways in which their behavior can *not* be explained. We have amassed a vast and exciting body of literature concerning the actual behavior of human beings in different parts of the world. We have discarded most of the ancient myths and fables about human beings that have so long interfered with the development of realistic undertakings. Most important of all, we have found out which kinds of questions are worth investigating. We have found out *where* we are going even if we are not quite sure how to get there.

My purpose in writing this unconventional text has been to present the basic questions and problems of cultural anthropology within a memorable theoretical framework built around the concepts of system and process. Naturally, since this *is* a textbook after all, it contains some facts and definitions that must be memorized. It is hoped that most of the facts are directly related to important questions. These are represented by the sometimes mystifying headings that appear at the head of each section. At the beginnings and endings of each section and chapter an attempt has been made to state the basic questions and problems that are dealt with with reasonable clarity.

Whenever possible, I have tried to use an "inductive" or "discovery" method. Sometimes the available data lends itself easily to this approach, other times it does not. Overall, I have attempted to present the questions and facts first, and the answers afterward. Although some may find this approach baffling, it is, nevertheless, important to spend some time thinking about the kinds of data presented and the kinds of questions data of that sort might be made to answer. My own interpretation of the data presented appears at the end of each section, so it is always possible to read a few pages more and find some sort of account of what is going on. Throughout, I have tried to help out as much as I could without destroying that sense of mystery and baffllement that must precede triumphant discovery.

An attempt has been made to keep *Culture in Process* short and inexpensive so that it may be used in conjunction with other materials. For example, in its previous editions it has often been used successfully with the Holt, Rinehart and Winston Case Studies in Cultural Anthropology, which, along with the Case Studies in Education and Culture, are listed on the last pages of this volume. In addition, a wide variety of short textbooks, collections of readings, articles, and pamphlets can be used to provide the student with alternative explanations of anthropological materials.

Although the reading of one or several books about anthropology is needed for an understanding of anthropological methods and viewpoints, some experience with the *practice* of anthropology is also desirable. *Culture in Process* contains examples and discussions of anthropological research methods. Suggested research projects are listed at the end of each chapter.

Without having collected at least one genealogy, without having done at least one interview, without having observed and taken notes on at least one activity, the individual is in a poor position to understand what anthropology is about. The student begins to *know* anthropology only on ringing the first doorbell or addressing the first question to a potential source of information. In recent years, governmental attempts to protect the victims of misguided medical research have imposed more and more bureaucratic difficulties in the way of student fieldwork in the social sciences. I believe that every effort should be made to overcome these difficulties.

In practicing anthropological fieldwork, I believe that students should enjoy the same privileges accorded to any other citizen. They should be free to observe or participate in any kind of public performance and to ask questions about the activities witnessed. Even further, they should have the right to talk to any other citizen and to ask questions and receive answers.

At the same time, students are not professional anthropologists and should not suggest to anybody that they are. They should be advised about the possible hazards of fieldwork and cautioned to avoid sensitive topics and confidential information. They should be warned that their instructors will not read or consider papers that involve invasion of privacy or the description of illegal activity. Although all of this sounds very serious, teachers of introductory courses have involved students in field research projects for many decades. For many students, the opportunity to do such research is one of the highlights of their college careers. As a reward, the instructor is provided with fascinating insights concerning the nature of American culture.

Where fieldwork cannot be carried out, students should be encouraged to make use of library resources, films, television programs, or self-analysis. There are abundant opportunities to compare different cultural systems, analyze texts, record behavior, or formulate taxonomies without making any direct use of human subjects.

For the previous two editions, chapters on cultural transmission and cultural change were contributed by George and Louise Spindler. In this edition, the chapters written by the Spindlers have been completely replaced with chapters I have written. In retrospect, I am not sure that the decision to rewrite the chapters completely was a wise one, for I found the task quite difficult and the results uncertain. The change represents a general desire to make the text more consistent and uniform in terms of organization and style. To this end, the beginning chapters also have been revised and reorganized.

The book now starts with what I hope will be a strong statement concerning the nature of culture and the approach to be used. The division of the book into separate parts is also designed to strengthen the emphasis on the interplay between the cultural message on the one hand and cultural processes on the other hand. In preparing this edition, I have received a great deal of assistance from the Spindlers, from my colleagues at the University of California, Riverside, and from my students. Among my students I would particularly like to thank Alexandra S. Maryanski for her help in criticizing the text and Robert Laidlaw for his help in providing photographs. Several authors of the Holt, Rinehart and Winston case studies have been most helpful in providing photographs. Their names accompany their photographs. The drawings, as in the previous editions, are the work of Joe E. Hargrove. I would like to thank Connie Watkins and Joye Sage for their help in typing the manuscript. David Boynton of Holt, Rinehart and Winston has continued to be a source of inspiration and encouragement. Finally, I should like to dedicate this book to Kathleen Truman Beals, to my neglected parents, and to my five children who tried so hard not to interrupt my labors.

A.R.B.

CONTENTS

CULTURE, PEOPLE, ANTHROPOLOGISTS

The three chapters in Part I provide basic information needed as a background for cultural anthropology; each represents a separate approach. The first considers the nature of humanity and culture. The discovery of humanity proceeds from a comparison of the Eskimo and seals through consideration of the genetic and linguistic codes and, so, onward to the nature of culture and process.

The second discusses cultural shifts toward the origin and development of the human species. In considering how beings became human, culture reappears as a part of the cause and explanation of Homo sapiens. *Toward the end of this chapter culture again becomes the dominant concept underlying a sketch of variation in human ways of life.*

The third chapter describes how anthropologists come to understand the variety of ways of life that are spread before them. This is as vital to the understanding of humanity as knowledge concerning the nature of culture or the history of humanity. We cannot understand culture or people until we understand how information about them is collected. To the extent that anthropology is what anthropologists do and culture is what anthropologists study, it is important to understand how anthropology is done and how culture is studied.

CULTURE: THE FIRST INVENTION

What is this chapter about?

This chapter begins with an example. The example of an Eskimo hunter in confrontation with a seal. What does the example suggest concerning the similarities and differences between humans, such as the Eskimo, and other living things, such as seals? Part of the similarity and difference lies in the nature of the genetic message. Answers are sought to the following research questions. What is the character of the genetic message? How does it change to create new species? What sorts of effects does it have on human beings? What are selection, adaptation, drift, and mutation?

Human beings speak languages and there are some important similarities between languages and the genetic code. Language makes possible (and/or results from) some special, human, ways of thinking. These ways of thinking permit the production of the cultural message. The cultural message, like the genetic message, provides a means of adapting and surviving. Culture replaces and supplements the genetic message in influencing a wide variety of human behavior.

The discussion of culture begins with an example from India: "The Railway Conductor's Song." The song is a part of a cultural message. But which part is it? And what are the things it tells people to do? Is the cultural message a set of instructions? If so, must we obey these instructions? Is culture the slave of humanity, or is humanity the slave of culture?

The next question concerns the ways in which the cultural message leads to and takes part in the formation of cultural systems. An example of children's play invites consideration of the nature of the parts of a cultural system. The next important question has to do with the nature of the things that cause human behavior and cultural systems. The example given has to do with the nature of the various things that determine the flight of an airplane. A village in Mexico and an island in the Pacific provide evidence that human cultural behavior originates in conscious and unconscious decisions made by groups of people. Because decisions generate activities and processes that anthropologists seek to explain, the examination of the nature of the culture turns to questions concerning the nature of processes and the ways in which they can be studied.

WHICH ONE WILL THE SPIRITS HELP?

Far north, the ice shelf rests upon the waters of the Arctic Ocean. There are holes in the ice where seals rise up to breathe. In season, following the wisdom of ancestors, the hunter waits beside the blowhole. With luck, after hours of waiting, the rising seal breaks the thin ice. Drawing upon the experience of friends and kinsmen, basing his actions upon years of play and practice, the hunter strikes the seal with his harpoon. The harpoon handle breaks away, leaving a barbed hook embedded in the seal's flesh. The seal dives, and the line attached to the hook burns across the hunter's gloved hands. The harpoon handle bobs against the ice. Centuries of experience lie behind the Eskimo's clothing, weapons, and hunting techniques. Even so, he has difficulty gaining a firm grip upon the harpoon line. His hands are stiff. He is half frozen and weak with hunger. The seal is bleeding and in need of air.

Two highly evolved and intelligent mammals are struggling for survival. Both may die. The hunter's feet are slipping. If he touches the water he will freeze. His whole being cries out for help. As he gives one last desperate pull, he feels behind him, tugging on the line, the hands of father, grandfather—all those who lived before. The souls of ancestors form an invisible procession stretching toward the mist and blackness of the distant shore. With a wild burst of strength, the hunter heaves the seal from the water, cuts its throat and drinks its steaming blood. The hunter has saved his own life. He will honor the seal in his rituals and divide its body among friends and neighbors.

WHAT GIVES THE HUNTER HIS STRENGTH?

Humans and seals are warm-blooded mammals. The flesh and blood and bones of the seal are much like those of the human. The seal is somewhat smaller and has slightly less brain tissue per pound of body weight. Humans learn very quickly, but so do seals. Both observe the world around them and discover things that help them to survive. They learn complicated routines; seals perform tricks and appear in circuses. Neither the eye of the camera nor the knife of the surgeon can uncover the precise mechanism that makes the human being the hunter and the carnivorous seal the hunted. Examination of flesh, bones, and blood fails to explain why seals never exhibit human beings in circuses. The Eskimo receives help from ancestors; the seal does not.

The difference between humans and all other animals is expressed in the Eskimo's harpoon, clothing, and brain—not just the shape of the brain, but what goes on inside it. The Eskimo made his harpoon following models furnished by other humans. His wife stitched his clothing according to patterns learned from her parents and her parents' parents. Originating from ancestors, a complex plan for the division of labor among old and young and between male and female frees the hunter's time to wait beside the blowhole. A traditional pattern of hunting handed down from one hunter to the next and enshrined in songs and stories explains the technique for hunting seals. The hunter's success rests upon a body of tradition reaching back uncounted millenia and involving the accumulated experience of vast numbers of individuals.

The seal learns by observation and experience and by imitating the behavior of other seals. When it dies, the seal's accumulated wisdom and knowledge dies with it. Seals and other mammals, because they are capable of learning by imitation and through social interaction, can pass on small amounts of traditional knowledge. The process is uncertain and there is no substantial accumulation of information. The human learns in all of the ways that the seal learns. On the whole, the differences between humans and other animals do not seem to be very great. Biologists who study desert wild flowers, honey bees, geese, monkeys, and other species of plants and animals find parallels between the species they study and the human species. Herring gulls, wolves, cats, dogs, porpoises, and seals often appear to be quite human in their behavior.

The Eskimo and the seal demonstrate the great and wonderful continuity of living things. All are made of the same materials and shaped by the same processes. Looking more closely at the Eskimo, some notable differences between humans and all other creatures emerge. First, almost everything about the Eskimo is artificial. The Eskimo's claws are barbs and hooks made out of bone. Body covering consists of the furs of other animals. A complex technology and a comparatively enormous variety of tools and equipment set the Eskimo and other humans generally apart from all other living things. Because the Eskimo for countless generations has grown and developed in an environment dominated by artificial constructions and equipment, it can even be argued that he is representative of an artificial or constructed species.

Second, the Eskimo talks. In the example above, the Eskimo hunter has learned his skills by talking to other hunters. He has acquired a religion, a faith in the spirits of his ancestors, which gives him hope and strength when needed. Although there are other animals that can be trained to make use of language at least to a limited extent, no other animal seems capable of inventing language. No other animal uses language to pass on the kinds of complicated plans and instructions that help the Eskimo hunter to kill the seal.

The unique properties of humans, the combined abilities to use tools and language, give rise to a complex organization called a cultural system. The following sections consider the nature of cultural systems and the nature of their parts. The single most important fact about humanity is that the life of every single human is dominated by two equally important messages: the genetic message and the cultural message. Because it is the genetic message that humans share with all other plants and animals, the first questions to be asked have to do with the nature of the genetic message.

WHAT IS THE GENETIC MESSAGE?

The genetic message is found in molecules of a chemical called deoxyribonucleic acid (DNA). The special property of molecules of DNA is that each molecule can divide to produce two new molecules that are virtually identical to each other. This is the chemical essence of reproduction. The message carried by any molecule can be repeatedly duplicated with almost perfect accuracy. At the beginning evolutionary biologists believed that chemical evolution resulted in the development of progressively more complicated compounds. In some place, under especially favorable circumstances, molecules of DNA or of some related chemical evolved and began to reproduce themselves. This was the origin of life and the beginning of biological evolution.

In complicated organisms, like humans, molecules of DNA, called genes, are strung together on even more complex molecules called chromosomes. Pairs of chromosomes exist in the cell as complicated messages involving thousands of molecules of DNA. When sexual reproduction or *meiosis* takes place, the pairs of chromosomes representing information received from the individual's male and female parents are separated. The chromosomes are grouped at different ends of the cell. Since the

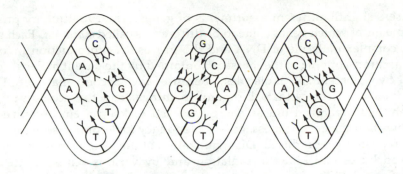

grouping occurs substantially at random with one member of each pair going to each end of the cell, the individual that is to be created will be unique. The next time a cell divides, the arrangement of the chromosomes at each end will be different.

When the cell divides, the pairs of chromosomes are separated forever. The egg or sperm cells that are now created have half of each pair of chromosomes or half as many chromosomes as an ordinary cell. In sexual reproduction an ordinary cell divides in such a way that one member of each pair of its chromosomes is donated at random to the resulting sperm or egg cell. Each grandparent has contributed one-fourth of his or her chromosomes to the grandchild, but, since the chromosomes have been contributed at random, there is no way to predict in advance which chromosomes the grandchild will get. Just to complicate matters, it sometimes happens that fragments of one chromosome get attached to another chromosome. This process of *crossing over* makes genetic inheritance even more complicated and unpredictable. *A variety of random processes guarantee that when the sperm and the egg cell come together an absolutely unique individual will be formed.* The individual will receive equal numbers of chromosomes from each parent, but it will never be known in advance what will be received or even if it will be received.

The molecule of DNA reproduces itself, but the process described above guarantees that it usually will not reproduce duplicate individuals. Even so, one trout or one human looks pretty much like any other trout or human. If there is a focus on the tiny differences between each newborn creature and all other creatures of its species, it is because the existence of variation is critical to the process of evolution. Change in the genetic message takes place because each individual is different from all other individuals. By the same token, each individual has a slightly different capacity to survive and reproduce. Some individuals have more children than other individuals. The individuals that have many children are the ones who transmit their genes, their genetic message to the future generations.

What causes the variation in the first place? Why do individuals possess slightly different assortments of genes? The evolutionary process by means of which genes come to be different is called *mutation*. Each gene is a complex molecule of DNA and the process of reproduction involves the accurate copying of the message contained by the parent molecule onto the two descendant molecules. Because the Second Law of Thermodynamics decrees that all organized things tend to become progressively less organized unless energy is used to keep them organized, it follows that the genetic message has a tendency to become disorganized as it is repeatedly reproduced. Disorganization of the genetic message can be caused by certain kinds of radiation and by various kinds of stress or interference.

Most mutations are lethal. The individual possessing the incorrect message simply fails to survive or reproduce. A few mutations are selectively neutral in the sense that they have little impact upon the ability to survive and reproduce. A few mutations represent improvements that enable their carriers to survive and reproduce more frequently than those who lack them. In each generation, many individuals fail to survive. There are spermatazoa that never fertilize eggs; there are eggs that never get fertilized. Many fertilized eggs fail to develop properly. Many of the eggs that are fertilized and develop into properly formed individuals fail to reproduce. Of all the seeds that are scattered, only a few are spared.

The males and females representing the eggs that survive more often than not tend to mate with other nearby individuals. This establishes a *gene pool* consisting of a set of organisms that share many of the same genes. The gene pool contains lethal, neutral, and advantageous genes. When genes are changed by mutation, *alleles* are created. That is to say, alleles are the result of two or more genes in the pool occupying the same place on the same chromosome and performing more or less the same functions. When the individual receives a different allele from each parent, one of the alleles may express itself while the other may not—or they may express themselves equally. In most species, albinism (the lack of pigment) is a *recessive* allele. Any gene for any pigment tends to be *dominant* over it. As a result, true albinos tend to appear only when both of the parents possess the same recessive gene and the individual happens to receive that gene instead of a gene for pigment from each parent. By contrast, in the plant world a cross between red and white four o'clocks produces pink four o'clocks, primarily because half as much pigment is made in pink four o'clocks as is made in red four o'clocks.

Because alleles at several different locations on the chromosome can influence each other, the situation is more complicated than the concept of recessive and dominant alleles would lead us to believe. Still, the message is clear: individuals who differ *genetically* may nevertheless resemble each other in appearance. This is the difference between the *genotype* and the *phenotype*. The phenotype is what you can see or measure and the genotype is the composition and arrangement of the genes. The phenotype arises out of a complex interaction between the genetic message and the environment in which it is located. The genes provide the plan, the phenotype is the product.

Because the egg receives its genes more or less at random and because the developing individual encounters all manner of totally unique environmental influences, it follows that all individuals possess unique qualities. This is not quite so wonderful as it sounds. All of the individuals in a breeding population must be similar if breeding is to take place and most will tend to have similar experiences in the environment. Identical twins have identical genotypes, but different phenotypes; for example, one twin is almost always smaller.

If the genetic message is to continue to be transmitted, substantial numbers of individual phenotypes must survive long enough to produce more fertilized eggs—and so more phenotypes. When individuals fail to reproduce themselves a fragment of the genetic message is lost. If individual reproductive failure occurs at random and the gene pool is fairly large, the gene pool will remain substantially unchanged. If the gene pool contains advantageous alleles whose carriers have a better chance of reproducing than do the carriers of less advantageous alleles it is only a matter of time, sometimes quite a long time, before the less advantageous alleles disappear.

When the environment changes or when individual members of a breeding population move to a less favorable environment, the *rate of selection* tends to increase; that is, fewer and fewer individuals survive to produce children. When this happens, a few individuals are likely to have a number of children, while many individuals fail to reproduce. In the new or changed environment, alleles that were advantageous before may turn out to be disadvantageous. Mutations that were lethal in the old environment may turn out to be advantageous in the new environment. The ultimate result of mutation and selection is the creation of a new and different gene pool and breeding population. If the differences between the two populations are quite marked and interbreeding between them is rare or impossible, biologists are likely to consider them to be two different species.

The process whereby some individuals survive and produce offspring while others do not is called *selection*. The end result of selection, assuming that the entire species is not selected against, is *adaptation*—the ability to survive and reproduce in the environment. In a stable environment, adaptation can only increase to the point where a stable population is maintained. If the population increases beyond a limit, it will destabilize the environment necessitating a new round of selection and adaptation. "Better adapted" is a contradiction in terms since the very best adaptation is only "good enough to get by." The process of adaptation is simply the process of running very hard to stay in the same place. Because the environment is always changing and thus creating opportunities and problems, all living things must continuously adapt or perish.

Selection is not the only cause of change in species. For various reasons, over time, and without regard to selective pressures, some genes will accidentally become increasingly frequent and others increasingly rare. This process is known as *drift*. It is especially important in small populations where small accidents can have large effects. Drift explains variation in genes that are selectively neutral—neither advantageous nor disadvantageous compared to their alleles.

We can regard different kinds of living things as representing different adaptive strategies. Here, once an animal has adopted the strategy of surviving by running fast, it is rather difficult to return to a strategy of wearing a turtle shell. Even though the strategies of running fast or wearing a shell might not be the world's best strategies, the animal that adopts a given strategy is more or less stuck with it. It must adapt and survive within the confines of that strategy.

The reason for this is that the production of advantageous mutations is a hit-or-miss affair. In an emergency, the species must accept whatever genes appear and hope that they are sufficiently advantageous to permit survival. The belief that a wise "Mother Nature" provided an optimum design for each plant and animal is a fantasy. Plant and animal species come into being when accidental errors in the transmission of the genetic message create changes that make it possible to continue to survive. Like all other plants and animals, *Homo sapiens* is a patchwork of modifications and repairs. Out of billions and billions of evolutionary accidents, the human species represents a single occurrence that has more or less accidentally survived.

Perhaps because we are human beings, we have a tendency to believe that the set of accidents that produced us is somehow special. Certainly, the unique aspect of human beings does not lie in our possession of the genetic code. Every living thing possesses that. From the human point of view the transcendent fact about human beings, the one thing that makes us absolutely unique among living things, is our possession of language and culture. Unlike all other plants and animals, human beings maintain their adaptedness through reliance upon plans and messages that are *not* genetic in character.

The rest of this chapter considers language, the cultural message, and the other unique features of the human pattern of adaptation. The genetic code is based upon combinations of four different molecules, which code for the production in sequence of some twenty different amino acids. The linguistic code is based upon a number of speech organs such as the lips, larynx, tongue, and glottis. These organs produce some twenty to sixty basic speech sounds. The genetic code always involves the same four molecules and the same twenty amino acids. The linguistic code involves, to some extent, different speech organs for different languages, and these speech organs are used to produce a variety of different basic sounds in each language. There seems to be no limit other than convenience to the number of basic sound types that might be used to form a language. For that matter, since the "sign language" used by nonhearing individuals in some cultures does not involve the use of speech, it is not always conceded that human language must involve the use of any particular speech organs.

The basic sound types or features in a language are called *phonemes*. Phonemes are the smallest elements of sound that can change the meaning of an utterance. Consider the contrasts between "pit" and "bit," "pack" and "back," or "cap and "cab." The difference in meaning between the two words in each pair is the sound we write as "b" and "p." Both phonemes are formed by using the lips to stop a flow of air through the mouth. The sound represented by "b" involves the vibration of the vocal cords (feel your throat) while the sound "p" does not. As children, speakers of English are trained to hear the result of this small difference in the way the sounds are formed.

When linguists study languages, they usually pay someone—an informant—to work with them. When the informant talks, an attempt is made to write down the sounds in terms of the methods used in making them. The written version is read back to the informant and corrected. Through such processes of experimentation, linguists discover the smallest units that make a difference in the meaning of utterances. Thus, in English it makes a difference whether a sound is voiced or unvoiced. It is this difference that causes "bit" and "pit" to vary in meaning.

Schaller, in his study of mountain gorillas (1963:211), recorded over twenty-two different meaningful sounds or cries. But gorillas and other nonhuman primates observed in the wild rarely combine their different noises in quite the way that humans do. Recent studies of chimpanzees show that they can be taught to perform most of the operations that are characteristic of human language. This is especially true if they use tokens or gestures rather than attempting to make speech sounds. The implications of this discovery are still being explored.

Human beings invent and use languages based upon the use of a few phonemes in various combinations. All of the findings of science and all of the poetry written in English derive from combinations of some forty-one speech sounds. The construction of meaningful sounds out of combinations of the same basic phonemes implies some interesting properties of human thought. The first thing to think about is that since words are simply combinations of basic sounds there is no natural meaning inherent in a word. The names of things are unnatural. English-speaking people have agreed, largely unconsciously, that a "chair" is something you sit

FIGURE 1–1 Social animals communicate in a variety of ways. Understanding such communication and discovering its relationships to human communication is a major research area. (PHOTO BY ALAN R. BEALS)

FIGURE 1–2 Gorillas, our close cousins, appear to be engaged in conversation. To what extent can gorillas and chimpanzees acquire communication skills resembling our own? (PHOTO BY ALAN R. BEALS)

upon and that a "mother" is something that has children and can be sat upon. English speakers could theoretically decide tomorrow to switch the meanings of these or any other words. It is difficult to think of a "mother" as something with four legs and a wooden back, but that is only because we are accustomed to thinking of a "mother" as something else. In *Brave New World*, Aldous Huxley predicted that "mother" would become a dirty word. In phrases like, "That mother bugs me," that is just what has happened. As Humpty Dumpty said, "a word means what I want it to mean."

HOW DO LANGUAGE AND THOUGHT AFFECT EACH OTHER?

The arbitrariness of language leads to the emergence of a new world of meaning. To be among the pine trees is not just to be surrounded by vegetation; it is to be in a place that has special meanings that have nothing to do with the reality of pine trees. For some it might be to be alone, on vacation, free; for others it might be to be endangered by witches or scalp-hunting Indians. We constantly exchange messages, and we convert all of the everyday objects around us into symbols that themselves convey messages foreign to their nature.

If things can be labeled in arbitrary fashion, as they must be if we are to label them with combinations of phonemes, it follows that labels stand for or replace the things that have been labeled. When someone says, "On the other side of the hill," we visualize the other side of the hill and the things that are there. The same memory system that permits us to remember thousands of words permits us to remember in detail things that no longer exist. According to Hans Kummer (1971: 30–31), nonhuman primates can communicate only about the here and now. A monkey can inform another monkey about the location of a distant plot of mushrooms only by leading him there. A monkey cannot say, "Let us meet at sunup by the old oak tree," or "There is a tree full of nuts three miles to the east." Although chimpanzees and other great apes, more closely related to human beings, can be trained to use gestures or tokens to make similar statements, they appear not to do so in nature.

All humans can speak about and think about things that are not present. We have been called "timebinders" because we have an ability to live in the past and future as well as in the present. The ability to speak about events removed in time and space is called *displacement*. It follows naturally from the fact that we can use words whenever we like and the words can refer to anything regardless of whether it is present or absent.

Very often when we combine words into sentences we produce expressions like "little green men," "flying island," or "time travel." Such

FIGURE 1–3   The human ability to form productive sentences may be related to the human ability to conceive new forms. From the Museum of Anthropology, Mexico. (PHOTO BY ALAN R. BEALS)

expressions appear to have meaning. They are grammatically correct, yet we know of nothing in nature that resembles such things. Language gives us the ability to fabricate, to make things up. This ability to use language to produce new things that did not exist before is called, not surprisingly, *productivity*. In a moment's dreaming, humans can create a world and then destroy it. Human creativity is related to the productive use of language.

The coding of language in terms of *phonemes* leads to the phenomena of arbitrariness, displacement, and productivity (Hockett 1973:98–121). At first glance, the use of these abilities appears to place the human species in a sort of cloud cuckooland far removed from reality. When a human being sees a lion, for example, the reaction is likely to be affected by symbolic associations. Humans don't just see lions, they see arbitrary and fantastic symbolisms that their culture has attached to the concept of lion. It is surprising that human beings are able to cope with the real thing. As with lions, so with all of nature. Humans beings create a world of meaning and symbols. They perceive reality, if they do so at all, only through a screen of rationalization and fantasy. If this is the case, how can it be claimed that language contributes to human adaptation?

Language permits the transmission of information between human beings and across generations on a comparatively enormous scale. Human beings have access to genetic information handed down to them by their parents. They also have access to linguistic information handed down and across by all members of their group and by all speakers of their language. Genetic messages, although they can conceivably become as informative as linguistic messages, are a somewhat accidental collection of information. They are messages without an author and edited by selection. Linguistic messages have authors. Much of the information transmitted involves practical detail: how to catch a seal, what to do when it rains, or how to find arrowroot for dinner.

Linguistic messages evidently convey sufficient information about reality to provide human beings with an adaptive advantage sufficient to make up for any loss associated with their propensity for fantasy. But that is not the whole story. The capacity for fantasy that permits us to visualize leprechauns in Ireland is the same capacity that permits us to conceive the transformation of natural materials into tools of various kinds. One of the problems for modern human beings arises precisely in our capacity for the radical transformation of nature. If our imagination leads us to the construction of ever more powerful explosive devices and of countless other technologies for the control and destruction of life, it is possible that we will destroy ourselves. The inventiveness triggered by language may be maladaptive after all. We will have been destroyed by speech.

For the present, barring such catastrophe, language seems to be adaptive and in many ways an improvement on the genetic code. Genetic messages can be altered only through a slow and destructive process of reproduction and selection. For example, if our reliance upon bread and beer were genetic, we might have to go through substantial genetic change before being able to consume bananas and yogurt. Centuries, nay millenia, of biological evolution would be required to make a change from English to French or Spanish. Because of these sorts of problems the human genetic code tends not to specify the details of behavior. The reason for this is that the function of controlling behavior has been almost entirely taken over by language. Put another way, the linguistic code and the cultural message represent a new system of adaptation in which genetic programming is partially replaced by cultural programming. Human beings can maintain a relatively unchanging genetic message while adapting and surviving by means of constant and rapid changes in the cultural message. What, then, is the nature of the cultural message?

DO YOU KNOW WHAT'S RIGHT?

In parts of South India, minstrels go from house to house singing ballads in return for gifts of grain or cash. One such ballad is the "Railway Conductor's Song." In this story, a young wife was sent to visit her parents in a distant village. As is the custom, her husband came some weeks later to take her home. Her father ordered her to remain in her parental home. The husband left, dejected. As the wife thought the matter over, she realized that it was her duty to obey her husband, not her father. She rushed to the railway station but discovered that her husband's train had already left. She was alone at the railway station with their baby. The railway conductor, seeing her plight, invited her to enter the second-class waiting room and sit there until the next train came. When the railway conductor attempted to follow her into the waiting room, there was a brief struggle and she succeeded in locking him out. Unfortunately, the baby was also locked out. The conductor threatened to tear the baby into small pieces if she refused to sleep with him. Despite this threat she kept the door locked and her virtue intact.

The "Railway Conductor's Song" is a part of the cultural message of a particular place, time, and group of people. Because a message must be received as well as sent, the importance of the message depends upon the extent to which people attend to it and base their activities upon it. The

FIGURE 1–4   A Muslim storekeeper considers an appropriate gift for strolling musicians. The music is free, but a reward is expected. Strolling musicians and minstrels carry portions of the cultural message from place to place. (PHOTO BY ALAN R. BEALS)

song, like other parts of the cultural message is a physical reality. People hear the song and it influences their behavior. What sorts of actions does the song encourage?

The song points up the problem that occurs when a young woman is asked to transfer her primary social allegiance from her parental household to that of her husband and his parents. Bad things will happen to the woman who forgets her primary obligation to "worship her husband as a god." The song is establishment propaganda dedicated to the proposition that marriages and the political and economic ties established by marriages must be preserved at all costs. South Indian women rather frequently forget their sacred obligations to their husbands. Nevertheless, they are always aware of what they are ideally supposed to do, and it is a factor in their behavior.

In ancient Greece, the Delphic oracle foretold the future with great exactitude (the gods are never wrong) but often in words that were ambiguous and subject to misinterpretation. The cultural message has the same faults. Divorce, remarriage, battles over custody of children, and fights over wedding jewels are a constant source of trouble in southern India. Do these activities represent violations of the cultural tradition, or is the "Railway Conductor's Song" somehow not a part of the cultural tradition?

The point is that the cultural tradition is a message, or better still, a set of messages. The messages can be contradictory or inconsistent. They may be simply what the old folks would like us to do or they may be commands or laws that carry severe penalties if violated. We may not get the message. We may receive only part of the message. It is up to us, as human individuals, to interpret the information we receive. The cultural message sets up an interplay or dialogue between the experience and information transmitted to us by our forefathers and fellow members and the realities that confront us at the moment. If we follow the well-worn path it is because we choose to do so. If the well-worn path is blocked by landslides, if we lose our way, or if we hear the beat of a different drummer, then we are free to head across country and into the brambles. Perhaps we go alone, perhaps others follow. In our going, the cultural message begins to be modified.

Traditionally, the cultural message has been viewed as a set of rules to be followed. Certainly, it is often the case that people do the things that other people expect them to do. It is also the case that people often behave as tradition urges them to behave even though it is hard to imagine a mother in South India allowing her baby to be torn to pieces. In this, normative, view of culture, the good people follow the rules and the rest are deviants or abnormal. In a more statistical sense, a normative view of culture can be thought of as a view in which individual variation centers about a norm or average that forms the standard of correct behavior.

It is not generally recognized that both of these kinds of normative views of culture are special cases of a *decision oriented* view. If everyone makes the "correct" decision, then everyone obeys the cultural rule or norm. If decisions vary normally around the "correct" decision, then normal behavior is conforming behavior and other behavior is deviant behavior. The real complexity of the interaction between human beings and cultural messages is best revealed when we think of human beings as constantly weighing alternatives and making conscious or unconscious decisions. In this view, following Ward Goodenough, *the cultural message is what you need to know in order to adjust your behavior to the expectations of the members of a group of human beings.* Your resulting behavior may be proper or improper depending upon whether you decide to meet such expectations or defy them. Beyond this, a cultural tradition contains explanations and rationalizations sufficient to convince at least some people that a particular cultural message is worth paying attention to.

At one level, that of norms and behavior standards, the cultural message can be described as determining behavior. This is true, for example, with regard to the language or languages that are spoken by any particular group of people. "Determine" is, of course, a strong word. None of us has to speak English. We speak English largely because it is practically impossible to survive in most North American cultural settings without speaking it. At least since Sumerian times, the older generation has felt that the younger generation was failing to uphold behavioral standards.* Changing conditions often encourage individuals to disobey rules and generally to seek changes in the cultural message. This leads to a feeling that the cultural message is a restrictive device; something that keeps people from doing what they want to do. In fact, because the cultural message represents the human means of survival, it must be regarded as the instrument by means of which human beings achieve their ends. In all fundamental ways, human beings adjust their behavior so that their relatives and companions will believe them to be proper and conforming members of society. Up to a point, conformity simply represents the easiest and most practical way of achieving individual goals.

Even so, no matter how great the rewards of conformity and no matter how stringently laws are enforced, there is always room for variation. Each person speaks the language of his group a bit differently from each other person. We conduct our lives as individuals. To the uninformed outsider, we may appear to be simply jocks, beauty queens, eggheads, Crow Indians, or Sherpas, each of us doing pretty much what the other members of our group are doing. From the inside, this dull uniformity of behavior is transformed into the sensitive interplay of quite different individuals,

---

* "Come now, be a man. Don't stand about in the public square, or wander about the boulevard." (Kramer 1959:14).

each doing a unique thing or each doing the common thing in a unique individual style. The forest is a green blob, a set of trees. Up close, each tree is separate and remarkable. Let us consider in a bit more detail the kinds of organization that emerge when a cultural tradition exists. The next section begins with an example of human behavior. What are the basic features of human cultural behavior?

What Makes Up a Cultural System?

The game of "seed" described below contains the major elements of a cultural system. In other words, it "stands for" or is "analogous to" a cultural system. There are many different ways of dividing such a slice of life into its components. The case provides an opportunity to consider these different possibilities. The terms used here—place, people, plans, paraphernalia, and process—are defined immediately afterward.

> In South India, an old man sits on a shady platform under a nim tree. With his hand he strokes a bundle of fibers against his naked thigh and twists it into a rope. Below, at ground level, Ganga and Bhima are sitting on a rock. Bhima, a three-year-old girl, is holding an empty tin can and a stick. She puts the stick into the tin can and causes the can to roll back and forth. A five-year-old girl comes out of a nearby windowless stone house. As she sits beside the old man on the platform, Bhima goes to her and says, "I will bring you two mango seeds and two for Ganga and two for me and we will play seed." The five-year-old answers, "Bring." Bhima disappears and returns with six mango seeds. Together the players arrange the seeds in a circle. The five-year-old takes a stone and throws it at the seeds so that they all bounce out of the circle. The five-year-old picks up all of the seeds. The five-year-old turns and runs away. Bhima says, "I won't play with you again."
>
> A two-year-old boy is sitting nearby on a rock. Bhima goes to him and pushes him off the rock, taking his place. The small boy sits on a different rock. Bhima pours sand on the boy. The boy rises and follows his sister into the house. In a minute the boy emerges from his house with a rock in his hand. He throws it in the direction of Bhima and then goes back inside the house. Bhima wanders off and the old man is left sitting under the tree, surrounded by gray, featureless houses, a stretch of sandy street, and a fractious goat. (Adapted from field notes taken by Constance M. Beals)

In this incident, a group of human beings came together, established a creative enterprise, and abandoned it leaving nothing but a circle in the sand. There are five major elements in the above scene: place, people, plans, paraphernalia, and process.

Place and People.   The village street is the place or environment within which the game of "seed" is carried out. The people, of course, are the players of the game, the *members* of the cultural system. The concepts

FIGURE 1–5   South Indian children enact the process of preparing food. (PHOTO BY ALAN R. BEALS)

of place and people or environment and membership are used by most social scientists. The concepts are defined somewhat differently depending upon theoretical context. These matters will be discussed further in later chapters.

Plans.   The members of a human group are the principal carriers of its *cultural tradition*, its plans for living. In the example given, the rules of the game of "seed" represent the tradition. The cultural tradition provides first of all the language that forms the basis for interaction among the members of a group. Communication by means of language provides names and significances to different parts of the environment and the different things that happen. The environment, now, is not just a plain old environment, it is an environment filled with symbols—things that have a special meaning as parts of a particular culture. Interaction among the members of a culture and between humans and their culture is symbolic interaction. The meaning of things lies in the interpretations contained within the cultural tradition. We understand humanity only as we understand the symbolic meaning of actions.

Paraphernalia.   Although the cultural tradition is transmitted primarily by the human members of a culture, it is also embedded in the *paraphernalia* of the group. Paraphernalia refers to the tools, equipment, artifacts, and constructions that are made and used by the memberships. These things, provided that they are made in the proper way, are literal embodiments of the cultural tradition. Everything built according to cultural plans is a material record of their nature.

Process.   A cultural system consists of place, people, plans, and paraphernalia—that is to say of an environment, warm bodies, a cultural tradition, and a material culture. This is like saying that a clock consists of springs, wheels, and hands. The important thing about cultural systems, or clocks, is the manner in which the parts are interrelated when in motion. The operation of a cultural system involves the carrying out of activities or processes. The cultural system exists as a functioning entity when its members are doing the various things that they are supposed to do as members of the cultural system.

A processual approach to the understanding of culture is simply an approach that places emphasis upon the things that get done and the rules for getting things done rather than upon abstract categories. Playing the game of "seed" is a process, so is making rope, or quarreling, or walking back to the house. Before considering the nature of such processes at length, let us first consider exactly what is meant by the expression "cultural system."

System: What Determines the Outcome?

A thing like a clock composed of functioning and interrelated parts is called a system. Because human social systems, unlike animal social systems, are unique in possessing cultural traditions, the system formed by the intersection of environment, people, culture, material culture, and process is best described as a cultural system. *A cultural system is a human social system composed of a setting, a membership, a cultural tradition, a material culture, and a set of processes.* Cultural systems, like other systems, derive their fundamental nature from the interrelationship of their parts.

Within a cultural system, the concept of straight-line causation is usually meaningless. None of the parts of the system causes or determines any of the other parts of the system. As cultural systems continue the various processes needed for their maintenance and perpetuation, there are dialogues and interactions among their various parts. Problems arise in the environment. The environment is changed. If the environment cannot be changed, then changes may take place in the cultural tradition or in the size and character of the membership. Interaction between the cultural system and the environment and between the parts of the cultural system takes place constantly and a change in any one part can cause changes in other parts. A systems concept implies that everything works together and that nothing "causes" anything else. Consider the case of the B–29:

The B-29 is an obsolete airplane which was designed to carry a crew of eleven men who, in the words of an air force general, were "to drop the bomb on the target." It belongs to a time when the dropping of bombs was considered "a good thing." If we were to follow a flight of such a plane, we would probably start with a briefing session in which the crew would be given precise instructions concerning the time at which the plane should leave the ground, the direction in which it should fly, the speed at which it should travel, the altitude it should maintain, the place it should go, and the things that should happen when it got there. These instructions, together with training, experience, and other relevant information, can be regarded as the cultural tradition of the crew. The members of the crew form a small and partial cultural system. The airplane is a constructed environment filled with the equipment and tools required for the maintenance and operation of crew culture.

As must the members of all cultural systems, the members of the B-29 engage in an immense journey. It is the duty of the anthropologist to make the best possible predictions about its course. We are to discover the things that determine the behavior of human beings in cultural systems. In particular, what determines the things that happen during a particular flight? Will the bomb get dropped on the target or will the mission be aborted as have so many ancient missions before? What determines the outcome of a flight?

"Groundpounders"—the people who decide where and when the plane is supposed to fly and who announce their instructions at the briefing sessions—tell us that the flight will follow the orders given. The groundpounders' hypothesis is that the behavior of the crew will follow the cultural tradition. "To predict human behavior, we need only know what the human beings have been instructed to do." Put another way, if we read the rule book carefully, we can easily become outstanding football players.

Captain Pennington, the aircraft commander, is aware that at the end of the flight he will have to explain why the airplane ended up in Tampa when it was supposed to be flying to Galveston. Because he believes that the best cultural systems can be operated only by the best people, Captain Pennington believes that the outcome of the flight will be determined by the quality of the biological message innate in his crew members.

Harris, the chief mechanic, says that the outcome of the flight is dependent upon the condition of the airplane. He points out that sudden tropical storms, adverse winds, and other things might cause turbulence that would force the crew to modify their flight instructions and so land at Tampa instead of Galveston.

The hypotheses put forward by the groundpounders, by the captain, and by the mechanic are rejected by the crew members. They agree that it is important to consider what goes on in briefing sessions and that it is important that each crew member be capable of learning his role and function. They consider the weather and the mechanical condition of the plane to be of great importance. They set forth the following example:

The manual of instructions states that if there is an oil leak in the engine, often a sign of breakdown, the leak should be reported immediately to the aircraft commander (pilot). Actually, B-29 engines leak oil in various quantities almost continuously. It is always difficult to determine whether there is a fresh leak or whether the engine is merely dripping oil in the usual manner. When a crew member looks out and sees oil dripping from the engine, his reporting depends upon his training and competence, the cleanliness of his glasses, the mood of the aircraft commander as revealed throughout the flight, the cultural tradition of the crew itself, or the visibility of the engine.

The reporting of oil leaks is a key element of the flight and might have a major bearing upon the success of a mission. The prediction of oil-leak reporting, only one of the many processes carried out by the crew, involves simultaneous control of a wide range of information having to do with the environment (the nature of the airplane, weather, the rest of the air force), the membership (who belongs to the crew and their attributes and abilities), and the cultural tradition (how people have been trained, what it says in the manual, the past experience of the group).

The groundpounder's or idealist's hypothesis is that the best prediction is based upon a knowledge of the rules, the cultural tradition. The captain's or individualist's hypothesis is that you have to understand the genetic or psychological character of the individual members of the crew. The mechanic's or environmentalist's hypothesis is that you just have to understand the airplane and the weather. In one form or another, these are the three major schools of thought concerning the prediction of human behavior. Each viewpoint seizes upon one aspect of a cultural system (rules, people, or environment) and attaches primary importance to that aspect.

What is the point? It is that there are many possible explanations of human behavior. Sometimes it is useful to think in biological terms and pretend that human beings are just like all other animals. Sometimes it is useful to think of human beings as robots responding automatically to the things that happen in the environment. Sometimes it is useful to think of human beings as slaves of their cultural messages blindly following the teachings of ancestors. In the end, the simple approaches to an understanding need to be combined. We need to consider the entire complex set of relationships among cultural messages, environments, and people. Human behavior is the emergent property of cultural systems, it is caused by the interaction of place (environment), people, plans (tradition), and paraphernalia (material culture).

What is the Cause?

There is no wonder in the fact that the settlement of Chan Kom decided to become a pueblo. Sooner or later nearly every settlement containing a score or more of houses in this part of Yucatan became a pueblo, or tried to, under leadership provided from the city and under the stimulus of ambition and the desire for material advantage. What is notable is the unusual zeal with which the Chan Kom people, above all others in the neighborhood, worked to attain their objective and the outstanding success they achieved. Once they had made the decision, they set their feet firmly on the path to progress, and no exertion was too great, no discipline too firm, for the enterprise. Beginning as a cluster of thatched huts deep in the brush, no different from several others similarly situated, in the course of thirty years the village became the recognized and authoritative community of an area fifty miles across (Redfield 1962:22–23).

The mutineers now bade adieu to all the world, save the few individuals associated with them in exile. But where that exile should be passed was yet undecided; the Marquesas Islands were first mentioned, but Christian, on reading Captain Carteret's account of Pitcairn Island, though it better adapted to the purpose, and accordingly shaped a course thither. They reached it not many days afterwards, and Christian, with one of the seamen, landed in a little nook, which we afterwards found very convenient for disembarkation. They soon traversed the island sufficiently to be satisfied that it was exactly suited to their wishes. It possessed water, wood, a good soil, and some fruits. The anchorage in the offing was very bad and landing for boats extremely hazardous. The mountains were so difficult of access, and the passes so narrow, that they might be maintained by a few persons against an army; and there were several caves to which, in case of necessity, they could retreat, and where, as long as their provisions lasted, they might bid defiance to their pursuers. With this intelligence they returned on board, and brought the ship to an anchor in a small bay on the northern side of the island, which I have in consequence named "Bounty Bay," where everything that could be of utility was landed, and where it was agreed to destroy the ship, either by running her on shore, or burning her. Christian, Adams, and the majority, were for the former expedient; but while they went to the forepart of the ship, to execute this business, Matthew Quintal set fire to the carpenter's storeroom. The vessel burnt to the water's edge, and then drifted upon the rocks (Shapiro 1962:53).

In both of these cases, a group of people decided to form a cultural system. More precisely, they decided to make changes in the cultural system they already possessed. The point is that the existence of *any* cultural system implies the existence of human beings interacting, communicating and, above all, making decisions. *A cultural system is the product of decision-making activity carried out by human beings.*

It is important, then, to see human life as emerging from chains of decisions. Decisions lead to actions. Actions produce changes in the environment. The changes made in the environment produce an environment that is somewhat different from the environment that existed before. Place, people, plans, paraphernalia, and process constantly interact with one another. Although in a given situation one of these five "P's" may be more important than the other four, the relationships among the five "P's" are in the nature of a dialogue or an argument. In deciding to become a pueblo, the people of Chan Kom required the sort of environment that would permit their growth to the status of pueblo. It was also necessary to make a variety of changes in their environment. This is the sense in which "dialogue" is used. The environment pushes on people and affects their plans, but the plans also push upon people and environment.

At Chan Kom and on Pitcairn, trees had to be felled and the environment drastically altered in order to make agriculture possible. The kind of agriculture to be practiced and the plants to be utilized depended upon the unique past history of the early settlers of both places. In both places, we may guess that one decision followed another. Not all decisions were good ones. Many decisions were irrevocable. Once the trees were cut and the ground leveled it was too late to decide upon an alternative way of surviving. We may guess, also, that the people of Chan Kom and Pitcairn made pretty good decisions on the whole. They survived. Their newly created adaptation was good enough to permit them to get by. Under the circumstances, although their adaptations may have been good, they could hardly have been perfect. Nevermind, the plants, animals, and people with whom they might later have to compete were probably not perfectly adapted either.

The important decisions that people make are decisions about how things are to be done. Because there are many such decisions and because cultural systems are almost endlessly complicated, anthropologists tend to focus their studies on particular sorts of decisions and on particular parts of cultural systems. One of the main points of this book is that we ought to be looking at the things people are doing, at activities, at processes. How are processes to be studied? What are the other things besides process that can be studied?

WHAT ARE YOU DOING AND WHY?

The fact that human beings talk to each other and produce plans and decisions is surely one of the most interesting things about them. What human beings actually do is, as we all know, somewhat different from the things they talk about doing. How, then, are the things people do to be studied, and how are they to be talked about? Consider some of the things that people do when people die:

Among the Cheyenne Indians of North America the body of a man is dressed in its finest clothing. It is wrapped in robes and transported outside the camp to be deposited in the crotch of a tree, on a scaffold, or on the ground under a pile of rocks. Favorite horses of the deceased are shot and left at the grave along with weapons or utensils which were used in life. Female relatives cut off their hair and gash their foreheads until the blood flows (Hoebel 1960:87).

In Mexico, in the village of Tepoztlán, a person who is about to die is placed on a mat on the floor. After death, the corpse is dressed in clean clothing and there is a day of mourning. The corpse is then placed in a coffin and carried to a cemetery where it is buried. Nine days after death, an offering of food is placed on the altar in the deceased's home in order to provide him with food during each of the months of the year. Wakes, in memory of the dead, are held on the night of the death, nine days later, and one year later. Mourning tends to be "restrained" (Adapted from Lewis 1960:84–85).

On Palau, an island in the Pacific, Doab's funeral took place as follows:

The corpse had been taken to the house of the headman of Doab's clan. It lay on a mat on the floor near one wall, dressed in its "best"—shirt, trousers,

FIGURE 1–6 Chamula Indian cemetery in Chiapas, Mexico. Other peoples cremate their dead or expose them on platforms. Explanation of these sorts of differences is a major task of cultural anthropology. Why is the Chamula cemetery different from other Catholic cemeteries? (PHOTO BY ALAN R. BEALS)

socks and shoes never worn in life and donated for the occasion by a relative. It had been washed with a heavily scented soap, in place of the old preparation of aromatic leaves, and its lips smeared with lipstick, a modern substitute for betel juice. A faded army cap lay on the pillow at one side of the head; on the other was a handbag containing the cherished possessions that were to accompany the corpse to the grave.

As the mourning women arrived to take their places around the corpse, the younger ones handed Doab's clan "mother" a few yards of dress goods; the older ones gave her finely made mats. These goods were to be used to reward the rest of the women for the food they brought and for their preparation of it. The mourners arrived one by one over the period of an hour. Some of them wept and brought tears to the eyes of the rest as they approached the body. Between their arrivals there were muted conversations among those already present and among the detached cluster of men. Betel nut was sent for and distributed by the head of the house to all persons in the room. A coffin maker was at work in the yard in the midst of a crowd of squatting men who gave advice. At one point he passed a tape measure in the window, asking one of the women to measure the corpse. Later he returned to ask for some of the dress goods with which to line the coffin (Barnett 1960:63).

Doab's funeral is an ethnographic case, a single observation of a funeral. The description of Cheyenne and Tepoztecan funerals are ethnographic hypotheses—predictions concerning appropriate or typical funerals. Each individual funeral, each ethnographic case, constitutes the carrying-out of a plan or program for dealing with persons that have died. Such plans and programs are the basis of the cultural tradition. Because the best laid plans tend to go wrong, each funeral is somewhat different from every other funeral. In the same way, no two tract houses are precisely the same even though they are all built from the same set of plans.

It is possible to carry out a proper funeral or to build a proper house in a variety of different ways. Cultural plans for funerals or for houses tell us about things that are needed in order to perform properly. It is understood that the plans will have to be modified in order to cope with scarce resources, personal desires, and other factors. A funeral involves economic activity. The band has to be paid, a few pounds of rice must be given to the priest, the mourners must be fed. A variety of aspects of culture—economics, religion, music, and social structure—are expressed in the funeral.

But we need not break down the funeral in this manner. We can consider it, instead, to represent the carrying-out of a plan, a plan that has developed over the years in response to problems and needs that have developed within the cultural system. The cultural system as a whole derives its nature from a succession of activities that are carried out within it. The operation or functioning of a cultural system is a process that is

FIGURE 1–7   Guambia Indians perform a ceremonial dance during the funeral of a child. Cauca Region, Colombia, May 1966. (UNITED NATIONS PHOTOGRAPH)

carried out over time. This master process, the working of the entire system, is easily divided into component processes or activities. A funeral process starts with the death or imminent death of an individual and continues until it comes to a specified end—such as disposal of the corpse, sending away the spirit of the deceased, or celebrating the last memorial feast. A funeral may be interrupted by some other process, but its participants, except for the corpse, are consciously aware that they are engaged in a funeral. *A process is a series of interlinked events commencing under culturally defined conditions, following a culturally defined plan or pattern, and reaching a culturally defined endpoint.* "Culturally defined" means that the members of a cultural system agree as to the meaning, form, and content of the process.

Everything that we do involves process—getting up in the morning, planting a crop, eating a meal, holding a funeral, graduating from college, sacrificing a goat, operating a filling station, giving a lecture, objecting to what has been said, greeting a fellow anthropologist, or disciplining the children. In many ways a process is simply a smaller version of a cultural system. There are places, people, and paraphernalia suitable for each process, and each process has to be carried out with reference to cultural plans if it is to be carried out properly. The difference between a cultural system and a process is that a cultural system is a sum of interlinked processes. Each individual process is carried out by a set of members of the larger cultural system. Participants in a process recognize their membership and regard the process as only one of the things they must do as members of the system. You cannot be a member of a process, only a participant.

For purposes of study and analysis, the various processes involved in the operation of any particular cultural system can be arranged or classified in a variety of ways. The third part of this book, the process part, deals with six processes considered essential for the maintenance and preservation of a cultural system. The six vital processes are (1) maintaining relationships to the environment, (2) regulating membership, (3) indicating status, (4) transmitting culture, (5) controlling behavior, and (6) adapting to changing circumstances.

These processes, or rather types of processes, are considered to be characteristic of and essential to the operation of any human group. The first process, maintaining relationships to the environment, includes all of the things that people do to obtain materials and resources required for the operation of the group. In a large-scale cultural system, this may involve obtaining food for the membership. In a small-scale, part system, it may involve only such things as obtaining cards for the bridge club.

The second major process or bundle of processes includes those things that are required to obtain members and to move members from position to position within the system. In all cultural systems the movement of members into and out of the group or into and out of subgroups is marked by ritual activity. Thus, the third major kind of process consists of rituals marking such things as position in life, succession to office, or initiation of life stages. Rituals range from informal greetings to complex religious ceremonials. Religious ceremonies often represent attempts to maintain or enhance the status of the system through appeals and constraints directed at the supernatural world.

The fourth and fifth major processes are the transmission of culture and the control of behavior. Cultural transmission involves teaching and learning ways of behaving properly and according to expectation. When individuals fail to exhibit proper behavior as defined by the cultural tradition, then mechanisms of social control are brought into play. Cultural transmission, both formal and informal, provides the individual with knowledge about the world and about the expectations of other people. It is what you need to know in order to do the right thing and to avoid committing a breach or crime. Once a breach has taken place, processes of social control are used to repair the damage and to restore the facade of correct behavior.

All five of the processes listed earlier have the effect of keeping things more or less as they are. As long as resources are obtained, membership regulated, status indicated, culture transmitted, and behavior controlled, there is very little new that can happen. On the other hand, circumstances change. Processes that once worked well may no longer work quite so well. Individuals may discover fresh incentives for doing the wrong thing instead of the right thing. Put another way, problems constantly arise in the smooth operation of the cultural system. As problems lead to increasing difficulties, various processes of cultural change are initiated. Alternative ways of doing things are considered; alterations are made in the cultural message. Eventually the problem is solved or reduced in importance. If problems were allowed simply to accumulate the day would come when membership dwindled and resources become unavailable. The cultural system would no longer be adapted to its setting and it would soon cease to exist.

HOW CAN PROCESSES BE STUDIED?

A description of a cultural tradition and of the processes that are carried out with reference to the information it provides constitutes an *ethnography*. Anthropologists have hardly begun the task of completing descriptions of all of the world's cultures. In addition to this stupendous task, anthropologists are seeking to discover general principles relevant to explanations of the behavior of all human beings and of the operation of all cultural systems. Cultural anthropology is the search for explanations of the similarities and differences among cultural systems. When discovered, such explanations permit us to reexamine existing cultural systems and to consider possible ways in which they can solve their outstanding problems.

As a means of arriving at general knowledge concerning culture and humanity, this book stresses the study of process. A wide variety of processes are characteristic of all human cultures. Other processes are characteristic of many but not all cultures. Going back to our previous examples of funerals carried out in different cultures (see page 26), let us now consider the kind of statement that might be made about funeral processes or mortuary proceedings in general.

> The mortuary proceedings show a striking similarity throughout the world. As death approaches, the nearest relatives in any case, sometimes the whole community, foregather by the dying man, and dying, the most private act which a man can perform, is transformed into a public, tribal event. As a rule, a certain differentiation takes place at once, some of the relatives watching near the corpse, others making preparations for the pending end and its consequence, others again performing perhaps some religious acts at a sacred spot. Thus in certain parts of Melanesia the real kinsmen must keep at a distance and only relatives by marriage perform the mortuary service, while in some tribes of Australia the reverse order is observed.

As soon as death has occurred, the body is washed, anointed and adorned, sometimes the bodily apertures are filled, the arms and legs tied together. Then it is exposed to the view of all, and the most important phase, the immediate mourning begins. There is always a more or less conventionalized and dramatized outburst of grief and wailing in sorrow, which often passes . . . into bodily lacerations and the tearing of hair (Malinowski 1955:48–49).

The above discussion of mortuary proceedings was set forth by Bronislaw Malinowski. It remains quite tentative, for anthropologists have been too busy with other things to spend time developing a theory about funerals. There are drawbacks to Malinowski's discussion as theory. For one thing, it doesn't tell us why people do these various things. Because the evidence has not been collected in any systematic fashion, it does not even convince us that all people actually do carry out their funerals in such a manner. Malinowski's discussion presents a descriptive theory. It lists the sorts of things that might be found or ought to be found in mortuary proceedings, but it does not attempt to explain why such things are present in one cultural system and absent in another.

Once a process has been sharply defined so that it can be recognized and identified in a variety of cultural systems, the way is open to a search for the various forces that will explain the differences and similarities among cultures. In this example, we have asked what funerals are and of what kinds of actions they might be composed. We might also ask why funerals are so common and what sort of needs they fulfill. In the end, we might ask about ways and means of designing funerals that would in some way work better to provide comfort and reaffirmation than do existing funerals.

The method for reaching such understandings was proposed in 1896 by Franz Boas:

We have another method, which in many respects is much safer. A detailed study of customs in their relation to the total culture of the tribe practicing them, in connection with an investigation of their geographical distribution among neighboring tribes, affords us almost always a means of determining with considerable accuracy the historical causes that lead to the formation of the customs in question and to the psychological processes that were at work in their development. The results of inquiries conducted by this method may be three-fold. They may reveal the environmental conditions which have created or modified cultural elements; they may clear up psychological factors which are at work in shaping the culture; or they may bring before our eyes the effects that historical connections have had upon the growth of culture (Boas 1948:276).

The study of the variation within a single process in a particular region provides an experimental control that helps to identify the kinds of factors that determine the shape of an existing process. If the members of one tribe fail to do so, then we must consider ourselves to be very close to an explanation of at least one of the causes of variation in the carrying out of funerals. As we expand our focus to consider the entire worldwide range of variation in the conduct of mortuary proceedings, we can then build an increasingly clear picture of their causes and of their value to humanity.

It may be that such information about mortuary proceedings will never be useful. Perhaps, indeed, they are not useful and not needed in modern societies. Perhaps we already have the perfect solution to whatever problems were originally solved by the creation of mortuary proceedings among early humans some tens of thousands of years ago. But there are other processes and other unsolved problems. The techniques of cross-cultural comparison outlined above can be applied equally well to child-rearing processes, marital conflict, play, courtship, learning, or discovery. All of the major processes, and quite a few of the minor ones, that are carried out in our cultural system are carried out in some other cultural system—somewhere. We can learn much that is practical simply by learning how other people do things.

A process acquires its particular form as a result of the interactions of universal human properties, particular environments, and particular cultural traditions. The general research strategy appropriate to a search for an understanding of the similarities and differences among cultural systems is to identify the role of each of these factors or clusters of factors in affecting the form of particular cultural processes and cultural systems. The work of the cultural anthropologist begins with the study of some particular cultural system. The relative importance of the different factors that have influenced the development of that cultural system can be understood only through cross-cultural comparison.

We have now considered the nature of culture. Our next questions have to do with how culture, and with it humanity, came into being. From a biological point of view, we should like to understand the status of human beings as animals and the importance of biological variation among them. Equally important is the history of the development of similarities and differences among human cultures. These things are the subject of the next chapter.

SUMMARY

Outside of a few superficial characteristics, there don't seem to be any very startling differences between seals and humans. Nevertheless, the Eskimo hunter is almost always successful in his contests with the seal. To the Eskimo, the essence of the difference between himself and the seal lies in the ability to call upon the assistance of the souls of his ancestors. Looking at a wide variety of other plants and animals, we see that there is a continuity in nature and that many plants and animals possess the same kinds of abilities possessed by humans. Looking more closely, it is apparent that almost everything connected to the Eskimo hunter and to human beings in general is artificial. Unlike any other living thing, the human being bases every action upon the presence of an elaborate *material culture* consisting of tools, equipment, and other constructed parts of the environment. Even more important is the fact that humans talk. The principal adaptation of the species lies in the ability to utilize the accumulated wisdom (and folly) of past generations passed on through the media of speech and material culture.

Similarity between humans and other living things derives fundamentally from the existence of the genetic message. The ability of living things to reproduce depends upon the existence of the genetic message. The genetic message is carried by molecules of DNA, which are capable of dividing in such a way as to duplicate the message. In sexual reproduction (meiosis), the process of reproduction guarantees that no two individuals will be precisely alike. Mutations arising in the physical law that no message can be duplicated endlessly without error are one source of variation. Other variations arise as the genetic materials of the individual's parents are recombined.

The fact that each individual is different from each other individual accounts for the fact that some individuals have more children (reproduce their genetic message more effectively) than do others. Selection, the process whereby some survive to produce children and some do not, leads to continuous change in the genetic message and, under proper circumstances, to the origin of new species. Such change permits species to maintain their adaptation to an ever changing environment. If the adaptations possessed by a species are not good enough to get by, then the species will become extinct. On the other hand, not all changes in the genetic message are related to adaptation. Many changes occur at random and have little or no adaptive significance. Biological or genetic evolution is a more or less accidental process subject only to the limitation that the accidents that cause genetic change cannot interfere too much with the survival and reproduction of the species.

Like the genetic code, the linguistic code derives its nature from meaningful combinations of a small number of basic units. The units of language are called phonemes. The use of phonemes enables human beings to assign *arbitrary* meanings to sounds and things. It also enables human beings to talk about things removed in time and space (displacement), and to produce new ideas (productivity). Unlike all other animals, human beings can tell lies and create fantasies. The ability of language to remove human beings from the real world is compensated for by the facts that language permits efficient use and transmission of information and the creation of new ideas and technologies. Because the linguistic code permits planned and rapid change in behavior, the linguistic code supplements and extends the potentialities of the genetic code in human beings. Human behavior is primarily determined by cultural messages transmitted by language rather than by genetic messages transmitted by DNA.

As suggested by the "Railway Conductor's Song," the cultural message consists of a variety of complicated and sometimes contradictory sorts of instructions and information. Although aspects of the cultural message may consist of "laws" that are invariably followed, the basic pattern is one of complex messages that are interpreted by individuals who then decide, either consciously or unconsciously, what is to be done. The cultural message is what you need to know in order to adjust your behavior to the expectations of your fellows. People tend to conform to cultural messages, to do what they think other people expect them to do, because they have learned that proper behavior is usually easier, safer, and more rewarding than improper behavior.

As people obey cultural messages, they create cultural systems. Observation of any cultural scene, in this case a children's play group in South India, permits identification of the five basic elements of cultural systems: place, people, plans, paraphernalia, and process. The place is the environment or setting; the people are members; the plans are the cultural tradition; pharaphernalia are the items of material culture that people construct; and process is what happens when the other parts of the cultural system are working.

The example of an airplane crew illustrates several different kinds of theories about how cultural systems work. For convenience, some scholars focus upon the environment and its influence, others focus upon human biology, still others upon the nature of cultural messages. A more complete understanding of human behavior depends upon a systems approach in which all aspects of human life are considered together.

In another sense, the cause of human behavior is the set of conscious or unconscious decisions that cause individuals to do the things they do. Thus, the settlement of Chan Kom decided to become a pueblo, and the mutineers decided to establish a colony on an unknown island. Thus, a cultural system is the product of human decisions. On balance, the fact that a cultural system survives is sufficient to indicate that most of the decisions made were good enough to get by. However, just as in biological evolution, some changes occur at random and not all changes are for the best. Because decisions are often irrevocable, mistakes often have to be repaid through ingenuity. Thus, cultural systems, like other biological systems, are something of a patchwork.

Although cultural systems can be interpreted in various ways, the most meaningful approach is in terms of the separate processes that take place when they are in operation. Many processes—funerals are used as an example here—are widely distributed among human groups. A process is defined as a series of interlinked events commencing under culturally defined conditions, following a culturally defined plan or pattern, and reaching a culturally defined endpoint. There are six processes considered vital to the operation of any cultural system: maintaining relationships to the environment, regulating membership, indicating status, transmitting culture, controlling behavior, and adapting to changing circumstances. The chapter ends with a discussion of the ways in which the study of individual processes can contribute to our understandings of cultural systems and of human behavior.

For Further Reading

Understanding the genetic code, leading ultimately to the ability to design and create life, has formidable technological and moral implications for all human beings. A good place to begin to find out about the genetic message is Watson's *The Double Helix* (1968), a personal account of one person's contribution to the great discovery. Any good biology or genetics textbook should provide an overview; somewhat less technical accounts are found in textbooks of biological anthropology such as Birdsell (1975) or Campbell (1974).

A background understanding of human language is more difficult to obtain. Sapir's early textbook (1921) and Greenberg's overview (1968) are good places to begin. Also of interest are Clark et al. (1972), Gleason (1961), and Gaeng (1971). Also worth considering is Gudschinsky's *How to Learn an Unwritten Language* (1967).

A readable introduction to the world of primates is Kummer's *Primate Societies* (1971). Summaries of research are to be found in Jay (1968) and DeVore (1965). Field studies by Schaller (1963), van Lawick-Goodall (1968), and Kummer (1968) are worth reading. See also Kummer's bibliography of primate studies (1971), and Lancaster's *Primate Behavior and the Emergence of Human Culture* (1975).

Kroeber and Kluckhohn (1963) provide an extensive review of the history of the concept of culture. Interesting, but not always readable, materials on culture and anthropology are to be found in Gaust and Norbeck (1976), Kaplan and Manners (1972), Bohannan and Glazer (1973), Jarvie (1977), Bateson (1972), and Hanson (1975).

Problems and Questions

1. Using a pencil and paper make some systematic observations of domestic animals. How do they resemble and differ from human beings? Why?
2. Compare "mother," "bow-wow," "anger," or other words in several different languages. What does this say about the ways in which words acquire their meaning?
3. Observe a film, a television program, or a dramatic performance. Is there any behavior that violates cultural norms or behavioral standards?

4. Read a folk tale from another culture. What is some of the content of the cultural message that it contains? (You should find folk tales from other cultures listed in the card catalogue of your local library under *Folklore*.)
5. Describe a small group or cultural system to which you belong. What are its parts?
6. How do you decide which course to take, what foods to eat, or what games to play? What sorts of factors influence your decisions?
7. Select a single process and see how it is carried out among several different peoples. How are the similarities and differences to be explained? (Ethnographic accounts of different peoples are likely to be listed in your library card catalogue under *Ethnology*. A number are listed in the Bibliography of this book.)

HOW WE BECAME
HUMAN

What are the problems?

The previous chapter dealt with the nature of similarities and differences between human beings and other animals. It raised questions about the genetic and cultural messages and the nature of people, cultural systems, and process. This chapter begins at the beginning. It asks questions about the origins of humanity. Who were our earliest ancestors? How far back can evolution in the human direction be traced? What caused our ancestors to develop into human beings? What were the outlines of the process of human evolution?

Several million years ago cultural evolution became the dominant means of human adaptation. There are questions about the early forms of culture; about possible explanations for the development of agriculture, cities, and industrial societies; and about the distribution of tribes and nations across the surface of the earth. Observation of the course of cultural evolution and of the development of a wide range of human cultures leads to further questions concerning human variation. Is there significant biological variation among the representatives of different cultural systems? Are there ways of evaluating the competence or intelligence of people from different backgrounds? Do they work?

Most of the questions covered in this chapter form a part of the ongoing research carried out in the subdisciplines of biological anthropology and archaeology. They have an important place in a textbook on cultural anthropology simply because, "What's past is prologue." Modern human beings are the product of millenia of biological and cultural evolution.

HOW DID WE BECOME HUMAN?

The processes of biological evolution result in the development of many different species. Each species takes its form as a result of a series of compromises between random change and selection. Like paper boats on troubled waters, species assume a variety of forms and survive for varying periods of time. As chance and selection result in the multiplication of forms, certain kinds of forms turn out to be more suitable than others. The single-celled organism, for example, is one of the most successful biological types ever to develop. Some are so perfectly adapted that they have probably remained virtually unchanged since they first evolved. Other single-celled organisms were less successful and consequently underwent adaptive changes that ultimately led to the development of multicelled organisms which include human beings.

The assumption that biological evolution proceeds according to some sort of plan, or design, directed by an intelligence, is no longer considered necessary to an explanation of the origins of humanity. Still, there are many ways in which humans can be regarded as a culmination of certain evolutionary trends. The development of language, writing, printing, and broadcasting represent tendencies in the improvement of communication that date back at least as far as the development of the spinal cord. Improved communication between body cells and, later, between different individuals has gone hand in hand with increasing complexity of organization culminating in the modern nation state and the United Nations. It has also gone hand in hand with the development of the ability to base behavior on learning as well as on genetic inheritance and to supplement direct learning with information storage by means of mnemonic devices, pictures, writings, and computer banks.

Essentially, the mammalian tendency is to develop an intelligent long-lived individual that learns a great deal by observing other members of the troop or group and draws upon the resources of memory to meet new environmental challenges. A long life span slows down the processes of biological evolution. Mammals tend to maintain their genetic messages relatively unchanged, while rapidly changing the learned messages stored, also by biochemical means, in the brain. Insects on the other hand have a dramatically opposed strategy. They learn little, but breed very quickly, changing their biological messages dramatically in shorter periods of time. The point here is not that mammals are more or less adapted than insects, but that mammals do things differently from insects.

Human beings are mammals. They nurse their young. They have hair. They have placentas. Among the mammals, humans are classified as primates because of their physical resemblance to monkeys and apes. Humans differ from other primates primarily because they use language to transmit complex cultural messages. Among the primates, human beings seem most closely related to the great apes, especially the chimpanzee and the gorilla. This being the case, we should expect to find in the fossil record a form resembling humans and great apes somewhere in our ancestry. *Ramapithecus*, a fossil ape that existed some fifteen million years ago, may be that fossil, although some scholars think he was just another ape.

Ramapithecus lived on the margins of forest and grassland regions at a time when many of the forests of Africa, southern Europe, and southern Asia were disappearing. It is interesting to speculate that the rapid decline of forest areas might have forced some "progressive" apes to attempt a grassland existence. In a grassland environment, vocalization, good eyesight, upright posture, and group cooperation may have had definite advantages.

A tendency to sit or stand in an upright position, besides permitting the individual to see over the grass, probably freed the hands for carrying or manipulating things. We can then imagine early protohumans (hominids) collecting small animals, roots, and nuts and carrying them to a safe and comfortable tree while using vocalizations to indicate location, direction of travel, kinds of resources available, and the presence of other animals. Because we know that wild dogs and other predators living in grassland regions seemed to hunt in groups, and because groups may have been needed for protection or to provide care for babies, it seems

FIGURE 2–1 Monkeys in a zoo keep their hands free for communication among themselves and with human beings. Note the family group. (PHOTO BY ALAN R. BEALS)

likely that the adaptation of protohominids to grassland living required improved organization of existing social groups. In turn, this need to get along with animals of one's own species, as well as animals of other species, required a good deal of crafty calculation and political savvy. Protohumans had to be pretty skillful in identifying other animals and keeping track of their activities.

This increased use of the hands, eyes, and mouth for social and economic purposes is believed to have led to the increasing sophistication of the human brain, which made possible even further use of hands, eyes, and mouth. Increases in brain-size relative to body-size may have been facilitated by upright posture in which the weight of the brain is supported directly by the spinal column instead of being held at an awkward angle by giant neck muscles. In turn, an upright posture and two-legged walking (bipedalism) caused changes in the shape of the female pelvis such that the birth canal became too small to permit the passage of a normally developed baby—thus probably forcing the early birth of hominid infants that were "not quite done." Like kangaroos, human beings give birth to immature babies that are unable to feed or otherwise care for themselves. Like the baby kangaroo, the human infant may find itself in a pouch, but the pouch is a cultural rather than a genetic artifact.

Because the human baby remains helpless for months after birth, arrangements must be made for the care of the infant and its mother. The assumption of male responsibilities for child care may well have been a crucial step in the separation of humans from the other great apes. It is true that one small ape species, the Gibbons, also forms family groups in which both males and females nurture children. But humans, unlike any other living species, are capable of recognizing many kinds of relatives and establishing special relationships with each. The development of upright posture, the manipulation of objects with the hands, and the need for a large brain to deal with social interaction and communication, probably precipitated a child-care crisis in hominid evolution. Over many years the evolved solution to that crisis may have been the development of language, culture, food sharing or exchange, and baby sitting.

HOW DID CULTURE INFLUENCE HEREDITY?

Human beings are the accidental creation of their ape-like ancestors. We do not know exactly how this accident took place, but it appears to have involved the beginnings of tool use, language, and increasingly complex group organization. With the emergence of these protocultural things, the evolution of ancestral species became dominated by interaction among the Australopithecines or other ancestors and their protocultural objects. The merest beginnings of language and the slightest use of objects for pounding, piercing, and throwing created a new environment which radically altered the course of Australopithecine evolution. The Southern Apes now became humans. Their evolution began to be influenced by the cultural message.

Among other animals, the tiger that acquires a longer tooth or a sharper claw is likely to outbreed any rival tigers, producing relatively more descendants and so perpetuating genes for longer teeth and sharper claws. Widespread introduction of the new-style tiger might take several generations. In the meantime, the environment might be changing in such a way as to place new demands upon tigers, perhaps for shorter teeth and duller claws. Among human beings, the person who discovered that flint made sharper knives than did other rocks, and the many other persons who have discovered ways to make even sharper cutting edges, did not have to rely upon genetic evolution to spread their new techniques. Once the ability to create culture existed, new evolutionary adaptations could be spread through the use of observation and speech. The first people to develop and use sharper knives may have had more children than the people who were still using dull knives, but this was not the way they spread the information required for adoption of the new adaptation. Most probably, the people who wanted sharper knives learned to make them themselves or traded some other useful object for them.

Human beings do not need genes for the use of flint knives or telephones because they already have genes for the building of culture and the development of language. Once the culture-building capacity existed, even in rudimentary form, the biological evolution of human beings was radically altered. Detailed genetic control of specific behaviors became even less important for human beings than for other primates. Genetic information concerning what to eat, how to mate, how to take care of children, how to cope with wild dogs, when to get angry, and almost every other aspect of existence appears to have been quickly and almost entirely replaced by cultural information. Under the principle of "use it or lose it," human beings even lost the canine teeth required for frightening enemies and making puncture holes. They could accomplish the same things with a few pieces of stone.

The thrust of human genetic evolution was in the direction of improving the human capacity to build culture. Up until 50,000 years ago, for example, there appears to have been a steady increase in the size of the human brain relative to the size of the human body and in its complexity. This increase was almost certainly a response to a need to improve human capacities for the use of tools and language. As language became the easy-to-use, flexible, and foolproof instrument that we know so well today, human beings became devices for carrying about an enormous brain that could be attached to various kinds of equipment largely by means of the fingers. Our genetic message has been stripped away until we stand naked, "sans fur, sans claws, sans fangs, sans everything."

After the Australopithecines transformed themselves into human beings, they naturally took advantage of their new adaptation. They radiated: their population increased rapidly; they began to spread outward. As they entered new environments, they adapted by altering their tools and equipment. Naturally, there was some genetic change as they traveled to new places, but such change may not have been sufficient to create geographical species. Among normal species, radiation into new environments leads to speciation as genetic adaptation to the new environments takes place. Speciation was not necessary for human beings. Therefore, it either did not take place or it took place only to a limited degree.

WHEN WAS THE FIRST PERSON?

The evidence concerning the early stages of human evolution is not highly detailed. Scholars agree that there was a transition from ape-like to human-like beings that is clearly marked in the fossil record, but they disagree about many of the details. In the early stages of ape-human evolution it is quite possible that several different species existed contemporaneously. There is even some evidence that more than one species of ape-human and human-ape existed together in the same spot. Still, apes and humans are quite variable species, and it is possible that individuals that look like they belong to different species really don't. As with dogs and other canines, it is possible that different species of human beings were interfertile and that developing specific differences were wiped out as the diffusion of culture promoted increasing intermarriage among human groups.

One of the Southern Apes or Australopithecines probably gave rise to *Homo erectus*. *Erectus* is the first indisputably human creature. Fossils of *erectus* have been identified in Africa, northern China, Java, and southern Europe. Geographically, *erectus* meets the basic criteria for humanity. *Erectus* occupied a wide variety of different environments, did not form any clearly marked geographical species, and used an elaborate tool kit which took different forms in different places. The lack of geographical speciation and the possession of variable tools indicates the supplementation of genetic evolution by cultural evolution.

Erectus improved upon the stone tools made by his predecessors and the quality of stone tools improves steadily over the period of the Lower Paleolithic (Old Stone Age), the period dominated by *erectus*. Several writers have questioned *erectus'* intelligence and humanity arguing that fully human beings would have developed improved tools more rapidly. *Erectus* may have been more concerned with inventions that left no mark on the archaeological record. For example, we don't know who invented or discovered the first piece of string, the first portable water container, the first fish net, the first medicinal plants, or the first portable baby carrier. We don't know who invented language or how difficult the task might have been. The technology used by early humans is so commonplace and widespread that we have little conception of the difficulties involved in developing and applying it. It is a sobering lesson in respect for our ancestors to attempt to make a piece of string adequate to fly a homemade kite; a basket that will hold water; a container that is ratproof; a stone spearpoint; a blowpipe that will kill a monkey at fifty paces; a bow and arrow that can kill a deer; a thatched roof; or even a decent broom.

And Who Was the First Wise One?

In China, *erectus* pushed at least as far north as Peking, surviving cold winters through the use of fire and the occupation of caves. Perhaps, as the winters grew colder, environmental pressures increased the rates of cultural and genetic evolution. About 100,000 years ago *erectus* had altered sufficiently to merit a new species designation, *Homo sapiens neanderthalensis*. The word *sapiens*, meaning intelligent, represents a judgment that the large-brained neanderthalensis possessed an intelligence comparable to that of modern *Homo sapiens sapiens*, ourselves. Another way of reaching this conclusion, brain-size being notoriously unreliable, is to consider the fact that many neanderthals exhibited funerary customs.

They buried, painted, and decorated dead people and their property. Such habits suggest an intelligence akin to our own.

This and other suggestions of religion or perhaps medicine, along with the increasingly complicated tools and equipment used for hunting and gathering, leads us to suspect that the neanderthals possessed a more highly developed ability to use language than their predecessors. As mentioned in chapter 1, modern languages possess properties of displacement and productivity that permit discussion of such things as life after death. We can only imagine what the neanderthals were thinking as they buried their dead, but it seems likely that complex ideas such as life after death were involved.

As language, culture, and tool use began to assume their modern form, the rate of human cultural evolution accelerated. The origin of *Homo sapiens sapiens* about 50,000 years ago represented the last step forward in biological evolution. No significant differences have been found between modern and early forms of *Homo sapiens sapiens*. This may reflect the comparatively small number of human generations completed in a mere 50,000 years. It may also reflect a change in the mode of evolution from genetic to cultural change. The next intelligent species is likely to be the result of invention and manipulation rather than the result of conventional biological evolution. *Homo sapiens sapiens* seems likely to achieve the ability to create life and supervise its evolution, thus completing the process that began when the Australopithecines first began to create the cultural environment that directed their evolution into human beings.

WHAT HAPPENED IN PREHISTORY?

The cultural inventions and genetic changes required to complete the evolution of the human capacity to build culture were probably completed with the emergence of *Homo sapiens neanderthalensis*. With the fluent use of language and the practice of cooking food before eating it, the heavy jaw and facial musculature characteristic of *erectus* and some of the neanderthals could be replaced by a more delicate apparatus suitable for the eating of mush and the making of light conversation. Neanderthals were probably replaced by modern humans, not because modern humans were smarter but because modern humans represent the biological changes that took place as *Homo neanderthalensis* accommodated to the sophisticated use of tools and language.

During the 50,000 years since the emergence of *Homo sapiens,* there is no evidence of biological evolution in any particular direction. To be sure, biological evolution continues, but there is no suggestion that the culture building and using capacities of the first *Homo sapiens* are any different from those of the last. One evidence for this is that the very earliest forms of art known—while sometimes very crude—may also be highly sophisticated. Another indication lies in the nature of language. All contemporary languages are fully modern and complete. There are no "primitive" or early forms of language. It seems probable then that all modern languages derive from a common ancestral stock, which came into being only a short time after *Homo sapiens* began to spread. If early *Homo sapiens* could use, and perhaps invent, "modern" language, then his brain could not have been significantly different from ours.

Important changes in the archaeological record begin with the neanderthals and continue through the development of *Homo sapiens*. On the whole, the continuous development of new technology suggests a gradual emergence into full humanity rather than any sudden "great leap forward" either in human culture or biology. As technology, and presumably linguistic and organizational skills as well, continued to develop, human beings moved into increasingly difficult environments. *Erectus* reached as far as Java, but *sapiens* went beyond to Australia, Melanesia, New Guinea, and the Pacific islands. *Erectus* spread its domain as far as Peking in China; *sapiens* moved farther north across the Bering Straits and into the New World. Ten thousand years ago, *Homo sapiens* occupied almost every part of the earth but Antarctica. The occupation of Antarctica took place within the last hundred years as a result of the sharing of technologies invented by the Eskimo and Europeans. At present, the movement of *Homo sapiens* into undersea environments, lunar environments, and perhaps space itself is a logical extension of the human ability to adapt through culture.

As *Homo sapiens* pressed against the retreating glaciers of Europe and Asia, a range of highly specialized hunting cultures developed. These cultures depended upon the use of semisubterranean dwellings to conserve heat energy. Clothing was tailored from animal furs and a complicated tool kit permitted survival in the coldest regions penetrated by human beings. Evidence of these cultures still survive in a broad belt reaching from Lapland across Siberia, Alaska, and northern Canada to Greenland.

In California, hunter-gatherers discovered ways of converting the bitter-tasting acorn of the oak tree into a useful food. On the northwestern coast of North America, specialized salmon fisherman created an elaborate permanently settled civilization characterized by extraordinary works of art. In Africa, Australia, and other desert regions, specialized adaptations to life in the desert were worked out. The Bushmen, now living in the Kalahari desert of South Africa, exemplify such an adaptation. In the jungles of what is now Zaïre and the rain forests of Southeast Asia, hunter-gatherers worked out specialized hunting techniques using nets or blowguns.

Why Are You Messing with Those Weeds?

Starting about eight thousand years ago, evidence of the existence of cultivated plants began to appear in a number of different locations throughout the world. It was first thought that the cultivation of plants began independently in the Near East and Central America and then spread to other locations. The examination of plant origins suggests that there may have been as many as five or six regions of the world that could be described as centers of plant domestication. There may have been as well a number of additional regions where a few wild plants were domesticated and cultivated.

There is little agreement concerning the factors that led to the first cultivation of plants. Changes in climate may have had an indirect effect, but it is noteworthy that marked climate changes appear not to have taken place in the specific regions where plant cultivation is thought to have developed. Some writers believe that population pressures—a need to feed increasing numbers of people—might account for the cultivation of plants. Others assert that hunter-gatherers tend to control their populations and use relatively small fractions of the available resources. That *Homo sapiens* occupied forbidding desert, jungle, and mountain regions that *Homo erectus* refused to touch suggests that population growth was always an engine that drove technological development.

As *Homo sapiens* developed more efficient ways of utilizing the environment, human population densities must have steadily increased. At the same time, the influence of human beings upon the environment must have become progressively greater. Under such circumstances, even without any marked deprivation, many things normally available must have become scarce. The response to such scarcity would have been the further development of sophisticated techniques for utilizing the environment.

While this was going on, the distribution of plants and animals in the environment would have changed. Some plants and animals were eliminated; others adapted to the presence of human beings. In particular, various edible grasses and tubers may have adapted to the point of spreading their seeds and sprouts by means of humans. This would be particularly true of weedy or "pioneer" species like wheat and maize that are adapted to growing in disturbed soil such as occurs at the edge of trails or on the margins of human habitation sites. Finally, human beings appear to have begun the deliberate cultivation of the weedy but edible plants that grew around their habitation sites and trash dumps.

Early or incipient food production was certainly carried out on a small scale. It is doubtful that early attempts at cultivation were very successful, or that people worked very hard to make them successful. The motive for the development of agriculture was probably a casual desire to make the collection of certain grasses and tubers somewhat more convenient. This

FIGURE 2–3 Adaptations required for food processing may have a significant impact upon human activities. Here, women at the North Fork of the Mono River in California grind acorns harvested from oak trees in preparation for the leaching or soaking process required to remove bitter tannic acid from them. (PHOTO COURTESY OF THE LOWIE MUSEUM OF ANTHROPOLOGY, UNIVERSITY OF CALIFORNIA, BERKELEY)

might have been particularly true with plants that were scarce and hard to find.

About six thousand years ago, a variety of plants (and some animals as well) had been domesticated. Furthermore, techniques of domestication had been developed to the point where it was scarcely worthwhile to spend much time in hunting and gathering. In any case, one result of increasing population is the creation of a scarcity of products that can be hunted or gathered. As people became increasingly addicted to agriculture, they soon realized the unfeasibility of planting crops in the same place for more than three or four years.

Agriculture then became shifting or "swidden" with people moving their fields, and often their houses as well, every few years. Thus, the large

FIGURE 2–4   Zapotec Indian field in Oaxaca, Mexico. In a few years, such swidden fields will be exhausted and abandoned, and brush will be cleared for the establishment of new fields. (PHOTO BY ALAN R. BEALS)

land areas required for this swidden agriculture and the sometimes forbidding mountain and jungle areas in which it was carried out created a tendency for swidden agriculturalists to be organized in terms of relatively small and often hostile communities. Swidden farmers still occupy parts of the Amazon rain forest in South America and in the remaining forested regions in New Guinea, Southeast Asia, southern Asia and Africa. Typically, swidden agriculturalists grow a variety of crops which are consumed almost entirely within the local community.

WHEN WERE THE CITIES BUILT?

In a few places, unique local conditions permitted the raising of crops year after year in the same place. This seems to have been true in parts of Central America where permanently established, and sometimes irrigated fields, appear to have been used. Similarly, the flood plains of the Nile and of other similar Southwest Asian and North African rivers permitted the development of permanent fields. Eventually, plow agriculture, with fields fertilized by cow dung, and wet rice agriculture provided the basis for most permanently occupied fields in the Old World. Highly productive and permanently occupied fields allow stable settlements, an increasingly

FIGURE 2–5 In the "unnatural" environment provided by a paddy (rice) field in Namhalli, South India, a husband and wife irrigate their small but productive patch of land using a bucket attached to a kind of see-saw arrangement made with a weighted and balanced beam. (PHOTO BY ALAN R. BEALS)

dense population, and ultimately, the creation of large-sized towns. If such towns are located on waterways or have other means of transporting large quantities of grain, they may develop into cities.

Another requirement for the development of cities is that a single farmer be able to produce several times the amount of food that he himself and his family can consume. It is not essential that every farmer be able to do this, but enough of them must be able to do so in order to supply the grain required for the support of an urban population. The farmer who grows substantially more than his family can eat becomes a specialist, a person who pursues a single task rather than a variety of tasks. Where a hunter-gatherer or a swidden farmer might typically manufacture virtually all of the equipment required for a variety of tasks, the peasant farmer is a specialist who relies upon other specialists for many of his needs. In a society characterized by the presence of cities, specialists are also required to collect taxes, defend the state, and regulate the economy. Thus, the city brings into being a class system. Slaves, landless laborers, and farmers occupy positions near the bottom of the class system while specialists in religious and military matters occupy positions near the top. Businessmen, skilled laborers, rural landlords and moneylenders, and artisans tend to occupy positions around the middle.

With the extensive trade required for a circulation of grain from the country to the city and services from the city to the country, elaborate economic systems involving markets, media of exchange, banking facilities, and taxes soon evolve. Such a system of marketing requires the keeping of records. Some form of writing or an elaborate system of record keeping is characteristic of all urban societies. Frequently, an urban society possesses a wealthy leisure class with special goods and services developed for the benefit of that class. Esoteric kinds of knowledge, special products, marvelous entertainments and artistic productions are demanded and provided for the benefit of gentlefolk and as a means of demonstrating their superiority over those who till the soil.

Farming, increased population, and the formation of cities and states led to increases in the complexity of the human tool kit. Copper, brass, and iron—in many cases worn first as jewelry—became the basis of metal tools. Special techniques for cutting and transporting stone were used to create the monumental buildings required for the military and religious needs of the upper classes. In the Old World, the use of the wheel revolutionized the making of pottery and the means of transportation. Elaborate weaving techniques were developed as specialists prepared elegant fabrics for the wealthy.

While the hunter-gatherer or swidden farmer works a relatively few hours each day, the peasant farmer begins his toil at dawn and ends it at twilight. His child, if lucky enough to attend a temple school, spends a similar twelve hours memorizing scriptures. Where the hunter-gatherer or swidden farmer dines upon a complex assortment of meat and vegetable products, the peasant farmer consumes mush or flat cakes wrapped around a tiny portion of vegetable and legumes. On festival days, which are quite frequent, a sheep, pig, turkey, or war captive may be sacrificed and a small portion of meat consumed.

The highly productive forms of agriculture practiced by peasant farmers required intensive labor, dense populations, and massive environmental changes. Often, environments failed to stabilize after the trees had been cut, the land leveled, and other improvements made. Unstable environmental conditions frequently led to drought, crop failure, and famine. Increasingly dense human populations provided ideal circumstances for the spread and perpetuation of a variety of epidemic and endemic diseases. Even earlier, with the introduction of swidden agriculture, which provides ideal breeding places for the anopheles mosquito, malaria spread across the tropics from India to Africa. Its ancient presence is verified by the presence of the gene for sickle cell anemia, which confers resistance to malaria, in widespread human populations.

Urban life depends upon the existence of taxation, transportation, trade, and other mechanisms that lead to the movement of grain and other food products from the country to the city. Because the ancient city produced relatively little in terms of goods that could be exchanged for farm produce, it follows that many an ancient city depended upon centralized control of a standing army. In addition, the city often provided a state religion and various entertainments. The ancient city provided the circuses, but the farmers provided the bread. Put another way, the city and the state or kingdom headquartered within it sold protection to the

FIGURE 2–7   Plowing a paddy field in Gopalpur, South India (PHOTO BY ALAN R. BEALS)

FIGURE 2–8 Participation in an urban society involves economic and ritual exchanges between town and village. Here, the Swazi Queen Mother inauguarates the agricultural season by plowing a special ritual field. She is accompanied by governors of royal villages and her close attendants. (PHOTO COURTESY OF HILDA KUPER)

farmer—doctors to cure illness, soldiers to defend the borders, and gods to provide rain.

Very often, especially when the soldiers failed to defend the borders, peasant farmers were cruelly exploited and their status was little better than that of the slaves and landless laborers that they themselves exploited. When greedy priests, rulers, and conquerors take more than the land can readily provide, the result is ecological disaster. Malnourished farmers fall prey to epidemic diseases; crops fail; banditry increases; irrigation works are destroyed; the city is burned; a wasteland is created.

Oppression, like small pox or cholera, is a self-limiting disease. In the best of times, the peasant farmer lived well enough. Taxes were light; wars were few; crops were good; and life expectancies long. The visitor to China, India, Mexico, Rome, or Peru during such a golden age would likely feel that peasant and urban life offered many advantages over the loneliness and isolation of the hunting and gathering way of life or the constant suspicion and warfare of the village farmer and/or swidden way of life.

After the Cities, What?

As of five hundred years ago a central portion of the New World, from Peru to possibly as far north as the Mississippi valley, was dominated by peasant farmers. In the Old World, China, parts of Southeast Asia, India, the Middle East, and the area surrounding the Mediterranean from Nigeria to Sweden were also largely devoted to peasant agriculture. In both the Old World and the New, hunter-gatherers and swidden agriculturalists continued to live in isolated regions. Swidden agriculturalists or independent village farmers dominated the rain forests of the Amazon and other rain forest regions ranging from the islands of Melanesia, north of Australia, across Southeast Asia, India, and Africa. Village farmers occupied eastern North America up to the point where early frost prevented the raising of maize. Pastoral peoples, living in association with agricultural peoples but depending primarily upon herded domestic animals, existed in plains and savannah regions in Central Asia and in Africa. The llama, the only domesticated animal in the New World that might have provided a basis for pastoralism, was limited in its distribution to the region of the Andes in South America.

Hunter-gatherers occupied the western coast of North America and an interior region stretching from the Mississippi region westward. From the southwestern part of the United States where hunter-gatherers lived in association with agricultural peoples, the hunting-gathering way of life reached beyond the Arctic circle from Greenland across the Bering Straits to Siberia. The entire continent of Australia was dominated by hunter-gatherers and so was much of South Africa. Elsewhere in Southeast Asia, India, China, the Philippines, and the rain forests of Africa, large populations of hunter-gatherers existed in relationship to agricultural civilizations.

Five hundred years ago, the voyages of Columbus and Vasco da Gama inaugurated European exploration of the world. The potato, maize, and other American Indian food crops were rapidly disseminated over most of the world. A rapid increase in population followed. In England, a colder climate and an increasing population resulted in deforestation and the use of coal to replace now unavilable wood. The Industrial Revolution was at hand. In less than two centuries, all but a handful of hunter-gatherers and their cultures were destroyed or confined to reservations. Swidden agriculturalists and tribal peoples generally were reeducated and integrated into national states. Peasant farmers have generally escaped the holocaust; their communities and ways of life still changing but identifiable in such far-flung places as Peru, Germany, India, and Swaziland.

The great cultural revolutions beginning with the use of fire and the spread of modern languages have caused particular ways of doing things to spread widely among the peoples of the world. With the invention of increasingly efficient methods of hunting and gathering, human population densities increased. Ultimately, societies became larger and more complex. Larger land areas were required to support them. With the agricultural and urban revolutions, the decimation of hunter-gatherer societies began. Uniform cultures began to occupy such large land areas as those of China, India, Mexico, Peru, and southwestern Asia. Increased efficiency in the production of food and in the organization of human societies led to the merger of populations and the intermixture of their cultural and biological inheritances.

WHAT KINDS OF PEOPLE?

The agricultural, urban, and industrial revolutions mark particular stages in which new technology was rapidly produced and disseminated. New ways of doing things triggered the movement of peoples from one place to another. It also increased the rapidity with which genes flowed from one biological population to another. Sometimes this happened as a result of such dramatic events as conquest, rape, or extermination. More often it happened simply because the exchange of goods and ideas facilitates acquaintanceship and the friendly exchange of genes between populations. In the preceding sections of this chapter, it has been shown how human beings can be classified technologically as hunter-gatherers, food producers, urban people and peasants, and industrialized people. It has also been indicated that the sum of human variation reached a peak before the food-producing revolution and has decreased rapidly, especially since the Industrial Revolution.

In biological evolution it is unusual for populations to be widespread, to diverge, and then to become increasingly similar. The general rule in biological evolution is that species originate, spread, diverge, and ultimately form separate species each adapted to a particular habitat. In human evolution, *Homo sapiens* spread over a large part of the world with considerable rapidity. Following this radiation, there can be little doubt that processes of divergence began. Because *Homo sapiens* populations were fairly large and because human generations are long, divergence could only occur slowly. Another factor limiting the rate of divergence of human populations is the existence of culture which permits adaptation to the environment without genetic change.

Rapid migration, where a few move and many are left behind, causes divergence because, for a variety of reasons, the genetic inheritance of those who migrate is likely to be somewhat different from the genetic inheritance of those who stay at home. The constant splitting apart and coming together of human groups can be considered to create genetic differences between human groups, but such differences are not likely to

be connected to adaptation or selection. Hence, they are not likely to have a cumulative effect. In other words, genetic divergence, when it occurs at random, does not necessarily lead to the development of species.

The division of a single species into separate breeding populations and then into separate species requires a process of gradual adaptation to environmental circumstances. The development of breeding populations into species proceeds most rapidly when (1) populations are small, (2) they are genetically isolated, (3) cultural adaptation is not possible, (4) generations are short, and (5) the rate of selection is high and the number of offspring high. Subspecies, described in nontechnical terms by such words as variety, strain, or race, are simply intermediate categories between breeding populations and species. Meaningful use of the concept of subspecies requires that the members of any postulated subspecies share a number of genetic traits which can be shown to have an adaptive value in their particular setting. These traits will be absent or comparatively rare in other breeding populations of the same species. For example, albinos are not considered a subspecies, nor are tall people. Both characteristics are widely distributed among human breeding populations and they do not occur in association with other characteristics as part of an adaptive strategy. Albinos and tall people do not necessarily have parents or siblings that are albino or tall.

If human breeding populations, generally defined as groups that interbreed more than 50 percent of the time, are to be combined into larger, subspecific groups then some logically consistent way of combining different populations must be found. Modern studies of the distribution of human characteristics indicate that there is little relationship between the distribution of one human characteristic and another. Tall, blond, and blue-eyed individuals are scattered fairly widely throughout the population of Europe, yet maps of the distribution of each of these characteristics show that there is little overlap. Many short people are

blond and blue-eyed; some blond-haired people have brown eyes; many blue-eyed people have brown or black hair.

Ultimately, the trouble with attempts to divide the human species into subspecies is that such classifications cannot be replicated and are not useful. Thus, no two schemes for the classification of human "races" have ever produced identical or even similar results. Although it was once thought that skin color, hair texture, head shape, nose length, blood type, or eye color might have some relationship to other human abilities, there has never been a single shred of evidence of any connection between the characteristics used to build racial classifications and the ability to perform particular tasks or develop particular kinds of cultures. A classification based therefore upon eye color, skin color, and hair form will have some value in predicting the eye color, skin color, and hair form of the populations to which it is applied. It seems to have no value in predicting anything else.

Ethnic groups called "races" are actually social groups based upon a few physical characteristics and a great many cultural and social characteristics. A young man having kinky red hair and a light brown skin will be classified as black if his parents are black. If his parents belong to the white or *Anglo* ethnic group, he will be classified as white. Evidently most of us carry stereotypes in our heads, which are equivalent to checklists of characteristics that we consider to be useful in identifying members of our own and other ethnic groups. Although very few individuals actually fit the stereotype, almost any individual will fit one stereotype better than others. When in doubt, people are assigned to the ethnic group of their parents or associates. Thus, a light-skinned, red-headed person with kinky hair, a southern accent, and a fondness for soul food is likely to be classified as a member of the black or Negro ethnic group. The criteria involved need not be biological at all.

Human beings differ biologically in many ways. The largest differences generally occur between individuals within breeding populations; fairly large differences also occur between nearby breeding populations. Differences between groups of populations occupying different geographical regions are comparatively small, certainly smaller than the differences existing within each geographical region. The concept of subspecies or "race" has not proven useful in anthropology. It does not help to explain the similarities and differences among human cultural systems.

BUT WHAT ABOUT DIFFERENCES IN INTELLIGENCE?

In the United States, it is an everyday observation that different ethnic groups in different geographic regions differ considerably in average school grades, test scores, and income. For some people, the differences in average scores between groups are an indication of some sort of biological difference between them. The thinking seems to be that anyone can grow up to be president of the country or at least of the local bank. Because the president of the country and of the local bank is almost always a male member of the "white" ethnic group, women and members of "nonwhite" ethnic groups are believed to lack the talent or motivation required.

The motivation for this kind of thinking is clear. It is a means of reserving prestigious jobs and other opportunities for "white" males. Such thinking is also embraced by those who are willing to accept an inferior role as long as they can regard themselves as superior to competing ethnic groups. The belief that the *average* performance of a group of people is somehow related to biological differences between groups leads people to emphasize the supposed biological superiority of their own group or to concede inferiority to some groups while insisting upon superiority to others. In time, the concept of hereditary abilities pervades society and almost all positions are assigned to one or another sex or ethnic group. Some people still seek to reserve the quarterback position in football to the male "white" ethnic group.

Because the current structure of our society and of many others depends fundamentally upon ethnicity, there have been repeated attempts to find scientific "proof" that ethnic groups are unequal. These attempts have centered around "intelligence" tests and *average* differences in test scores between groups. The fact that on the average one group scores higher than another does not mean that individual members of the low-scoring group have lower scores than all members of the high-scoring group. There is always substantial overlap between groups. Knowing that Group A has a higher test score than Group B on the average does not permit the prediction that individual number three from Group B will score lower than individual number six from Group A. Individual A–6 may be the lowest-scoring individual in both groups. Individual B–3 could well be the highest-scoring individual in both groups. Differences in *average* performance or *average* anything between groups do not permit discrimination. If it could be shown that *all* "whites" are capable of playing quarterback and that *all* "blacks" are incapable of playing quarterback, such knowledge would be useful to football coaches. Because such a belief is demonstrably false, coaches who act upon it are likely to deprive themselves of the services of excellent quarterbacks. Put another way, the fact that the *average* person can carry fifty pounds doesn't mean that the baby ought to carry fifty pounds.

Granted that average differences between groups on "intelligence"

tests are meaningless figures, what about the use of such tests to determine differences in individual ability? Consider how the tests are made. The first step is to assemble a list of questions that are thought to be answerable by intelligent people and not by unintelligent people. The next step is to identify some intelligent people. This is not at all difficult. We might choose graduate students at Harvard, bank presidents, or undergraduates with very good grades. Most of these people would tend to be male and "white." We now determine which questions these people, who form our "criterion" group, can answer and which questions they cannot answer. We throw away the questions they can't answer. The questions they can answer form the "intelligence" test. Basically, such tests measure an individual's knowledge of the cultural tradition of middle- and upper-class "white" males.

Such tests need not be direct demonstrations of knowledge. For example, the "Draw-a-Man" test, which was designed to be "culture free," involves simply asking children to draw pictures of a man. Right there, when the child is asked to draw a "man" rather than a woman or a child, is the first plainly culturally biased part of the test. The test is scored by examining the amount of detail in the picture and comparing it with the child's age. A middle-class American child or a Hopi Indian child will normally score quite high on this test. Children in both cultures are trained to draw and are accustomed to seeing men dressed in fancy costumes. By contrast, "black" children raised in urban ghettos sometimes refer to themselves verbally as "nothing." Such children tend to draw pictures of individuals with blank faces. Although such a drawing would receive a low score on the test, some reflection might suggest that it is a highly intelligent way of depicting a disregarded person. The examples of the "Draw-a-Man" test suggest the futility of attempts to relate numerical test scores to the biological makeup of human groups. Any kind of test is bound to be affected by culture and by the past experience of those to whom it is administered.

Some years ago, a few communities in the southwestern United States were able to generate substantial federal funding by administering standard intelligence tests, written in English, to Spanish-speaking children. Because the Spanish-speaking children uniformly flunked the test, they were classified as mentally retarded, allowing the school district to receive additional federal funding. Such extra funding was then frequently used to improve the education and recreational activities of the English-speaking children. This is the extreme case of the misuse of intelligence tests, but the objections made to this absurd practice can be extended to many other uses of the tests.

Even aside from the fact that people have rather different backgrounds in terms of culture, education, and general experience, questions remain concerning what it is that an intelligence test measures. In the case of some physically handicapped people, a pencil and paper test might simply be a measure of the ability to hold a pencil in one's hand. In other cases, a test might measure the individual's experience with written tests, the ability to write quickly, or practice in following verbal instructions. Written or verbal tests may also measure linguistic dialects or language differences such as that between Spanish and English. Should the verb, "to con," be defined as a nautical expression or as the art of convincing prison officials that one is ready for parole?

An "intelligence" test score is affected by a variety of quite different abilities. It is also affected by many aspects of the individual's background and experience. Many kinds of intelligence are not measured by such tests. Certainly, it might be suspected that persons having high grade-point averages and high test scores might not be very effective if it comes to throwing a harpoon, stalking a kangaroo with a spear thrower and spear, or getting a fix. On the whole, people are good at doing the things they have been trained to do—not so good at other things.

Without question every single human being who is not an identical twin possesses a unique assortment of genes and, correspondingly, of abilities. These abilities develop out of the interaction between the individual's biological message and the individual's experience in a cultural and natural environment. The maximum development of human potentialities depends upon the existence of an environment in which each individual is encouraged to develop unique abilities to the point of excellence.

There remain individuals who seek to demonstrate that "intelligence" tests form some sort of measure of inherited capacities. Here, it is important to remember that two individuals with the same training will differ primarily in terms of heredity because there is no place else for them to differ. On the other hand, two individuals with the same heredity will differ primarily as a result of training because it is impossible for them to differ as a result of heredity.

For example, one-egg twins brought up in the same household show a mean difference in intelligence test scores of 5.9 points (Bodmer and Cavalli-Sforza 1970:25). Twins coming from different eggs show a mean difference in intelligence of approximately 10 points. Because twins are likely to be quite similar in terms of training and experience, the study of twins appears to show that biologically identical persons tend to have similar test scores while biologically different persons have different test scores. The difference, however, is only about four points, and it could be argued that twins coming from different eggs are scarcely affected by the sizable biological differences that exist between them. Interestingly, when the same person takes an "intelligence" test twice, the difference in scores is likely to be about twelve points.

A further test is to look at identical twins that are raised apart. The fact that twins brought up apart had similar scores on "intelligence" tests was once considered to be a proof that "intelligence" tests measured a biologically inherited ability. But what does "apart" really mean? What happens when the parents of identical twins die or when identical twins are given up for adoption? Well, usually, they are *not* separated. Twins are frequently raised by relatives. If not, arrangements are often made so that they can keep in close touch with each other. It would be quite startling, if not psychologically damaging, if identical twins who were actually brought up apart and in ignorance of each other's existence should meet. Twins, then, are likely to be cared for together by relatives. Failing that, they are likely to grow up in the same community and social class. There is no record of twins being raised truly apart; that is, in different cultures. If one twin were raised in Kansas City and the other twin among the Bushmen of South Africa, it is a certainty that their intelligence-test scores and abilities would differ markedly.

While most people who have examined the matter would agree that the individual's performance on an intelligence test is a result of nature and nurture working together—an interaction between the genetic message and the individual's life experience, there appears to be no easy way of estimating the relative contribution of each component. In fact, we should expect that, depending upon the individual, nature and nurture would play quite different roles. A person raised in a closet would have to depend heavily upon biological potentialities. A person subjected to heavy and constant training and stimulation would rely far more heavily upon the cultural message. The size of the contribution made by nature and nurture would also vary depending upon the particular task to be performed. The ability to run very fast might involve a genetic contribution of between 20 and 50 percent and a training-experience contribution of 50 to 80 percent. By contrast, the ability to drive an automobile would be almost entirely a matter of learning. At the expert level, where competition takes place between superbly trained individuals, biological factors become overwhelmingly important because differences due to nurture have almost been eliminated.

If differences between individuals and groups are treated as biological in origin, it follows that little can be done about them. For this reason, any assumption that any kind of illness or deficiency is due to biological causes is dangerous. Such a conclusion should be reached only after all other possibilities have been explored, and only when irrefutable evidence of a genetic origin can be produced. Here, the fact that an individual shares certain characteristics with parents or siblings is not proof of genetic inheritance. Very often, unless a clear pattern of Mendelian inheritance can be traced, it is proof that the shared characteristic is a cultural characteristic of the individual's family.

In all cases where individuals can be seen to differ in health or ability, the safest assumption, in the absence of any clear proof, is that the difference is due to environmental factors—to cultural and experiential differences. Very likely such differences have a biological component; nevertheless, the probability is that the impact of any real biological difference can be substantially eliminated through an emphasis on treatment and training. It is better to err on the side of nurture and attempt a cure than to err on the side of nature and do nothing.

In conclusion, we know that individual human beings differ greatly, more than the members of most other species, in their genetic inheritance. It would be surprising if that variation did not have an impact upon the things that different individuals can do. There is a probability that human genetic variation, by permitting each human population to possess a wide range of different kinds of individuals, is an important factor in the adaptation of the human species. There is no doubt that it makes life more interesting.

The differences between human groups are less marked than the differences between individuals, and there is great genetic overlap between groups. To the extent that human genetic and other characteristics can be mapped geographically, it has been found that there is no consistent pattern of genetic difference or similarity among human groups. The distributions of individual genes do not correlate with each other or with the distribution of human languages or cultures. There is no present benefit and no likely future benefit to any approach that assumes that existing differences in behavior and culture between any two human groups are due to differences in biological inheritance.

SUMMARY

The emergence of humanity represented the culmination of evolutionary trends toward improved communication, increasing complexity of organization, and the development of the ability to learn. The Rubicon, the uncrossable river separating humans from all other animals, was the supplementation of the genetic message by the cultural message. This process may have begun with an ape-like, human-like creature called Ramapithecus. It almost certainly began with the emergence of the Southern Apes or Australopithecines some five million years ago. The Australopithecines continued an earlier primate emphasis on learning and manipulation and required the ability to make and use tools. At some, not precisely identified point, an interaction between such protoculture and the genetic message led to the invention of true culture and the beginnings of humanity. A troop of Australopithecines became human by inventing culture. In other words, the late Australopithecines created their human descendants by inventing culture and so changing the course of evolution.

Following this, the first undeniably human beings were the diverse and widely distributed group of fossils known collectively as *Homo erectus*. Such fossils began to appear over one million years ago and dominated the human fossil record until they began to be replaced by *Homo sapiens neanderthalensis* some 150,000 years ago. Neanderthalensis in turn was replaced by *Homo sapiens sapiens* some 50,000 years ago.

During all of this time, the archaeological record, consisting of the stones, bones, and other material traces left behind or buried in the earth, shows a continuous development of increasingly sophisticated and refined tools for the hunting of animals and the gathering of plants. About eight thousand years ago, evidence began to appear of the domestication of animals and the cultivation of plants. With the development of agriculture, rapid increase in the size of the human population soon led to the emergence of cities, states, and empires. Large areas of the world came to be occupied by swidden agriculturalists and peasant farmers. Less than five hundred years ago improvements in transportation led to the introduction of new food crops in many parts of the world. Increasing population and possible changes in climate created an energy crisis in Great Britain and other parts of northern Europe. The development of technologies based upon the use of coal as fuel then precipitated the Industrial Revolution.

The recent evolution of *Homo sapiens* and accelerated genetic exchange between populations, caused by frequent and great cultural revolutions, has created a modern form of humanity that is characterized by the existence of relatively large biological differences between individuals and relatively small biological differences between groups. Attempts to map the distribution of human biological characteristics have failed to demonstrate any significant tendency toward the development of separate varieties, races, or subspecies of human. Insofar as biology is concerned, the members of so-called racial or ethnic groups differ more among themselves than their group differs from other groups. The overlap of genetic characteristics between different groups means that most people cannot be clearly identified on biological grounds as belonging to one group or another.

As with "race," so it goes with intelligence tests and other proposed measures of ability. Different sorts of groups often differ on average test scores. Such averages are meaningless ways of reporting differences because the distributions overlap. Measures of ability, especially pencil and paper tests, tap a wide range of abilities. We cannot say which abilities contributed to any particular person's test score. Finally, no such test is culture free—all measure experience and training as well as the abilities that they are supposed to measure. Studies purporting to demonstrate that intelligence-test scores or other measures of ability are the result of hereditary factors are generally set up in such a way as to prevent or severely limit the extent of variation produced by cultural and environmental influences. For example, studies of identical twins are never based upon identical twins brought up in different cultures.

The assumption without proof that individual or group differences in performance, health, or ability are due to hereditary factors raises serious ethical questions since heredity cannot easily be changed using current technology. Because all human performances and abilities are the result of interaction between biological and cultural messages in particular environments, the strategy that would allow each individual to develop unique abilities to the point of excellence is recommended as the most ethical and most effective way of dealing with human problems.

Further Reading

In the last few years, many new discoveries of human or human-like fossils have been announced. Analysis of these materials has not yet been completed and, in the meantime, controversy rages over almost every aspect of early human prehistory, and written sources are out of date before they are published. Clark's work on African prehistory (1970) provides a useful summary of information to that time. A more general, but often overenthusiastic, summary is Pfeiffer's *The Emergence of Man* (1978).

Materials dealing with the other primates include van Lawick-Goodall (1971), Jolly (1972), and Lancaster (1975). General treatments of prehistory and archaeology include Butzer (1971) and Fagan (1977). The agricultural revolution is thoroughly explored in Struever (1971). A number of fairly recent works such as Basham (1978) deal with urban anthropology and the nature of cities.

The best way to obtain a sense of the dramatic variation among human cultural systems is to read Bates' *Gluttons and Libertines* (1958), which covers a wide range of dietary and sexual customs. Alland (1971, 1972) also deals with human variation and the role of biology in human behavior. Race is dealt with by Montagu (1969) and more recently by Loehlin, Lindzey, and Spuhler (1975).

Problems and Questions

1. Children in many hunter-gatherer and peasant groups obtain a good part of their own diet by finding, killing, cleaning, cooking, and eating small mammals or birds. Can you invent and make the tools required for such a task using stone, bone, or wooden materials?
2. Compare a small group containing less than fifty members with a very large organization. What are some differences that you think might be due to size?
3. Compare a group that practices farming with a nearby group that practices hunting and gathering. Suggest possible explanations for some of the similarities and differences.
4. Using photographs or glancing discreetly at passersby, can you identify any specific body or facial characteristics that permits you to classify them consistently? How often do groups of characteristics show up together? Would another person classify the people involved in the same way?

WHAT CULTURAL ANTHROPOLOGISTS DO

How do you find out?

Chapters 1 and 2 discuss similarities and differences between human beings and other animals, and the overall pattern of evolutionary events that created or maintained those similarities and differences. The two chapters together are intended to provide the background knowledge of humanity and culture required for the study of cultural anthropology. Another closely related, but quite different problem, has to do with the methods to be used in the understanding of people and culture. The question for this chapter, then, is "How do you find out what people are really like?"

We begin with a broad discussion of fieldwork. What is anthropological fieldwork? What is the proper way to begin to learn and study a cultural tradition other than our own? In the next section, the experiences of several anthropologists in the course of their fieldwork illustrate the problems of gaining admittance to the group or putting oneself in "good conditions of work." The ambivalent comments made by anthroplogists such as Malinowski and Chagnon illustrate the problems of maintaining objectivity while living on intimate terms with people who differ not just on some high mental plane but in basic and physiological ways. Culture shock and ethnocentrism are threats to personal welfare as well as to the accurate description of other cultures. These points are illustrated with references to John Ross, Tacitus, and the Abbé Dubois.

The process of learning another culture involves the carrying out of "childlike" experiments. Unlike the child, the ethnographer keeps a written record of what he has done. The basic technique of ethnography is illustrated by an example from linguistics. The object of ethnographic research is to make guesses or hypotheses about the content of the cultural message or the processes that are being carried out. Crude experiments and other tests are then used to see if the guesses are correct.

Another important technique of fieldwork is direct observation. Here, a comparison of an observation of some baboons with observations of human beings indicates the additional complexities that develop out of the study of animals that talk. A rather poor observation of a Mexican funeral is used as a means of illustrating how inadequate data can be used to generate increasingly detailed and sophisticated questions leading toward a complete description.

It is not enough that ethnographers come to believe that they understand the cultures they study. Most people believe that they understand their own culture and others with which they are familiar, yet very few understand more than a small piece of it. On some matters, we are prepared to trust the ethnographer completely because it seems almost impossible to make an error. Thus, impressionistic and anecdotal presentations are a common and acceptable way of presenting many kinds of ethnographic data. What should be done if the data are controversial or involve highly specialized interpretations?

As anthropology matures as a scientific discipline, impressionistic and anecdotal accounts (natural history accounts if you prefer), tend to give way, as they have in the physical and biological sciences, to increasingly formal methods. When formal and standardized methods of asking questions or making observations are employed, then it is possible to understand precisely how the resulting findings were made. It is also possible to repeat the investigation and determine if the results are the same or to make formal comparisons between those results and studies carried out elsewhere. Formal methodologies are illustrated by reference to the Spindlers' work with the Rorschach projective technique and then by reference to genealogical and census methodologies. Agar's use of the simulated situation as a means of studying and understanding cultural scenes that could not be observed provides a final example of a formal methodology.

The next problem concerns the kinds of things that ought to be included in a description of another culture. A complete description is impossible, but what kinds of things should be included? Should an ethnography contain the kinds of things that people in the group consider to be important or should it emphasize the kinds of information that are scientifically important? Can the views of members and scientists be reconciled? It is suggested that an ethnography should describe the major parts of the cultural message and the fundamental processes that are carried out within the cultural system.

FIELDWORK: HOW DO YOU BEGIN?

Imagine yourself suddenly set down surrounded by all your gear, alone on a tropical beach close to a native village, while the launch or dinghy which has brought you sails away out of sight. Since you take up your abode in the compound of some neighboring white man, trader or missionary, you have nothing to do, but to start at once on your ethnographic work. Imagine further that you are a beginner, without previous experience, with nothing to guide you and no one to help you. For the white man is temporarily absent, or else unable or unwilling to waste any of his time on you. This exactly describes my first initiation into fieldwork on the south coast of New Guinea. I well remember the long visits paid to the villages during the first weeks; the feeling of hopelessness and despair after my obstinate but futile attempts had entirely failed to bring me into real touch with the natives, or supply me with any material. I had periods of despondency, when I buried myself in the reading of novels, as a man might take to drink in a fit of tropical depression and boredom (Malinowski 1961:4)

Because human behavior is so deeply conditioned by the influence of verbal and nonverbal cultural messages, the scientific study of human beings requires that the observer or *ethnographer* place himself in a position to receive and learn the cultural messages transmitted among the members of a group. Unlike any other kind of scientist, the cultural anthropologist must become a part of the object of study, gaining acceptance by the group (establishing rapport) and learning to display at least some of the behaviors appropriate to group membership.

The quotation from Malinowski represents the extreme case in which the ethnographer, without the help of prior knowledge, must single-handedly establish contact with persons whose way of life is different from his own. Because the ethnographer's training differs radically from that of the people he studies, the cultural message is thrown into sharp relief. Where the ethnographer works with his own group or with a closely related group, the content of the cultural message is not easily perceived. People tend to view the characteristic behaviors of their own groups as natural and proper. Because they have learned their own traditions without conscious effort and often without conscious awareness, they are incapable of recognizing what they have been taught. Without a basis for comparison, such customs as eating with a fork or having only one wife may appear to be expressions of universal human tendencies. Although many anthropologists study their own culture or closely related cultures, they do so with knowledge of other cultures. The recognition of culture and the existence of cultural anthropology as a discipline depend upon the cross-cultural method, the conscious or unconscious comparison of the group being studied with other different groups. Our knowledge of the range of human behavior and the varieties of human culture depends, in turn, upon the ability of individual ethnographers to encounter strangers and to secure their help and acceptance. Like a good salesman, a good ethnographer has the courage to raise his arm and press his finger upon a strange doorbell. What happens next?

WHEN THE DOOR OPENS, WHAT THEN?

Napoleon Chagnon began his fieldwork among the Yanomamo with the aid of a missionary who was familiar with them. He describes his introduction as follows:

> My heart began to pound as we approached the village and heard the buzz of activity within the circular compound. Mr. Barker commented that he was anxious to see if any changes had taken place while he was away and wondered how many of them had died during his absence. I felt into by back pocket to make sure that my notebook was still there and felt personally more secure when I touched it. Otherwise, I would not have known what to do with my hands.
>
> I looked up and gasped when I saw a dozen burly, naked, filthy, hideous men staring at us down the shafts of their drawn arrows! Immense wads of

green tobacco were stuck between their lower teeth and lips making them look even more hideous, and strands of dark-green slime dripped or hung from their noses. We arrived at the village while the men were blowing a hallucinogenic drug up their noses. One of the side effects of the drug is a runny nose. The mucus is always saturated with the green powder and the Indians usually let it run freely from their nostrils. My next discovery was that there were a dozen or so vicious, underfed dogs snapping at my legs, circling me as if I were going to be their next meal. I just stood there holding my notebook, helpless and pathetic. Then the stench of the decaying vegetation and filth struck me and I almost got sick. I was horrified (1968:5).

When Christoph von Fürer-Haimendorf began his study of the Apa Tanis of Assam, he insisted upon entering their country without the military escort eagerly proffered by government officials. The members of this "hostile, treacherous and unpredictable" tribe were so astonished at the sight of a peaceful visitor that they welcomed him with open arms. A mob of over two thousand armed tribesmen surrounded his party, examining his equipment and body and so trampling the ground that he could scarcely find a place to set up his tent (Fürer-Haimendorf 1956:17–18). In other places enthusiasm may be tempered with understanding:

We arrived at Tonghia in the middle of a bright, clear November morning. The long rainy season was recently over, the marshes below the village were green, and the men and women were in the fields gathering the last of the crops. We sat on a low wooden platform in front of the chief's house and waited for him to return from his labors. Children peeked from behind fences, an audience assembled in the courtyard, the tall and ancient chief arrived, and my assistant introduced me. He said that I was a student who had come to learn the language and observe the customs of the Badyaranké, and that I was hoping to become ateacher—as part of my education, I had come to Africa to learn how they live and work, and to write about them for others in America to read. The chief accepted this introduction, praised the motives, and gave us a tidy thatch-roofed house in his compound. He ridiculed the bag of rice which I had brought, for rice was then abundant in his village. Tonghia proved to be a happy choice, and I passed the ensuing year in the chief's family, i.e., with the persons living in his compound, and shared the food from his granaries (Simmons 1971:5–6).

In his encounters with strangers, the ethnographer copes with reactions ranging from deadly hostility to smothering friendliness. The fact that different peoples have different ways of dealing with strangers and different levels of understanding of the ethnographer's task represents one of the central problems of cross-cultural study: How can you make general statements about encounters with groups of people who are so different in their behaviors and in their way of thinking? We can deduce certain rules of thumb, but always with the certainty that an exception will be found somewhere.

First, friendliness and openness are essential to gaining acceptance. Feelings of contempt or dislike are, in the long run, difficult to conceal and are likely to be heartily reciprocated. Elaborate cover stories or phony justifications of the ethnographer's activities usually represent an unfounded contempt for the intellectual powers of those being studied. Where people sense a lack of genuineness, they are not likely to be cooperative or truthful. Most people are flattered when they encounter a stranger who is friendly and interested in their way of life and will go out of their way to provide the correct information. Although Simmons' explanation of himself approaches the ideal, not all peoples understand such concepts as research or teaching. Here, the ethnographer must limit his explanations to easily understood propositions such as, "I am interested in learning your language" or "I am studying your folklore or your local history." It is unethical and an invasion of privacy to study people without their knowledge or without explaining the possible consequences of the study.

Second, and particularly as the ethnographer's stay lengthens, it becomes increasingly important to contribute to the life of the group. This derives from a moral obligation not to exploit people who are very often defenseless, as well as from the fact that exchange is fundamental to social life. Although direct payment is possible and necessary in many situations, it may create and maintain the social distance characteristic of master–servant relationships. Often, the ethnographer returns favors by being interesting or by giving people the opportunity to display a powerful and exotic stranger. Depending on circumstances, it is possible to provide aspirin, trade goods, advice on educational matters, or free photographs. Keiser's presence among the vice lords of Chicago was made legitimate by the fact that he was writing a book (Keiser 1969:228), but the Rohners achieved general acceptance from the Kwakiutl only when they helped to recover the community motion picture projector from the Indian agent (Rohner and Rohner 1970:12). There are limits to the magic of friendliness and generosity: Chagnon discovered that he could work with the Yanomamo only when he became "sly, aggressive, and intimidating" (Chagnon 1968:9).

Third, as illustrated by the plight of Malinowski, who received little help, fieldwork is always made easier when there is a Mr. Barker or a "field assistant" who can mediate initial communications between the fieldworker and the people he studies. Sentences like "So and so said you could help me" will open many doors. With the exception of a few isolated groups like the Polar Eskimo, human groups have relationships with other human groups. These relationships are mediated by various contact-persons. "Contact-persons" tend to have a cosmopolitan outlook and may serve to introduce the ethnographer to the most hostile of groups.

Finally, because the accuracy of an ethnographic report depends upon the establishment of trust and fluent communication, a period of six months to two years of residence and participation in the activities of a group is often required:

> Indeed, in my first piece of ethnographic research on the South coast, it was not until I was alone in the district that I began to make some headway; and, at any rate, I found out where lay the secret of effective field-work. What is then this ethnographer's magic, by which he is able to evoke the real spirit of the natives, the true picture of tribal life? As usual, success can only be obtained by a patient and systematic application of a number of rules of common sense and well-known scientific principles, and not by the discovery of any marvellous short-cut leading to the desired results without effort or trouble. The principles of method can be grouped under three main headings; first of all, naturally, the student must possess real scientific aims, and know the values and criteria of modern ethnography. Secondly, he ought to put himself in good conditions of work, that is, in the main, to live without other white men, right among the natives. Finally, he has to apply a number of special methods of collecting, manipulating and fixing his evidence (Malinowski 1922:5–6).

The following section deals with the problems of bias and prejudice as they affect our ability to describe other cultures as they really are.

What Does It All Mean?

Despite his possession of "real scientific aims," the ethnographer, like Malinowski or Chagnon, may yet encounter difficulties in coming to terms with the "real spirit of the natives." Human beings are slaves of their cultural traditions. All are influenced by the biases and preconceptions they carry as representatives of a particular group of people at a particular time and place. The encounter with persons whose basic conceptions of morality and proper behavior are radically different from one's own and whose conceptions of the very structure of the universe and of the way things are to be named and classified are completely unfamiliar, can be a shattering experience perhaps best described by the term *culture shock*. Entering an alien world, the ethnographer encounters problems of communication and translation. How do you explain what people think when the very terms of their thought are radically different from your own? Consider the Polar Eskimo:

> In search of the Northwest passage, while following the shores of a cold and barren land, John Ross and the members of his party heard voices hallooing across the ice. As they sailed toward the distant sound, figures on the ice resolved themselves into Eskimoes driving their dog sleds back and forth. When the ships tacked to avoid drifting ice, the Eskimoes fled. John Ross and his men placed a pole upon the ice with a flag bearing a representation of the sun and the moon painted over a hand holding a sprig of heath (the only notable vegetation on that stony shore). To the pole was attached a bag

containing presents and a picture of a hand pointing toward a ship. When the Eskimoes failed to approach the pole, Sacheuse, an Eskimo who had volunteered to sail with the expedition, walked across the ice shouting "Kahkeite" ("Come on."). To this the strange Eskimo replied, "No, no, go away" (Adapted from Ross 1819:80–81).

After some four hundred years of isolation, the Polar Eskimo, confronted with the opportunity of rejoining the human species, could only say, "No, no, go away." Only the presence of Sacheuse, and his knowledge of the Eskimo language, prevented the failure of the encounter. John Ross and his men did all that they could, hoisting a flag bearing "universal" symbols and relying upon the "universal" value of gifts. Universal though the message might have been, it could not be translated by the men John Ross encountered.

Humans do not communicate by means of universal symbols. They communicate by means of symbols that are given an arbitrary meaning within a system of language and social interaction. People differ in the way they arbitrarily subdivide and measure the universe around them. They differ in the things they recognize and in the labels they apply to things (see chapters 5 and 6). The existence of the "translation" problem means that the ethnographer cannot study a cultural system without understanding the system of meanings and perceptions characteristic of that system. Having learned the system of meanings, ethnographers still face the task of expressing an alien way of thought within the confines of their own language and culture. Although the problem of translation has been partially solved, it remains one of the most difficult and controversial obstacles to the scientific description of other cultures.

Ethnographers, like all other people, tend to perceive reality in the light of their own culture-bound experience. Chemists came to the study of salt filled with attitudes and beliefs about salt acquired at their mother's knee. As a rule, people do not *feel* very strongly about salt, and the chemist does not feel a need to praise or condemn the substance studied. It is different with people:

> Their physical type is everywhere the same—wild blue eyes, reddish hair and huge frames that excel only in violent effort. They have no corresponding power to endure hard work and exertion, and they have little capacity to bear thirst and heat. When not engaged in warfare, they spend some little time in hunting, but more in idling, abandoned to sleep and gluttony. They show no self-control in drinking. You have only to indulge their intemperance by supplying all that they crave, and you will gain as easy a victory through their vices as through your own arms (Tacitus 1960:4, 113, 120).

Here, writing less than a century after Christ about the tribes of northern Europe, the Roman historian cannot conceal his disgust. Later historians might wonder whether the Romans ran out of alcohol or the Germans became temperate. Writing of South India, the French cleric, Dubois, states: "It has struck me that a faithful picture of the wickedness and incongruities of polytheism and idolatry would by its very ugliness help greatly to set off the beauties and perfections of Christianity" (1947:9). The Abbé also notes: "Being fully persuaded of the superlative merits of their own manners and customs, they think those of other people barbarous and detestable, and quite incompatible with real civilization" (1947:303).

Ethnocentrism is the feeling that one's own culture is somehow more important or more central than any other culture. It usually takes the form of negative value judgments (idolatry is ugly) or of selective reporting which emphasizes the "bad" features of another culture. What Malinowski called "real scientific aims" include the attempt to describe other cultures objectively, without bias or prejudice. For some anthropologists, the desire to avoid ethnocentric reporting gives rise to the doctrine of *cultural relativity*; namely, that all cultures are equally good and/or equally bad. Although some consider this doctrine parallel to, "Each to his own taste as the lady said when she kissed the pig," the habit of passing judgment upon other peoples appears to be immature and pretentious. If there are divinely inspired individuals who are competent to pass judgment upon other cultures, then the best means of helping them in their judgments is an accurate and objective description of what others do. The "ethnographer's magic," then, has to do with the ability to

overcome ethnocentric feelings, and this ability, in turn, rests upon the ability to arrange "good conditions of work."

What Is the Secret of Fieldwork?

If, as Malinowski suggested, we imagine ourselves stranded on a beach, not far from a collection of houses occupied by the members of an unfamiliar culture, we will be confronted with problems affecting our ability to survive as well as our ability to collect useful information. When, like Chagnon or Simmons, we enter the settlement, we are at once confronted with concrete evidence concerning the manner in which strangers are received. As we attempt to obtain food, to form sentences, or to make friends and acquaintances, we are again confronted with evidence of the responses to the stimuli we provide.

Because our initial attempts to behave properly in a strange setting seem bumbling, incompetent, and confused, our first reaction parallels the culture shock described by Chagnon.

> As we walked down the path to the boat, I pondered the wisdom of having decided to spend a year and a half with this tribe before I had even seen what they were like. I am not ashamed to admit, either, that had there been a diplomatic way out, I would have ended my fieldwork then and there. I did not look forward to the next day when I would be left alone with the Indians: I did not speak a word of their language, and they were decidedly different from what I had imagined them to be. The whole situation was depressing, and I wondered why I ever decided to switch from civil engineering to anthropology in the first place. I had not eaten all day, I was soaking wet from perspiration, the gnats were biting me, and I was covered with red pigment, the result of a dozen or so complete examinations I had been given by as many burly Indians (Chagnon 1968:5–6).

In walking the few steps from the beach to the settlement, we have lost control of ourselves and our lives. Where we were once competent and self-confident adults, we are now a curious hybrid, part clown, part lunatic, and part child. The secret of anthropological fieldwork lies in the ability of the ethnographer to become as a little child, to learn as a child learns, but at the same time record what he learns. Anthropological fieldwork is the science that every child knows but that most adults have forgotten.

Children commence the process of learning to speak by babbling incessantly. When people respond to some noises and not to others, certain noises are made more frequently. As they proceed, children form hypotheses and make unconscious experiments to test their validity. Hearing, "Yesterday, I walked in the park," the child attempts, "Yesterday, I runned in the park." Laughter, rejection, or other negative reactions inform the child that the experiment has failed. The hypothesis is modified, fresh experiments are attempted. Eventually, the child confidently asserts, "Yesterday, I ran in the park."

Every human being is an ethnographer. Each of us, through careful, prolonged, and often painful research has developed a theory concerning the nature of the cultural system in which we were raised. For the majority of human beings, this internalized theory of culture is sufficient to permit the generation of appropriate behavior and successful participation in the activities of the group. Because ordinary human beings perform only a few of their experiments at the conscious level and never attempt a rigorous description of their theories of culture, ordinary human beings cannot explain the nature of their culture any more than they can explain the grammar of their language. The ethnographer attempts to keep a written record of experiments conducted in another culture. Steps in the development of a theory of that culture are carefully explored and cross-checked. Consider the manner in which linguists, students of language, construct their theories of grammar.

ETHNOGRAPHY: CAN YOU SAY IT RIGHT?

As Bloomfield says, "The ancient Greeks studied no language but their own; they took it for granted that the structure of their language embodied universal forms of human thought or, perhaps, of the cosmic order" (1933:5). Unlike the child or the ancient Greek, the anthropologist is aware of the artificial nature of languages and has some idea about what might be found when studying a different language. Knowing that all known languages consist of a small number of basic sounds or *phonemes*, the anthropologist-linguist is able to begin work with a series of systematic experiments, designed to identify the phonemes of the language. The anthropologist points to a dog and a native who is assisting him utters a series of sounds that may or may not be relevant to the anthropologist's actions. The anthropologist attempts to write down or "transcribe" the sounds uttered by the speaker. The speaker bursts into laughter and repeats what he said before. In extremity, the fieldworker may seize a dental mirror and thrust it into the mouth of the native speaker to discover how the sounds are produced. Eventually, the ethnographer learns to make the correct sounds, but still doesn't know which sounds are important or significant in determining correct pronunciation.

The speaker of a language makes all kinds of noises in saying "dog," but only some of the noises are essential to meaning. In the initial stages of experimentation, the ethnographer attempts to write down the sounds in such a way that they can be read out loud with correct pronunciation (that is, so that the listener finds them informative and not laughable). Gradu-

ally, the ethnographer assembles a box of file cards with a different "word" written on each card. Searching through the cards, words are found that are different only in minor details. For example, having started with "dog," the ethnographer might eventually encounter the word "bog." When pointing to a dog and saying "bog," the ethnographer encounters a burst of laughter. Plainly, the difference between dog and bog is significant or meaningful. The hypothesis now is the "d" and "b" are both phomemes; that is to say that the difference between them makes a difference in the meaning of utterances.

Shuffling through his file cards, the fieldworker encounters "bug" and "dug." Again, the difference between "b" and "d" is meaningful. After a few weeks of hard work, a list of the thirty to fifty basic types of sounds out of which the entire language is constructed is compiled. With more effort, it can be discovered how these thirty to fifty sounds may be combined to form words or parts of words (morphemes and bound morphemes). Using similar techniques, ways of combining words to form phrases and sentences are uncovered. The grammar of one language might consider "Dog digs" to be a correct sentence, while the grammar of another language might favor "Digs dog." Word order is arbitrary, not part of the cosmic order.

A grammar of a language is a set of rules that enables the fieldworker, or for that matter anybody else, to generate formally correct sentences. Because there might be several different ways of formulating a grammar and because the same effect might be produced by a different sort of grammar, the grammar developed by a fieldworker is not necessarily identical to that used by native speakers. All that can be asserted about it is that it is a part of a theory of culture that meets the test of predicting the behavior of native speakers.

There is much more to the study of a language than the formation of correct sentences. It helps to know what the words mean and when particular grammatical sentences are appropriate. The meaning of a word is determined by when and where it is used (its distribution and context) and by its effect on human behavior. The sentence, "Bring me a turnip," is appropriate only in certain contexts. Used in such an appropriate context, the fieldworker learns what a turnip is. The word "turnip" is an arbitrary label assigned in a particular culture to a particular object. There is no guarantee that a different language would contain a word for turnip or that if it had a word for turnip it would be used in the same way or in the same context. When we point to a turnip and say, "What is this called?" the word we elicit may or may not mean the same thing as the word "turnip" in English. It is no simple problem to determine the meaning of a word, and even when the meaning is established it may not be possible to translate it into another language.

The grammar or rules of language enable the individual to generate correct sentences. Other kinds of rules permit him to make such sentences at appropriate times and in appropriate places. By extension, we can think of a cultural tradition as consisting of a series of grammars which enable the individual to generate not just correct speech but correct behavior upon any occasion.

When people actually talk, they may speak in ungrammatical or improper ways, and when they carry out other forms of behavior they may also deviate from correctness or propriety. Thus, an ethnographic account of a group of people consists of replies to the following two types of question: (1) What is the proper way of doing X? (2) How do people actually do X? The symbol "X" may represent any kind of process or activity: going through a doorway, sitting in a class, giving a lecture, making a date, planting potatoes, tuning a violin, getting dressed, eating breakfast, going for a walk, or training a dog. Because all of these processes are carried out within particular settings and in terms of particular social roles and kinds of equipment, an ethnography also contains statements of the general form: "What are the circumstances surrounding X"? Such circumstances include the environment within which the activity takes place, the kinds of people involved in the carrying out of the activity, and the kinds of clothing, tools, buildings, or other items of material culture involved in the activity. A complete ethnography also indicates the manner in which each of the activities described is related to other activities.

An ethnography represents the fieldworker's best guess concerning the nature of life in a particular group. It is, then, a theory concerning a particular cultural system and the various statements in it represent hypotheses concerning the nature of the culture. How does the ethnographer go about assembling the data required for the testing of these hypotheses?

What Do You Observe?

07.30   Circum utters a contact grunt and goes *northward* along the riverbed. Again the entire party follows for some 20 yards and then stops.

07.31   Circum again rises; he briefly looks back at Pater and then goes another 30 yards *northward*. No one follows. He stops, comes back until he is only 20 yards away from his closest female and sits down. All the while Pater has been watching him.

07.32   Circum rises and begins to move *west*, straight across the riverbed. Only his youngest female follows him. After a few seconds both come halfway back and sit down.

07.33   Circum sets out again, this time in a *southwest* direction. Now, Pater rises, and the whole party follows Circum in the same marching order as above (Kummer 1971:64).

The above represents an observation of the behavior of a troop of baboons. Ethologists, who are zoologists concerned with animal behavior, base their findings primarily upon written observations of the above kind. Human behavior may be studied in the same way:

Maud, with Otto following, circled back to the children's room and stopped just inside the doorway.

She started away, as though to lead Otto again.

Otto asked in a serious tone, "Can I be the horse:"

Maud immediately agreed in an equally serious tone, "O.K."

In a loud, commanding voice Maud yelled, "See, you run away and I catch you." This was a new angle to the game.

Otto mater-of-factly gave Maud the rope and immediately darted through the hall and into the living room (Barker and Wright 1955:364–365).

Both of these observations place a primary emphasis on social interaction, decision making, and leadership. Both emphasize movement from place to place. Both describe vocalizations, but neither one gives much detail concerning hand, face, or eye movements. The difference between the two observations lies primarily in the fact that human beings talk about what they are doing. The baboons, in fact, spent nearly half a day deciding to go southwest, where Pater wanted to go. Of course, Kummer was not able to ask the baboons what they were doing, nor was he able to ask them about the meaning of the grunts and gestures they exchanged. The presence of verbal communication among human beings complicates the task of making observations (you have to learn the language) but it also provides additional evidence concerning what people are doing and why.

Each of the fieldworker's observations contains a heading giving the date, the place, and the observer's name. Depending upon circumstances, an observation may contain a description of the setting and the persons involved and references to the time of day at which each separate notation was made. Each observation is copied and at least one copy is stored in a safe place. Ethnographic observations must often be written in code or stored under lock and key to protect the privacy of the individuals involved. After making an observation, the fieldworker reads it over, making comments in the margin concerning things to look for next time or questions to ask about what he saw and heard. When a series of observations have accumulated, the ethnographer arranges them in terms of a system of classification and compares those that are similar in kind. A single observation of children playing horse is an inadequate basis for making any very firm statements.

In many situations, the fieldworker is unable to follow people around making notes, and his observations, written after the fact, look something like this:

FUNERAL   A.R.B. *July 15, 1967* Santana
Not far from the village, near the approach road, is an adobe wall surrounding a large open space. At one side of the construction facing the road is an arched doorway upon which is written in fading letters, the Spanish words, "Ashes to ashes, dust to dust." [Spanish translation needed here, also more detailed description of the graveyard.] Inside the doorway are the mounds of earth, the crosses and the monuments constituting the graveyard in which the fathers and grandfathers and perhaps most often the young children of Santana have been buried for more than [how many?] years. [Note: what is the Zapotec vocabulary relevant to this setting; what is the evidence that death is a significant cultural theme?]

Standing in front of this monument to the futility of life . . . [Strike this out, meaningless editorializing and artsy craftsy.]

Sometimes, a passerby standing in front of the cemetery can look down the road just at dusk and see moving toward him myriad points of light. To his right, he can see the evening star and on the clouds the last remnants of daylight. The strong winds of the afternoon have died with the evening. In the distance the sounds of a band are heard. [Find out if there are two bands or not and if one plays only American Indian music; also what about recruitment to the band?] [Does the above belong here?]

Soon the procession is visible. At the front, walking almost in darkness comes the band. A relative [what relative?] of the deceased [why not say dead man?] is circulating among the players offering them an occasional sip of mescal. There are about fifteen men in the band carrying drums, trumpets, flutes, clarinets [get a better list and put it in a table or appendix]. Marching with the band is a small boy carrying a bottle of orange pop in his hip pocket. From time to time he hands it to his trumpet-playing father who takes a swig. [Is this an idiosyncrasy or does orange pop really help?]

Following the band is a figure of Christ on the cross. The figure hangs in a contorted position and in a better light it would be possible to see the agonized expression, the blood dripping from the wounds, and the phrase [what is it?] inscribed upon the cross. Behind the cross comes a plain black coffin of the standard octagonal [?] shape. It is carried by four pall bearers [Was it four, how were they selected, paid? Connie says, they were almost too drunk to stand]. Following the coffin is a group of women carrying candles. Every so often a candle blows out and the carrier holds it in the flame of another candle, lights it and continues to move solemnly in tune to the music. Behind the women come a group of men [check this]. Both men and women have been drinking heavily [were all of the women drinking?], but most can navigate reasonably well.

The procession is the concluding portion of the funeral of Luis Martinez, an old man who died, evidently of heart failure on the previous day [Connie says he was 85 and died during the night]. (From field notes taken by Alan R. Beals)

Such an observation, perhaps written in more detail, might serve as a basis for further investigation of the nature of the funeral process in the community of Santana in Mexico. Because Santana is a fairly small community, it might not be possible for the ethnographer to observe any other funerals. In such a case, the ethnographer has to collect information about other funerals by asking residents of the community what they remember about them. In presenting material on funerals, the ethnographer may simply describe the funeral observed and discuss the extent to which it was typical. Alternatively, the ethnographer might describe a typical funeral. Ideally, the ethnographer would present a set of rules, a grammar if you like, which could serve as a means of explaining and predicting any kind of funeral likely to be held in the community.

At the funeral, one man turned to the ethnographer and said, "Look at this man, he is dead. Soon I too will be dead. You too will die. We must all die." Statements like this might lead an ethnographer to wonder about the meaning of death and funerals to the people of the community, with the hypothesis that the attitude toward death plays some kind of important role in regulating a wide variety of different kinds of behavior. From an analysis of a wide variety of observations and interviews, the ethnographer might identify a general organizing principle of the following kind. "Because we are all going to die, we must preserve proper behavior at all times, acting without regard to physical danger or self-interest."

In this way, each observation made by the anthropologist leads to further questions about what is going on. As these further questions arise, the ethnographer applies a variety of additional research techniques in an attempt to find definitive answers. Having derived a variety of questions about the meaning of death from his observations of funerals, the ethnographer might formulate a series of specific questions and administer them to a randomly selected sample of individuals. Such a systematic questionnaire would provide data that could easily be manipulated by means of standard statistical techniques. A problem arises in that the questions are those of the ethnographer. There is always the danger that the questions reflect the ethnographer's view of life rather than that of the persons being interviewed. Other data concerning death and its significance might be obtained from casual conversations, from nondirective questions or statements (What did you think about last night's funeral?), or from an examination of gossip or folk tales.

In both observations and interviews, ethnographers are likely to select materials of special interest to themselves or reflecting the biases of their own culture. One way of correcting for this sort of bias is to train members of the group studied to make observations or carry out interviews. In general, interview situations are more susceptible to bias because every gesture and statement made by the ethnographer may be used by the informant as a source of information concerning the answers sought by the ethnographer. When a person who has never thought about funerals at all is asked, "What did you think about that funeral?" there is little choice, particularly if being paid or otherwise rewarded for cooperation, but to formulate a convincing answer.

In attempting to describe how other people live, the ethnographer inevitably introduces some degree of distortion and error. The best ways of reducing the extent of such errors are to spend a considerable period of time in the field, to learn the language, to allow the people being studied to speak for themselves as much as possible, and to apply a variety of formal and systematic methods, particularly in those areas where the findings are most likely to be subject to question. The observation that people live in thatch- or tile-roofed houses with walls of adobe brick is unlikely to be questioned, while a statement that they are incapable of forming strong emotional attachments to others requires extensive documentation. The ideal test of an ethnographic description would lie in the ability of another person to behave properly within the culture described on the basis of the ethnographic description. Where a given group or community cannot be restudied by an independent observer, the value of an ethnographer's account must be tested indirectly in terms of comparison with other studies of similar communities. Let us consider this matter further.

How Do We Know It's So?

In his history of Arctic explorations, John Barrow has the following to say about John Ross's observations of the Eskimo:

> Ross, indeed, suspects that this account "may appear in some points to be defective"; he may safely satisfy himself that it will not only *appear*, in some points, to be *defective*, but will be so pronounced by all: in point of fact, he never set his foot on shore, and could not, by any possibility, have known anything of the stuff he has set down, which is of that kind of manufacture not worth the paper on which it is printed (1846:33).

Years later, Knud Rasmussen's Eskimo informants corroborated John Ross's description. From the time of Marco Polo, also branded a liar, accounts of strange peoples and unusual customs have been greeted with incredulity.

A laboratory scientist who discovers an unusual effect can usually find another scientist willing to repeat the experiment and test the findings. The field scientist tends to work alone or in small groups and has no organized way of replicating findings. Robert Redfield, who conducted an early study of a village in Mexico (Redfield, 1930), was much concerned about replication and encouraged Oscar Lewis (1951) to conduct a restudy of the village of Tepoztlán. Where Redfield had found a peaceful and harmonious community, Lewis found a community filled with conflict and disagreement. Although Redfield and Lewis agreed concerning most of the features of Tepoztlán, they disagreed concerning the basis of social interaction in the community. Because Redfield was interested in quite small communities, he may have focused his interest and attention on outlying hamlets, while Lewis emphasized the more urban-influenced central community of Tepoztlán. Because some years had passed between the study and restudy, it is possible that the community had undergone rapid change. Perhaps the differences in the two accounts are nothing more than an expression of differences in the personalities or theoretical viewpoints of the two men. In this case, Lewis's replication of Redfield's study failed to lead to any very general confirmation or disconfirmation of Redfield's findings. In the end, verification of the Lewis and Redfield studies has had to rest upon the gradual accumulation of evidence concerning the nature of communities in Mexico. The general feeling arising from this sort of comparison is that, while Lewis's work contains certain characteristic biases, it represents a more detailed and better documented description of the community than does Redfield's work. In view of the fact that Lewis had the advantage of Redfield's experience, this is hardly surprising.

What Are Your Impressions?

Faced with the probability that for years to come he or she will be the only reliable source of information about Tepoztlán or some other community or group, the ethnographer feels a need to provide as much information as possible. Every minute or hour the ethnographer spends documenting one kind of fact is a minute or hour not spent documenting some other kind of fact. In preparing the final account of what a particular group of people is like, the ethnographer finds that the bulk of the information consists of little more than personal impressions of what the people are like. Because the impressions of a knowledgeable person are more useful than no information at all, some of the information contained in an ethnography represents little more than a series of assertions supported only by the fact that the ethnographer was there. Such statements take the following form:

> An individual normally worships the deity of his father, and some also worship their mother's deity as well. Many deities are identified with a particular clan in which case all members, male and female, are worshippers by virtue of birth into it. After marriage women return home for the annual festival of their own deity, but they assist in the performance of the annual festival of their husband's deity. If a woman is childless, despite prayers and sacrifices to her husband's and her own deity, she may seek the help of another deity (Bascom 1969:77).

Such a means of presenting data is particularly acceptable if: (1) the materials covered are so obvious as to make error unlikely, or (2) similar accounts exist elsewhere in the literature. Because such descriptions rest upon the ethnographer's impressions, they are generally described as *impressionistic*.

A slightly more convincing method of presenting data is the *anecdotal* method, where the ethnographer's impressions are supported by direct reference to observations or by direct quotations from informants. For example, Bascom supports his comments about institutionalized friendship with a quotation from a legend:

> Once there were two men who were best friends. One of them had a fight with another man and killed him. Escaping, he ran to the house of his friend and told him what had happened. He said that the king would arrest and punish

him. His friend advised him to act like a crazy man, to dress in rags, and, when questioned, to speak nothing but nonsense (1969:47).

Where available and relevant, photographs (Collier, 1967), motion pictures, tape recordings, or various kinds of documents may be used to support ethnographic statements.

Over the years, ethnographers have developed impressionistic and anecdotal accounts of a wide variety of peoples. The existence of these "natural history" accounts have tended to release ethnographers from the burden of providing "complete" descriptions of the peoples they study. It is now becoming increasingly acceptable to produce ethnographies that focus upon particular topics and apply relatively sophisticated methodologies to more limited areas of culture. Fifty years ago an ethnographer having the opportunity to study a tribe of Indians living in the jungles of the Amazon would have been ridiculed if he had studied nothing more than their hunting techniques, their language, or their methods of raising children. Today, when a number of general accounts of these tribes already exist, the ethnographer is expected to carry out more detailed investigations of some particular aspect of life. Such detailed investigation permits the application of formal methodologies.

Formal Approaches: How
Do You Know?

In carrying out their study of the Menomini Indians of Wisconsin, George and Louise Spindler confronted a situation in which there already existed a considerable body of published material concerning the tribe. Most of this material attempted to deal with the way the tribe was organized before it had experienced changes resulting from the modernization and urbanization of the part of Wisconsin in which they lived. For the Spindlers, the problem was not, "What are the Menomini like?" but "How have the Menomini adapted to the changing world in which they live?" To answer this question it was necessary to find some way of measuring the degree to which individual Menomini or groups of Menomini had adapted to modern circumstances and to find some way of describing the different kinds of adaptation characteristic of different groups of Menomini.

One of several ways in which the Spindlers attacked this problem was to use the Rorschach projective technique on individuals from each of several different groups of Menomini. This technique consists of presenting a series of cards depicting inkblots to the individual and asking the individual what he sees. The advantage of the technique is that it provides the informant with relatively few cues concerning what he is "supposed" to see. Particular characteristics of the responses such as references to color

FIGURE 3–5 Among the Menomini Indians of Wisconsin some groups have struggled to maintain a traditional way of life. (PHOTO COURTESY OF GEORGE SPINDLER)

or to movement can be analyzed in numerical terms and a measure of the similarities and differences of individuals and groups to each other can be constructed. "Acculturated" Menomini gave responses similar to those given by white Americans, while "native-oriented" Menomini gave quite different responses (George and Louise Spindler 1971:28–29). Through the use of this and other systematic measures, it was possible to develop a consistent and well-documented description of the kinds of differences existing between different groups of Menomini. The resulting positive evidence concerning the least acculturated or native-oriented Menomini lends special conviction to the Spindlers' consequent description of the way of life of the native-oriented group.

The methods used by the Spindlers developed logically out of the kind of research question they were asking. The study of acculturation is improved by methods that measure its extent. A great many ethnographic questions are fundamental to a wide range of human groups and the methods for finding answers to such questions have become relatively standardized. A case in point is the method for studying language described previously. A similar case, reflecting a different sort of method, arises in the need to identify the individual members of a cultural system.

WHAT IS YOUR NAME?

Fairly early in the conduct of their research, ethnographers wish to assemble basic information such as the name, age, and sex of the people they study. The most common means of assembling such information is through a household census. Typically, the ethnographer goes from door to door getting a list of the names of each person in the household along with qualifying information such as sex, age, relationship to household head, birthplace, years of schooling, occupation, income, and, if relevant, the previous relationship of husband and wife. From this information, the ethnographer can construct a population pyramid showing the distribution of individuals in terms of age and sex, and can compute estimates of fertility, divorce, or migration. It can be determined whether or not the households represent nuclear families (father, mother, son, daughter) or some other kind of arrangement. If informats report that married couples always live in the household of the husband's parents, their report can be checked against the facts revealed in the census.

Depending upon his interests, the ethnographer may also collect censuses dealing with house styles, household equipment, expenditures, political opinions, or religious beliefs. In a small community of less than one hundred households, the census is the only accurate way of collecting detailed information concerning the group as a whole. Where households are numerous, the same sorts of questions might be answered more economically by numbering the households and using a table of random numbers to select between twenty and one hundred households for systematic study. The sample survey has the drawback of providing information about what the group is like on the average, but not providing information about exceptional households or individuals. It would be easy, for example, to conduct a sample survey which would omit the households of particularly wealthy or influential individuals. In a small community people may become indignant if they are omitted from a sample survey.

Generally, a census or a sample survey fails to provide information concerning the kinds of relationships that may exist between households. Kin relationships between households are generally obtained by collecting genealogies that include all of the households in the community. The most common tactic, here, is to interview an older person concerning the identity of his ancestors and decendants. To begin with, the informant, or Ego, might be asked the name of Ego's father's father or his father's father's father. Emphasis on the father assumes a tendency to trace relatives patrilineally (in the male line) because such a tendency is considerably more common than tracings in the female line or in both lines. If the father's father had any older brothers or sisters or any younger brothers or sisters, their names are written down. The name, birthdate, deathdate, and other similar information about each individual mentioned are taken down, and the names of their wives, children, children's children, and so on are then taken. Kinship terminologies are elicited by asking how Ego addresses and refers to each of the individuals in the geneaology, and how each of these individuals would address and refer to Ego. One way of organizing materials in a genealogy is to assign the letter "A" to the oldest male in the genealogy. Capital letters are used for males and lower-case letters are used for females. The oldest male's oldest son would be AA and the oldest son's oldest son would be AAA. Thus, the number of letters in the code name indicates the generations. "A's" younger brother would be "B," and their younger sister would be "c." The younger brother's oldest son would be "BA." Thus, birth order is indicated by alphabetical position with A being the first born and B being the second born.

When enough genealogies have been collected, it is possible to determine how every household in the community is related to every other household. Marriages to cousins or other close relatives can be traced, or the genealogies may provide information essential to an understanding of the inheritance of property. Genealogies provide evidence of membership in lineages or clans and this may be useful in understanding how people choose sides in disputes or why a particular individual is influential.

WHAT IF YOU CAN'T BE THERE?

The ideal way of finding out what people do is to be there and to observe and record everything that happens. Given money enough and time, it is possible to consider surrounding a group of people with sound motion picture cameras continuously in operation. Unfortunately, massive operations have a way of altering situations. Even unsophisticated persons can detect the difference between "carrying on one's daily life" and "making a motion picture." Flooding the scene with motion picture cameras or note-taking graduate students, even if it could be done without altering the situation, is also likely to produce vast quantities of information that no one knows what to do with. Science does not really study reality; it studies small pieces of reality.

It is usually impractical to observe and record everything. Even if it is not, many things that people do are private, hidden in some way, or infrequent. Much of ethnography involves reconstruction. We ask people what they do when they get sick or we ask them what happened last time they were sick. Another approach is through the use of simulated situations:

> BILL: How much bread you got?
> BRUCE: Uh, wow, y'know like, uh, I'm not too good man.
> Like you know, like I got, uh, about ten bucks and that's it, y'know?
> BILL: Yeah, well I got twenty. I can carry you for some.
> BRUCE: You got twenty bills, man?
> BILL: Yeah, right.
> BRUCE: Solid. I got a set of works.
> BILL: Yeah? Ha, ha. That's cool, let's go.
> BRUCE: Yeah, OK, let's split. (Agar 1973:135)

In this case, anthropologist Michael Agar asked five white male inmates of a drug treatment center to demonstrate the process of "getting off." Because this process is totally illegal, direct observation of the process involves danger both from members of the group and from the authorities. In theory, a series of accurate simulations or enactments should provide a basis for a reconstruction of the entire process including the various alternative ways of carrying it out and the frequencies of each.

There is a problem, though. How can the ethnographer be sure that the enactment is true to life? What if—a likely event with drug addicts—the people are staging a "put on." Agar checked the reliability of his simulated situations in three ways. First, he checked over each situation to determine how frequently there were interruptions, breaks in continuity, references to the recording equipment, or other "unreal" happenings. Then, he played the tape-recorded simulation to the group and asked the members to comment on any mistakes or "unreal" happenings. Finally, he played the tape to other groups of addicts and noted their reactions. In this case, the ultimate test, comparison of the simulations with observations of real events, is impossible.

Because the simulated situation provides an opportunity to observe gestures, facial expressions, and movements and to hear the words spoken, it provides a more complete and accurate reconstruction than might be obtained by simply asking people, "How do you 'get off'?" or "What things do you do to 'get off'?" The systematic interview, in turn, provides a more detailed account of what happens than might be obtained by a formal questionnaire containing questions like : "How often do you get off; Do you get off with other people; How many other people do you usually get off with; or, Who usually gets to get off first?"

Rorschach projective techniques, censuses, genealogies, and simulated situations represent only examples of the many kinds of formal methods now used in the collection of ethnographic information. Other examples will be given in later chapters. Essentially a formal method involves the collection of information in terms of a standardized set of procedures often leading to mathematical or statistical analysis and verification. The standardization of procedures limits the ethnographer's ability to bias his data through unconscious selection. It permits others to verify his results by applying the same methodology and seeing if it leads to the same results. Because the formalization or standardization of methodology has a way of introducing its own kinds of biases, it is unwise to depend upon a single method such as sample surveys or life history interviews to the exclusion of other methods. An ethnography is a systematic description of a cultural system. It is built up over a prolonged period of fieldwork through the application of a variety of informal and formal methods. What might an ethnography contain?

WHAT IS INCLUDED IN AN ETHNOGRAPHY?

Ideally, an ethnography is a complete description of a cultural system. It tells us about the people, the setting, the equipment, the cultural tradition, and the ongoing activity. A regular or traditional ethnography is written by someone who has lived, hopefully for at least a year, among some particular people and asked questions and taken notes concerning a variety of topics. Heider's description of the Dugum Dani of New Guinea has the following chapter headings: subsistence, social organization, conflict, man and the supernatural, language and categories, art and play, the natural environment, the body, and artifacts of culture (1970:xi). Elwin's *Bondo Highlander* (1950), a study of a tribe in India, discusses setting, social organization, economics, marriage, religion, ceremony, maladjustment, and Bondo character.

In general, the table of contents of an ethnography represents the ethnographer's interpretation of the kinds of parts into which a cultural system can be divided with special reference to the cultural system at hand. Because each ethnographer forms unique ideas about what is important about the people studied, it follows that attempts to compare different cultural systems are often frustrating. Variations in the training and theoretical interests of different ethnographers combined with variations in the nature of different cultural systems make it difficult or impossible to formulate a universal framework for the description of culture.

For most purposes, a good eyewitness description of another cultural system is perfectly adequate. The advantage of the natural history, or "see it, write it," method is that it permits broad general description of the cultural system. The disadvantage of the method is that it depends largely upon our ability to trust the individual ethnographer. When Heider tells us that the Dugum Dani eat yams or when Elwin tells us that the Bondo hunt with the bow and arrow, we are inclined to believe them. Such facts would tend to be obvious. Even more important, there would appear to be no reason for error, falsehood, or bias. Although it is impossible to write an ideal "complete" ethnography, it appears reasonable that the first thing an ethnographer should do is to prepare a general, natural history, description of the cultural system being studied.

Even here, where the ethnographer sets out to describe a cultural system in terms of his own observations and experiences, there are problems. Should a cultural system be described in terms of a standardized table of contents that could be applied to all cultural systems or should it be described in terms of the categories that people in it consider to be important? For example, the Hopi Indians live in a desert environment and their central concern is rain. Other peoples are more concerned with money, disease, warfare, or pleasure. The question is, should we permit the Hopi to talk about the things that interest them or should we insist that a Hopi ethnography deal with the things that interest anthropologists or academicians?

It is possible to compromise. First, it is extremely difficult to get people to talk about things that they don't think about and that don't interest them. The Hopi ethnographer who attempted to discover the beliefs and attitudes about rain and rain-making held by urban New Yorkers would be doomed to frustration. Similarly, there are many things that interest New Yorkers that do not interest the Hopi. Ethnographers and the people they study have a common interest in developing topics that are important to both.

Even though it is impossible to predict in any detail which sorts of topics will be broadly interesting, the ethnographer can begin his work with a list of those various things that groups generally find interesting. One way of developing such a list is to consider things that can be expected to be present in any cultural system. By definition, every cultural system must possess a cultural tradition. People are interested in their own cultural traditions. If they were not, they would not bother to pass on their cultural message to their neighbors and children.

Thus, as in chapter 4, a description of a cultural system might well start with a description of world view, philosophy, religion, and science. Certainly people must have, either explictly or implicitly, a firm view of what the world is like and what their place in it is. Questions to be asked might be: "What's the meaning of this; what are you guys up to; what's going on here; what's the object of the game?"

A notable part of world view or perhaps a whole separate section by itself consists of the names of the players and their roles and duties. People are going to have ideas about what people are like, what kinds of people there are, and what is to be done about them. This field, sometimes called social structure, involves questions like, "Who's in charge here; who do I see about doing 'X'; how do you know who the members are; or who's that out in left field?" This topic is covered in chapter 5.

In addition to these general aspects, cultural traditions define specific processes routinely carried out by the membership of the cultural system. Although specific processes are rarely universal, some general types of process may be considered universal because they are necessary to the operation of a cultural system. Thus, every cultural system must have ways of maintaining environmental relationships, regulating membership, indicating individual and group status, transmitting culture, controlling behavior, and adapting to changing circumstances. These processual categories are described in the third part of this book.

SUMMARY

Scientific explanation of the similarities and differences among cultural systems is dependent upon the ethnographer's ability to arrive at detailed and objective descriptions. Objective descriptions depend upon the ability of the ethnographer to establish rapport; that is, to establish relationships with the people he studies that will permit him to collect information from them. This usually involves openness, a willingness to contribute to the life of the group, use of intermediaries or contact-persons, and prolonged participation.

Once rapport has been established the ethnographer still faces the translation problem and the problem of his own ethnocentrism. The strangeness of a new situation and the ethnographer's incompetence in coping with it may lead to culture shock. As this is overcome, the ethnographer, like the child, begins to learn a new culture. The ethnographer learns faster and more effectively than the child because he maintains a record of his experiences and because he has special methods of "fixing his evidence." This process is illustrated by the methods used by linguists in studying unknown languages.

The evidence collected by the ethnographer involves the answers to such questions as what is the proper way of doing X, and how is X related to other activities or processes. Much of the ethnographer's information derives from his formal and informal observations of behavior and from interviews of various kinds. Such data, written in the form of field notes, provide the basis for further questions or observations.

As data accumulate ethnographers must consider the kind and variety of documentation required for a convincing description of those aspects of the cultural system they choose to emphasize. Some description is presented in impressionistic or anecdotal form, but other description requires the use of formal methods. Such formal methods, illustrated by Rorschach projective techniques, censuses, genealogies, and simulated situations involve the collection of information in terms of a standarized set of procedures. For example, in Agar's use of the simulated situation, a group of people act out a happening. The resulting material is then systematically tested to determine the extent to which it is "real" or "unreal." Where possible, evidence concerning matters that are controversial or uncertain is collected through the use of a variety of formal methods. Because an ethnography or description of a way of life tends to represent those aspects of culture considered vital to its operation, an ethnography is likely to be a theory of how some particular human group operates. The ideal test of such a theory is for a third person to read the ethnography and on that basis to generate behaviors acceptable to members of the group described.

For Further Reading

General problems of research in anthropology are considered in Pelto (1970). Considerations relevant to professional careers in anthropology are given in Frantz' *The Student Anthroplogist's Handbook* (1972) and in Fried's *The Study of Anthropology* (1972). The carrying out of fieldwork is discussed, often from a highly personal point of view, in Spindler's *Being an Anthropologist* (1970), Golde's *Women in the Field* (1970), and Freilich's *Marginal Natives* (1970). There are numerous accounts of ethnographic experiences such as *A Diary in the Strict Sense of the Term* (Malinowski 1967), *In the Company of Man* (Casagrande, 1960), *Return to Laughter* (Bowen 1954), *Travels in Arabia Deserta* (Doughty 1888), *The Oregon Trail* (Parkman 1849), and *Incidents of Travel in Yucatan* (Stevens 1871). Anthropological fieldwork for beginners is discussed and illustrated by student papers in *The Cultural Experience* (Spradley and McCurdy 1972).

An introduction to more specific fieldwork techniques is provided by Maranda's *Introduction to Anthropology* (1972) and by the variety of specialized publications in the "Studies in Anthropological Method" series by Holt, Rinehart and Winston. Several of the case studies, such as Newman's on the Gururumba (1965), and Turner's on the Highland Chontal (1972) provide good discussions of the problems of the anthropologist in the field. Useful surveys of anthropological methods are Pelto's *Anthropological Research: The Structure of Inquiry*, 2nd ed. (1978) and Brim and Spain's *Research Design in Anthropology* (1974). Lofland's *Doing Social Life: The Qualitative Study of Human Interaction in Natural Settings* (1975) may also be of interest.

An idea of the nature and content of ethnography can be obtained by examining any of the Holt, Rinehart and Winston "Case Studies in Cultural Anthropology" or any of the ethnographies referred to in the bibliography, especially those by Arensberg and Kimball, Colson, Elwin, Evans-Pritchard, Firth, Kaberry, Lowie, Malinowski, Nadel, Sahlins, Rasmussen. Lewis, Whyte, West, Wilson and Warner.

Recent case studies stressing field methods include Chagnon's *Studying the Yanomamo* (1974), Heider's *Grand Valley Dani: Peaceful Warriors* (1979), Dentan's *The Semai: A Nonviolent People of Malaya*, rev. ed. (1979), Barnett's *Being a Palauan*, rev. ed. (1979), and Keiser's *The Vice Lords: Warriors of the Streets*, rev. ed. (1979).

Problems and Questions

1. Observe the entrance to a crowded library, store, or cafetaria. What rules would predict who goes through the door first and how?
2. Observe some human beings for fifteen minutes. Try to write down everything they say and do. What sorts of things did you leave out?
3. Collect several genealogies from your friends or colleagues. Is there any variation in the way that people in the same culture apply kinship terms to their relatives?
4. Compare some folk tales from two different cultures. How frequently are humans, animals, plants, colors, machines, or other categories of things mentioned?
5. Write down the "proper way of doing X" in sufficient detail so that anyone could do it. Stick to simple and noncontroversial topics such as "What is the proper way of putting on a shirt, waxing a car, or writing a term paper?"

TRADITION: THE CULTURAL MESSAGE

Ideally, an ethnography consists of two major parts: a description of the cultural message and an account of the major processes involved in the operation of the cultural system. The second and third parts of this book deal with tradition and process respectively. Because the cultural message is somewhat analogous to the rules of a game, it follows that the first of the two chapters dealing with tradition begins with a discussion of world view. The questions are, "What is this game about?" "Why are we playing it?" "How do we score?" World view conceived as containing both science and religion consists of the general answers contained in the cultural tradition concerning the nature of things and the purpose of life.

The second of the two chapters dealing with tradition is concerned with a narrower question but one that is especially interesting to human individuals. It is, "What are the names of the players and what are they expected to do?" In anthropological terminology questions about role and status, about who the members are and what they are supposed to do, are classified as belonging to the domain of "social structure."

WORLD VIEW, RELIGION, AND SCIENCE

What are the major questions?

World view is a self-defining term. It refers to the view of the world contained in the cultural tradition. It includes religion, philosophy, and science—the things that people know and believe. After discussion of the nature of world view, this chapter continues with descriptive material concerning Hopi world view. The Hopi case raises a number of problems. Why do the Hopi believe that "Whoever is mean will surely die?" Why do they possess their particular religious beliefs concerning witchcraft, the kachinas, and the bringing of rain? Are these views somehow useful to the survival of the Hopi? Do they lead the Hopi to formulate specific and useful strategies for survival?

To aid in thinking about these sorts of problems, a second view of the world is presented, that of the Saora in India. Here, the glorious life after death envisioned in our cultural tradition and that of the Hopi is replaced by a dim and pessimistic view. Again, what is the work of a system of world view? Why do some people hold ideas that are different from those held by other people, yet still in some way convincing and real? In connection with the Saora world view, we pose questions about function and adaptation. Does world view really help people survive, or might it sometimes contain misconceptions that are harmful and lead to unrealistic and impractical behavior? Does world view arise in response to specific needs or does it consist merely in tales told to children? It is important to consider these difficult questions.

Another problem has to do with the relative value of different systems of world view. The Iglulik Eskimo attempt to conduct their affairs in a hard-boiled and practical way. Is their world view, then, more useful than that of the Saora or the supposedly frivolous citizens of New York City? Why not develop a rational and realistic system of world view such as might be designed by a committee of natural scientists?

In pursuit of answers to these difficult questions, or perhaps in an attempt to find more meaningful questions, anthropologists have begun to pay increasing attention to the small details of world view. Special techniques have been developed for the construction of taxonomies and other "pictures" of the nature of things. Examination of the Tikopia concept of direction leads to questions about the fundamental categories of thought. Do "up" and "down" actually exist or are they mere constructs that differ from one culture to another. Looking at the kinds of animals recognized in the English language can we identify basic principles that might be fundamental to human thought or, at least, characteristic of some particular culture? Is a numerical system derived from four basic digits biologically determined because that represents the number of sticks that can be held between the fingers of one hand?

When we ask questions like, "What are all the things in the world?" what determines the nature of the answers? How can so much information be filed away in the human brain, and yet be produced instantaneously and in vast quantity? Ethnoscience and cognitive anthropology seek to answer some of these questions. There must be order in the cultural message because people could not remember so many things if they were not organized in some fashion. Ethnoscience attempts to tell us about the things that exist in the world; cognitive anthropology attempts to tell us how the human brain processes such information. What sort of magic key enables the tiny human brain to respond so quickly and efficiently with the correct answer or the proper behavior? This is a complex chapter because anthropologists are only beginning to understand the questions that must be asked. The questions are about how people think and beyond that, setting aside all existing religion and science, about the true nature of the universe. To understand reality, we must understand the human brain; not the brain itself but what goes on inside it. The work has hardly begun.

WHY IS THE WORLD THIS WAY?

If we ask why human beings build cultural systems and preserve cultural messages, part of the answer is that people seek explanations of things. They wish to predict and control the natural and social forces about them without sacrificing their own freedom and individuality. The cultural message provides expectations concerning the things that happen. Very often these expectations become predictions about what is going to happen. In our own culture, science assumes that there is one and only one real reality. It may be complicated; it may be perceived in different ways, but somehow it exists independently of human opinion. Drugs or ecstatic experiences, trips, do not take us to a different reality; they merely give us a different view of the one and only reality. In thinking about real reality, physical scientists have concluded that it is probabilistic. In other words, we cannot know exactly what will happen; we can only know that some things are probably going to happen. Medieval philosophers knew that the sun would rise in the morning because they knew that the sun had been placed in the changeless heavens by Jehovah. Because the heavens were changeless, there was no way the sun could fail to rise. A modern physicist also believes that the sun will rise tomorrow; he considers dawn to be a high probability event. In the same way, anthropologists consider that there is a high probability that a child will learn the language and culture of his or her parents and teachers.

An interpretation of the goal of modern scientists would be that they seek to understand reality in increasing detail so that more and more of the events in it can be predicted with a high probability of success. Like clever gamblers, scientists maximize their winnings by confining their bets to relatively sure things. Science moves slowly into fields where probabilities are low and predictions often wrong. Sciences that deal with complicated events, such as anthropology and meteorology, do not always enjoy high prestige; quite possibly, because many of their predictions involve low probabilities of success.

All cultural traditions include the knowledge of reality required to make reasonably correct predictions about nature and humanity. In this informal sense, science could be said to be universal. The characteristic activities of people in different cultural systems and the fact that more people survive are evidence that much human behavior is realistic. It is true that most human beings abuse the environment, use up scarce resources, and generally behave with a certain amount of impracticality. We suspect that some ancient cultures and civilizations perished as a result of misjudgments. Even so, the disappearance of most human cultures and civilizations has to be put down to very rapid environmental changes such as dramatic failures of rainfall or unprecedented invasion by more powerful peoples. Humanity has gotten by, as the saying goes, by the skin of its teeth.

In all cultures, people have a sufficient store of exact knowledge to permit survival. They know enough to get food, to train their children, and to resolve most kinds of conflict. Science or practical knowledge does not, however, promise a perfect understanding of all things. It does not always inform people concerning what they are to do when things go wrong. There are illnesses that cannot be cured; there is lingering doubt that the sun will rise in the morning. People wonder; they become anxious.

Esoteric and mysterious knowledge is now added to practical knowledge. That which cannot be cured by herbs and bed rest can surely be cured through magic or appeal to the supernatural. Deaths that cannot be explained in other ways can be seen to be the result of a malignant enemy who has used magical powers to introduce noxious foreign objects into the body. Even as human beings achieved the capacity to sterilize the earth by jacketing an atomic bomb with cobalt, other human beings began to receive messages from mysterious and unseen creatures from outer space.

Just so do the Guardians from Planet Clarion replace the Angels of the Lord. Faith in science converts religion to psuedoscience.

Scientific knowledge covers so little and explains so poorly that it is inevitable that humans go beyond it in search of more pleasing explanations. The different kinds of knowledge are like candles—each lighting up a tiny portion of reality. Human beings create myths and other pleasing stories that explain the relationships between the regions of brightness. Such myths also describe the things lurking in the darkness.

Mythological and practical knowledge are those aspects of the cultural tradition that inform the individual concerning the things believed to exist and the things that can be done about them. But there is more to life than knowledge. The individual requires a rationale, a set of reasons for doing the things that are to be done. Philosophy and religion are intertwined in the formation of a world view, a grand explanation of what life is all about. A world view provides convincing answers to the questions: why are we here; what's happening; what comes next; what is our purpose; where are we going; what's it all about anyway? The world view is the intellectual cement that attaches the individual firmly to a cultural system.

The following section provides materials relevant to an understanding of the Hopi world view. It is intended to demonstrate the nature of world view and also to provide a sense of the kinds of things that make any particular world view attractive to the individuals who learn it. What are the really important things in the Hopi world? Believing these things to be true, what kinds of actions seem advisable?

WHAT CAUSES THE RAIN?

My child, tomorrow morning you will go for a bath. Just as the sun comes out you will pray (wish, will) that your life shall be good. Then the sun will come out and give you life. And you shall live happily. Here you happily will work for me and I'll eat those good things. With them I will grow strong. I shall continue to live well. I won't be sick. Going on (my road) I shall always be happy. And these people having something to live by will think only of continuing their good lives. And having made the good life for them, don't ever be mean (angry). Whoever is not mean will live long. Whoever is mean will surely die. Therefore anyone who is happy always sings. And so go take your bath. If you do that you will be strong, and your mothers and fathers (clouds, katchinas, the dead) will be happy when you work for them. They will be parents to your plants. One who lives thinking this way has a peaceful (Hopi) life and is always happy (Kennard 1937:491).

Certain things seem important to the Hopi: the good life, sunshine, living happily, having sons to work for you, eating good things, being strong and well, and having a peaceful (Hopi) life. Because the Hopi appear to think of themselves, assuming the above translation is correct, as "the peaceful people," it is easy to conclude that being peaceful is one of their major values. To achieve *values* such as the good life or being peaceful, the important thing is not to be mean or angry. People who think mean thoughts will die. People who think good thoughts and are always happy and singing will have a good life. The "mothers" and "fathers" (clouds, ancestors, kachinas) will water their plants, and they will eat well and be happy. Suffering and sacrifice are also involved, for the father is asking his child to take a ritual bath, which involves running to the foot of the mountain (mesa) and quite possibly breaking the ice film on top of the water in order to plunge in and bathe. After that, the warm morning sun will surely bring happiness.

The father's speech is sufficiently public and official that we may guess that it reflects the official Hopi view of the world. Examination of such statements combined with prolonged observation of Hopi activities have permitted anthropologists to develop a fairly consistent account of the Hopi world. The Hopi view of reality is different from ours, but it is based, as is ours, upon reasonalbe inferences drawn from observation of the real world. For many centuries, the Hopi experience has been unique, and the things that they have sought to accomplish have involved values somewhat different from those of other people.

Hopi culture, originally represented by a collection of loosely related villages, has occupied a series of connected mesas about ninety miles north of Flagstaff, Arizona, for more than one thousand years. This desert region is only marginally suited for agriculture, and it is probable that the Hopi became established there at a time when water was much more easily available than it is now. In their traditional pattern of growing corn (maize), the Hopi often had to plant the seeds more than a foot deep. When the seed sprouted, each hill or cluster of corn plants had to be protected from the desert wind with a screen. Survival of the Hopi required great skill and hard work. Hundreds of ruined settlements throughout the southwestern United States testify to the many villages, similar to those of the Hopi, that failed to survive. For centuries, now, the Hopi have faced the reality of a hostile world.

Perhaps the secret of Hopi survival lies in the fact that the Hopi people have always demanded from each other a high level of cooperation, conformity, and discipline. The basis of these demands lies in the Hopi view of the world, most spectacularly in the belief that mean thoughts are the primary source of trouble and confusion in the world. Although we can make categorical distinctions among Hopi values (good or bad), Hopi beliefs (true or false), and Hopi behavior (done or not done), the Hopi view of the world wraps up the central elements of all of these categories in one simple and all-embracing package.

Directly south of the mesas are the often snow-covered and cloud-embraced San Francisco mountains. On these almost always visible peaks live the kachinas, variously defined as the ancestors of the Hopi—the clouds, the spirits, the mothers and fathers of the corn plants. The kachinas are impervious to cold and snow, but their success in raising their own crops and carrying out their own existence is dependent upon the adequacy of the rituals conducted by the Hopi and upon Hopi good thoughts and good behavior. When the Hopi are good and think good thoughts, then the kachinas are happy and the clouds (the kachinas) drift north from the San Francisco peaks and water the corn plants of the Hopi.

In the olden days, when the Hopi first came to this world, they came in order to escape the "two-hearts." Two-hearts are people who think mean thoughts, develop a double heart, and, in order to survive, must eat the life substance (the animal soul) of at least one close relative each year. The two-hearts managed to follow the Hopi into this world and, according to some Hopi estimates, there are now more two-hearts in the world today than there are right-thinking people. People who think good thoughts are impervious to the two-hearts. Not only that, good thoughts tend to damage two-hearts, and there is nothing more painful to a suspected two-heart than to be treated to a display of friendliness and goodwill. In sum, every Hopi carries upon his or her shoulders the awesome responsibility of defending the world from the two-hearts, of making the rains come, and the corn grow. In some ultimate sense, this is the rationale for the Hopi way of life. It is a committed, religious way of life dedicated to the perfection of the world and the elimination of evil.

This summary of Hopi world view provides some idea of what world view is. It includes basic ideas that cannot be described simply as science or religion. What else can be said about world view on the basis of the Hopi example? Perhaps the most obvious conclusion is that the world view provides a credible reason for being a Hopi. The Hopi are just about the only people in the world who are not two-hearts. They have an important role in fighting the evil and danger inherent in the world. To fight evil and danger successfully, all Hopi must concentrate upon thinking good thoughts and performing proper actions.

Historically, many elements in the Hopi world view were exchanged among a variety of American Indian and even Asiatic groups. Still, we may speculate that the Hopi forefathers, confronted with an environment that is known to have been slowly drying up, struggled to find ways of obtaining the conformity and cooperation that were required for survival against the odds. At some periods in history different ideas about such things as the nature of two-hearts or the reality of kachinas must have struggled for acceptance. The Hopi chose among such ideas on the basis of their intellectual appeal. Perhaps the ideas chosen were not the very best ideas from an adaptive standpoint. There is no way of knowing. What is known is that the Hopi survive and that their system of world view provides a framework that seems to encourage their survival.

What, then, does a world view accomplish? First, it makes people wish to be members and to do the things that members do. Second, it provides a picture of the universe that is generally useful or, at least, seems generally useful. The ultility of world view as a means of adaptation is perhaps best seen by comparing Hopi world view with a rather different world view. The Hopi world view seems to help to solve the really important problems that confront the Hopi. Now consider the Saora and the sorts of problems that they confront.

WHY ARE THE DEAD SO LONELY?

The Saora are a tribe of some 100,000 people living in a mountainous district in India. For centuries they have preserved their way of life despite continuous pressure from the great civilizations of the Indian plains regions. Much of the time they have been subjugated:

> The Saora's threshing floor in Ganjam is indeed one of the saddest places in India. This symbol of a lifetime's toil, this shrine into which Mother Earth pours her choicest gifts, is the scene of persistent and wholesale economic trickery and exploitation (Elwin 1955:60).

Despite the necessity for paying tribute to powerful neighboring peoples, the Saora way of life and the Saora themselves continue to survive. The Saora are efficient collectors and producers of food. Each day, the men obtain quantities of the nutritious and mildly intoxicating sap of the palm trees surrounding their villages. Between meals there are snacks of land crab, chili, and mush. Protein-rich foods are easily obtained and include buffalo, land crab, fish, field rats, and red ants with mushrooms. The Saora suffer heavily from malaria and other endemic diseases, and there are always problems in dealing with avaricious members of powerful neighboring groups. The Saora explain their situation in the world, more or less as follows:

There are two separate worlds, this world and an underworld. When a man dies, his spirit descends briefly to the underworld. Later, the spirit finds his way out of the underworld and wanders about the earth pestering everyone. When the spirit's friends and relatives sacrifice a buffalo and give an expensive feast to their kinsmen and neighbors, the spirit returns to the underworld and temporarily refrains from bothering the living.

Although most Saora are contented with their roles as farmers and members of an unimportant tribe, a few Saora seek a life of greater usefulness and importance. Such individuals are likely to become shamans. That is, they are likely to be visited by the spirits of wealthy and

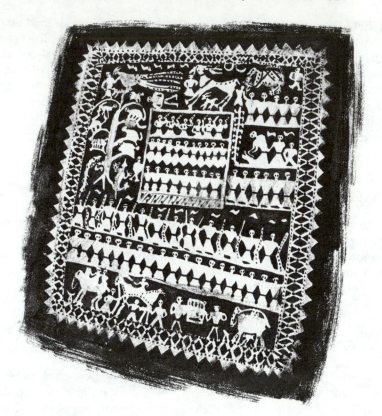

important Hindus who threaten them and quite literally drive them out of their minds until they agree to marriage. Once married to such a Hindu tutelary spirit, the living Saora undertakes a variety of special obligations including communication with the underworld and the healing of the sick. In carrying out these obligations, the shaman may visit the underworld and be possessed by individual spirits and speak with their voices. This direct experience gives the Saora detailed knowledge of the nature of spirits and the underworld:

> The underworld is like this world; there are hills, rivers, rocks, and trees, but it is always moonlight there. There is no brighter light than that, there is no sun and the clouds are very low. You cannot recognize people at a distance, the light is so dim. The tutelaries (spirits of Hindus) are the officials and the ancestors are the peasants of the land. Since there is so little light, the ancestors cannot get about very much. But when they do find a path, they come to this world and cause a lot of trouble.
> It is hard to get sufficient food, though the ordinary dead plough their fields. But the rulers, the tutelaries, who dress and behave like Hindus, are rich and prosperous; they sleep on beds; sahibs and forest officers come to

their marriages; they keep many servants and soldiers; they ride on elephants and horses and have lizards, snakes and tigers as pets. As men keep dogs, they keep tigers in their houses. But the ancestors who are the peasants of that country, look just as they did at the time of death, thin, weary, deformed and sad. They cannot get proper clothes to wear and it is always cold under the infernal moon. The wind too blows so hard that it carries their thin bodies up into the air. When they can find the way, they come to their old homes on earth and give their relatives fever and ague; that is why we shiver when we get fever, because the dead who give it are themselves shivering with cold; they do not let us be until we give them clothes (Elwin 1955:69–70).

Pathetic creatures, neglected by their living relatives, the spirits desperately attempt to attract the attention of the living. Acting through grief, loneliness, and dire need, deceased parents attempt to carry off sons or grandchildren so that they will have someone to care for them in the underworld. Through the shamans, the living hear the pleas and demands of the dead and conduct appropriate ceremonies to cure the living and provide for the economic needs of the spirits.

There are also a variety of deities. These deities, as well as the spirits, are continually journeying from place to place. Although they are invisible to man, they may be encountered anywhere:

You who live in clearings now overgrown with trees, you who live in pits, you who live above, you who live in water, you who live in bones, you who live in the bones of men, you who live in the stone walls between fields, you who live in the trees of the forest, you made us and gave us birth; come all of you to take your offerings (Elwin 1955:328).

Walking along a trail, a Saora may inadvertently interfere with the activities of spirits or deities invisibly picnicking there. Should he accidently kick over their bowl of rice, they will be enraged and he will fall ill. Illness, then, is the consequence of failing to provide proper offerings to the ancestors or of accidentally or deliberately failing to treat deities with proper respect. Illness is cured through the holding of a ceremony in which the spirit or deity possesses the shaman, explains the cause of his anger, and is propitiated by means of gifts of food and drink. Any serious illness requires the sacrifice of a buffalo. The buffalo is obtained by borrowing money from neighboring groups so that most Saora are in debt to the moneylender. Although this sort of indebtedness is an aspect of the economic exploitation of the Saora by neighboring groups, it is worth noting that the moneylender now has a vested interest in the economic success of his client. Indebtedness, by providing the Saora with the protection of powerful moneylenders, may be one of the means by which the Saora have maintained themselves as a group despite pressures to adopt the customs and religion of their more powerful neighbors. Another characteristic of illness among the Saora is that wealthy men fall ill with greater frequency than do poor men. The man of wealth apparently establishes his social status and his importance through a form of hypochondria in which he provides gifts of food and drink not only to the spirits, but to the living as well.

The Saora world view presents an organized picture of the Saora world and provides explanations for the great questions of life: why do some men fall ill and not others; why do men die; why is the world the way it is? The concept of an underworld occupied by spirits that cause disease leads to the performance of shamanistic healing rituals. These rituals have the purpose of curing disease, but in practice they appear to be multipurpose instruments that contribute to the solution of a variety of Saora problems. The role of shaman provides an outlet for those who might otherwise fail to find satisfaction in the Saora way of life. The feasting and buffalo sacrifice provides an opportunity for joyous unification of the community and for the display and circulation of wealth by the rich. Because male buffalo are economically useless, except for eating, the buffalo sacrifice helps to control their numbers. Finally, because buffalo sacrifice leads to indebtedness to members of neighboring groups, it provides an avenue of social and economic interaction between the Saora and their neighbors. The Saora world view seems useful, but is it really?

DO THESE WORLD VIEWS WORK?

The Hopi world view appeared to be consistent with the kinds of interest and problems of a group of people attempting to practice agriculture in a desert region. In pursuing questions concerning the possible adaptive value of systems of world view, consideration has now been given to the Saora world view.

Where the Hopi world view expresses the idea of dedication to good thoughts and good deeds, the Saora world view expresses a grudging acceptance of the obligation to feed their greedy neighbors and their poor, cold, starving ancestors. Anyone feeling a desire to complain about life as it is has the consolation of knowing that it will only get worse in the next life. One might almost say that the Saora are so concerned with making hay while the sun shines that they do not even give consideration to the fact that they ultimately cease to exist even as spirits. Having determined in advance that life and death are both painful, the Saora take a perverse pleasure in enjoying themselves. For those who do wish for something more out of life, there is "involuntary" marriage to a high-caste Hindu spirit and the subsequent adoption of the role of medium and healer.

In some crude way, Saora world view is consistent with being a Saora and with survival in a world that is not harsh like the Hopi world, but that

traditionally offers few avenues for economic progress or social better-
ment. Assuming that these explanations, rationales, and values making
up the Saora world view are in some way useful to Saora individuals, it
can be hypothesized (guessed) that part of the work of a system of world
view lies in the fact that it convinces people that it is worthwhile to be a
Saora and worthwhile to do the things that good Saora do. The role played
by a part of a cultural system in maintaining that system is called its
function. Very often the parts of a system will have several functions. One
of the functions of the Saora world view and all other world views as well
would appear to be strengthening the commitment of the individual to a
particular way of life.

Acting in terms of their world view, the Saora hold curing rituals
presumably for the purpose of curing people. Although a nice ritual
undoubtedly makes a sick person feel better, there seems to be no very
realistic connection between what happens in the ritual and the problem
of treating a disease. Possibly the curing ritual doesn't really cure anybody
even though it might be helpful for some kinds of psychological ailments.
In fact the people attending curing rituals eat a lot of special food and
drink a lot of beer. The comparatively well-to-do Saora are ill somewhat
more often than others. This leads to the hypothesis that curing rituals are
a means through which people entertain their friends and display their
wealth. A generalization would be that the ritual functions as a means of
preserving the Saora system of wealth and status.

In examining Saora world view, we might well be concerned about its
value to the Saora as a means of maintaining their society or surviving in a
changing world. We should like to know in some measurable or at least
definitive way whether the Saora curing ritual does some job and whether
it does it well or badly. For example, the government of India considers
animal sacrifice to be unsuitable behavior in a modern nation and might
well wish to ban the custom among the Saora. What would this do to the
Saora? Would they become totally demoralized and lose their desire to
live? This has happened to some peoples and individuals as a result of
similar meddling by outsiders. On the other hand, would they quickly
find some substitute that would please the government and at the same
time fulfill *their* needs? As a third possibility, perhaps the banning of
animal sacrifice would not affect anything. In this last case, we would have
evidence that animal sacrifice has no particular functional or adaptive
value. If, as a fourth possibility, animal sacrifice were dysfunctional and
maladaptive, then the Saora might well enjoy psychological and economic
benefits when it was banned. In parts of New Guinea people have welcomed government action to prevent head-hunting, saying something
like, "Thank goodness! We've been trying to figure out how to stop this
thing for years!"

One test of the function of a custom is to see if it feels better or worse

FIGURE 4–2 Maze in South India is a visual symbol possibly reflecting a view of the world as a place of complexity and choice. (PHOTO BY ALAN R. BEALS)

when you stop it. Experimental tests, however, are difficult to arrange. In most cases, they are illegal or unethical. Other ways of testing function might involve various kinds of historical or comparative research. How did animal sacrifice develop? What are the differences between peoples who practice animal sacrifice and those who don't? Almost certainly investigations would show that animal sacrifice occurs in quite different contexts in different places and originated for a variety of historical reasons. Very likely, since all places are unique, the precise role of animal sacrifice in different places would be quite different. Still, in the end, we might have some ideas about the value of this and other Saora customs.

We have been dealing with the research question: "How do you evaluate the contribution of a custom to the cultural system within which it is found?" We have tried to point out that such evaluations are very difficult to make. Even when we can distinguish between true and false beliefs, we cannot always be sure that true beliefs are more necessary or more valuable than false beliefs. Concepts of function and adaptation help us to think about these matters, but we lack any foreseeable and effective ways of measuring either one. In the end, we take refuge in the idea that world view is useful because people use it. It is the acceptance of the Hopi or Saora world view that makes people into Hopi or Saora. It is the job of world view to provide a reasonable if not a rational explanation of why they are expected to be and behave in the ways considered appropriate for members of the cultural system.

It could be said that the Hopi and the Saora both have patterns of world view that are otherworldly. The Hopi work, not for themselves, but for the defeat of evil. The Saora are more playful than the Hopi, but seem more concerned in a kind of happy-go-lucky way with the welfare of their ancestors than with the nature of reality. The next example deals with the Eskimo and to a lesser extent with the scientific view of the world. Both of these world views emphasize the importance of dealing with concrete reality. Pleasing the gods, perfecting oneself, all those other *religious* goals are put aside. The goal is knowledge, for the Eskimo the knowledge required for survival.

DOES THE ESKIMO WORLD VIEW WORK BETTER?

The Iglulik Eskimo have reason to believe that danger and hardship are everywhere. They consider themselves to be hard-boiled and practical, and their world is governed and dominated by the "rules of life." All living things contain "souls" and "names" which render them sensitive to the rules. If the rules are violated by sinful and unclean human beings, the souls of animals killed in the hunt become evil spirits causing harm and death. All animals taken from the sea are controlled by the sea spirit and many of the rules of life are designed to appease her. When men are out hunting, the rules of life insist that they must sleep each night a considerable distance from the water. If they sleep on the ice-edge, they are likely to be caught by the sister of the moon spirit. She will creep up and cut out their entrails with her semicircular knife. "The sea spirit does not like her creatures to smell human beings when they are not actually hunting" (Rasmussen 1929:76). In the same way, children who play noisily inside the house while their parents are away are likely to attract the attention of the spanking monster. Rasmussen tried to find out why the Eskimo had so many rules:

It had been an unusually rough day, and as we had plenty of meat after the successful hunting of the past few days, I had asked my host to stay at home so that we could get some work done together. The brief daylight had given place to the half-light of the afternoon, but as the moon was up, one could still see some distance. Ragged white clouds raced across the sky, and when a gust of wind came tearing over the ground, our eyes and mouths were filled with snow. Aua looked me full in the face and pointed out over the ice, where the snow was being lashed about in waves by the wind, he said:

"In order to hunt well and live happily, man must have calm weather. Why this constant succession of blizzards and all this needless hardship for men seeking food for themselves and those they care for? Why? Why?"

We had come out just at the time when the men were returning from their watching at the blowholes on the ice; they came in little groups bowed forward, toiling along against the wind, which actually forced them now and again to stop, so fierce were the gusts. Not one of them had a seal in tow; their whole day of painful effort and endurance had been in vain.

I could give no answer to Aua's "Why?" but shook my head in silence. He then led me into Kublo's house, which was close beside our own. The small blubber lamp burned with but the faintest flame giving out no heat whatever; a couple of children crouched shivering under a skin rug on the bench.

Aua looked at me again and said: "Why should it be cold and comfortless in here: Kublo has been out hunting all day and if he had got a seal as he deserved his wife would now be sitting laughing beside her lamp, letting it burn full without fear of having no blubber left for tomorrow. The place would be warm and bright and cheerful. The children would come out from under their rugs and enjoy life. Why should it not be so? Why?"

I made no answer and he led me out of the house into a little snow hut where his sister Natseq lived all by herself because she was ill. She looked thin and worn, and was not even interested in our coming. For several days she had suffered from a malignant cough that seemed to come from far down in the lungs, and it looked as if she had not long to live.

Aua looked at me again, and said. "Why must people be ill and suffer

pain? We are all afraid of illness. Here is this old sister of mine; as far as anyone can see, she has done no evil; she has lived through a long life and given birth to healthy children, and now she must suffer before her days end. Why? Why?"

This ended his demonstration, and we returned to our house to resume with the others the interrupted discussion.

"You see," said Aua, "you are equally unable to give any reason when we ask you why life is as it is. And so it must be. All our customs come from life and turn towards life; we explain nothing, we believe nothing, but in what I have just shown you lies our answer to all you ask.

"We fear the weather spirit of earth that we must fight against to wrest our food from land and sea. We fear Sila.

"Our customs all come from life and are directed toward life; we cannot explain, we do not believe in this or that, but the answer lies in what I have just told you.

"We fear.

"We fear the elements with which we have to fight in their fury to wrest our food from land and sea.

"We fear cold and famine in our snow huts.

"We fear the sickness that is daily to be seen among us. Not death, but the suffering.

"We fear the souls of the dead, of human and animal alike.

"We fear the spirits of earth and air.

"And therefore our fathers, taught by their fathers before them, guarded themselves about with all these old rules and customs, which are built upon the experience and knowledge of generations. We do not know how or why, but we obey them that we may be suffered to live in peace. And for all our angakoks (men who deal with the spirit world) and their knowledge of hidden things, we yet know so little that we fear everything else" (Rasmussen 1929:55–56).

When things go wrong, when even the most careful attempts to follow the rules and customs fail to ensure good weather or good hunting, the Eskimo gather together, and, under the leadership of an *angakok*, confess to all of the violations they have committed. When the spirits and the

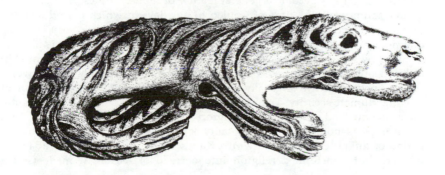

souls of the dead are satisfied that all sins have been confessed and forgiven, the sky clears and the animals emerge once more where they can be hunted.

Because the Eskimo live in one of the harshest and most demanding environments known to man, their world view is presumably as helpful to them or at least noninjurious. The habit of conforming to a wide variety of rules and the mechanism of group confession in a sort of sensitivity session appear to contribute to the smooth functioning of the tiny and isolated communities in which the Eskimo live. The conformity of every person to the rules of life seems to be an asset in maintaining stable relationships with the environment. Would it not be better, then, if the Saora believed as the Eskimo do?

The Eskimo system works for small communities in a harsh environment, while the Saora system works for larger communities where the physical environment is rich and complicated and where the main problems of life have to do with disease and neighboring peoples. The Saora world view works for the Saora and the Eskimo world view works for the Eskimo. These different forms of world view do not arise directly from the environment; rather they develop slowly as a result of a continuing process of interaction between the cultural system and the environment. Different cultural systems with different world views might well be adapted to the same environment. One system might support more people, survive for a longer time, or be more or less subject to change than another system. Where there are two cultural systems and two world views, it is not always easy to decide that one is more functional, more adaptive, or better than another.

We might argue that world view based upon truths established through science would be superior to any other world view. We might even argue that such a world view exists and that we possess it or are so close to possessing it that it makes no difference. But does man live by truth alone?

The overestimation of the reliability of scientific results is not restricted to the philosopher; it has become a general feature of modern times, that is, of the period dating from the time of Galileo to our day, in which period falls the creation of modern science. The belief that science has the answer to all questions—that if somebody is in need of technical information, or is ill, or is troubled by some psychological problem, he merely has to ask the scientist in order to obtain an answer—is so widespread that science has taken over a social function which originally was satisfied by religion: the function of offering ultimate security. The belief in science has replaced, in large measure, the belief in God. Even where religion was regarded as compatible with science, it was modified by the mentality of the believer in scientific truth. The period of Enlightenment, into which Kant's lifework falls, did not abandon religion; but transformed religion into a creed of reason, it made God a

mathematical scientist who knew everything because he had a perfect insight into the laws of reason. No wonder the mathematical scientist appeared as a sort of little god, whose teaching had to be accepted as exempt from doubt. All the dangers of theology, its dogmatism and its control of thought through the guarantee of certainty, reappear in a philosophy that regards science as infallible (Reichenbach 1959:43–44).

Only if science were infallible and contained the answers to every important question would it be possible to construct a world view based upon a perfect understanding of the nature of things. World view must go beyond the ordinary to provide answers to questions that have no answer. It must do this because it must succeed in convincing the membership of the cultural system that what they are called upon to do is worth doing. Where a cultural system exists, it exists, in part, because the membership retains its allegiance to a particular world view consisting of explanations and understandings which reach beyond science and above truth.

The members of any cultural system regard their own particular view of the world as more accurate, useful, beautiful, or in some way better, or better for them, than any other world view. If they did not, they would change their views. Our own particular view of the world leads to questions about the effectiveness of other views. Is the Eskimo world view more or less consistent, more or less realistic, or more or less effective in its functioning than the Saora world view? Is it better to view the things in nature as something to be used up and consumed or as something to be cared for and preserved? Is it more useful to think of human beings as high class apes or as supernatural beings? Would it be be better for the species as a whole if all the human beings in all the cultural systems shared the same world view or would it be better if they all had different world views?

It is easy to grade world views, cultural traditions, or cultural systems along various dimensions, but it is difficult to establish the value of any particular system of grading. Even if the rating of world views did not involve important moral and philosophical questions, most cultural anthropologists would feel that two other sorts of questions would have to be answered first: "How may we investigate and describe world view?" and "How may we explain the similarities and differences among different world views?" Because it is impossible to answer any questions about world view without achieving descriptions of world view that are accurate and comparable, a major thrust of current anthropological research deals with the problem of description.

DESCRIPTION: WHERE IS THE PATTERN?

In the beginning God created the heaven and the earth. And the earth was without form, and void; and darkness *was* upon the face of the deep. And the Spirit of God moved upon the face of the waters. And God said, Let there be light: and there was light. And God saw the light, and it *was* good; and God divided the light from the darkness. And God called the light Day, and the darkness he called Night. And the evening and the morning were the first day.

And God said, Let there be a firmament in the midst of the waters, and let it divide the waters from the waters. And God made the firmament, and divided the waters which *were* under the firmament from the waters which *were* above the firmament: and it was so. And God called the firmament Heaven. And the evening and the morning were the second day.

And God said, Let the waters under the heaven be gathered together unto one place, and let the dry *land* appear: and it was so. And God said, Let the earth bring forth grass, the herb yielding seed, *and* the fruit tree yielding fruit after his kind, whose seed *is* in itself, upon the earth: and it was so. And the earth brought forth grass, *and* herb yielding seed after his kind, and the tree yielding fruit, whose seed *was* in itself, after his kind: and God saw that *it was* good.

The above statement is a myth, an authoritative or trusted explanation of things. It is accepted by a variety of cultural systems sharing access to the *Old Testament*. If we could simplify some aspect of this statement and reduce it to order or identify some part of the pattern in it, it would provide a starting point for an understanding of the world view of these cultural systems.

One way of beginning an analysis is to regard the statement as a kind of classification or taxonomy. The statement is among other things a list of certain things that exist in the world. Within the list things are arranged in a particular order. Some things precede other things in a temporal way

and some things are on top of or within other things. An analysis of the statement might then lead to a diagram of the following sort:

WATERS					
WATERS ABOVE	FIRMAMENT (HEAVEN)	WATERS BELOW			
		SEA	LAND		
			GRASS	HERB	FRUIT TREE

To persons steeped in the particular world view of which this genesis story forms a part, most of the distinctions made seem perfectly logical and natural. Surely it is only human nature to distinguish heaven from earth, land from water, fruit from seed, and so on. But consider an aspect of Tikopian classification and Tikopian human nature.

Can You See Things as They Are?

> It is hard for anyone who has not actually lived on the island to realize its isolation from the rest of the world. It is so small that one is rarely out of sight or sound of the sea. The native concept of space bears a distinct relation to this. They find it almost impossible to conceive of any really large land mass. I was once asked seriously by a group of them, "Friend, is there any land where the sound of the sea is not heard?" Their confinement has another less obvious result. For all kinds of spatial references they use the expressions *inland* and to *seawards*. Thus an axe lying on the floor of a house is localized in this way, and I have even heard a man direct the attention of another in saying: "There is a spot of mud on your seaward cheek" (Firth 1963:19).

On Tikopia, an island in the Pacific, the world view contains, as we might assume that all world views must, a way of expressing the spatial relationship among things, but the Tikopians approach the problem of defining location in a fairly unique way. It may be natural and human to have a system of coordinates for locating things in space, but there is evidently nothing in nature that says that all human beings must use the same set of coordinates. World views often differ in terms of the most basic and fundamental ways of classifying things:

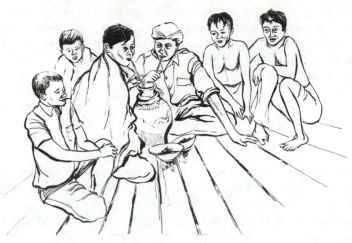

To dispose things spatially there must be a possibility of placing them differently, of putting some at the right, others at the left, these above, those below, at the north of or at the south of, east or west of, etc., etc., just as to dispose states of consciousness temporally there must be a possibility of localizing them at determined dates. That is to say that space could not be what it is if it were not, like time, divided and differentiated. But whence come these divisions which are so essential. By themselves, there are neither right nor left, up nor down, north nor south, etc. All these distinctions evidently come from the fact that different sympathetic values have been attributed to various regions. Since all the men of a single civilization represent space in the same way, it is clearly necessary that these sympathetic values, and the distinctions which depend upon them should be equally universal, and that almost necessarily implies that they be of social origin (Durkheim 1961:23–24).

Durkheim's argument is that the basis of human thought and perception derives from the arbitrary or "made-up" nature of the principles, coordinates, or relations that are used to divide up the space-time continuum. If, as Durkheim suggests, fundamental categories are simply invented by the members of cultural systems and passed along as a part of the cultural tradition, it becomes impossible to perceive reality except as one's perceptions of reality are conditioned by culture. Because the scientific method itself depends fundamentally upon the idea of intersubjectivity; namely, that different observers will perceive the same experience in the same way, Durkheim's suggestion places an obstacle in the way of all general scientific theories about the nature of things. Modern physical theories, involving such violations of common sense as *N-dimensional space* or *relativity*, illustrate both the strength of such obstacles and the possibility of overcoming them.

Although it is easy to understand that concepts like "landward" and "seaward" are arbitrary categories made up by members of a group, many anthropologists suspect that there might be fundamental categories that arise from common human experience or the biological similarity of human beings. Psychoanalytic theories sometimes argue that the early experiences and the development of the human infant lead to the development of universal symbols and ways of perceiving. It might be argued, for example, that because the human infant's first experiences have to do with ingestion, defecation, and urination, all later experiences are likely to be classified in oral, anal, and genital terms (Erikson 1950). Biologically oriented theorists might argue that such things as the structure of the human eye place fundamental limitations upon the human capacity to divide up the space-time continuum. Because none of these possibilities have gained general acceptance, the safest guess would seem to be that there are universal categories of thought but that we cannot speak of them with precision because they lie hidden in a thicket of arbitrary or culturally derived categories of thought.

In linguistics, the relatively small number of distinctive speech sounds made by people speaking different languages suggests that biological factors having to do with the nature of the speech organs place powerful limitations upon the kinds of noises that can be made.

That some peoples produce highly distinctive speech sounds and that every language has its own particular set of speech sounds suggests the power of arbitrary or cultural categorizations in overriding or distorting biological limitations. An examination of the numeral systems of various peoples appears to indicate that counting is almost universally associated with the number of fingers and toes that people possess. The decimal system is based upon a unit of ten fingers, other systems are based upon five fingers or the sum of the fingers and toes. There are peoples who count the spaces between the fingers instead of counting the fingers and toes, and they end up with systems that run: 1, 2, 3, one hand, one hand plus 1, one hand plus 2, one hand plus 3, two hands, two hands plus one, and so on. The early experience of having ten fingers and ten toes creates a predisposition to divide up the world not in some particular way, but in a limited variety of particular ways. There appear to be no methods of counting based upon 3, 6, 7, or 9, and the binary system (one, one hand, one hand plus one, one hand plus one hand) appears to be a recent invention. The creation of a numeral system to the base three poses no problem (1, 2, trio, 1 trio 1, trio 2, 2 trio, 2 trio 1, 2 trio 2, and so on), and is, therefore, natural enough even though uncommon in nature.

To the extent that human beings see things as they are taught to see them, speak as they are taught to speak, and count as they are taught to count, human beings are dreamers living in dreamworlds of their own, or rather of their ancestors' construction. Is it possible for a man immersed in the dreamworld of his culture to enter the dreamworld of another culture? If so, we must assume some common basis underlying all constructions of reality. The most common assumption is that all systems of belief represent a division of the space-time continuum into subjects or items and relationships between them. In other world, there must be things related to each other in terms of specific principles of classification such as sex, number, location, developmental state, origin, or temporal order. How may we discover what the principles of classification are?

WHAT ARE YOUR PRINCIPLES?

The following table by Hjelmslev, quoted by Sidney Lamb (1964:68), represents a way of classifying animals. The manner in which the items in the table are related serves to indicate their meaning.

ANIMAL	ADULT		INFANT
	Male	*Female*	
sheep	ram	ewe	lamb
horse	stallion	mare	foal
chicken	rooster	hen	chick

The fact that sheep, horses, and chickens may all be placed in the same table suggests that they are in some way things of a kind. Thus, within something which might be called the domain of animals, there is a type of animal whose subdomain is divided in terms of the principles given in the table. What are the principles of classification? There is a distinction between infant and adult animals and between male and female adults. These distinctions could be labeled principles of sex and maturation. In the culture represented by the table, one way of dividing the space-time continuum is in terms of principles of maturation and sex. Further study would be needed to determine how widely these principles are applied. Is everything in the world classified in terms of sex and maturity; if not, what kinds of things are so classified? Because all animals of the sheep, horse, and chicken kind are classified in terms of maturity, but only mature animals in terms of sex, it might be guessed that in this culture developmental state is more important than sex.

Here is another list (Lamb 1964:68):

Size	*Big*	*Little*
length	long	short
width	wide	narrow
depth	deep	shallow

In this table, the space-time continuum is divided into things that have size, and presumably things that do not, and the domain of size is divided into big and little things. The implications for the perception of things and behavior toward things are striking. If this were the only way of dealing with the domain of size, it would be impossible to describe a box of average size. The anthropologist brought up as a speaker of English and having a tendency to think of the animal domain or the size domain in these particular ways would have difficulty navigating in a cultural world that used different principles of classification or even the same principles in different ways or with different emphases. One of the goals of modern anthropology has been to find ways of eliciting or discovering principles of classification different from those of English.

What Is It That There Is?

Q: In the world, what is there?
A: Houses, trees, water, huge factories, ordinary factories, bus stops, railroad stops, airplane companies, and hills, working people, cattle, birds, and snakes.
Q: In houses, what is there?
A: Roof tiles, beams, men, radios, pictures, cooking utensils, cows, and rats.
Q: In roof tiles, what is there?
A: Flat tiles from Bangalore, flat tiles from Chikkballapur, ordinary tiles, and VJI tiles.
Q: In beams, what is there?
A: Main beams, supporting beams, and rafters.
Q: In men, what is there?
A: (Gives names of household heads in his family)
Q: In radios, what is there?
A: Radio, pocket radio, and hand radio.

The inverview method used here involves the use of a linguistic frame. A single question, "In the _____, what is there?" is asked repeatedly making use of words supplied by the informant. The object of linguistic frame interviewing is to obtain as much information as possible from the person being interviewed while minimizing the bias that might be introduced by a series of perhaps unrelated questions asked by the interviewer. After the first question, in effect, the person interviewed supplies all future questions.

The example given above leads to a taxonomy, to a classification of the things that exist in the world. An example of a taxonomy is given in the table on page 121. What kinds of questions can we ask about such a taxonomy? Presumably, it tells us something about the processes of human memory. How many items can there be in a list? How finely

WORLD														
HOUSES											TREES	WATER	HUGE FACTORIES	ORDINARY FACTORIES	ETC.
ROOF TILES				BEAMS			MEN	RADIOS			PICTURES	ETC. COOKING UTENSILS, COWS, RATS			
BANGALORE TILES	CHIKKABALLAPUR TILES	ORDINARY TILES	VJI TILES	MAIN BEAMS	SUPPORTING BEAMS	RAFTERS	HOUSEHOLD HEADS FROM 1 TO n	ORDINARY RADIO	POCKET RADIO	HAND RADIO					

detailed can a classification be? It also tells us something about the person being interviewed. What are his interests? What are his areas of knowledge? How typical are his responses compared to those of other members of his group? Finally, such a classification, when compared with classifications given by other members of the group tells us something about the culture. What aspects of the environment are considered important? What principles are used in classifying? Is there any pattern in their scheme of classification? How closely does their scheme of classification resemble a similar set of responses, perhaps given by a college student in another culture? Finally, how do people generate such lists and classifications? Is there method in their madness?

In the example, everything listed exists in nature. From the scientific standpoint, the view of the environment is perfectly accurate, but it is difficult to imagine anyone but an urban-influenced South Indian interpreting a house as containing roof tiles, beams, radios, pictures, cooking utensils, cows, and rats. That persons in different cultural systems propose different world views does not mean that they are out of step with reality, it may only mean that they classify and interpret the world around them in different but equally valid ways.

In anthropology, the term *ethnoscience* has come to refer to highly systematic and formal studies of the systems of labeling and classification which the members of different cultural systems apply to the things they believe to exist. A history of the development of the ethnoscience approach is given in Sturtevant (1964) and formal methodologies are discussed by Frake (1964) and by Metzger and Williams (1963). Although ethnoscience has sometimes been treated as if it were a "new ethnography" with the implication that older forms of ethnography are therefore obsolete, it is in fact a useful and efficient way of gaining access to at least some of the content of the cultural message. Several writers, perhaps infatuated with the success of new methodologies in understanding cultural messages, have given the impression that an adequate cultural anthropology would dedicate itself solely to the study of cultural traditions. The position taken in this book is that full understanding of the similarities and differences among cultural systems is to be attained only through an understanding of the complex and systematic relationships among cultural traditions, environment, and actual behavior.

Ethnoscience is, in fact, a part of a new ethnography which has arisen as cultural anthropologists of all persuasions have brought increasingly systematic methodologies into the study of all aspects of cultural systems. The wholesale borrowing of methodological approaches from psychology, linguistics, statistics, mathematics, and computer science has not so much rendered the "old ethnography" obsolete as it has enhanced it by providing access to more accurate and systematic information about cultural systems. The new methods, perhaps most particularly the use of linguistic frames, lead specifically to questions about human behavior. One of the most important of these questions, considered in the following sections, has to do with the relationship between individual behavior and the cultural message. Specifically, how do individual members of a cultural system generate behaviors their fellows consider to be appropriate?

Where Do You Get Your Ideas?

In his responses to the linguistic frame, "In the _____, what is there?" the young South Indian generates a classification which reflects the cultural tradition of his particular village. Within the framework provided by his culture, his responses are unique. No other human individual would provide precisely the same responses to that particular linguistic frame. A key questions in anthropology is, "How is it possible to be a unique and creative individual and at the same time to exhibit the behavior characteristic of a particular cultural system?" One possible answer to this question, proposed in connection with language by Noam Chomsky (1966), is that cultural tradition exists in the form of rules, analogous to the rules of grammar, that permit the generation of uniquely individual behavior which nevertheless is accepted as culturally appropriate.

In South Indian culture, for example, two of the rules used in generat-

FIGURE 4–10 Shiva, one of the forms of the Hindu diety. The image permits the worshipper to focus upon the ultimate reality, the truth concealed beneath false desires for such things as sex and wealth. Taken near Gopalpur, South India. (PHOTO BY ALAN R. BEALS)

ing classifications seem to be: (1) that the environment is divided into a series of places; and (2) that each place contains characteristic things, plants, animals, people, and supernatural figures. Although not every place contains things in all of these categories, it seems likely that people respond to a question like, "In houses, what is there?" by listing some of the things—plants, animals, and so on—that they remember as being characteristic of houses. The order of listing and the number of things in each category reflect the individual's personal interests and experience, but the particular things that can be in a house and the general method of classification reflect the cultural tradition.

What Kinds of Nails Are There?

Table 4–1 offers a taxonomy or classification of the kinds of nails that exist. The obvious function of such a classification is that of permitting communication among the members of a cultural system. To order a nail of a

Table 4–1 Nails Advertised by Smith Nails and Fasteners (What dimensions are involved in the classification?)

	COMMON NAILS		BOX NAILS	FINISHING NAIL BRAD HEAD	
	Length *(in inches)*	*Gauge*	*Gauge* *(length is same)*	*Gauge*	
60d	6	2	(not listed)	00	(not listed)
50d	5.5	3	(not listed)	00	(not listed)
40d	5	4	8 ("nonstock")	00	(not listed)
30d	4.5	5	9 ("nonstock")	00	(not listed)
20d	4	6	9	10	("nonstock")
16d	3.5	8	10	11	("nonstock")
12d	3.25	9	10.5 ("nonstock")	11.5 ("nonstock)
10d	3.00	9	10.5	11.5
9d	2.75	10.25	11.5 ("nonstock")	12.5 ("nonstock")
8d	2.50	10.25	11.5	12.5
7d	2.25	11.5	12.5	13 ("nonstock")
6d	2.00	11.5	12.5	13
5d	1.75	12.5	14.00	15 ("nonstock")
4d	1.5	12.5	14.00	15
3d	1.25	14	14.5	15.5
2d	1.00	15	15.5 ("nonstock")	16.5 ("nonstock")

Casing nails, countersunk head, are the "same length and guage specification as Box Nail."

Additional Information
1. "All types of nails available with ring or screw shank for greatly increased holding power."
2. "Galvanized finish provides maximum rust resistance and may be specified in any Keystone nails."
3. "Cement coated—an adhesive resin coating that increases holding power may be specified on any type of nail."
4. "Other popular Keystone nails" include:
    a. concrete—"oil quench hardened, plain or screw shank".
    b. flooring—"nonslit blunt point."
    c. lath—"sterilized blued."
    d. plasterboard—"blued, flat head."
    e. pole barn—"stiff stock ringshank."
    f. roofing—"large head polished or galvanized."
    g. scaffold—"double head."
    h. spikes—"up to 12" in length."

particular kind over the telephone, it would be necessary to have a grasp of this classification. In order to communicate, the individual must be capable of exhibiting behaviors other people can interpret accurately. To start a fight with another person, it is necessary to exhibit an angry frown, a threatening gesture, or some other indication of opposition. Human beings live in a forest of symbols and classifications, and, if they are to do the right thing at the right time, they must know how to generate correct behaviors and interpret the behaviors generated by others.

Lacking access to the system of classification and meaning, the member of a cultural system finds himself unable to function or compelled to seek the assistance of someone who does understand the system. Most people cannot order nails over the telephone; they must take the nail to a hardware store and ask a specialist to classify it for them. If so simple a thing as a classification of nails is too difficult for an ordinary person to learn, we are left with the puzzling question: "How do people manage to exhibit meaningful behavior most of the time?" In other words, how can the human individual have filed away in his head and instantly accessible all of the things he needs to know in order to function as a member of his cultural system? When the anthropologist asks, "How many kinds of trees are there?" how is it possible for the individual, acting virtually without hesitation, to generate an appropriate list of trees? How is it possible for a student during an examination to respond to a question with an answer that is interpreted by the instructor as correct, but is at the same time unique and so individualistic that the instructor is convinced that the student obtained the answer from his own head?

The conclusion is almost inescapable that when a human being performs such routines as classifying trees, buying nails, starting a fight, plowing a field, making a date, or passing through a doorway, his behavior depends in part upon habit or memorized sequences of behavior, but it depends perhaps even more upon the presence somewhere inside his body of a mechanism which permits him to generate behavior that is at once uniquely individual and culturally appropriate. For example, people do not remember all of the numbers in their numeral systems, rather the numbers are supplied by applying a succession of rules to a small number of basic terms. Presumably these rules themselves are not independent of other rules and might themselves be generated by some set of even more basic rules. These considerations lead to two kinds of questions: first, what is the nature of the rules or, if you like, the grammar underlying a particular classification or a particular type of behavior, and second, what are the basic and general rules underlying a particular cultural tradition? Consider how the first of these questions applies to the making of beer.

What Makes Good Beer?

One of the important items in the culture of the Subanun of the Philippines is beer. The making of beer requires yeast cakes, and yeast cakes require the mixing of spices, rice, water, and old yeast. The quality of Subanun beer is believed (by the Subanun) to depend upon the particular spices that are added to the yeast cakes. Using linguistic frames to determine what sorts of things could be added to spices, Charles Frake (1964:139–140) received the answers "young leaves," "underground parts," "fruits," and "stems." Such expressions as "young leaves" do not mean the same in English that they do in Subanun, but with practice and further interviewing and observation, the ethnographer can learn, or come to think that he has learned, to make the same distinctions that the Subanun make.

Continuing with the use of linguistic frame questions, Frake arrived at the following rules governing the making of spices: Select plant parts which include: (1) the "fruits" of "chili"; (2) the "stem" pieces of "sugar cane"; (3) "young leaves of selected trees"; and (4) the "underground parts" of selected "herbs" including "ginger" and "rice" if available. These reflect only a small proportion of the rules that must be followed if good beer is to be made, but they are sufficient to indicate the general properties of the grammatical rules that impose cultural limitations upon behavior. The first two rules give little scope for individual behavior; the second two rules provide a wide range of options. All Subanun beer spice is the same in that it is likely to contain chili and sugar cane, yet each individual recipe is different in that it is likely to contain different young leaves and underground parts. In the same way, a correct response to an examination question must involve both the correct information and an individual or personal style. There are many ways of making good beer, but you can't make good beer in just any way.

When the ethnographer, using systematic interview techniques or carrying out careful observations, arrives at a list of items and a set of rules he believes can be used to generate correct behavior with reference to the items, he may test his selection of items and set of rules by attempting to generate correct behavior. The test of a set of rules for beer-making would lie in the ability to make good beer by using those rules. Having formulated a set of rules that work, it is tempting to assume that those are the rules that people actually use, but that too is a question for investigation.

There is nothing earthshaking about knowing how to classify nails or make good Subanun beer. The importance of the study of such trivial matters is that the reduction of a complicated variety of behaviors to a set of comparatively simple items and rules increases the possibility of making comparisons both within and between cultures. Because it must be assumed that there are certain fundamental rules governing the generation of proper behavior within each cultural system, cultural systems might ultimately be compared in terms of relatively small lists of basic principles or orientations. Each cultural tradition or each cultural system might be reduced to a simple form or structure which would be comparable to the structure of other traditions or systems. Can it be done?

WHERE IS THE MAGIC KEY?

Indeed, what we find among the Zuñi is a veritable arrangement of the universe. All beings and facts in nature, "the sun, moon and stars, the sky, earth and sea, in all their phenomena and elements; and all inanimate objects, as well as plants, animals, and men," are classed, labeled, and assigned to fixed places in a unique and integrated "system" in which all the parts are co-ordinated and subordinated one to another by "degree of resemblance."

In the form in which we now find it, the principle of this system is a division of space into seven regions: north, south, west, east, zenith, nadir, and the centre. Everything in the universe is assigned to one or another of these seven regions (Durkheim and Mauss 1963:43).

In writing about systems of classification in 1903, Durkheim and Mauss sought to reduce systems of world view to a simple scheme in which all aspects of culture could be shown to be simple reflexes of a single overall classificatory scheme. They sought a kind of magic key which would not only unlock the secrets of Zuñi culture but permit the systematic comparison of Zuñi culture with that of the Australian aborigines, other American Indian cultures, and ultimately the cultures of China and Europe.

Writing somewhat later, Ruth Benedict attempted to approach the question of fundamental cultural structure in more psychoanalytic terms. Benedict saw the great range of possible personality types as being in some way fundamentally divided between Dionysian and Apollonian emphases. The Dionysian pursues the values of existence through escape into extraordinary and even frenzied experience, while the Apollonian avoids excess and seeks moderation and temperance. The materials of culture were then seen as deriving from differing emphases upon different personality types.

Psychoanalytic theorists like Benedict, Kardiner, and Erikson have sought to explain culture as a kind of secondary expression of individual personalities. By contrast, Durkheim and Mauss, and the more recently celebrated Lévi-Strauss, have sought to explain culture in terms of systems of classification which they tend to see as originating or finding their basic expression in terms of the categories of kinship. These different searchers for the magic key have attempted to grasp the fundamental structure of culture by means of dramatic intuitive leaps. They have tried to grasp the essence of culture, not by the slow accumulation of data, but by means of a sudden and, very generally inexplicable, understanding of the whole. Both sets of theorists place the handles of their magic keys in very nearly the same place. The psychoanalytic theorists tend to emphasize early childhood experience, while the classification-oriented theorists tend to place their emphasis upon classifications of kinsmen, which must surely be among the first classifications learned by the growing child. If there is a magic key to culture, it is certainly to be found among the cultural materials made available to the new member of the cultural system.

In a different frame of mind, Bronislaw Malinowski (1961) sought to arrive at a "clear outline of the framework of the natives' culture in the widest sense of the word" by the method of "statistic documentation by concrete evidence." Ultimately the bits of concrete evidence were to be gathered and arranged in a basic master chart expressing the fundamental structure of the culture. Because the Trobriand culture studied by Malinowski, like all cultures, is exceedingly complicated, Malinowski never arrived at a clear outline of a cultural framework. Franz Boas, the "father of American anthropology," believed that any search for a magic key or basic framework was premature. Thus most American and British anthropologists, following Malinowski and Boas, have either postponed the search for fundamental unities of culture or attempted to develop a groundwork for such a search through the refinement of methodological approaches. In recent years, the search for a magic key has been guided by the thought that once sufficiently rigorous and formal descriptions of culture are available, the search for uniformities among the rules and classifications characteristic of particular cultures might take advantage of the modern computer's prodigious capacity for the storage and manipulation of data. For the present, the possibility of simplifying and reducing to order the vast and complex content of cultural traditions is supported only by the fact that it is hard to see how cultural traditions could exist in any other form.

SUMMARY

Life turns upon simple questions. Why does it rain? Why does the sun rise in the morning? Why are we here? Many of these questions can be answered in terms of scientific and practical knowledge; many of them cannot. A world view is a system of thought that includes practical knowledge, the answers to simple questions, and grand explanations of why things are the way they are. World view includes religion, philosophy, science, and all of knowledge. Because it provides answers to the key questions of life, world view provides the intellectual cement that binds the individual firmly to the cultural system.

In the Hopi world view, wishes become prayers, and prayers become the good thoughts that inspire the spirits (the kachinas) to bring rain, good crops, and good food. Mean thoughts result in the illness of others, the failure of rain, and the starvation of people. Seen as a whole, Hopi world view includes the basic ideas required for acting as a good Hopi. The world view provides a credible reason for being a Hopi. It seems also to provide a way of living that would be advantageous to people living under the conditions of hardship that the traditional Hopi face each day. A world view makes people wish to be members and to act like members. It provides a useful picture of the universe.

The Saora live in close association with spirits that move easily between this world and an underworld that many Saora claim to have visited. When such spirits become annoyed they cause people to fall sick. Sick people must be cured by shamans, individuals who are "married" to spirits. These aspects of Saora world view seem relatively unconcerned with problems connected to survival in a natural environment. In fact, the greatest problems for the Saora are disease spread by human beings and exploitation by neighboring groups of people. Saora world view, like Hopi world view, appears to have the functions of strengthening the committment of the individual to the system and of encouraging behaviors that are advantageous from an adaptive standpoint. The Saora seem to enjoy life and their habit of buying buffalo from neighboring peoples seems to encourage good relationships with the powerful. Saora rituals, unrealistic though they may seem, apparently function to make people feel better and they function as a means of entertaining friends and displaying wealth.

Although a common-sense feeling that most of what people do must be advantageous to them in some way informs us that most aspects of world view ought to have positive functions, most of our interpretations of function are merely plausible arguments. Careful research is required in order to establish the actual functions of a belief or practice. Experimental tests that might help to answer questions about function are almost always illegal or unethical. Because a false belief may have important social or psychological functions, the supposed truth or falsity of a belief is not an indication of its value for the support of a cultural system. In the end, we assume that world view must be useful because people use it.

By contrast to the Hopi and the Saora, the Eskimo emphasize the absolute realism and practicality they feel is necessary for survival in the Arctic. They see their life as founded upon the accumulated wisdom and knowledge of preceding generations. This brings up the question as to the extent a practical world view is practical. Reichenbach's reference to the mathematical scientist as God emphasizes the shortcomings of truth and knowledge as practical guides to the conduct of life. People need to know more than science or practical knowledge can provide. In the end, a faith in "Science" differs little from a faith in spirits. World view deals with questions too fundamental to be answered by the scientific method.

Anthropological descriptions of world view may be stated in general terms along the lines of the description of Saora and Eskimo world view, but they may also, following the various approaches used by students of ethnoscience, center upon the problem of exposing the principles of classification used to organize the various things in the world. Such principles of classification may, like the Tikopian concepts of landward and seaward, represent artificial or arbitrary conventions, or they may in some sense derive from psychological or biological characteristics of the human species. Limitations upon the kind and number of speech sounds characteristic of human languages and the limited number of possible numeral systems actually encountered in real life suggest the powerful influence of universal human characteristics upon human behavior, but they also indicate how easily such universals may be overridden and how difficult it is to be sure what they are.

One common interpretation of all systems of world view is that they may be analyzed in terms of items and relationships. The differences among sheep, horses, and chickens illustrate how the various items within the domain of animals may be classified in terms of maturation and sex. Similarly the domain of size can be divided in terms of bigness and littleness. The domain of cultural anthropology that deals with these problems is called ethnoscience, and an illustration from South India shows how linguistic frames can be used in the discovery of taxonomies.

Although the individual members of a cultural system share the same cultural message and classify the things around them more or less in the same way, individuals tend to behave in markedly different ways. Variation in the behavior of individuals sharing the same cultural tradition seems to be accounted for by the existence of grammars or sets of rules which permit them to generate behavior that is at once uniquely individual and culturally appropriate. The example of Subanun beer-making illustrates some of the ways in which a person who follows the rules of beer-making may nevertheless make a uniquely individual beer. One of the tests of our understanding of Subanun beer-making or of any other aspect of a cultural tradition is to see if we can develop a grammar or a set of rules which will permit us to make beer or do something else in a manner that is both creative and acceptable.

The possibility of discovering basic mechanisms which permit the generation of culturally appropriate behavior within limited spheres leads to the even more fascinating possibility of discovering magic keys or basic structures representing underlying uniformities in cultural systems. Whereas Durkheim and Mauss and Lévi-Strauss sought such uniformities in terms of classifications of kinsmen, psychoanalytic theorists sought them in early childhood experiences. Both kinds of theorists attempted to grasp such fundamental unities by means of dramatic intuitive leaps. Malinowski and Boas, in contrast, appear to have believed that such fundamental unities, if they existed, could be reached only through the careful assembling of detailed evidence. Today, the rigorous methodologies characteristic of the new ethnography combined with the use of computers offer new approaches to the discovery of such "magic keys."

For Further Reading

Textbooks in the anthropology of religion such as Lowie (1948) and Norbeck (1961) provide useful overviews of patterns of religious thought. Some of Malinowski's ideas about religion and funerals are to be found in *Magic, Science and Religion and Other Essays* (1955, First edition 1925). Lessa and Vogt's *Reader in Comparative Religion* (Third edition 1972) is a collection of useful articles. Sahlin's *Culture and Practical Reason* (1976) is a useful exploration of the material and immaterial causes of human behavior.

Durkheim and Mauss' *Primitive Classification* (1963, First edition 1903) is one of the early attempts to explore human cognition. More recent attempts include the work of Berlin and Kay on color categories (1969) and Gay and Cole's *The New Math in an Old Culture* (1967). Tylor's *Cognitive Anthropology* (1969) contains a number of highly specialized articles.

Case studies emphasizing various aspects of world view include Kearney's *The Winds of Ixtepeji* (1972), Dentan's *The Semai* (1968), Beals' *Gopalpur* (1962), and the Spindlers' *Dreamers without Power* (1971). Basso's *The Cibecue Apache* (1970) and Hoebel's *The Cheyennes* (1960) provide different sorts of formal statements of systems of world view.

Problems and Questions

1. Observe several episodes of the same television program. How often are particular values or purposes mentioned? Discuss in relation to world view.
2. Examine some folk tales, stories, life histories, or other accounts of two different peoples. What do these suggest about the object of the game or the purposes of life?
3. With regard to the above two questions, ask a friend to examine a different program or a different culture, ethnic group, or social class. Compare results.
4. What kinds of "X" are there? Let "X" equal trees, flowers, foods, or some other class of thing. How would you explain disagreements between informants?
5. Talk to some old people and some young people about the things they consider important. Is our world view changing or do people at different ages have different world views?
6. Discuss. What is the purpose of life, should different people or peoples have different purposes?

5 THE HUMAN DOMAIN

What should be asked about the people?

This chapter deals with social structure, essentially with the answers to "What kinds of people are there in the world and what should be done about each kind?" The first case, taken from the Makah Indians of the northwest coast of the United States, has to do with the relationships between what people say about their social structure and the kinds of social structures that actually exist. Did the Makah have classes such as slave and commoner or do they just like to think that they did or do? Why did they think they had classes? What sort of relationship was triggered by the constant need to demonstrate that one was not a slave? Cultural messages dealing with social structure may be as baffling as cultural messages dealing with the theory of relativity or supernatural figures. Discrepancies between what is and what ought to be make people uncomfortable. An example illustrates how a Tikopian resolves such a strain.

In most societies, perhaps all, the earliest learned and most basic aspect of social structure involves the relationships between Ego, the individual, and Ego's relatives by descent and marriage. An example from the English kinship terminology introduces an inquiry about kinterms and kintypes. The Kannada kinship terminology leads us to wonder: "What is the one and only one right way to describe kin?" What is the nature of classifications and terminologies? How do English speakers avoid marrying their parallel cousins, and how do Kannada speakers recognize their own mothers? More broadly, why do people have kinship terminologies? How is it possible to make "sense" out of them?

The Crow Indians have a variety of formal roles that are assigned to different kintypes. One rule governing the formal role of mother-in-law is that Ego should never speak to his mother-in-law. But even among the Crow, some people liked their mothers-in-law. How is such a problem to be resolved? In modern Canada and the United States, the relationships between kin may be strong, but roles are relatively informal. Why are familial relationships important to the formation of relationships with nonkin?

132

Beginning with Croatans in the United States and ending with Crow Indians, also in the United States, some examples of problems encountered in the classification of nonrelatives and relatives are given. How do we know which status and which role the individual is occupying at the moment? In the next section, an examination of Australian social structures leads to the question: "How is it possible for individual human beings to keep track of the many complicated relationships that go into the formation of a cultural system? It is easy enough to keep track of a hundred or a thousand people, but what about ten thousand or a million? How do the Hopi and Tewa approach this problem? The Swazi? Finally, why does much of India seem culturally homogeneous while much of traditional Mexico appears not to have been?

WHAT KINDS OF PEOPLE ARE THERE?

A woman of the Makah Tribe (Indians of the northwest coast of the United States) describes a portion of her social world as follows:

> They just had to get married to the same kind of class they belonged. For one reason, them chiefs wanted to marry the same class of people as they were themselves. So when they got children, they didn't want their children—well, like if I got mad at you and said, "You're low class, part slave!" you'd be hurt. So they wanted to get married same class generation after generation so all the children were the same class. So if I married a low-class person, then well my niece could call my son a low-class boy. That's what my father used to tell me. That's how I found out. That's why they used to marry the upper class, so all the time they would stay the upper class; the middle class, the middle class; the slaves, the slaves. Only crazy ones didn't obey orders. Even to my day they used to say that, "Slaves!" Now (turning to her niece), I know that your family was chiefs, and I tell you this. They didn't want no slaves for their children! They didn't want anybody to be able to say that to them (Colson 1953:206).

When Elizabeth Colson tried to find out if the Makah continued to maintain class distinctions, she discovered that "the line-up of important men of earlier days changed, a man would shift from slave to commoner to chief with the particular informant questioned."

In this example, Makah tradition suggests that there were three major kinds of Makah and it gives some indication of the kinds of relationships supposed to exist among them. The relationship of marriage was supposed to occur only within each type and the types were related to each other hierarchically with the chiefs being high and the slaves low. Evidently, orders and instructions flowed down this hierarchy from chiefs to middle class to slaves, while obedience was extended upwards.

We could regard the Makah situation as a case of *cultural lag* in which, possibly under the liberating influence of democracy, every man has become a chief while the cultural tradition continues to refer to a previous situation in which some men were commoners or slaves. We could also

argue that the cultural tradition in this case represents *ideal culture*, rather than *real culture*. Perhaps the three-class system represents an ideal pattern, a plan or program, which no one ever paid any attention to. It might well be that no Makah ever willingly admitted to being a slave or a commoner.

Why, then, should there be a discrepancy between the ideal described in the cultural tradition and the behavior actually exhibited by the members? One way of answering this question is to consider the effect of the classification upon the behavior of the members—everybody tries to exhibit chiefly behavior and to avoid slavelike behavior. The function of the official class system might be to promote a struggle for status in which each person attempts to acquire the attributes and behaviors of a chief. Among the Makah this struggle was often acted out in elaborate ceremonies or *potlatches* in which men advanced their claims to chiefly status by providing lavish gifts and entertainments to their competitors. When Indian agents, horrified by these acts of conspicuous consumption, forbade such costly displays, the Makah adopted elaborate birthday and Christmas parties. It is not, after all conspicuous comsumption itself that is bad, but the other fellow's conspicuous consumption.

Although members of cultural systems, as in driving on the right-hand side of the street, often obey the dictates of their cultural traditions with diligence or even slavishness, the case of the Makah illustrates that it is unwise to assume the literal existence of all of the kinds of people ("abominable snowmen?") described in the tradition or to believe that all of the rules and regulations ("Thou shalt not kill.") are literally and slavishly followed. A cultural tradition is a long and complicated message. Some parts of the message are poorly and vaguely worded; some parts, like *Catch 22*, are well-guarded secrets; some parts have nothing to do with past or present reality; and some parts mean things quite different from what they seem to mean. Thus, the "real" meaning of "Thou shalt not kill" is "Thou shalt not kill without legal sanction."

That part of the cultural message that deals with the kinds of people in the world and what to do about them provides information about a *social structure*. A social structure consists of a set of defined positions or *statuses*, each occupied by an individual or a group (*subcultural system*). The cultural tradition provides *labels* or names for some, but not necessarily all, of these statuses such as "chief" or "slave." It indicates the arrangement of these statuses or the *relations* between them (chief is higher than slave or above slave), and it defines the *roles* each is to perform (chief supervises, slave does manual labor). Bearing in mind the differences among labels, statuses, and roles, consider the following set of puzzling events reported by the Tikopians of the South Pacific:

> . . . a lad went down to surf at Namo, leaving his *maro*, his waistcloth, near a canoe house. When he returned from the beach it had disappeared. Peering around he located it in the possession of a woman at the back of the shed. He called out to her:
> "Bring me, mother, my *maro*."
> "Come and take it away," she replied.
> "Bring me, grandmother, my *maro*."
> "Come and take it away."
> "Bring me, aunt (unmarried mother), my *maro*."
> "Come and take it away."
> "Bring me, sister, my *maro*."
> "Come and take it away."
> "Bring me, friend, my *maro*."
> "Now that's it then!" (Firth 1963:182)

Here, the young man, whom we shall call Ego, has been placed in an awkward predicament by a young woman whose status is unknown to Ego. Because the young woman has already adopted the role of a person qualified to view Ego's nude body, Ego attempts to resolve his predicament by assigning an appropriate status to the young woman. He begins by reciting a series of labels, "mother," "sister," and so on, which apparently apply to close relatives who can look upon Ego's naked body without sexual risk. When the young woman refuses to accept the status assignments implied by the labels, Ego has no recourse but to label her "friend." Although we may assume that a Tikopian person having the label "girl friend" may sometimes look upon the naked body of her "boy friend," our own cultural experience may lead us to believe that there is something not quite legitimate about the equation of the status, "friend," and the role of *maro* bringer. Ego resolves this last problem by seizing his "friend" firmly by the wrist and taking her to his house where they are married. She now has the label and status of "wife" and may legitimately play the *maro*-fetching role for many happy years to come.

KINSHIP: WHAT DO YOU CALL YOUR MOTHER'S CHILD?

The anthropologist, seeking to understand the system of names and labels that the members of a cultural system apply to each other, often begins with questions of the following kind:

Q: What do you call the woman who gave birth to you?
A: Janet.
Q: I see. That's her name. Isn't there some more general way of referring to her?
A: Do you mean, "mother"?
Q: Would "mother" refer to any woman who gave birth to children?
A: Yes.
Q: What does Janet call you?
A: She calls me "son."
Q: Is there anyone else you call "mother?"
A: Yes. My wife's mother.
Q: What's a "wife"?

In this series of questions, a rather naive anthropologist is trying to discover terms that Ego, the informant, uses for kinsmen. The anthropologist's goal is to obtain a list of primary kinterms including "mother," "father," "son," "daughter," "brother," "sister," "husband," and "wife." From such a list of primary kinterms, a genealogy can be developed by combining the primary terms.

Q: What is the name of your father's father's father?
A: I don't know.
Q: What about the name of your father's father?
A: Horace.
Q: What was his wife's name?
A: Charity.
Q: Did he have any brothers or sisters?
A: Yes, I think he had an older brother.

Once Ego's genealogy has been collected, it can be arranged in the form of a genealogical diagram (Figure 5–1). In the diagram, circles represent females and triangles represent males. Marriages are indicated by an "equals" sign and descent is indicated by the vertical and horizontal lines.

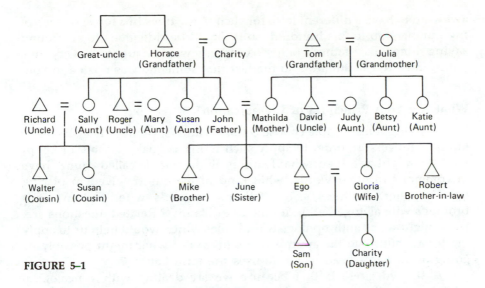

FIGURE 5–1

Essentially, the genealogical diagram illustrates the network of persons who are connected to Ego through the relationships of marriage and descent. Relative age of a set of siblings (brothers and sisters) can also be indicated by placing the oldest sibling at the left. Other material such as age, date of birth, or birthplace can be written directly under the circle or triangle representing each individual. The death of an individual can be indicated by drawing a slanting line through his circle or triangle or by writing in his date of death.

Now, with the genealogy in hand, the anthropologist can ask Ego how he refers to each of his relatives. He writes a *kinterm* ("uncle," "cousin," "sister") under each of the individuals in the diagram. Looking at the diagram among the set of persons one generation older than Ego, we find that both of John's sisters are called "aunt." Because both Sally and Susan are Ego's father's sisters, they can be regarded as occupying the same position on the diagram; that is, as representing the same *kintype*. A kintype is any type of relative that can be referred to by the same combination of primary terms (father's sister, mother's brother's daughter, or father's brother's wife's brother's daughter).

The appropriate kinterm for the kintype, father's sister, is "aunt." Is "aunt" a descriptive kinterm like "father" which applies to one and only one kintype or is it a classificatory term which applies to several kintypes? Looking at the diagram again, we find that "aunt" is also applied to mother's sister, father's brother's wife, and mother's brother's wife. The term, "aunt," covers four different kinds of relatives. Why should this be so? For one thing, it is very inconvenient to have a different term for all of the different kintypes that a given Ego might have. Just as it would be awkward to have a different term for each of the trees in a forest or each of the numbers up to one hundred, so it would be ridiculous to go around saying things like "father's father's brother's wife's daughter" every time you wanted to call attention to the fact that someone was related to you.

What Are Your Principles of Classification?

In classifying trees, people choose certain features, perhaps leaf shapes or kinds of flowers, in order to apply such terms as "oak," "ash," or "poplar." We might ask, then, what features all the people called "aunt" have in common? In other words, what kind of logic is involved in placing father's sister, mother's sister, father's brother's wife, and mother's brother's wife all together under the term, "aunt"? Related questions are: How might we as anthropologists find rules which would help us to apply the term, "aunt," to the appropriate kintypes or what might possibly be going on in Ego's head when he uses the term "aunt"?

A shrewd guess is that because we are dealing with genealogical relationships, the answers to these questions are likely to be found in the

genealogical properties of the various individuals labeled "aunt." We might say that an "aunt" is the sister of a parent or the wife of a parent's brother. Or, thinking about the qualities of "auntness," we might observe that an "aunt" is a female one generation higher than Ego. Because "aunts" are found on either side of the direct line of descent leading to Ego, we might use the term *collateral* (on the side) to express the distinction between "aunt" and "mother." Thus, a "mother" is a female *lineal* relative one generation higher than Ego, while an "aunt" is a female *collateral* relative one generation higher than Ego or the wife of a male collateral relative one generation higher than Ego.

In thinking about the English kinship system as a whole, it would appear that all of the kinterms except "cousin" involve more or less the same distinctions that can be observed for "aunt." In effect, relatives are differentiated in terms of sex, generation, and closeness to Ego (for example, lineal-collateral-distant). For a great many Egos, "cousin" seems to be used to refer to any distant relative, while the term "in-law" tends to be used for relatives by marriage. For Ego, who has made use of the English kinship terminology throughout his lifetime and has no knowledge of any other method of classifying relatives, the English terminology seems right and proper even though he can't explain exactly how the classification works.

Consider, now, the Kannada (South Indian) kinterms given in the genealogy in Figure 5–2. Here, at least in the simplified version given in the diagram, it turns out that there are only four terms used to describe all persons one generation older than Ego. As in English, a distinction is made on the basis of generation and sex, but there is no apparent distinction between lineal relatives and affinal relatives and there is no apparent distinction among close, collateral, and distant relatives. As anthropologists, what are we to say about the rule governing the use of such terms as "amma" and "atti"? If we asked which term is the Kannada term for "aunt," we would be asking a nonsensical question because both terms include kintypes covered by the term "aunt."

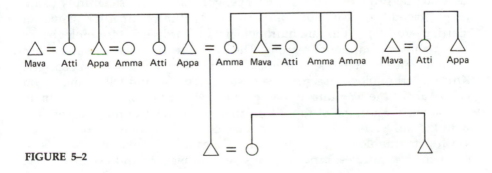

FIGURE 5–2

The problem appears to be simple, for all we have to do is find a rule that would permit us to divide all the women in the generation above Ego into two classes. One interpretation of this situation would be to assume that all siblings of the same sex are considered similar and that they always marry spouses of the same kind. In terms of this rule, an "amma" is any female one generation older than Ego who is his mother, his mother's sister, the wife of an "appa," or the sister of an "amma." A "mava" is any male one generation older than Ego who is his mother's brother, the brother of an "amma," or the husband of an "atti." A wife's father is a "mava" because, if he were an "appa," Ego would be marrying his "sister." Because Kannada speakers regard all human beings as kin, terms like "amma" and "mava" can be applied to any older man or woman whom Ego thinks of as being like a father's wife or a mother's brother. When Ego is asked what "mava" means he is likely to reply, "Bridegiver." Thus, "mava" is any man who might conceivably have a daughter that Ego might marry or any man to whom the respect due to a father-in-law is owed.

One interpretation of this situation is that "mava" is basically a kinship term referring to mother's brother, but that its meaning is extended to cover all persons whom Ego wishes to treat like a mother's brother. Another interpretation would be that there are two kinds of older men in the world, "appas," who are treated with a warm and personal respect, and "mavas," who are treated with a cold and distant respect, the differences being similar to those between neighbors and strangers. In the Kannada terminology, Ego's relationship to such men is not fictitious because Ego starts with the supposition that all men are related. Similar extensions of kinship terms in English are regarded as fictitious. The term "aunt" may be applied to a friendly neighbor woman who gives cookies to the children, or, historically in some southern communities in the United States, to a black woman who is old enough and close enough to merit some degree of respect, but not white enough to be addressed properly by name.

Kinship terminologies refer to people who are classified in terms of genealogical principles such as sex, age, generation, consanguinity (common "blood" or common descent), and affinity (marital status or marriage-ability). Cultural anthropologists regard such terminologies as important for a variety of reasons. The most fundamental is that kinship terminologies exist in one form or another in every known human society. Kinship terminologies seem to be basically human and tell us important things about the way human beings think about the world around them and about the origins of those fundamental social groupings associated with the early evolution of the human species. On a more frivolous level, kinship terminologies provide neat puzzles which, like other kinds of mathematical puzzles, can often be solved in elegant and exciting ways.

Perhaps, in the end, it is the ability to make some kind of sense out of kinship terminologies that gives cultural anthropologists the hope that they may someday make sense out of the rest of culture.

Whatever it might be about kinship terminologies that fascinates anthropologists, the people who use them are concerned with identifying people towards whom they are to act in particular ways. How should relatives be treated?

WHAT DO YOU DO TO YOUR "AMMA" AND WHAT DOES SHE DO TO YOU?

In 1907 I experienced a good sample of the relevant behavior. I was in the tent of David Stewart, my interpreter, and wished to draw out his mother-in-law concerning the games played in her youth. Though she was only a few feet away, Stewart did not ask her directly, but put each question to his wife, who repeated it to her mother and then repeated the answer to her husband. In 1910 James Carpenter did not speak to his wife's mother or grandmother and would not pronounce the Crow word for "to mark, to write" because his mother-in-law's name was Marks-plainly. In 1931 he still kept up these taboos. Even a man of preponderantly white blood may maintain the rule, presumably in deference to the old women's feelings (Lowie 1956:31).

The quotation above provides an example of what anthropologists call a *formal* role. When a person is termed, "mother-in-law," Ego behaves toward her in certain specified ways. What makes the avoidance relationship described above interesting is why such formality should be necessary.

In the case of mothers-in-law, the fact that the wife's mother is so frequently the target of avoidance relationships, mother-in-law jokes, and even accusations of witchcraft leads us to suspect that the frequent formalization of relationships to mothers-in-law has to do with the possibility that Ego and his mother-in-law might get along too well or not well enough. Adams and Romney have argued that mother-in-law avoidance develops to prevent conflict between husband and mother over control of the daughter-in-law (1959). More broadly it can be argued that formal relationships are a means of preventing individual decision making in areas where conflict is likely to occur. Where Ego's obligation to his mother-in-law is simply the formal one of attending Sunday dinner, Thanksgiving, and Christmas, Ego's status as a good son-in-law is easy to evaluate and there need be no conflict over whether or not Ego is doing the right thing by his wife's mother.

What, then, happens to a formally defined relationship when power-ful informal ties develop between the relatives involved?

> The taboos described are never conceived as the expansion of hostility but rather of the utmost respect. A substantial gift can, however, sometimes abrogate the taboo. If a man gives two or three horses to either parent-in-law, the ban may be lifted; according to one informant, a donation of a hundred dollars might suffice. Further, abolition of the customary rule occurs particu-larly after a wife's death; then her mother may absolve her son-in-law from all prohibitions by addressing him as "son," whereupon his relationship to her is assumed to have become filial and is not dissolved even if he should remarry. It is also possible for the son-in-law to take the initial step.
>
> There was some variation in this procedure. Sometimes gifts were of-fered, yet the taboo persisted. Thus, Gray-bull once gave a horse to his father-in-law, and another to his mother-in-law, but spoke only to the former thereafter. The same informant gave his son-in-law Yellow-brow one or two horses, pronouncing the formula of adoption: "You, too, I shall make my child." Since then he would speak to Yellow-brow and smoke with him as if he were his son, but Gray-bull's wife was not affected by this arrangement (Lowie 1956:31–32).

It is easy to see how useful an avoidance relationship can be, particularly in connection with relatives one would prefer to avoid. Other kinds of relationships, such as Hopi joking relationships, are more difficult to explain:

> There is a joking relationship between a boy and the husbands of his father's sisters. In fun these uncles are called "grandfathers" by the boy. There is no such relationship among the girls and women. A grandfather may come and sprinkle cold water on the boy early in the morning, or may carry him out and dip him in the spring, or may continually tease him by word and manner or play practical jokes on him.
>
> The boy retaliates in kind. The boy may offer to carry a load which his "grandfather" has just gotten to the top of the mesa, but upon being trusted with it, he may proceed to take it back down the trail and deposit it at the foot of the cliff. Another trick is to dig a shallow pit in a trail frequented by a "grandfather" and to camouflage it so that he will step into it. Other tricks are improvised as the occasion warrants. A "grandfather" is the only adult who may be teased by the boy; least of all would he tease his true grandfathers (Dennis 1940:65–66).

Because boys may often have close relationships with their fa-ther's sisters, the father's sister sometimes undertaking responsibilities for the sexual education of the male child, the joking relationship may well serve to institutionalize and therefore control very real feelings of jealousy and hostility. Of course, relationships between relatives need not be sharply defined, and they may in fact be quite vague:

In America the family, in the Roman and aristocratic signification of the word, does not exist. All that remains of it are a few vestiges in the first years of childhood, when the father exercises, without opposition, that absolute domestic authority which the feebleness of his children renders necessary and which their interests, as well as his own incontestable superiority, warrants. But as soon as the young American approaches manhood, the ties of filial obedience are relaxed day by day; master of his thoughts, he is soon master of his conduct.

In a democratic family the father exercises no other power than that which is granted to the affection and the experience of age; his orders would perhaps be disobeyed, but his advice is for the most part authoritative. Though he is not hedged in with ceremonial respect, his sons at least accost him with confidence; they have no settled form of addressing him, but they speak to him constantly and are ready to consult him every day (Tocqueville 1960: 2 203–206).

FIGURE 5–3 Where physical and emotional closeness are vital missing persons must be replaced by appropriate substitutes. In Malitbog in the Philippines, the father's sister takes his place while he is away. (PHOTO COURTESY OF F. LANDA JOCANO)

More recent students of the North American family than Alexis de Tocqueville, who wrote in the 1830s, have found that the father often does not know what to do. In the quotation below, Crestwood Heights is a suburban community in Canada.

> Both father and mother, within and without the home, perform their various roles largely, as we are now aware, "for the sake of the children." With only rare exceptions, Crestwood parents pretty well take for granted their responsibility for the physical care and social training of their children. But beyond their fundamental and obvious legal responsibility, Crestwood Heights parents often wonder "what to do next" with their children, since they are given no support by traditionally sanctioned methods of child-rearing. There is great variation in the patterns of child care and control, and considerable parental uncertainty.
>
> Nor are the father and mother commonly agreed even in uncertainty as to how this function is to be discharged (Seeley, Sim, Loosley 1963:193).

In a relatively unchanging society, parents know what to do because they are permitted and encouraged to do substantially the same things their parents did. Neighbors and relatives also know the right thing to do. The North American father and mother, after debating with the Italian grandparent, the French grandparent, the Egyptian grandparent, and the Norwegian grandparent, finally turn toward books as a source of information concerning the definition of proper role relationships between parent and child. It is almost a case of the ethnography becoming the cultural tradition.

Anthropologists, and human beings in general, tend to place great emphasis upon kinship and particularly upon the supposed biological ties connecting the persons who occupy the same kinship diagram. For the anthropologist and members of cultural systems, kinship is often a convenient fiction. Human beings do not love, honor, or obey their biological relatives unless they have an appropriate sociological relationship to them. For example, in the South Indian kinship terminology, an "appa" or "father" can be a very distant relative, by the standards of the English kinship terminology, not a relative at all. In some aboriginal Australian kinship systems, all human beings and many other living things are classified as kin and ways of acting toward them are specified. The belief in a mystical tie among biological relatives is probably the force which leads people to attempt to extend their kin relationships as far as possible. The mystical brotherhoood of church, lodge, labor union, or clan is in many ways superior to actual brotherhood, for mystical brothers can be endowed with virtues that real brothers may lack. If a stranger can be treated as "daddy" or "buddy," it is unnecessary to learn new ways of dealing with him.

Varieties of consanguinity and affinity appear to be recognized by all human beings. For most people, the earliest experiences of life are in a family-based household. Real and supposed kinship relationships and ways of treating kin probably form the basis of the bulk of human social classifications and are of psychological importance even where kinship is not overtly present. At the same time, there is probably no society where biological kinship is the only basis of human relationships. The following sections deal with terminological classifications of human beings that are either distantly related or totally unrelated to kinship terminologies.

WHAT OTHER KINDS OF PEOPLE ARE THERE?

You know, we have some Negroes in this country that are as white as you and I, and when I fill out marriage licenses for them I have sometimes put them down as white and they have told me they are Negroes. Of course, this is no insult to them. They know they look white, and being taken for white is no new experience for them. But the ones I have trouble with are these Croatans. We always record them as white in this office, and when I think someone is a Croatan I just mark the license white and say nothing about it. But the trouble is with the dark ones. Really, some of them do look for all the world like Negroes, or like mulattoes anyway. And you know I hate to come right out and ask them, because they don't like that (Berry 1969, p. 48).

In the United States, the people in the world are often thought of as divided into different *racial groups* such as "white," "black," oriental," "Mexican-American," and "Indian." Very often these racial classifications are further subdivided into *ethnic groups* in terms of religion or tribal and national origin. Most people believe that membership in a racial category is easily determined on the basis of such superficial physical traits as skin color, eye color, hair color, hair form, or various facial characteristics. Very often it is believed that members of some or all ethnic groups can also be identified by such characteristics. Where the supposed racial characteristics fail to make positive identification possible, it is often assumed that habits of speech, occupations, gestures, or other behavioral characteristics are infallible indicators of group membership.

In the above example, the judge in charge of issuing marriage licenses encounters the fact that actual or real membership in racial or ethnic groups has to do not with the individual's physical characteristics but with such sociological factors as who his parents are, to which church he belongs, or which school he attends. The Croatans, who may or may not represent some complex mixture of ethnic groups, consider themselves to be quite distinct from "Negroes" and may violently resent being classified as such. Should the judge fail to apply an unworkable racial classification correctly, he may consider himself fortunate to escape with a punch on the nose. The point is: It is fairly easy for Ego to classify people in terms of kinship and it is fairly easy for the anthropologist to arrive at an understanding of what the classification is about; other kinds of classification are likely to be much more complicated and to involve criteria which are poorly understood both by Ego and the anthropologist.

Ethnic groups in the United States seem to be classified in terms of various combinations of biological attributes and behavioral characteristics. Terms like "Jewish mother," "Irish policeman," or "white Anglo-Saxon Protestant," bring to mind stereotyped images of individual physical characteristics and at the same time images of characteristic behaviors. Of course, many other statuses are defined within North American culture. Consider "fireman," "boss," "New Yorker," "Rotarian," "Episcopalian," "radical," "friend," "roommate," "suburbanite," "patient," and "neighbor." Some of these terms imply classification in terms of occupation or activity, some imply status hierarchies ("boss"), some imply equality, some make reference to birthplace or residence, others make reference to group membership. In all cultures each individual has many statuses and plays many roles. Ego's slection of, or assigment to, some particular status depends upon the nature of the process that is being carried out at any particular moment. A man who carries out the process of "visiting mother" is a son, but when he carries out the process of "putting out a fire," he may be a fireman. Even in less complicated societies, such as that of the Crow Indians of the North American Plains, part of the interest of the game of culture and part of the problem of predicting human behavior lies in Ego's multiplicity of statuses and roles. How should Ego really treat his *barā'ace*?

A man is extremely circumspect in the presence of his brother-in-law, whom he addresses as bā'aci and refers to as barā'ace. These terms embrace the wife's mother's brother as well as the wife's brother and his sister's husband, since a maternal uncle always figures as an older brother. Two brothers-in-law are supposed to be extremely friendly and to exchange gifts. They are permitted to speak lightly on impersonal matters, but under no condition must they bandy personal remarks savoring of obscenity. There is apparently no objection to telling an obscene myth before a brother-in-law, but according to Leforge even this was deemed gravely indecorous. The bond and the taboos linked with it sometimes outlast the marriage on which the relationship rests. On the other hand, adoption into a society might transform a brother-in-law into a "son." A distinction is drawn between the wife's own brother and her remote kinsmen addressed by the same term. It is her closest "brothers" that enjoy the greatest respect, while some jesting is possible with the others, especially on military matters. Thus, White-man-runs-him married one of Old-dog's clan sisters, and the two men would jocularly say to each other, "You have never been on a war party." Similarly, Gray-bull was wont to chaff Scolds-the-bear, who was at a disadvantage, being afraid to respond because of Gray-bull's superior prestige as a warrior.

Even in such distant relationships of the brother-in-law category personal allusions to sex are rigorously barred. I once pretended to be Arm-around-the-neck's brother-in-law, but mispronounced the proper term of address so that it was mistaken for a reference to my informant's genitalia. Playing the assumed part, he at once dealt me a light blow. Even outsiders respect this taboo. A man at once breaks off a ribald remark if he sees his victim's brother-in-law entering the scene (Lowie 1956:29–30).

STRUCTURE: WHAT ARE YOU BUILDING HERE?

When the ancient Babylonians attempted to contrive a tower reaching up to Heaven, the deity destroyed the common enterprise by assigning a different language to each of the builders. Without a vehicle for the transmission of the cultural message and without the means of assigning appropriate roles and statuses, the cultural system of the builders of the tower of Babel promptly collapsed as did their building later. The curse that afflicted Babylon still afflicts the human species, and, when our cultural systems become so large as to threaten Heaven, difficulties of communication and understanding develop.

Among nonhuman primates, who lack language altogether, the largest possible group—the equivalent of a tribe or nation—is called a troop. A troop of primates is generally associated with a particular piece of land or territory and generally has little to do with other troops. Troops have been observed numbering anywhere from two to seven hundred individuals, but the most common range of variation for all primate species is between ten and eighty animals (Kummer 1971:31). Modern tribes of hunters and gatherers, whose means of coping with the environment resemble those of archaeologically known early human groups, consist, on the average, of about five hundred individuals. Joseph Birdsell suggests that one limiting factor affecting the size of such human groups is

language (1968:229–240). In other words, as groups of human beings become increasingly large, the development of different dialects in different subgroupings makes communication increasingly difficult. Particularly in desert regions, hunter-gatherers tend to form relatively tiny bands or subgroups which are isolated by geographical distance. Increasing distances and numbers make it difficult for the different bands to maintain close contact and the result is that their languages and cultural traditions tend to diverge.

How, then, can there be large tribes of hunter-gatherers, agriculturalists, or industrialized peoples within which many thousands of millions of people share common languages? One answer is to use roads, horses, or airplanes as a means of transcending the limitations of geography. Another is to use writing, printing, telephones, or radios as a means of promoting communication among individuals separated by geographical distances. Another technique, perhaps more basic and fundamental, is exemplified by the case of Dimal, a two-year-old aborigine from the Kimberly Division in Western Australia:

> Dimal was generally referred to by her subsection name of Nambin, as was also her half-sister, Buma, aged about nine. The mother belonged therefore to the nadjili subsection and her father to the djangala. Dimal like all others had a djering, in this case, dilly-bag, and was found at Mindjari, a water-hole in her father's horde country of Bibiban, lying about 40 miles to the northwest of the camp in the Lunga territory. Her subsection totem was opossum, and from her father she had inherited his *guning*, dream totems, which were *tfimili* (baobab tree) and *ngali* (paper-bark). Buma, since she had another father, possessed a different horde country and a different *guning*, but like Dimal had the right to live in her mother's horde country, her *kamera*.
>
> Dimal's name was that of another woman of the same tribe and subsection whom she had never seen, but whom she would regard henceforth as her *naragu* or namesake (the same term being used also for the subsection totem). The elder woman on hearing that the small child had been named after her, had sent a frock and for the rest of their lives, the two would continue to exchange gifts and visit one another when possible.
>
> Dimal then, from the moment of her birth was equipped with a *noera: da:m*, a *wanyegoara da:m*, four totems, a namesake, and a subsection; i.e., her relationships were already defined in regard to certain strips of territory, the tolemic system, and to individuals, since the subsections stand in a kinship relation to one another (Kaberry 1950:49–50).

The trick involved in providing Dimal with all of these statuses and roles consists of dividing the membership of the tribe into a variety of groups and classes and providing the individual with different patterns of interaction or relationship which she may use in dealing with members of the different groups or classes. Dimal and the other members of her tribe escape the limitations of geography and biological kinship by creating systems of classification in which geographically or biologically distant persons are brought affectively or emotionally close by belonging to the same group or class as Ego or persons close to him.

One of the techniques used by Dimal's people to extend the membership of their groups and hence to extend the circle of individuals with whom close communication is possible is to deny the facts of paternity:

> Questioned on the function of sexual intercourse natives admitted that it prepared the way for the entry of the *djinganara:ny*. "Him make 'em road belonga picanniny: young girl no got 'em road." Most women believed that the semen remained in the vagina and had nothing to do with the child. "Him nothing," was the trenchant reply, when after circuitous inquiry I finally suggested the facts in the case (Kaberry 1950:40).

Due to the denial of paternity, Dimal, besides being able to inherit statuses from her actual mother and father, is in a position to acquire statuses and memberships by virtue of the fact that her "spirit" was found in a distant water hole and possessed particular properties associated with the "dilly-bag." Dimal has a lot of connections, and it is only natural that in the course of her life she will make practical use of them in communication and social interaction. Such interaction will involve linguistic communication with people who are geographically and biologically distant and will have the effect of counteracting in some degree the Babylonian curse.

What Can You Do for Me?

The easiest way to deal with stangers, as in traditional Tiwi culture, is to kill them. Such a response to those who cannot be named or classified as members has an inhibiting effect upon trade or other useful contacts with people outside of Ego's close group of kin and neighbors. As in the case of Dimal, above, a system of categorizing people which provides statuses and roles for at least some strangers facilitates communication and makes these strangers psychologically, economically, or socially useful and acceptable. Once large groups of people have been divided into kinds or classes, it is useful to imagine that all of the members of any particular category fulfill some function that is of special importance to Ego or to the group as a whole. Consider the case of the Tewa, a group living in close association with the Hopi Indians of Arizona:

> I am of the Bear clan. Our mothers' mothers' mothers and our mothers' mothers' mothers' brothers were Bear clan people. They came a long time ago from *Tsawadeh*, our home in the east. Our sisters' daughters' daughters' children, as long as women of my clan have children, will be of the Bear clan. These are our clan relatives, whom we trust, work with, and confide in. My

mother's older sister guards the sacred fetish which is the power and guardian of our clan and which was brought in the migration from *Tsawadeh*. My mother's older sister feeds our fetish and sees that the features are always properly dressed. At important ceremonies, my mother's brother, erects his altar and sets our fetish in a prominent place within the altar. My mother's older sister and my mother's brother make all the important decisions for our clan, and such decisions are accepted with respect and obedience by all Bear clan members. My mother's older sister and her brother are called upon to advise, to reprimand, and to make decisions on land and ritual affairs for all of us who are of the Bear clan. My mother's older sister's house is where our fetish is kept, and therefore it is a sacred house to us and there we go for all important matters that concern our clan (Dozier 1966:42).

Other neighboring tribes and groups such as the Hopi and Navajo have clans which can be identified with Tewa clans when it is convenient to do so.

When I asked if the Hano (Tewa) Corn clan was also similarly related (i.e., to Hopi clans), my informant, a Corn clan woman, replied that the Tewa were not Hopi and she could not believe that a Hopi clan, even though similar in name, could be related to a Tewa clan. With regard to the association of Fir and Bear clans with certain Hopi clans, she remarked that these people "were trying to deny their Tewa heritage and wanted to be like Hopi." Yet when this same woman was on a visit to Mishongnovi in the winter of 1951, she sought out Patki (a theoretically related clan) households. At that time she remarked: "These are our people; they treat us kindly when we visit them, and when they come in our village they stay in our houses" (Dozier 1966:45).

The above example shows how the concept of clan brotherhood and sisterhood can be used to convert perfect strangers into helpful relatives. Clan solidarity, as in the case of the Capulets and Montagues or Martins and Coys, may lead to situations in which rivalries or feuds poison the relationships between clans. In the Romeo and Juliet story or the story of the Martins and the Coys, the conflict between clans was resolved quite typically by the affection of a boy in one clan and a girl in another. That clans tend to be exogamous—that marriage must take place outside of the clan—contributes powerfully to the cementing of relationships among clans and to the fact that feuds between clans tend to be better regulated than wars between strangers. The mothers' brothers, the male members of a matrilineal clan, must always consider that the enemy includes some of their wives, wives' children, and sister's husbands.

How else may clans be made interdependent?

The *Sumakolih* is a curing association whose members wear masks like Kachina impersonators. The *Sumakolih*, now controlled by the Cloud clan, was formerly owned and managed by the extinct Sun clan. The association cures "sore eyes"; but any Tewa or even a Hopi from First Mesa may request the association to dance, either to effect a personal cure or to secure well being for the community in general (Dozier 1966:78).

Most of the Tewa clans are assigned the management of particular associations charged with practical and religious duties vital to the carrying out of life. Individuals from a variety of different clans, sometimes voluntarily, sometimes at the request of their parents, and sometimes as a result of accidental involvement in the affairs of the association, are initiated into some particular association, and thus, in collaboration with members of other clans, carry out important duties. War between clans now threatens to become war between members of the same club and among its costs must be included the disruption of those vital practical and ceremonial activities which prevent illness, bring rain, or secure the general well being. The case of the Swazi illustrates some more complicated ways of joining clans together.

Why Do You Have So Many Wives?

The Swazi form a political state in South Africa consisting of thousands of people occupying a region the size of Hawaii. The Swazi are organized into large patrilineal clans, but also in terms of a complex and hierarchical political system dominated by a king and a queen mother:

> . . . clan exogamy is recognized as an effective way of extending and creating social ties, and the king is expected to unify and centralize his position by taking women from all sections of his people. When he marries a clan sister (a special privilege reserved for kings), her father is automatically removed from the royal Nkosi Dlamini clan, and becomes the founder of a separate subclan. This also limits the number of Dlamini; a nobility always tries to maintain itself as an exclusive minority (Kuper 1963:17).

The king puts himself and his clan above clan rivalries by making his own clan rather small and special, and he may eliminate rivals within his own clan by marrying their daughters. He ensures that important clans have access to the kingship by taking additional wives, one king had forty, from a variety of different clans. The king was also surrounded by "blood brothers" who performed important parts of the rituals of kingship and government and were also drawn from a variety of clans.

At lower levels there were regimental age classes:

> Age groups cut across the boundaries of local chiefs and across the bonds of kinship, incorporating individuals into the state, the widest political unit. Between members of the same regiment, and particularly those in permanent residence, there is a loyalty and camaraderie. They treat each other as equals,

FIGURE 5-4 Clothing is an important part of the demeanor of an individual. The four oldest daughters of the Swazi King wear identical clothing, indicating that they are of approximately the same age and status. (PHOTO COURTESY OF HILDA KUPER)

eat together, smoke hemp from the long hemp pipe that is part of their joint equipment, work together, and have a central meeting place or clubhouse in the barracks. They call each other "brother" or "my age mate," "my peer," and the ties between them are said to be stronger than those between kinsmen of different generations. Towards other age sets there is often openly expressed rivalry and occasional fights. . . . (Kuper 1963:53).

Because the individual Swazi recognizes and belongs to a variety of groups and classes and because the activities of all of the complex organizations are orchestrated by a powerful political hierarchy, many thousands of people can be brought into a cultural system which seems to operate as effectively as an Australian tribe containing five hundred individuals. The institutions of the Swazi—the kingship, the clans, the age classes, the households, and other territorial groupings—constitute a social structure which may be appreciated in architectural terms in the same way that we appreciate the structure of a crystal, a mollusk, or a symphony. Though we may appreciate their beauty, it is more difficult to evaluate the effectiveness of the structures built by the Australian aborigines, the Tewa, or the Swazi. Would some other system provide for better communication, more cooperation, or more efficient regulation of internal conflict? To compare such systems in terms of numbers is not unlike judging a symphony by the number of instruments involved or

FIGURE 5–5   Swazi warriors in their everyday uniforms. The army is recruited from the age sets. (PHOTO COURTESY OF HILDA KUPER)

judging a house by the number of square feet it contains. Consider the sharp parallels and remarkable contrasts existing between India and Mexico.

Should You Marry Out and Trade In or Trade In and Marry Out?

Throughout most of India, the ideal pattern of social structure consists of a series of ranked castes or *jatis*. Birth into a high ranking jati is usually considered to be a reward for virtuous conduct in a previous life, while birth into a low jati is a punishment for previous sins. For the most part, jatis are divided into exogamous clans, and marriages take place between the clans but within the castes. The reward or punishment, the "fate," assigned to each caste consists of particular occupations, special ritual duties, special restrictions on the foods that may be eaten, and special dress or other characteristics. Each village or group of related villages consists of representatives from a variety of different jatis. In theory, and to a considerable extent in practice as well, the representatives of each of the jatis, in the process of working out their fate, have the right and obligation of performing particular religious or economic tasks vital to the welfare of the village. A member of the Barber jati has the unique privilege of cutting hair. The farmer raises grain, the Carpenter makes plows, and the Potter makes pots. If the Barber wishes to arrange his daughter's marriage, members of other jatis in the village perform special services essential to the ceremony. Thus, the Priest conducts the ceremony, the Goldsmith manufactures the bridal jewelry, and the Astrologer determines the future prospects of the bride and groom.

Because one Barber can serve many persons, a village is unlikely to contain many practicing families of Barbers. Naturally, if the Barber is the victim of unfair competition or if he wishes to raise prices, he calls upon the members of his jati in other villages to support him. Here, the Barber jati operates like a trade union. When the Barber arranges his son's marriage, he must communicate with his kinsmen in other villages in order to find a bride. Because the Barber jati is a small one and there are only a few Barbers in each village, the son's bride may come from a considerable distance. Intermarriages within the Barber jati create a network of kinship involving many villages and covering many square miles

FIGURE 5–6 The young man in the center of the picture has inherited the privilege of serving as village astrologer in a group of seven villages. On New Year's Day, usually in April, he foretells the future using a sacred Hindu almanac written in Sanskrit. Traditionally, the privilege of reading this holy language was largely restricted to members of Brahman castes. Such specialization is characteristic of urban societies. Gopalpur, South India. (PHOTO BY ALAN R. BEALS)

of countryside. A small village containing perhaps twenty jatis, might find itself in the center of twenty kinship networks covering several hundred different villages.

Under these circumstances, in contrast to the more typical human situation where a man lives within a community composed largely of relatives, the local community may consist almost entirely of persons who are not considered relatives of Ego and with whom marriage is unthinkable. Because the village is the setting for Ego's daily life, almost every other kind of important social tie operates across jatis within the village. Ego's friends, the people he works with, his neighbors, the fellow members of a drama company, and his fellow worshippers at the village temple are very largely members of other jatis. Regardless of Ego's jati, he must maintain smooth relationships with the members of most other jatis or face a situation in which he cannot get a haircut, have his sheep butchered, hold a wedding, or even be buried. The basic pattern of the Indian village community enfolds millions of people and has persisted for several thousands of years.

The pattern of the Indian village is basically one of marrying outside the village and trading or economic exchange within the village. The result has been the creation of large areas or regions within which people speak the same languages, raise children in similar ways, accept the same religion, and so on. What would happen if the pattern were reversed so that marriages took place only within the village, but different villages tended to manufacture particular necessities of life? Something like such a mirror image of the Indian situation exists in parts of Mexico.

In the Valley of Oaxaca, marriages take place almost entirely within the village. Whereas individual families in Indian villages exhibit considerable differences in wealth, occupation, and social status, individual families in Oaxaca villages tend to be of roughly equal wealth and status and to follow the same occupations. Persons of relatively high wealth and status in Oaxaca villages are often chosen to direct and financially support elaborate religious ceremonies or fiestas. Thus, if a man does become wealthy, he may be compelled to donate a considerable portion of his wealth to the community.

Specialists who provide the goods and services required for the day-to-day carrying out of the life of the village are located in market towns or in other villages having unique economic specializations. One village weaves blankets, another produces grinding stones, another bakes bread, another makes pottery, and another sells milk products. Relationships between villages take place at weekly markets where large numbers of people congregate for purposes of conviviality and for the buying and selling of goods produced in different villages. In Oaxaca, attendance at weekly markets is practically compulsory, while in India, weekly markets tend to be small and to offer relatively few products for sale.

In both India and Oaxaca the basic pattern of organization involves the exchange of products between economically specialized endogamous groups. In India marriage takes place within castes and economic exchange takes place between castes within the village; in Oaxaca marriage takes place within the village and economic exchange takes place between villages. What are the consequences of these two different arrangements? In the Valley of Oaxaca, several different languages are spoken and differences in dialects often make communication, except in Spanish, difficult between persons from different villages. Even following the advent of modern roads and systems of communication, Mexican national culture retains great regional variation, while the cultural uniformities characteristic of India seem much greater. While this difference can be attributed in part to the mountainous nature of the Mexican terrain and the difficulties of communication between villages, the patterns of social structure governing the relationships among individuals and villages offer more important explanations. In particular, it would seem that market relationships are less effective than kin relationships in promoting similarities between villages.

In comparing the social structures of traditional India and Mexico it is possible to reach judgments concerning the effectiveness of the structures for particular purposes. Marrying out and trading in is plainly more effective in maintaining linguistic and cultural similarities over large regions than is marrying in and trading out. One of the costs of this kind of effectiveness is the disappearance of interesting people such as the Zinacantecos of Mexico (Vogt 1970), but perhaps their traditions are doomed in any case by the advent of roads and transistor radios.

SUMMARY

A social structure consists of a set of defined positions or statuses, each occupied by an individual or group. The cultural tradition provides labels or names for some statuses, such as "chief" or "slave," but not for others. As the Makah example illustrates, it also provides information concerning the ranking of statuses and the relations between them, and the role that individuals are supposed to play when assigned to one or another of the statuses. Labels, statuses and roles are different things. A young man from Tikopia resolves a conflict between role and status by marrying the girl who saw him nude.

A genealogy is an arrangement of individuals in terms of their real or supposed biological relationships. The individuals in a genealogy, consisting of relatives by descent and marriage, are the kin of Ego, the person whose genealogy it is. Each position on the genealogy is a kintype. The label given to any set of kintypes is a kinterm. Thus, father's sister and mother's sister are both "aunt." Why not call each person by name? Presumably because systems of classification simplify information storage and retrieval in the human brain. Who wants to remember a great long list?

Kinship terminologies refer to people who are classified in terms of such genealogical principles as sex, age, generation, consanguinity, and affinity. The choice of principles of classification expresses fundamental conceptions of the nature of reality as well as patterns of relationship among different kinds of relatives. Kinterms provide information concerning the way particular individuals are or should be treated. Thus, the term "mother-in-law" tells the Crow Indian to avoid close contact with the person he would normally address by that term. But this is a formal rule and people have ways of getting around formal rules. A gift of two or three horses might cement an arrangement in which the in-laws treated each other as "mother" and "son."

Relations to kinspeople are among the first sorts of relations the individual comes to know. It may be that kin relationships play a fundamental role in all cultural systems as a means of establishing precedents for varieties of social relationship.

Croatans, like other people who are given a label inappropriate to their social position, are likely to respond violently to errors in classification. In even the simplest social structure, a variety of statuses, roles, labels, and situations creates difficulties both for the individual and the anthropologist. Among the Crow Indians, for example, adoption into a warrior society might transform a "brother-in-law" into a "son," creating awkward problems.

Joseph Birdsell has suggested that there are cognitive limits to the size of human groups; by his measure five hundred should be just about right. However, there is nothing that says the human individual cannot belong to numerous overlapping groups. Thus, Dimal has many kinds of relationships that she can claim with other people. Among other groups, such as the Tiwi, any cognitive dissonance or mental disarray caused by the presence of strangers is dealt with readily by killing all strangers. The Hopi and Tewa deal with strangers by identifying their clan. Strangers are thereby converted into helpful relatives. Because clans are normally exogamous, tendencies toward conflict between clans are prevented by the fact of marriage between them. Membership by members of one clan in an association managed by another clan also creates links of affection and mutual aid. In a clan society, as in many others, overlapping memberships tend to prevent the division of society into warring groups. Swazi social structure demonstrates the elegant complexity of human relationships.

In India and Oaxaca, Mexico, products are exchanged between economically specialized endogamous groups. In Mexico, the endogamous groups are villages; in India, they are jatis distributed across numerous villages. The Indian pattern tends to promote linguistic and cultural homogeneity, while the traditional Mexican pattern leads to a fascinating variety of lifeways. How can large societies be constructed without destroying the unique lifeways of the different peoples out of whom they are assembled?

For Further Reading

General techniques for the analysis of kinship terminologies are discussed in Schusky's *Manual for Kinship Analysis*. Also worth consulting are *Kinship and Marriage* (Fox 1967) and *Kinship and Social Organization* (Buchler and Selby 1968). Other aspects of social classification are dealt with in *Politics, Law and Ritual in Tribal Society* (Gluckman 1965) *Social Anthropology* (Bohannon 1963), *Primitive Social Organization*, 2nd ed. (Service 1971), and *Comparative Political Systems* (Cohen and Middleton, eds. 1967). Graburn has edited a useful set of *Readings in Kinship and Social Structure* (1971).

   In the Case Studies, kinship and social classifications are emphasized in Dozier's *Hano* (1966), Beidelman's *The Kaguru* (1971), Basso's *The Cibecue Apache* (1970), Beattie's *Bunyoro* (1960), von Fürer-Haimendorf's *The Konyak Nagas* (1969), and Kuper's *The Swazi* (1963). Works dealing with relationships among men and women include China's *The Isthmus Zapotecs: Women's Roles in Cultural Context* (1973) and Friedl's *Women and Men: An Anthropologist's View* (1973).

Problems and Questions

1. Collect a genealogy from a speaker of a language unfamiliar to you. What are the kintypes and kinterms used? What are some of the principles of classification used?
2. For any formal organization with which you are familiar, draw an organization chart indicating the different officially recognized statuses.
3. What is the proper way to give a lecture; i.e., to play the role of lecturer?
4. For the building trades industry or any other large organization, what are the different jobs or statuses? Which are the best ones? Why?

PART

PROCESS

The operation of a cultural system involves setting in motion the various processes normally carried out by its members. Although the operation of a cultural system can be viewed as a single encompassing process, it is convenient to define a number of separate processes. In the following six chapters, six basic or fundamental processes are described. Chapter 6 deals with the problems involved in maintaining relationships with the environment; chapter 7 with the problems of regulating membership; chapter 8 with the use of ritual and symbolism to define situations and establish statuses; chapter 9 with the transmission of the cultural message; chapter 10 with the control and coordination of the activities of the membership; and chapter 11 with adaptation to changing circumstances.

In Part 2, discussions of the cultural message covered the equivalent of such things as "object of the game," "the playing field," and "the names of the players." More detailed rules of the game define the different things that the players can do—the processes. The cultural tradition tells people what they ought to do and how they ought to do it. Very often people do not know exactly how to carry out a process; very often they know what they are supposed to do but believe that they see a more profitable or more efficient way of doing it. The aim of this part of the book is to examine the game as it is actually played. What are the real world effects of the things that people actually do?

6 ENVIRONMENT AND ECOLOGY

What are the questions about environment?

Cultural systems take form when groups of human beings begin to act in terms of policies defined by an emergent cultural tradition. Cultural systems, like all systems, require inputs of energy from the outside environment. Developing technology must permit the maintenance of appropriate relationships between the environment and the cultural system. Because the culture-building capacity appears to be a remarkable adaptive device and because human beings tend to exaggerate their importance in the scheme of things, it is hard to believe that they and their cultural systems might slip into oblivion as easily as did the passenger pigeon or the dodo.

This chapter opens with an exploration of the ruins of Mohenjo Daro. In what ways are humans and their cultural systems subject to the dread hand of natural selection? The next problem, introduced through reference to the experiences of some Menomini Indians, has to do with the nature of reality and the kinds of things that are to be described in the environment. What is the difference between scientific reality and cultural reality? Is there a difference?

In examining the Tiwi of Melville and Bathurst Islands, it seems that almost everything they do is directly related to problems of survival in the environment. Can we consider Tiwi culture to represent a direct response to environmental pressures? Was Tiwi culture the one and only culture at the level of stone age technology that might have developed in that particular environment? Does environment determine culture?

The next case considers the presence of two kinds of agriculture in certain parts of South India. What are the advantages and disadvantages of each kind? What kind is most suited to the environment? Can two or more different ecological adaptations prove more adaptive in a single region than one adaptation alone? Will cultural systems developing in the same environment or in similar environments and having quite different histories be (1) quite similar, (2) alike in some respects, or (3) quite different?

Does humanity survive by virtue of adaptation to the natural environment

161

alone? What happens to a democratic airplane in an autocratic environment? Is it needful to adapt to preexisting social structure or to items of equipment as well as to nature? Does a good adaptation deal with problems posed by the natural environment or does it simultaneously solve problems in the artificial and social environments?

But what about adaptation? How do we know if the Karimojong or the Tsembaga are adapted? Because we can make up a good story about why they are adapted? What about the superpotato? Was it an improvement on the Peruvian Indian practice of raising a wide variety of potatoes in each plot? Did human beings succeed in nature and in life because of mistakes like the superpotato? Why do humans seem to have evolved and changed rapidly, first through biological evolution and then through cultural evolution, while clams have remained about the same?

A rigorous definition of adaptation creates problems for the understanding of human religious practices. Why do people like Yowana practice sorcery? Why are parents in the United States accused of transmitting insanity to their children? Is there adaptive value to religion or sorcery? Because people often do not know why they do the things they do and because they sometimes think that they know when they do not, it is difficult to make a connection between the nature of a process and its impact upon the environment. What was the problem that the solution solved?

WHERE ARE THEY NOW?

From the Himalayas to the Arabian Sea, the valley of the Indus River is over one thousand miles long. Four or five thousand years ago, a civilization spread across the valley. Mohenjo Daro, one of the great cities of that civilization, was three miles in circumference and contained granaries, bathing pools, citadels, broad streets, a drainage system, great houses, and artistic works in clay and metal. Today, the city and civilization are in ruins, their once fertile lands covered with useless brush and scrub. Overgrazing, the silting up of irrigation works, accumulation of salt in the soil, destruction of forests to make bricks and smelt metals, flooding, an upthrust of coastal lands, overpopulation, internal dissension, and invasion by barbarians—some or all of these things led to the fall of the city and the destruction of the Indus civilization.

In every part of the world abandoned campsites, wrecked villages, or ruined cities bear testimony to the difficulties of coming to terms with the environment. In the process of their dying, ancient cultural systems have contributed to new cultural systems so that over the years the sum of knowledge and experience accumulated in the cultural traditions of humanity has increased. The Indus civilization contributed to the rise of a new civilization in the Ganges Valley which, through a process of constant change and adaptation, has persisted to the present day.

FIGURE 6–1 These are the ruins of Yaguul in Oaxaca, Mexico, where people once lived in spacious houses overlooking their fertile lands. Somehow their adaptation failed. (PHOTO BY ALAN R. BEALS)

The example of the Indus civilization is proof that human cultural systems are not excluded from the necessities of adaptation and survival. It is a proof that an adaptive capacity, such as the culture-building capacity, is useful only when it is used in an adaptive way. The building of cultures can take place only within limits and restrictions imposed by the environment. The research questions underlying this chapter and serving to define the subdiscipline of environmental or ecological anthropology have to do with the relationships between cultural systems and their environments. As already indicated, the environment consists of the entire set of physical, biological, and cultural circumstances within which a given cultural system operates. The relationships between an environment and a cultural system constitute the *ecology* of that system. Ecological anthropology is concerned with the description of environments, the description of relationships between cultural system and environment (the ecological system), the explanation of the impacts of environments and cultural systems upon each other, and assessments of the adaptive value of particular cultural systems or processes. A first step in answering such questions is the discovery of suitable ways to describe human environments.

FIGURE 6–2 In Yadgiri, South India, an impregnable fortress well supplied with water and once surrounded by the houses of the wealthy stands in ruins. The cutting of trees and erosion may have impoverished what was once one of the great centers of civilization. (PHOTO BY ALAN R. BEALS)

WHAT IS OUT THERE?

In the heart of the country they inhabited when first encountered by white men, the Menomini Indians . . . reside today on nearly 400 square miles of heavily timbered reservation on the Wolf River in northeast central Wisconsin. The natural environment—consisting of many waterfalls, streams filled with trout, and pine forest inhabited by bear, lynx, and wolves—remains the same.

The largest portion of the reservation is thickly forested and provides a sharp, oasis-like contrast to the flat, cleared farmlands of the white farmers to the north. This abrupt change in the terrain experienced as one enters the reserve from the north has an interesting psychological effect upon the tourist. Cars slow down as they approach the veritable wall of trees, and all of the superstitions and beliefs regarding the "scalp hunting Indians of the forest" are brought to the fore. Members of the Mitawin Dream Dance group living in this area relate with great amusement the fear-ridden condition of tourists who have been forced to come to their houses at night for various kinds of assistance (L. Spindler 1962:21).*

A few Menomini have experienced other things:

That's how my aunt died. They said after she died they watched her grave and found a bird and a couple of dogs they couldn't kill. My dad caught a dog one time. If any relatives were sick he watched with a gun, but the best way to catch one is to hide. My dad saw the light in the dog's eyes and just kept still. They put you to sleep if they catch you. Dad hollered at him and it was some old woman from Keshena. He hollered first before it saw him and it changed into a woman. When he surprised her she didn't have anything on but a necklace of tongues and hearts of people she had killed. She said not to do anything to her and she would quit witching (adapted from L. Spindler 1962:71).

Having defined a cultural system and specified the boundaries of the environment within which it operates, the ethnographer prepares a description of the environment. Such a description may involve elaborate maps and photographs or careful measurement of rainfall, wind velocity, temperature, and other variables, but its particular goal is to identify and classify those things that have or are likely to have an influence upon the cultural system and its members.

The description of the Menomini environment leads to a major problem: Is the environment to be regarded as consisting of those things that can be recognized by the anthropologist or is it to be regarded as consist-

---

* The Menomini Reservation became a county in the state of Wisconsin upon termination of federal support in June 1961, and the wolves have departed.

FIGURE 6–3 Modern Menomini Indians prepare for a social dance. Like everything else it is deeply affected by the shape of the Menomini environment. (PHOTO COURTESY OF GEORGE SPINDLER)

ing of those things that are recognized by the members of a cultural system? Assuming that Louise Spindler in her role of scientific observer might never encounter an old woman from Keshena attired in the tongues and hearts of her victims, there is a discrepancy between the real world of the scientific observer and the real world of the Menomini. By the same token, a scientific observer is likely to note many things in the environment that influence the Menomini but which the Menomini fail to recognize.

It is convenient to define the environment perceived by an outside observer as representing *scientific reality* and the environment perceived by the members of a cultural system as representing *cultural reality*. A more accurate, if less convenient, assumption would be that the observer perceives reality in terms of *his* culture, while the Menomini perceive reality in terms of a different culture. Whether we distinguish between scientific reality and cultural reality or see both as two kinds of cultural reality, there is a difference between them, and it is instructuve to consider its implications. The remainder of this chapter deals with environment and ecology perceived in terms of scientific or observer reality, while chapter 4 dealt with environment perceived in terms of cultural reality. Whether people survive or not depends upon the extent to which they are adapted to the environment as it is, but what people do depends upon what they think the environment is like. Because survival depends upon adaptation to external conditions, it is fruitful to look upon cultural systems as devices for solving adaptive problems. Because any cultural system is by definition adapted, at least in the short run, there must be some sense in which it "fits" its environment. Consider the Tiwi from this perspective.

DO CULTURE AND ENVIRONMENT DOVETAIL?

The Tiwi live on Melville and Bathurst Islands off the coast of Northern Australia in an environment containing a relative abundance of edible wild plants and a fair amount of game. Extremes of temperature and climate appear not to have presented problems, nor is there much disease or ill health. Tiwi women and children spend most days gathering vegetable foods in the region surrounding their campsites. Young men often spend their time hunting, but are probably none too successful. Tools used by men consist of spears and throwing sticks, while the women use baskets and various digging implements. Women spend many years learning when and where to find food. Men become skilled hunters after years of effort. That survival requires the maintenance of extensive and

FIGURE 6–4   Threshing ground and permanent fields at the hill village of Elephant in South India. Use of cow manure on these fields permits maintenance of soil fertility. Dependence upon rainfall limits production to only one crop per year. (PHOTO BY ALAN R. BEALS)

complicated skills was demonstrated by the famine which took place between 1942 and 1946 when warfare cut off the supply of imported foodstuffs upon which the Tiwi had become dependent. They had lost their traditional skills and could no longer survive without outside help.

In the traditional Tiwi household, the old men collect as many wives as possible, and the younger men—unable to marry—are treated as hangers-on, marginal members of the family. The wives, under the leadership of a skilled older woman, handle the collection of vegetable foods. Young men hunt for animal food and, because they are marginal, are free to move to other households when the supply of wild animals shifts. The old men, freed from the labor of the food quest by their multiple wives, are able to devote themselves to artistic, ceremonial, and political affairs.

The Tiwi cultural system appears to dovetail at every point with the requirements of the environment. Tiwi young men are freed for hunting; Tiwi women are organized into efficient work groups; and Tiwi old men are given freedom to manage political relationships among the different groups of Tiwi. The Tiwi seem to exist in almost perfect equilibrium with their environment. They appear to eat well and to have peaceful relationships with other Tiwi (Hart and Pilling 1960). Granted the limitations of Tiwi knowledge and technology, the Tiwi cultural system appears almost

FIGURE 6–5 The rice paddy is an environment created by human beings. Once it is created it helps to shape their culture and their experience. Gopalpur, South India. (PHOTO BY ALAN R. BEALS)

to have been dictated by its external conditions. Can we, then, explain the similarities and differences among the external conditions that affect them? Does the goodness of fit between cultural system and environment justify an environmental determinism of the kind discussed earlier?

Must We Conform to the Environment?

In South India there are two major kinds of agriculture. Where water is abundant, irrigated rice is grown; where water is scarce, various millets and legumes sown together form the major crop. The environment offers a vast range of possibilities—hunting, collecting vegetable products, spice raising, coconut growing, wheat farming, sweet potato raising, tea planting, and so on. Although there are a few communities devoted almost exclusively to each of these types of subsistence activities, most communities specialize in the raising of rice or millet or a combination of both. Are all of these adaptations equally suitable and can the existing diversity be accounted for by the external conditions affecting each community? Consider some of the characteristics of rice and millet farming as practiced in South India.

To grow irrigated rice using the usual South Indian methods it is necessary to redesign the environment, leveling the ground and forming a kind of artificial swamp. Once the swamp is formed, constant attention is required to keep the water where it belongs and prevent it from washing away the crop. There are many weeds where there is much water, and where the yield is great the application of fertilizer must be great. In some places there are two or three crops per year, and the life of the rice farmer is one of steady labor. Because the crop requires extra attention during certain periods, a supply of temporary agricultural laborers is required. Rice land, when it has to be leveled and irrigated, is expensive. Men who are rich enough to buy such land are usually too rich to have to work for a living. Rice farming, then, tends to involve classes of investors or capitalists, farmers, and laborers. Millet farming requires little preparation of the land. There is usually only one crop per year. The farmer owns his own land and hires relatively little labor. Millet-farming communities support relatively few investors or laborers.

In both of these cases, the choice of an agricultural technique has sweeping implications. Rice agriculture, of the kind described above, does not encourage social equality:

> . . . their masters may beat them at pleasure, the poor wretches having no right either to complain or to obtain redress for that or any other ill-treatment their masters may impose on them. In fact, these Pariahs are the born slaves of India, and had I to choose between the two sad fates of being a slave in one of our colonies or a Pariah here, I should unhesitatingly prefer the former.

This class is the most numerous of all, and in conjunction with that of the *Chucklers*, or cobblers, represents at least a quarter of the population. It is painful to think that its members, though so degraded, are yet the most useful of all. On them the whole agricultural work of the country devolves, and they have also other tasks to perform which are still harder and more indispensable. . . .

They live in hopeless poverty, and the greater number lack sufficient means to procure even the coarsest clothing. They go about almost naked, or at best clothed in the most hideous rags.

They live from hand to mouth the whole year round, and rarely know one day how they will procure food for the next. When they happen to have any money, they invariably spend it at once, and make a point of doing no work as long as they have anything left to live on (Dubois 1947:49–50).

South Indian rice agriculture requires a large class of laborers who work but do not own or control the land on which they work. Millet agriculture, particularly where the soil is poor and the yield small, cannot support a large laboring class. In the "poor" sections of South India, where little rice is grown, most people are artisans or small farmers. The class of agricultural laborers is small and relatively prosperous. In rice areas, village councils tend to be made up exclusively of members of the land-owning castes, whereas in millet areas village councils tend to be made up of one man from each caste, lineage, or household.

The traditional situation in South Indian millet-raising areas is comparable to that of the United States of more than a century ago:

In America there are, properly speaking, no farming tenants; every man owns the ground he tills. It must be admitted that democratic laws tend greatly to increase the number of landowners and to diminish that of farming tenants. Yet what takes place in the United States is much less attributable to the institutions of the country than to the country itself. In America land is cheap and anyone may easily become a landowner; its returns are small and its produce cannot well be divided between a landowner and a farmer. America therefore stands alone in this respect, as well as in many others, and it would be a mistake to take it as an example (Tocqueville 1960, II:96).

Today, in many parts of the United States, yields have become large, agriculture has become industrialized, population has increased, and "democratic institutions" have changed their form. In India, "democratic institutions," developing perhaps as a result of industrialization, have begun to have an impact upon those places where rice agriculture is practiced. In earlier times, the spread of rice agriculture and irrigation works may have pressed upon the democratic institutions of millet-raising villages, just as urban industrial democratic institutions now press upon rice-growing villages.

But Which Choice Is Adaptive?

In South India rice agriculture ordinarily produces more pounds of food than does millet agriculture, but in many places the silting up of dams and irrigation works limits to a few hundred years the time period during which effective rice agriculture can be practiced. Rice agriculture under these conditions fails to lead to equilibrium between external conditions and the cultural system. It is not clear, then, that rice agriculture in South India is necessarily a more adaptive choice than millet agriculture. Rice agriculture also requires more water than other equally productive crops. Why, then, rice instead of coconuts, black pepper, or sweet potatoes? In broader terms, what accounts for a variety of adaptations and cultural systems coexisting within the same environment or occupying similar environments?

One possible explanation is that cultural systems form a part of the environment of other cultural systems. Therefore the growing of a given crop in a given village community depends in part upon the demand for that crop in village communities that do not produce it. The presence of a variety of cultural systems within a given environment may, then, increase the adaptability of each one of them. If millet was the most adaptive crop and everyone therefore raised it, the overall adaptive advantage might be much less than that provided by a situation in which many different crops were grown.

Another not necessarily alternative explanation has to do with commitment or entailment. When the members of a cultural system decide to raise rice, their commitment to rice agriculture entails modification of the environment and cultural system. Once the commitment has been made, the cost in effort and adaptive loss involved in deciding to do something else is increased. In the case of rice agriculture, where the environment may have been irreversibly changed, some alternative ways of adapting may have been placed out of reach forever.

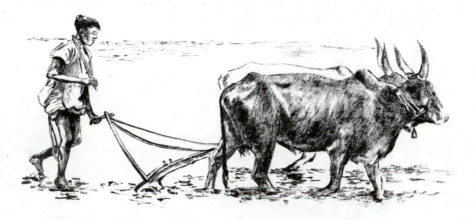

Acting within the limits of the information contained in their cultural tradition or in the cultural traditions of neighboring peoples, human beings select particular technologies or means of coping with the environment. If they always chose the most adaptive technology, the correlation or goodness of fit between environment and cultural systems would tend to be quite high. In real life, human technologies usually do not permit the discovery of the one and only one best solution to human problems. People make mistakes and then adapt to their mistakes by making additional decisions about what to do.

Because each decision involves a cost, it become increasingly difficult to go back to the beginning and start all over again with a different crop or a different technology. As in the case of the Indus civilization, a long series of maladaptive choices may lead to ruin. In the case of two neighboring cultural systems where one is somewhat better adapted than the other, there is always the possibility that one will replace the other; that is, unless both cultural systems taken together are more adaptive than either one taken separately.

Two cultural systems operating in virtually identical desert environments in Africa and North America are not likely to be identical in character because: (1) they are likely to base their decisions upon different sources of traditional information; (2) they are likely to make different sorts of mistakes in the search for the one and only one best solution to their adaptive problems; and (3) they are likely to have different social environments. If, besides controlling the environments so that they are identical, we control the level of technology so that both groups consist of deer hunters or potato farmers, other similarities between the two cultural systems will increase.

As an explanation of the similarities and differences between cultural systems, then, the environment can be seen as setting limits upon what can be done with the technology at hand. The environment alone, or even the technology and the environment alone, cannot determine exactly the nature of particular cultural systems. Although a severe environment, one in which there are only a few possible ways to survive, has a greater effect than a more permissive environment, human beings and their cultural systems survive, not because they have achieved the one and only correct solution to each of the problems posed by the environment, but because they have solved their problems well enough to get by.

So far, adaptation to the environment has been considered primarily as adaptation to the *natural* environment. With reference to nature, we can classify cultural systems in terms of such processes as hunting, fishing, collecting, growing crops, practicing plow agriculture, herding, or using machinery. These processes differ in the extent to which they consume resources available in the natural environment and capture energy or materials which can be used to increase the population size or complexity of the cultural systems. Although the natural environment is critical in the sense that it is the ultimate source of the energy and materials required for the support of cultural systems, the impact of *artificial* and *social* components of the environment upon particular cultural systems may be of equal importance and may even dictate the choice of technologies used in coping with the natural environment. Consider the following.

WHY NOT CHANGE THE ENVIRONMENT?

The crew of a B-29 consisted of eleven men. In order to "drop the bomb on the target," the crew carried on its operations within a complex machine. That machine, the B-29, was, at once, the major portion of the crew's environment and an instrument for dealing with the natural environment. External conditions, instead of being primarily a series of natural things, consisted of the machine itself and the crew's status as a part of a military hierarchy composed of other human beings.

The machine itself was built by civilian designers and builders whose main concern was to find a means of carrying heavy loads long distances at rapid speeds and great altitudes. The plane also had to be a superfortress, relatively immune to attack. In effect, then, the environment within which the aircrew was to operate was designed and built without too much regard for the cultural system of the aircrew or for the role of the aircrew in the larger military cultural system within which it also operated.

The aircrew came from the Army Air Corps, later the Air Force. These men had originally been civilians, but had been trained to interact in terms of a military organization which had developed in response to the problems encountered in land warfare by an infantry platoon. Because the activities of the infantry platoon were relatively simple and the men in it relatively untrained, members of such a platoon operated under control of a platoon leader whose orders were to be followed with "unthinking obedience." For the purposes of land warfare, an authoritarian organization in which a well-trained leader directed the activities of untrained followers was probably efficient.

In adapting this organization to the B-29, it was decided that there should be a commanding officer, very much like the platoon leader or the captain of a ship. He would possess absolute authority while the plane was in flight. Under the captain there would be a staff of officers consisting of a bombardier, a radar operator, and a copilot. Other crew members, the flight engineer, radio operator, and gunners were usually noncommissioned officers. Of the four gunners, several were likely to be privates. According to organizational charts, even the gunners were ranked— central gunner, right gunner, left gunner, and tail gunner.

Although all the members of an aircrew were more highly trained,

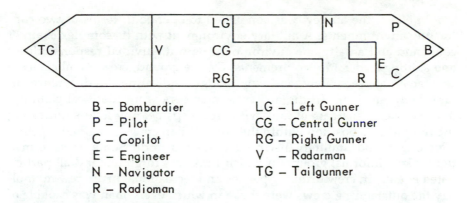

B — Bombardier
P — Pilot
C — Copilot
E — Engineer
N — Navigator
R — Radioman

LG — Left Gunner
CG — Central Gunner
RG — Right Gunner
V — Radarman
TG — Tailgunner

better paid, and higher ranking than most members of an infantry platoon, the operation of the crew was considered parallel to the operation of an infantry platoon: The aircraft commander gave orders, the crew members followed them. In practice, things were different. Few of the officers were in a position to observe, let alone supervise, the activities of the enlisted men. The tail gunner was completely isolated from the rest of the crew and beyond supervision. In flight, perhaps because of close confinement and boredom in the small tail compartment, he often fell asleep leaving the rest of the crew to wonder if he had set himself on fire or jumped out of the airplane. The aircraft commander, being trained almost exclusively in the complex art of piloting the airplane, had little or no idea what the other members of the crew were supposed to be doing. Each man on the crew was a trained specialist whose activities were often mysterious and incomprehensible to the others. Theoretically, the bombardier was an armaments officer, who supervised the activities of the relatively untrained gunners. Because the bombardier was situated in the nose of the plane and had other duties as well, he was in no position to oversee the gunners. In practice, because the central gunner was located in a bubble in the center top of the plane and had access to the gun controlling machinery and a good view of the action, the gun crew, including the bombardier, was directed by the central gunner.

In flight, the flight engineer, who alone possessed the equipment and skills required to calculate most efficient speeds and altitudes, instructed the aircraft commander concerning the speed and altitude at which he was to fly. The navigator, radarman, and radioman told the aircraft commander where he was and what he should do to get back on course. When the plane reached the target area, the aircraft commander was required by regulations to obey the orders of the bombardier. In the event of attack by enemy airplanes, it was the task of the gunners to instruct the aircraft commander concerning the maneuvers required to evade attack and to bring maximum firepower to bear upon an enemy he often could not see.

In effect, the aircrew was compelled to operate in terms of two contrasting environments: A military environment with its complex chain of command and an airplane environment with its divided responsibilities and shifting leadership requirements. On the ground, crew members lived separately, ate separately, and wore badges indicating the differences in rank between them. In the air, crew members wore identical clothing, often replacing insignia of rank with crew caps bearing letters indicating the individual's position within the crew. When crews remained together over long periods, military discipline tended to erode. Some crews formed tightly knit informal groups in which rank was forgotten and all participated equally in crew drinking parties and recreations. In aircrew mythology the outstanding crews were those in which every man was capable of performing the duties of every other crew member.

From the standpoint of the traditional military organization, the environment provided by the B-29 was clearly wrong. By 1952 Air Force generals were publicly advocating the development of new aircraft which would require small crews of very highly trained men; ultimately, there were to be no enlisted men or noncommissioned officers aboard. An all-officer crew could fraternize and be "democratic" without violating military tradition.

The case of the B-29 illustrates, among other things, that the requirements of a cultural system may generate powerful pressures toward the finding of problem solutions consistent with existing patterns and procedures. It is for this reason that people "pre-adapted" to the practice of rice agriculture and its various social and economic consequences are likely to attempt rice agriculture even in a situation where it represents a less efficient problem solution than might a new technique. Intensive rice agriculture, the construction of a city like Mohenjo Daro, or replacement of one airplane by another represent a great deal more than simple adaptation to the natural environment. They represent planned and systematic destruction of an existing environment and its replacement with one thought to be more suitable.

WHAT IS A GOOD ADAPTATION?

Rice agriculture can be regarded as an adaptation to the natural environment, while the building of a new airplane to replace the B-29 can be regarded as an instance of adaptation to the social environment. The trouble with thinking in such terms is that it obscures the fact that an adaptation can be successful only if it works simultaneously within the natural, artificial, and social environments. Rice agriculture can be successful only in appropriate artificial and social environments; a new airplane representing a successful adaptation to the social environment is useful only if it also flies.

In these terms, we can think of every process carried out within a cultural system as contributing to the solution of a problem existing simultaneously in the natural, artificial, and social environments. As a problem solution, a process must be reasonably compatible with other processes and consistent with the varieties of knowledge and experience contained within the cultural tradition. Writing about religion, Emile Durkheim, said:

> There are basically no false religions. All are true in their fashion. All stem from the conditions of human existence (1912:3).

Durkheim argued that anything that was false and therefore inefficient or maladaptive would sooner or later meet an obstacle it could not overcome. In other words, every process carried out in every cultural system must be adaptive because anything that is maladaptive will be edited by processes of selection. Because the editing might often take place later, rather than sooner, it cannot be concluded that "all that is" is adaptive.

In sum, the survival of a cultural system involves much more than the solution of problems posed by the natural environment. It involves coming to terms with changes in the environment resulting from the operation of the cultural system. It involves coming to terms with characteristics of the cultural system itself because anything that people do must be in some degree consistent with all the other things that they do. And finally it involves meeting possible competition from other cultural systems. The complexity of the survival problems handled by each of the processes carried out during the normal operation of a cultural system makes it difficult to estimate the extent to which a given process is adaptive or even what it is an adaptation to. More than a thousand years passed before the Indus civilization encountered an obstacle it could not overcome; before that it would have been hard to say just how the civilization was mal-adapted. A cultural system could not long survive if all its processes were maladaptive, but it can long survive when only some of its processes are. To the optimist most human cultural systems appear to be ingeniously adapted in almost everything they do. To the pessimist almost nothing seems adapted. Consider, in the following section, the difficulties in-volved in judging the adaptive value of the Karimojong way of life.

Are the Karimojong Adapted?

The Karimojong live in the southern part of Karimoja District in Uganda and depend for their subsistence upon cattle raising, hunting, collecting, and agriculture. The Karimojong maintain large herds of cattle which tend

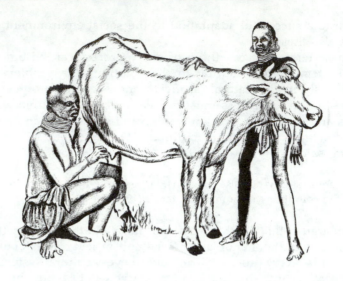

to overgraze the regions surrounding the campsite and force migrations to other regions. Cattle are regularly milked and all cattle, except pregnant or lactating cows and bulls reserved for breeding, are bled to provide blood for human consumption. Despite the large herds, the Karimojong eat relatively little meat. Oxen and sometimes a barren cow may be slaughtered to provide food at religious ceremonies or when other food is not available, but there is no attempt to slaughter surplus male cattle or cows that produce little milk or few offspring.

As individuals, Karimojong dedicate themselves to the acquisition of as many cattle as possible and treat them with great affection. As a boy, a Karimojong is given a specially named male calf. He decorates the calf elaborately, sings songs about it at dances and beer parties, and makes references to it in naming himself. It is hard to imagine how overgrazing or the maintenance of inefficient milk cattle can be adaptive, particularly if adaptation is considered in terms of maximizing the production of milk, meat, and blood. Is there any way in which Karimojong cattle raising makes sense?

One of the most significant factors in the Karimojong environment are enemy tribes who themselves seek greener pastures. If the Karimojong reduce their herds to maintain lush and abundant grasslands, the neighboring tribes may redouble their efforts to take them away. The need for unity in preventing cattle and land theft requires each cattle herder to have the support of friends and neighbors. In Karimojong society, this support is gained through gifts of cattle to relatives and in-laws. The man who owns a large herd has many friends and much protection. The rainfall in Karimojong country is uncertain and crops often fail. Here, again, a large herd of cattle provides insurance against famine. Cattle represent a means of storing wealth and rendering it portable where there are no banks, insurance companies, or elaborate food storage facilities.

> Even in modern times, the market for Karimojong beef is none too good. Four hundred pounds of dressed meat will buy less than three hundred pounds of cornmeal. (Dyson-Hudson 1969:76–89).

After reviewing only a few of the complexities of Karimojong life, it is difficult to reach enthusiastic judgments concerning the extent to which it might be considered adaptive or maladaptive. The Karimojong world is hardly the best of all possible worlds, but what other world is better? With these same questions about adaptation in mind, consider the equally complicated world of the Tsembaga.

Are Tsembaga Pigs Necessary?

The Tsembaga of New Guinea hold a periodic ritual called the *Kaiko*. At a Kaiko observed by Rappaport (1967), some 105 pigs were slaughtered yielding between 7000 and 8000 pounds of meat. Of this meat, between 4500 and 6000 pounds were distributed to 2000 or 3000 guests from 17 neighboring groups.

Pigs are useful in keeping residential areas free of garbage and feces. In gardens, they root up weeds and soften the ground. They also eat tubers and other materials that human beings would normally throw away. When there are too many pigs, it becomes expensive to feed them and they are inclined to invade gardens and to compete with human beings for the available food. One function of the Kaiko ritual, and of other similar rituals, would appear to be to reduce the pig population to manageable size, but this could also be accomplished by simply killing and eating pigs.

On the other hand, groups in New Guinea tend to be rather small and, at least in former times, often engaged in warfare. Frequent and uncontrolled warfare might have unfortunate consequences for the human population; carefully regulated warfare might help to control human populations or might contribute to the smoothing out of man/land ratios by forcing smaller groups to relinquish lands to larger groups. Traditionally, the waging of war and the making of peace was closely tied to ritual activities. The Kaiko ritual apparently served to promote contact and trade between otherwise isolated groups and it also led to marital and military alliances. To fight a war, it was necessary to have a lot of pigs which could be used to hold rituals and gain allies. Rituals held at the termination of a war created alliances which could only be changed after the enemies had again accumulated pigs and formed appropriate alliances.

Rappaport argues that this constitutes a "ritually regulated ecosystem," adaptive because it establishes an equilibrium among pigs, people, and the environment. Although it might turn out that ritually regulated ecological relationships are more or less adaptive than other kinds (if there are other kinds), it appears likely that change in any important part of the Tsembaga system of relationships would create severe adaptive problems. Without completely redesigning the cultural system, it would be difficult to improve upon the traditional adaptation. The Tsembaga, like the Karimojong, pass the major tests of adaptation. They have managed to survive over substantial periods of time, and, in terms of their tightly knit traditional cultural systems, it is hard to find much that has a demonstrably negative effect upon their chances of survival.

Who Needs a Superpotato?

The potato was developed in ancient Peru at least two thousand years ago. In Peru, there are many varieties of potatoes and traditional farming practices until recently ensured that the potatoes in any one field were of many different kinds. Instead of carefully selecting the best potatoes and using them for seed, the Peruvians traditionally used whatever was handy. Around 1588, potatoes were introduced into Ireland. Due to problems of shipping and the need to transport only the best potatoes, it is probable that these potatoes were superpotatoes, perhaps representing only one variety. After several centuries of selection by Irish farmers, who tended to plant only the biggest and best of potatoes, the Irish potato crop was totally destroyed in 1845 and 1846 by the previously unknown fungus *Phytophtora infestans.* Within a few decades, the population of Ireland had fallen from nine million to four million people. In the process of selecting potatoes for cultivation, the Irish farmer had apparently eliminated those varieties of potatoes that were resistant to *Phytophtora infestans* (from Salaman 1952).

The question of the superpotato raises some interesting problems concerning the ability of modern civilizations to disseminate new technological adaptations rapidly across wide areas. Might not atomic power, insecticides, new crops, or supersonic airplanes, like the superpotato, carry hidden within them the seeds of destruction? Might not the spread of a single set of closely related cultural systems over the entire planet create a kind of superculture every bit as vulnerable as the superpotato? Were all men and all cultures essentially the same and adapted to their environments in essentially the same way, would the human species have the same protection against rapid environmental change that it now possesses through the existence of a variety of cultures and kinds of man? The poet has many kinds of grass, dandelions, and daisies in his lawn; the efficiency expert has a lawn consisting entirely of the "best" variety of bluegrass. Who has the lawn most fitted to survive? For that matter, is the poet or the efficiency expert fitted to survive? The next section considers the possibility that the culture-building capacity itself is maladaptive.

Why Are Clams Happy?

Over the millennia, the so-called "higher" animals embarked upon a course of evolution emphasizing the importance of cooperation within the species and of learning through experience. Using hindsight, it appears almost inevitable that this should lead in time to the emergence of a culture-building species such as *Homo sapiens*. Ultimately, should the culture-building capacity prove adaptive (that is, if we survive as a species), it seems inevitable that this capacity will overwhelm the biological message so that human biological evolution becomes a reflex of the cultural message. This next great evolutionary step is implicit in our developing capacity to understand and hence to modify the genetic code.

The evolutionary "success" of the so-called higher animals might be thought of as a consequence of their adaptive failures. The higher animals, most particularly *Homo sapiens*, have rarely achieved a state of equilibrium with the environment. Like the flying Dutchman, the ancestors of *Homo sapiens* and our own species have fled through the corridors of time seeking, first through biological and then increasingly through cultural evolution, new solutions to the problems of survival. Through these same milennia and more, the happy clam has merrily reproduced itself, maintaining, with few apparent changes, the genetic message with which it started its career.

With the emergence of the culture-building capacity, human survival appears to have depended upon the increasingly rapid development of new means of adaptation. Following the first inventions, leading to the use of tools and the hunting of large animals, human cultures changed but slowly. Then, with the invention of agriculture less than ten thousand years ago human beings began to alter and sometimes to destroy their environments with increasing rapidity. Human beings are not the only life forms that destroy their environments. It has been pointed out that if the first plants had preserved the "balance of nature," the earth would perhaps still have an atmosphere of methane and ammonia.

Whether we speak of the use of bows and arrows, fire, plows, bulldozers, or repeating rifles, the impact of human inventions upon the environment has been to simplify it and to dramatically reduce the number of plant and animal species. Humanity has solved its probems with a meat-axe, cutting out those species which were useless or threatening and replacing them or allowing them to be replaced with species which were more useful or better adapted to the presence of humanity. More and more, human beings have adapted the environment to themselves rather than adapting themselves to the environment. Without exception, certainly from the time of the Indus civilization, such drastic revisions of the environment have failed to promote the kind of equilibrium that might be described as adaptation. With the creation of superpotatoes, pesticides, and atomic bombs, it would appear that the survival of the species has come more and more to depend upon the solution of problems that the species itself has created. As *Homo sapiens artificialis* or synthetic humanity emerges from the drawing boards of the biologist, is there any guarantee that our redesigned species will be better adapted than the superpotato?

Unlike the clam, the human species has never reached the safe harbor of relative equilibrium. In every environment and cultural system there have always been problems that were not solved and human beings who were considerably less happy than clams. What is the impact of such problems upon the development of cultural systems? Consider the case of the Nyoro, a tribe of East Africa.

WHY THIS, WHY NOW, WHY TO ME?

Yowana bought a piece of timber to make a door with, but it was stolen before he could use it. After searching the village he found it in the house of a neighbor, Isoke. He accused Isoke of stealing it, but since Isoke denied the theft and there were no witnesses, the charge failed. A few days later Yowana's house was burned down and he lost all his property. He did not know who had done this (though he suspected Isoke), so, informants afterwards said, he obtained from a vendor of powerful medicines a substance which if smeared on those of the posts of the burned house which remained standing would cause the incendiarist to suffer from dysentery and burning pains in his chest. Yowana is said to have applied the medicine as directed, and four days later Isoke became ill. His brothers consulted the local diviners, who said that Yowana's medicine was the cause of the illness. Isoke then summoned Yowana, confessed to him that he had burned his house and also that he had stolen the timber, and promised to make restitution. Isoke's brothers begged Yowana to get an antidote from the vendor of the original medicine so that Isoke might be cured. Yowana promised to do so, but unfortunately Isoke died. In this case complaints were made to the Protectorate police and Yowana was arrested for suspected murder, but an autopsy on Isoke's body showed no signs of poisoning, and Yowana was released. Nonetheless, nobody doubted that Yowana had killed Isoke by sorcery, least of all Yowana, who was heard to boast at beer parties of his prowess (Beattie 1960:74).

Throughout the world men like Isoke, strong enough to carry away another man's timber and mean enough to become involved in neighborhood quarrels, have a tendency to fall ill, sometimes to die. It appears likely, although Isoke's confession was obtained under duress, that he had committed the crimes of which he was accused. In other cases, perfectly innocent men may die as a result of sorcery or perfectly healthy men may die quickly and unpleasantly of unknown and unusual diseases. The germ theory of disease, however useful it may be for some purposes, fails to explain why Isoke got sick and not Yowana.

The Nyoro explain the matter as follows:

> A sorcerer is a person who wants to kill people. He may do it by blowing medicine toward them, or by putting it in the victim's food or water, or by hiding it in the path where he must pass. People practice sorcery against those whom they hate. They practice it against those who steal from them, and also against people who are richer than they are. Sorcery is brought about by envy, hatred, and quarreling (Beattie 1960:73).

In some ultimate sense, perfect adaptation would involve perfectly stable and predictible relationships with the environment. Because the rains do not always come on time or are too heavy when they do come and because men die inexplicably or encounter misfortune, human beings inevitably face the problem of explaining that which cannot be explained. Such explanations, often partaking of the qualities of religion, may have adaptive consequences. For the Nyoro, sorcery and illness may be avoided by avoiding envy, hatred, and quarreling. Thus, the unsolved problem of illness appears to be used to promote qualities of behavior that enhance the adaptive virtues of unity and cooperation.

North Americans explain colds and other illness by saying, "I guess I've been staying up too late," "not eating properly," "too much boozing around," or "I should have worn my sweater." The fact that others who got drunk or forgot their sweaters did not get sick is ignored. Here, illness is not the result of sorcery, but the result of one's own misbehaviors. Small wonder that a sick person is confined in a small room, dressed in special clothing, deprived of the companionship of friends and family, forced to consume poorly cooked food served on a tray, allowed to do things only at rigidly specified times, and forced to undergo pain and humiliation. Criminals are punished in much the same way.

The North Americans also believe in sorcery:

> There are many roads to insanity and our culture has probably trod them all. It is difficult to find in any other society a form of madness, or a pathway to it, that cannot be duplicated by us. The opposite is not true: that all cultures have developed as many forms of psychosis or found as many ways to attain it as we. In this we are secure in our riches. We are as highly developed in psychopathology as in technology.
>
> Psychosis is the final outcome of all that is wrong with a culture. Coming to intense focus in the parents, the cultural ills are transmitted to their children, laying the foundation for insanity. The parents, blinded by their own

disorientation, confusion, and misery, sometimes half mad themselves, make fearful mistakes; but only an observer who sees these with his own eyes can really know exactly how the tragedy was prepared (Henry 1963:322–323).

Science tells us that human beings sometimes cause their own illnesses and that their illnesses are sometimes caused by others. There is a tendency, as among the Nyoro and the North Americans, to convert these sometime explanations into general explanations. The resulting processes of diagnosis and treatment are directed not so much at coping with the environment as at coping with the anxiety and hostility that arise because it is impossible to explain why one man became ill and not another.

In thinking about the problem of the relationships between cultural systems and their environments, it is useful to think of the various processes carried out within the cultural system as involving solutions or attempted solutions to problems posed by the environment. Because not all problems can be solved, because the correct solution is not always found, and because some problems are solved by radically changing the environment, it is not easy to draw direct connections between what the problem is and what people do in response to it. Because designing a process to solve a problem involves some sort of recognition of the nature of the problem, one of the problems of studying the environment is that of recognizing the problem and discovering the connection between problem and process.

BUT WAS THAT THE PROBLEM THE SOLUTION SOLVED?

Raymond picked himself up and started pulling the wagon westward, along the side of the Vocational Training building. As he walked along, he muttered to himself, "I'll go get my crate." He ran around the back of the building and headed for the pit, where he had been playing with the crate in the afternoon. When he reached the pit, he crawled down into it and went straight to the crate. He began tugging and pulling at the crate, trying hard to raise it up to the level of the vacant lot. He worked hard (Barker and Wright 1955:242).

Had Raymond not announced the nature of his problem, the outside observer would have had difficulty understanding what Raymond was up to. It is not obvious that he was getting the crate, for he might have been cleaning out the pit.

In South India, an outside observer might see something like the following: In the rice fields ten women are standing in line. At one end stands an elderly woman who is peering along the line. She begins to sing

a strongly rhythmic and repetitive song. As she sings, the women step backward one step, bend over, and thrust rice seedlings into the ground. Looking at this behavior, the outside observer is likely to conclude that the environmental problem here is that of planting rice seedlings in straight rows, and that this is solved by the process observed. Even here, where the problem seems easily identified and where the women would almost certainly say that they were planting rice if they were asked, other problems are mixed in. The songs the old woman is singing involve a kind of instruction and, in this sense, the observed process is educational. Similarly, the arrangement of the women under the leadership of the old woman could be interpreted as a process of assigning status or social position.

As Raymond or the women of South India carry out particular activities and processes, they exert impact upon the environment. The sum of the human activity carried out within a cultural system determines the nature of the ecological relationships between the cultural system and its environment. In many cases, the carrying out of a particular activity represents a conscious plan, such as "getting the crate," formulated with a view toward establishing some particular relationship to the environment. Of course, there is a distinction between planning to get the crate and actually getting the crate and there is a difference between planting a crop of rice and harvesting a crop of rice. In many cases, as noted in the Bible, people quite literally "know not what they do," and processes carried out with one purpose in mind may lead to undreamed of consequences. Human beings may solve their adaptive problems without planning to do so, or in planning to solve some particular problem, they may create new ones. A part of the problem of understanding cultural systems and their relationships to the environment is that of understanding why a given process is carried out and what its specific impacts are, not only on the environment, but upon other aspects of the cultural system. In thinking about ways of planting rice, women in South India cannot think solely of the one and only one best way of planting rice, for they must also consider a variety of social and educational impacts that any method of planting rice must have. In selecting ways of doing such things as planting rice, human beings are guided by their general understanding of nature of the environment and of the place which they occupy within it.

SUMMARY

The disappearance of the Indus Valley civilization and of many other cultural systems throughout history is evidence that adaptation is required of people and their cultural systems just as it is required of all other living things. Discussion of the nature of adaptation begins with a consideration of the nature of the environment. The case of the Menomini illustrates the dual nature of human realities and environments. We must attempt to consider the environment as it really is, scientifically; we must also consider that it might contain witches. The Menomini view is important and it has an impact upon what the Menomini do.

The Tiwi seem to fit closely to their environment in everything that they do. This does not mean, however, that Tiwi culture was determined by the Tiwi environment. It means that the Tiwi found solutions to the problems posed by the environment, but not that these were the only possible solutions. This theme is pursued in thinking about the alternation between rice and millet agriculture in South India. Rice agriculture represents the case where culture determines the environment every bit as much as environment determines culture. The coexistence of alternative technologies may represent a more efficient adaptation than the presence of either technology alone. An environment may permit a wide range of effective adaptations.

An effective adaptation must deal with the artificial and social environments as well as with the natural environment. The conflict between the functional requirements of the B-29 and the functional requirements of the Air Force social system was met by designing a different kind of airplane.

Another problem has to do with assessing the effectiveness of an adaptation. The Karimojong and the Tsembaga appear to be adapted to their environments. Both groups were able to maintain their traditional cultural systems until quite recently. A plausible story can be made up which explains how everything that they do is reasonable and adaptive. The problem is to make the transition from plausible to demonstrable.

The point that not all human activities are adaptive is illustrated by the case of the superpotato, which caused what may have been the greatest disaster in human history. The case of the superpotato illustrates the point that not all new ideas are good and that it is dangerous to go about simplifying and changing environments and species. The maintenance of diversity is an important means of adaptation.

The case of the superpotato and of the clam raises questions about the quality of human adaptations to the environment in general. Extremely rapid biological and cultural evolution may well terminate, as it did in the case of Mohenjo Daro and in the case of the superpotato, in extinction. Human beings sometimes seem to have fled through the corridors of time desperately papering over the mistakes of their ancestors.

Another problem in considering human adaptation is the human use of religion and fantasy in apparent attempts to solve problems. The Nyoro believe that their illnesses may be caused by sorcery. In the United States, people sometimes believe that their psychoses are passed down to them by their parents. Religious beliefs, or unrealistic beliefs generally, may represent useful ways of adapting to the persistence of unsolved problems. Religious beliefs may provide vital psychological reassurance or encourage cooperation. On the other hand, there may be false religions after all.

Finally, the cases of Raymond and the South Indian women illustrate the difficulties involved in determining just what it is that a process is supposed to accomplish. Much more needs to be known concerning the specific impacts of the various processes carried out in cultural systems.

For Further Reading

General works on anthropological ecology include Netting (1977), Hardesty (1977), and Bennett (1969). The "Worlds of Man" series edited by Walter Goldschmidt is now published by AHM publishing corporation and includes Beals on South India (1971), Kennedy on *Beer, Ecology, and Social Organization* (1978), Bennett on the northern plains (1969), Alkire on the coral islands (1978), and Sutlive on the Iban of Sarawak (1978).

More technical ecologically oriented ethnographies include *Moala, Culture and Nature on a Fijian Island* (Sahlins 1962), *The Nuer* (Evans-Pritchard 1940), *Pigs for the Ancestors* (Rappaport 1967), and *Hill Farmers of Nigeria* (Netting 1968). Case studies dealing with environment and adaptation include *Dreamers without Power* (Spindler and Spindler 1971), *The Tiwi* (Hart and Pilling 1960), *Padju Epat* (Hudson 1972), *The Magars of Banyan Hill* (1965), *The Barabaig* (Klima 1970), and *Fields on the Hoof* (Ekvall 1968).

Problems and Questions

1. Select cultural systems that share similar environments such as the Hopi and Tewa (Dozier 1967) and the Navaho (Down 1972). Consider the relationship between environment and culture.

2. Consider a substance or resource necessary to the maintenance of an existing cultural system. How long will that resource last? What will happen when it is used up?

3. Taking any kind of group or organization with which you are familiar, what sort of environmental problems does it face? How are they solved?

4. For any cultural system, examine a major ritual and consider some of its effects upon relationships between human beings and the environment.

5. Review the history of any place with which you are familiar. Can you relate any changes to changes in the environment?

6. The library contains many books dealing with the spread of technological innovations, new crops, or deadly diseases. Consider the impact of such a dramatic change upon the cultural systems affected by it.

7 THE REGULATION OF MEMBERSHIP

The chapter opens with a discussion of the regulation of membership. Next, Malthus's calculation concerning the rate of increase of the human population is presented. World population has grown with alarming rapidity over the past few years; why, then, is it that human beings do not now occupy every square foot of available space? There is some encouragement in recent and successful attempts to limit the growth of world population.

Next, the system of population regulation used in Tikopia is described. Given the traditional system, what effects would follow if some traditional practices were forbidden while others were permitted to continue? In the case of Ireland, a system that avoids contraception, abortion, and infanticide is described. How do the Irish do it?

In complex societies, different ethnic groups and subpopulations possess unique systems for the regulation of their populations. The retention of wealth and a dominant political position is sometimes dependent upon careful population regulation on the part of dominant ethnic groups. How do the Brahmins restrict population growth? What are the general ways in which human societies regulate their populations? What are the economic and moral costs of each technique?

Although maintaining a reasonable relationship between the number of deaths and the number of births is the fundamental problem of population regulation, the process of human reproduction poses some other problems as well. An example from South India presents the problem of relating family household composition to the jobs that a family household is supposed to carry out. Chance variation in birth ratios and the accidents of life make it more difficult than might be expected to assemble the perfect household. What do you do if you want a son and a daughter and end up with five sons and no daughters? Try again?

Ways in which the Nunivak Eskimo and the Alorese adjust their household composition are described. What, now, are some of the processes that permit a household to replace missing or ineffective members?

Various factors including a range of economic and environmental factors, cause some villages and cities to need additional population while some other villages and cities may have a surplus. What are some of the kinds of arrangements that lead to permanent and temporary migration? An additional case describes patterns of marriage in the French village of Peyrane. How does marriage contribute to the exchange of population between places? What are the effects of different marriage rules? How does marriage help to maintain a constant relationship between village population and resources in South India?

Finally, looking at the Tsembaga again, what is the possible relationship among pigs, people, rituals, marriages, and wars? What sorts of things are likely to happen when population regulating mechanisms begin to fail or when population cannot be transferred from one place or group to another?

WHERE WILL WE GET THE MEMBERS?

If a cultural system is viewed as a social structure, as a set of statuses or positions to be filled by members, then processes for the regulation of membership are those by which the cultural system obtains the persons it needs and moves them from status to status within its structure. Given limits on the loaves of bread that can be won from the environment and on the capacity of the cultural system to provide jobs or statuses for human beings, processes for the regulation of membership must provide enough warm bodies to solve manpower needs, but not so many as to exhaust environmental resources or available positions. Because human beings grow old and die, because they lose interest or move away, the membership of every cultural system must be constantly renewed. Because too many human beings are little better than too few, so far as survival is concerned, processes designed for the renewal of membership must be balanced by processes designed for the limitation of membership and for the circulation of members from job to job or status to status.

The fundamental processes that regulate membership are, of course, those that concern the regulation of human biological reproduction. Processes that simply transfer members from one status to another within the social structure would soon lose their point unless the supply of human beings were constantly replenished through birth. In discussing processes for the regulation of membership, then, the distinction between a society, which includes all of the processes required for the reproduction and survival of human beings, and a part- or subcultural system is extremely important. Processes carried out within societies and having to do with marriage, fertility, birth, life support, and mortality encounter special problems posed by the biological characteristics of the human species. What are some of these problems?

HOW MANY PEOPLE CAN THERE BE?

In 1798, Thomas Malthus published an essay concerning the rapidity with which the human species might reproduce:

> . . . if the necessaries of life could be obtained without limit, and the number of people could be doubled every twenty-five years, the population which might have been produced from a single pair since the Christian era, would have been sufficient, not only to fill the earth quite full of people, so that four should stand in every square yard, but to fill all the planets of our solar system in the same way, and not only them but all the planets revolving around the stars which are visible to the naked eye, supposing each of them . . . to have as many planets belonging to it as our sun has (Malthus 1798: quoted in Heilbroner 1961:86).

For his computations, Malthus assumed only that the human population would double each twenty-five years. For this, all that is required is that each living family produce, on the average, two living female children along with an occasional male. Considering that human females have the capacity to produce children roughly every two years while they are in their teens and retain that capacity for more than twenty years, Malthus' predictions are modest.

Under the assumption that the necessities of life can be obtained without limit, the earth should have been filled with people many centuries ago. Lacking the benefit of any accurate knowledge of human behavior much beyond what he could see, Malthus believed that the failure of human populations to reproduce at the expected rate was the result of an absence of necessities. He arrived at the anthropological law that the members of any society would reproduce themselves until they attained a state of overpopulation that could be remedied only by famine, pestilence, or mass killing. Actually, this law is false. Almost all cultural systems engage in some degree of population regulation.

How Fast Is the Population Growing?

Although even today, we are only beginning to make accurate estimates of the size of the human population, there have been several attempts to estimate the rate of increase of the human species. Choosing, as did Malthus, the quite recent beginning of the Christian era for his estimate, Dorn (1962:285) arrives at the following figures:

FIGURE 7–1 Control of epidemic diseases, improved sanitation and medical care, and multiplication of the necessities of life have led to a sharply decreased infant mortality and a corresponding increase in population. Gopalpur, South India. (PHOTO BY ALAN R. BEALS)

Year (A.D.)	Population in Billions	Number of Years to Double
1	0.25 (?)	1650 (?)
1650	.50	200
1850	1.1	80
1930	2.0	45
1975	4.0	35
2010	8.0	?

These figures do not take into account the time, perhaps starting ten thousand years ago, when the development of agriculture triggered one great increase in the size of the human population; nor do they take into account earlier population explosions such as might have been triggered by the invention of language or even fishnets. The limited information available points to a rapid increase in the human population over the last few hundred years. Foerster, Mora, and Amiot (1960:1291) go so far as to predict that we will all be literally squeezed to death on November 13, 2026, when the human population approaches infinite size.

The recent vast increase in the human population is the result of the introduction of new crops and technologies which have *seemingly* led to the multiplication of the necessaries of life without limit. It may also have to do with rapid changes in the character of human cultural systems which have swept away traditional processes for the regulation of population. Because unlimited increase in the production of the necessaries of life leads to unlimited consumption of irreplacable resources (including space), it seems to be only a matter of time before we run out of air, water, energy, space, or some other vital resource and become extinct.

Long before vital resources are completely used up, the planet will probably be swept by famine, pestilence, or mass killings which will substantially reduce world population. Such a solution to the population problem, usually called a *Malthusian solution*, has undesirable features. Human reproduction is a costly and time-consuming process, and so, even without considering moral issues, it seems stupid to raise people to maturity and then kill them off. A more practical solution would appear to be to discover, perhaps rediscover, methods of regulating population so that the number of individuals conceived and born is just large enough to maintain equilibrium with the environment—using resources, but not using them up. In the last few decades, fear of such a Malthusian catas-

FIGURE 7–2 Very often people have many children because children are economically useful. The two boys serve the customers at Malitbog in the Philippines. (PHOTO COURTESY OF F. LANDA JOCANO)

trophe has caused more and more governments to encourage population regulation. Contraception and legalized abortion have resulted in sharp reductions in the birth rate all over the world. Some recent estimates now place world population at the beginning of the next century at a figure closer to five billion than eight billion. Current resistance to abortion and disastrous side effects from some forms of contraception may yet signal or trigger a rejection of the concept of population control. Modern nations, with all their technology, unlike some other cultural systems have not yet arrived at a reliable means of population regulation.

The regulation of human populations involves, as does the regulation of any other species, the interruption of the normal biological life cycle in such a way as to produce a balance between the number of individuals who are born and the number of individuals who die. Such regulation can take the form of the prevention of mating, the prevention of conception, the prevention of live births, or the killing or weakening of infants, children, or adults. In one form or another, most of these techniques are used, not always deliberately, in all human cultures, but cultures differ greatly in the frequency and manner in which these techniques are applied. Consider some of the ways in which population is regulated on Tikopia, an island in the South Pacific.

REGULATION: DO THEY CASTRATE THEIR SONS IN TIKOPIA?

According to Dillon, the population of Tikopia in the early years of the nineteenth century was in an anomalous state. The number of females was "at least treble that of the males." This discrepancy he attributed to artificial means, alleging that all males except the first two were strangled at birth, the reason assigned by the natives being to prevent an undue increase in population. The Englishmen found on the island by Dumont D'Urville denied this. Gaimard speaks of the number of children in a family as varying from three to eight, while John Maresere, eighty years later, stated that the family was limited in size to four, any number beyond this being buried alive as a rule. Moreover in contradistinction to Dillon, he said that girls rather than boys were destroyed. Durrad, who lived for two months on the island and was a careful observer, stated that the people had large families and that there was an excess of males over females. . . .

The utter worthlessness of casual observation derived from the stay of a day or so which the *Southern Cross* and other vessels make was demonstrated by a statement which I received as a serious explanation from an engineer on the way down to the island. He said that he believed that large numbers of the boys were castrated soon after birth, and alleged that he had ripped off the waistcloth of three and found this to be the case. Hence he accounted for their great stature—almost a legend among white people—and their general mild nature. This, as I noted with some skepticism at the time, would account for restriction of the population, but not for a differential sex ratio. Moreover, the effects should be perceptible in families without children, if such lads afterwards married. The statement, as might be imagined, I found later to be entirely without foundation, but it is true that the Tikopia do endeavor to control their population in ways that are hardly less striking (Firth 1963:367–368).

Firth found the population of Tikopia to be distributed as follows:

	MALE		FEMALE	
	Married	*Unmarried*	*Married*	*Unmarried*
Children and adolescents (under 18)	00	338	00	249
Adult to middle-aged (18–40)	132	117	149	101
Above middle age (over 40)	85	15	76	19

Among the children there are substantially more males than females. Among the eighteen to forty group there is a balance of males and females, while the above forty group shows slightly more males than females. The large number of children under eighteen cannot be accounted for by lowered mortality such as might result from better diet or improved medical care because there is no particular increase in the number of females. Firth suggests that the discrepancy between the number of males under eighteen and the number over eighteen can be accounted for by the fact that sizable numbers of males are killed or disappear during long and dangerous sightseeing voyages. Female infanticide might explain the relatively small number of females under eighteen, but while Firth was in Tikopia slightly more females were born than males. A tendency to neglect female children would, however, have the same impact as deliberate infanticide. In former times, Tikopian population was controlled by the following methods: Younger brothers in a large family were expected to remain single, both unmarried and married people with "sufficient" children practiced *coitus interruptus*, abortion was practiced by unmarried girls, infanticide was practiced at the discretion of the family head, and young or unmarried men often set out on sea voyages from which they did not return. When the island became crowded, one section of the population was attacked and forced to emigrate. Such attacks sometimes involved conflict between districts and sometimes involved attacks on persons of low rank by persons of high rank. The principal means of controlling

population on Tikopia was probably the prevention or delay of the marriage of large numbers of women.

In the Tikopian case, the introduction of laws forbidding abortion or infanticide would tend to increase the frequency of long and suicidal sea voyages and/or genocidal conflicts. The prevention of sea voyages and killing, measures often adopted by colonial powers in the South Pacific, leads to overpopulation resulting in famine, the importation of the necessities of life, and/or mass migration. The processes involved in the regulation of membership in the Tikopian cultural system can be evaluated in terms of cost and effectiveness. Assuming the unavailability of any modern technology for birth control, what might be an ideal means of controlling Tikopian population? Consider how population in Ireland was regulated following the great famine.

Ireland: After the Famine, What?

Tom Casey, K———, is a very poor holder with thirty acres of mountain and a bog. Two sons and a daughter are still at home, and a bachelor brother works with him. Another daughter works for herself as a domestic servant in Ennis. One son, Tom, is apprenticed to a carpenter in Ennis. A daughter emigrated through the good graces of her aunt.

Michael Dunn of T——— has twenty acres, but has not prospered. His two sons left at eighteen and twenty respectively to drive hackney automobiles in Ennis, an uncle there giving them a start. Another son now thirty and a daughter are still at home working the farm.

In a mountain townland, Pat Looney's father prospered, won the good graces of the landlord's agent; amassed four farms, the largest fifty acres, the smallest eighteen. He married off two daughters with two-hundred-pound fortunes, settled three sons and a daughter with her husband in each of the farms. Pat himself, the eldest, now about eighty, got the largest farm but not the one he wanted. He has beeen warring with his brothers and his neighbors ever since. He held out against his father for five years, refusing to marry and take his farm. In Pat's youth, land agitation and reform had not yet prevented the subdivision and acquiring of new farms by a successful tenant. Pat, on his fifty-acre mountain farm, has married off a daughter locally at three hundred pounds and sent two sons out to America. Another daughter works in England. Two sons, aged forty-three and thirty-six, are at home and Pat hasn't made up his mind yet which one shall get the land (Arensberg and Kimball 1948:147–148).

It will be recalled that the introduction of the superpotato to Ireland led to a dramatic increase in the Irish population and, ultimately, to a disastrous famine. Over one hundred years after the famine, Ireland still maintained one of the highest rates of fertility in the world, over 250 births per one thousand *married* women. The typical Irish wife was producing one child every four years. Presumably the cause of this high rate of fertility was that both the Irish government and the Catholic church strongly opposed birth control and encouraged large families.

Despite the high rate of fertility, Ireland's rate of population growth remained small. Her annual birthrate was twenty-one babies per thousand people. How was it possible for each thousand married women to produce 250 babies, but to have only twenty-one babies for each thousand people? Taking note of the above quotation concerning Tom Casey, imagine a small family farm just large enough to support a married couple and their children. Assuming that the family has at least two male and two female children and that the male children will farm the land while the female children marry men farming other small plots, it would be evident that the small farm could not produce sufficient resources to support both sons and their wives and children. One son (in Ireland this was generally the oldest) had to leave the farm and take his chances in the city, England, or the United States. If they remained on the farm, the daughters would have to wait until a farmer came along who had sufficient resources to support them. All other things being equal, the daughters might wait a very long time before such a prince appeared. Most probably, one daughter might never marry and bear children, and the other daughter might not begin to bear children until she was thirty. Even if the married daughter produced a child every two years until she was forty, she could only produce five children, while the unmarried daughter would produce none at all. Irish population, then, appears to have been controlled by a combination of emigration and spinsterhood.

We are often led to believe that the control of human populations depends entirely upon the development of safe, cheap, and effective devices which will prevent the conception of children. The Irish case is one in which population control was achieved, at least for a time, by creating circumstances that delayed or prevented the marriage of women. For such a method to be effective, cultural rules forbidding sexual relationships outside of marriage must be effectively enforced.

INDIA: Can You Afford It?

In K. Sagar's *Modern Complete Letter Writer*, the following is given as a typical matrimonial advertisement:

> Match for M. A., 25 years, beautiful employed Arora virgin. Early decent marriage. Dowry seekers please excuse. Apply Box 2589 Hindustan Times, New Delhi 1. (Sagar N.D.:220).

To the reader, this advertisement conveys the information that this is a Brahmin lady, well past the normal age of marriage, who is unable to provide the dowry usually regarded as a requirement. Brahmins are one of the highest ranking of all the Hindu *jatis* (castes). This is partly because they are a pure, vegetarian, and priestly jati, but it also derives from their control of land, their access to higher education, and their great wealth. Over most of India, Brahmins are a numerically small jati with a birthrate that is lower than that of most other jatis. How is this small birthrate achieved?

The lady in the advertisement is twenty-five years old and has no dowry. Over much of India, a Brahmin woman can be married only if her father is comparatively wealthy. Even in villages, the minimum dowry required amounts to some three times the annual earnings of an ordinary laborer. In the city, the bride's father may well have to provide for the bridegroom's education, perhaps even for years of foreign study. Already ten to fifteen years past the normal age for an early decent marriage, the Arora virgin may hope to marry only some gentleman sufficiently modern or wealthy to disregard dowry or, if she herself is modern, a gentleman from some other jati. The *Modern Complete Letter Writer* offers a reply from a civil engineer of active habits and good disposition but who is a member of a non-Brahmin jati.

In a complex society, such as that of India or the United States, where people are divided into jatis or ethnic groups and where membership in a particular class, caste, or ethnic group has an impact upon the life chances of the individual, differential access to medical care or other resources may also have an impact upon population size. In the United States, poor people, American Indians, American Negroes, and Mexican-Americans may lack access to education, medical care, and jobs and consequently tend to have a lower life expectancy than do members of other groups. Often high mortality is balanced by a high birthrate to produce a net increase in population mostly consisting of children doomed to early death. Among poor people in the United States, especially those living in urban slums, the depressing prospects of future survival, combined with a virtual absence of effective or responsive law enforcement, sometimes leads to heavy use of dangerous drugs and high rates of crime, murder, suicide, and divorce. Where the mother must work to support her children, the absence of public child-care facilities may lead to the neglect and death of younger children. In many societies malnutrition, disease, child neglect, and other similar factors may press as heavily upon the reproductive capacities of the rich as upon the poor.

In most complex urban societies, casual or calculated inequalities in the distribution of goods and services lead to a kind of cryptogenocide in which some kinds of people have high rates of infant mortality and short life expectancies. In all societies, the distribution of opportunities and resources helps to determine who shall be married, who shall have children, how long the children will live, and whether or not those children shall, in turn, have the opportunity to bear children.

What Are All the Methods of Control?

In sum, human populations everywhere are regulated by a variety of mechanisms operating at every stage in the life cycle. Before marriage or mating takes place, the high cost of marriage, institutionalized forms of spinsterhood such as convents, malnutrition, poor medical care, or drug taking severely limit the prospect that some individuals will bear children. Once married the high cost of childbirth or the presence of numerous children may lead the husband and wife to abstain from sexual relationships, to practice interrupted sexual intercourse, or to use birth-control devices. Once a child has been conceived, drugs or mechanical means may be used to secure abortions. Amateurish, illegal, or self-help abortions often limit population by destroying the mother as well as the fetus. Where abortion is legalized and performed effectively, it has roughly the same impact as birth-control devices. As of 1969, for example, the populations of the United States and Japan were both growing at the rate of about 1 percent per year, presumably as the result of legalized contraception in the United States and legalized abortion in Japan. The widespread use of contraception in Japan and illegal abortions by perhaps one fourth of all mothers in the United States make this a less than perfect example. As abortion has become more common in the United States and contraception more common in Japan, both countries have had further declines in the birth rate.

As in the story of Moses, the abandonment of unwanted children has a long history in human society. In the United States the beating to death of unwanted children has recently been recognized as a social problem. In South Indian villages, first-born and second-born male children are generally taken to scientifically trained medical practitioners when they fall ill. Later-born male children and female children often receive no medical care at all. There is some evidence that a mere absence of affection may often lead to debilitation, illness, and even the death of human infants. Certainly the love and attention which greets the first-born child can hardly be expected for the fifth-born child. In most societies, although there are exceptions, the first-born child receives the education or expanded opportunity. Very often it is the first-born who makes the "proper" marriage and has the greatest chances of bearing children. The seventh son of a seventh son has dreary prospects indeed. Neglect in infancy is one of the major causes of human mortality.

For all human societies, extraordinary drought, newly introduced epidemic diseases, or other temporary restrictions upon resources or life chances may result in sharp increases in mortality. New technology or more successful adaptations may also lead to needs for rapid reproduction. When this happens, restrictions on population growth tend to be removed and sometimes forgotten. The resulting increase in population may produce a situation in which there are more people than required for efficient operation of the cultural system and more people than the environment can conveniently support. The consequences of such unlimited increase are mass migration, famine, pestilence, or killing.

All cultural systems deal with the problem of having just enough, not too many or too few, warm bodies. The problem is complicated because changing environmental factors and technologies cause constant fluctuations in the size of populations and the need for bodies. Because children are born ten to twenty years before the need for them can be determined and because the number of children born depends upon the number of women who become pregnant, regulation of population requires a degree of knowledge, accurate prediction, and detailed calculation which no cultural system has achieved. For the United States, we do not know how many women have illegal abortions or how many die as a consequence of one. We do not know how many children die of neglect or beatings. We do not know in any detail how many people we need to man our institutions or to maintain our equilibrium with the environment, especially twenty years from now.

Human reproduction can be achieved with little training and vast enjoyment by almost any human male and female. Almost certainly, it was the puritanical belief that pain must follow pleasure which led Malthus to conclude that human societies must commit the sin of overpopulation and suffer the punishments of famine, disease, and genocidal war. Comparative examination of a variety of human societies suggests that although these deadly processes occur almost everywhere, their impact is lessened by more benign processes which limit human marriage and fertility. Once processes for the regulation of population have provided a reasonable balance between numbers of people and resources available, other processes are required to ensure the movement of people among the various subcultural systems within the society and the occupation of the various statuses provided within the social structure of each of these systems. What are the processes involved in the movement of people within and between cultural systems?

WHAT IF YOU WANT A MALE CHILD?

Each time a woman bears a child there is a 50 percent chance that it will be male. If a woman bears two children, there is a 25 percent chance (0.5 times 0.5) that both will be male. In thinking about such things as kinship terminologies and family structures, anthropologists like to visualize nuclear families composed of father, mother, son, and daughter. In real life, a host of factors may create situations in which a nuclear family household lacks a mother or a father or possesses two sons and no daughters. If the adequate operation of the tiny cultural system represented by the nuclear family requires that it be staffed by some particular set of people, severe problems are created by their absence.

In South India, according to one version of the cultural tradition, "A woman should have nine children and treat her husband as the tenth." Most women do not have such proverbial ambitions, but nearly all wish to have four or five children, and, because male children inherit the family farm and may often support the parents in their old age, most women wish to have one or two sons. Because household tasks such as bringing water from the well, grinding grain, and preparing food require large amounts of time, it is very difficult for a single individual to live alone and still have time to earn his living. As a kind of minimum, a household should consist of a working husband, a housewife, and a male heir. Any other condition threatens survival. Consider the following table representing all the households in a single jati in a South Indian village:

Household Number	Household Composition
1	husband, wife, 3 sons
2	husband, wife, 2 daughters
3	husband, wife, 2 sons, 2 daughters
4	husband, wife, 4 sons, 3 daughters
5	adult male
6	adult female
7	mother, 3 sons, 1 daughter
8	adult male, his mother, his sister, his sister's daughter, his sister's husband, his brother's wife
9	husband, wife, husband's father, husband's 3 sisters husband's 2 sister's daughters

Out of nine families, only three possess husband, wife, and male heirs. In Household 8, the role of the missing wife is filled by a mother and a brother's wife. In Household 8 and 9, the absence of male heirs has been attacked by bringing in women likely to produce sons. There are other things that can be done. If a wife is childless or produces only daughters, she can be divorced or a second wife, often the wife's sister, can be obtained. Where there are daughters and no sons, or where a household owns more land than can be worked by the existing number of sons, it is possible to "adopt" the daughter's husband. In former times, more rarely today, a daughter could be married to one of the deities. Following the marriage, she could have intercourse with persons of any respectable jati who contributed money to the temple of the deity. Her male offspring could inherit her father's property. A husband who suspected that he was responsible for the childlessness of his wife, might prevail upon a friend to have secret intercourse with his wife with the hope of producing a male heir.

A woman, living alone with her children, might rent her fields on a sharecropping basis to a brother or close relative or might earn a living through prostitution, concubinage, or the sale of cooked food. A single adult male would generally remarry as quickly as possible. During the interim, he might obtain cooked food from a neighbor or obtain a concubine, often belonging to another jati. A childless husband and wife might borrow or purchase a son, usually from a close relative. The roles played by missing or sick household members can be filled by visiting relatives or by hiring replacements.

All of these arrangements for the exchange of persons between households have to do with the regulation of membership, and all of them depend upon the existence of a larger cultural system which permits cooperation and the exchange of personnel between households. Because chance factors deeply affect the membership of households, means for the permanent or temporary exchange of personnel between households seem essential. Households tend to be linked together to form bands, neighborhoods, or communities which carry out, among other things, processes regulating the membership of households.

Can You Use Another Hand?

The following excerpt from the life history of a Nunivak Eskimo indicates how such processes may affect the individual:

> First thing I remember, I was riding in a sled, but I don't remember where I was going or whom I was with. Next thing I remember, I was living with an old couple. I thought they were my parents, but they were really my grandparents, I learned later. After a while, some children told me they were my grandparents. At first, I wouldn't believe them, but gradually I believed them.
>
> Then my grandfather died. That was the first time I had seen a dead person. I went to live with my father's sister named AMa'Gakh. She was poor and I had a very bad time while I was with her.
>
> I don't know how long I lived with my grandparents or with my aunt. Then Isaac Aiya-qsaq took me: he was my father's brother.
>
> When I went to Isaac, I learned for the first time that I had a real mother and real brother somewhere.
>
> I tried to help Isaac; I wanted to help him. But then Isaac died, the year the church was built. A year later, or a little more than a year later, I married Agnes, Lewis's daughter, Dick's sister, and I came to live with Lewis at Nash Harbor. Lewis's home was a good place. Lewis was like a father to me.

I have had four children. My little girl died of measles in 1942. I have three boys now (Lantis 1960:84–88).

The same sort of thing happens on Alor in Indonesia:

Once my mother wanted me to cut (clear) the fields, but I didn't want to, so she tied my hands together and left me in the house. I gnawed the rope through and ran away to Alurkoma (mother's mother's sister's husband, called grandfather). I lived with Alurkoma for about a year. But I thought about my mother's tying my hands, and so I got part of a knife blade and pounded it to make it hard and went to cut the field. When it was all cut and burned over, my father and mother came to plant it. Then I cared for the field myself and weeded it. When the food was ripening, my mother came to harvest it. I remember her tying may hands, and I said she could not take the food. She remembered how I had gnawed through the cord and ran away, and she said the crop was hers. She told me I could not cut her gardens any more, and if I wanted to cut gardens I had better go to my father's. She herself got the corn.

All this time I was living with Alurkoma. Alurkoma's wife, Tilamau, said I had better go work at Ruataug, where my father's garden was. So I went there to cut the garden. The first year I got a hundred bundles of maize and sold them in Likuwatang and bought a knife. The next year I got only forty bundles, the year after only thirty, the year after only twenty. Then I stopped working there. (Question) Mother and father lived together all this time. (How many years did you live with your grandparents?) Four years. (Then?) Then I returned to live with my mother and father. At this time I had a friend called Fanmale. We used to shoot at a banana trunk target. When Fanmale hit the target many times, I would beat him over the head with a bow. When I hit the target many times, he would hit me over the head with a bow. We were always quarreling. Then we said we had better stop target shooting. We stopped being friends, and I made friends with Malemani. I threw out Fanmale I was maybe twelve or thirteen at this time.

Malemani made a house in the fields. His mother was dead. Young men and women gathered. Girls and boys planned whom they would marry. They slept together in this house. The house was near the Limbur ravine. We played there for three years. I stayed there and didn't live with my mother and father. There were many gardens there and enough to eat.

After we had been there awhile I said, "We play only with women and do not think of anything else. Let us think of collecting a brideprice" (DuBois 1961:194–195).

During his childhood, Mangma, who gave the above account, lived with several other relatives including his father's first cousin:

I liked him because he took good care of me. Langmai had no wife. I followed him around, ran errands for him, getting areca, water, fire, tobacco, or whatever he sent me for. I was there alone with him. Langmai said, "My older brother has many children; you come and stay with me" (DuBois 1961:197).

A year later, Mangma went off to stay with another family. On Alor, in contrast to most human societies, the relationships between parents and children appear to be particularly fragile. This is reported to have an impact upon the kinds of people Alorese children turn out to be, and it may have great ecological importance in that it eliminates the role of chance factors in affecting household composition. An Alorese household can apparently contain whatever assortment of male and female children appears desirable at the moment.

ALL IN THE FAMILY?

Next to the human individual, the individual family household is the fundamental operating unit out of which most cultural systems are constructed. The chances of biology and the life chances of individuals war constantly upon the household, depriving it of needed members and interrupting its functioning. Processes of adoption, marriage, visiting, and employment mobilized within the larger cultural systems represented by bands, neighborhoods, and villages permit replacement of missing or ineffective household members and the continued effective functioning of the unit. Just as the human infant cannot survive without the support of human adults, so the human household cannot survive without the support of larger cultural systems. As households exchange their memberships in order to maintain themselves, a network of communication and interaction between households is established with the result that different households come to share virtually the same cultural tradition.

A community of interacting households may be quite small and it, too, is affected by the problem of getting the right person in the right place at the right time. Small and isolated communities tend to produce a large proportion of their memberships and to rely upon their internal processes for the staffing of the various statuses required for effective operation. More commonly neighborhoods and communities are engaged in wider processes for the permanent or temporary exchange of membership with other cultural systems. The following sections consider the special case of exchange between the city and the small community.

Where Have All the Young Men Gone?

The city of Bombay is located on a peninsula which forms one of the largest and most beautiful harbors in the world. To this harbor come ships laden with the oil, manufactured products, and foodstuffs of Europe and the Near East. Foreign and domestic industrial concerns build their factories and the stately mansions of their managers here. Because the penin-

sula is small and because factories and stately mansions require considerable space, Bombay, like Manhattan Island or San Francisco, is crowded.

Men who work as laborers in the city take up their residence in crowded slums with unpaved streets. The flushing toilet is unknown; there is no garbage disposal, running water, electricity, or municipal service of any kind. The climate of Bombay is warm and wet and people shelter themselves in impromptu shacks just large enough to contain a bed and a one-burner kerosene stove. To get to work in the morning, the factory worker puts on hip length rubber boots and wades, sometimes for miles, through the mixture of feces and garbage constituting his environment. People who are unable to obtain factory jobs which permit them to buy or rent shacks may find employment in stone quarries located outside the city. Here, there is slightly better housing, trees, and an occasional blade of grass. The barefoot, barehanded worker, his wife, and children gather rocks dynamited from a cliff-face and load them into trucks.

People come to Bombay from the village of Gopalpur, three hundred miles away, for a variety of reasons, but mostly because they are poor and even the stone quarries pay a wage four times larger than can be obtained in the village. Although the population of Gopalpur has grown very slowly and there have been few changes in the village or its region over the past

FIGURE 7–7 This particular rock crusher in Bombay is the source of the cash that is transforming agriculture in Gopalpur, South India. (PHOTO BY ALAN R. BEALS)

years, people have had an increasingly difficult time maintaining their traditional forms of agriculture. Traditionally this depended upon the presence of a kind of landed aristocracy, which made agricultural loans available to the community and preserved wealth in the form of stored grain that could be released to clients in time of need. With modernization, the rural aristocracy began to move to urban areas and to use their resources for such personal benefits as the education of their children. Over the past two decades, those aristocrats who remained have begun to purchase tractors, jeeps, and other equipment with which to farm their own large acreages. Gopalpur lies, then, in the center of an increasing competition between industrialized farmers and peasant farmers. For the moment, the poor people of Gopalpur maintain their traditional form of agriculture and their competitive position by importing money from Bombay.

For many individuals the traditional form of peasant agriculture has become a kind of hobby supported by remittances from the city. Typically a man works in the city until he manages to save enough money to marry. Leaving his wife and children in the village or, in some cases taking them with him, he returns to the city until he earns enough money to buy land and cattle. His sons then plow the land until they, in turn, require money for their marriages and for expansion of the family agriculture. Permanent emigration to Bombay, while it takes place in some cases, is ruled out by the abysmal living conditions there. Many find it impossible to support their wives and children in the city, and, even if they take their wives, they often find it necessary to leave some or all of their children with grandparents or other relatives. There is a tendency for Gopalpur to become a village of children and old people with most of its young and middle-aged men living in the city.

For many families, the bright promise of a few years spent working in Bombay is marred by susceptibility to fatal and contagious diseases. In one family of Muslims, two brothers emigrated to Bombay and obtained prestigious jobs working in the railroad yards. A younger brother was left behind to care for the agricultural properties and the aged parents. In due time, one of the older brothers sent back his daughter who had contracted tuberculosis of the bone. Daily, the younger brother carried his niece to the dispensary two miles away, but one day, as we started out with our notebooks, we passed him in the Muslim cemetery. He had buried his niece quietly in the cold dawn and was weeping silently while he smoothed and decorated the mud over her grave. In another family, one of the young sons returned from Bombay with tuberculosis. The disease spread through his family, the search for wealth in Bombay ending in the death not only of the son but of most of the members of his household as well. For Gopalpur, the city of Bombay may well represent a kind of ecological trap into which she must pour her young men and thereby

FIGURE 7–8 They hate the work, the housing, the city, and the people. Bruised by the stones, underfed, and weary, they come because the pay is four times what they can earn in Gopalpur, South India. (PHOTO BY ALAN R. BEALS)

maintain a precarious existence between the tractor on the one hand and the cesspools of Bombay on the other.

Where Else Does This Happen?

The movement of rural populations to urban areas has an ancient history. An old Tamil (South Indian) poem translated by Dr. K. Gnanambal describes a city where the rain is falling and the entire population cowering indoors beside the glowing hearth. Everyone, that is, except the Greek mercenaries who are wandering about in the rain, singing and drinking wine. Perhaps, like the men of Gopalpur, they were thinking about wives and children left behind on rocky and unproductive farmsteads.

The following advertisements appeared in the *American Weekly Mercury* of February 18 and May 22, 1729:

> Lately arrived from London, a parcel of very likely English servants, men and women, several of the men Tradesmen; to be sold reasonable and Time allowed for payment.

> There is just arrived from Scotland, a parcel of choice, *Scotch Servants*; Taylors, Weavers, Shoemakers and ploughmen, some for five and others for seven years; . . . (Quoted in Parrington 1927, 1930:134).

With a few changes in working conditions and in the definition of terms, the North American territories have continued to require cheap labor:

> The most dramatic occupational change and one which has become a major new source of income to the village is the *bracero* movement. In 1948, fewer than thirty Tepoztecans were *braceros*—that is, temporary agricultural workers

in the United States; by 1957, over six hundred men had been *braceros* for periods that varied from forty-five days to over a year. This occupational change has made for other great changes in the village. In 1943, Tepoztlán suffered from an acute land shortage. Now, because in many cases the *braceros* return to the village only to rest a few months before setting out for another period in the United States, it suffers from a shortage of manpower, and many *milpas* go uncultivated (Lewis 1960:97–98).

In Ireland, parts of India, Scandinavia, Greece, Central Asia, all over the world, younger brothers hear of far-off places they will never visit; spinsters wait patiently beside hearths grown cold. A community of old people, women, and children wait for lovers who have gone to war, sons migrated to America, or older brothers working in the factories. In some cases, overcrowded communities become residual communities occupied by grandparents, mothers, and children while the able-bodied men serve in distant wars or factories returning in their old age to retire and raise their now departed children's children.

The above examples deal with the special case in which rural communities producing a surplus of population maintain an integration with urban communities by exchanging their young men for retired factory workers or soldiers. Such a condition is most likely to obtain when new territories, new occupations, or high urban death rates create a population shortage in urban centers. There are many other devices for the exchange of population between communities. One of them is marriage.

MARRIAGE: WHO SHALL BE CHOSEN?

Marriage, and practices affecting the likelihood of marriage, may play an important role in determining who shall bear children. It is also an important means of regulating the exchange of persons between households and the creation of new households. At this level, incest taboos, forbidding sexual and/or marital relationships among members of the household, have the effect of compelling exchanges between households. Exogamous rules forbidding marriage with particular individuals or classes of individuals and endogamous rules requiring marriage within particular groups or classes, place further limitations upon marriage. Rules that the bride or groom must be beautiful or hardworking or a college graduate or older or younger also work to control the movement of individuals by marriage. Consider the situation in the French village of Peyrane:

By the time young people are ready to marry they are acquainted with other young people from the whole area of the Apt Basin and even from more distant parts of the department. Family connections, visits, *promenades*, and, above all, the dances which they have attended have enlarged their circle of acquaintances beyond the limits of Peyrane.

Choosing a husband or wife from among these acquaintances is limited by both legal and popular restrictions. It is forbidden by law to marry a lineal relative, whether the relationship is legitimate or illegitimate, whether the relationship is by blood, marriage, or legal adoption. Marriage is also forbidden between brother and sister, uncle and niece, aunt and nephew, brother-in-law and sister-in-law (if divorced). . . . Popular and canonical restrictions go even one step further, to forbid marriage between first cousins. . . .

It may be that a common but less recognized prejudice still further limits the field of choice; young people apparently prefer to find a spouse living beyond the boundaries of the commune rather than to marry someone from the village whom they have always known. Unfortunately, the census records are incomplete on this point, so that we cannot know exactly to what extent people go outside of Peyrane to find a spouse. Of the eighty-two married couples for whom we have information, only seven were endogamous [both spouses from village] and seventy-five were exogamous [one spouse from outside the village] (Wylie 1964:124).

In addition the girl's father must give his consent to the marriage. He does this when the family feels that the young couple are truly in "love" and that both are *serieux*. Being *serieux* involves fidelity, hard work, frugality, and a host of other virtues. Because "a fool and his money are soon parted," the present financial status of the prospective bridegroom is not stressed. On the other hand, a father is unlikely to approve his daughter's marriage unless the prospective bridegroom has some means of support and the couple has a place to live. In order to get married, then, a young man has to establish himself economically. This process is usually delayed because the young man must complete his military service before his marriage. The period of military service begins at the age of twenty, and a considerable time elapses before a young man completes his military service, establishes himself in an occupation, and locates the right girl.

Although a young man may inherit a family farm and therefore bring his wife to his family homestead, such patrilocal residence is often impossible. Whether the new family lives patrilocally, matrilocally (with the wife's family) or neolocally (in a new place), depends upon the availability of occupations and houses. Thus, the concept of *serieux* requires the bride and groom to establish themselves in some location where they may be productively employed. The marriage pattern, then, creates a system for the exchange of brides and grooms between communities, and, by influencing the residence of the bride and groom, it adjusts the population of each community to the available resources. Complaining about the effect of military service upon marriage, Wylie states: "The State loses far more in economic productivity and a lower birth rate than it gains from their services [in the military]." On the other hand, France has been relatively free of overpopulation or high rates of unemployment.

In Peyrane, marriage and the selection of a place to live after a marriage depend primarily upon the earning capacity of the bridegroom. It is a fair guess that the goal of establishing a lasting relationship upon a sound economic foundation is fundamental to all systems of marriage. The individual who embarks upon the process of "getting married" or more likely upon the process of "arranging someone else's marriage" follows a complicated decision-making process which determines who shall be married and where the married couple will take up residence. Consider the preliminary steps involved in entering into the marital search procedure in South India (See Figure 7–11).

When Do We Search for the Bride?

The groom's father, uncle, or older brother must be prevailed upon to set in motion a process of bride-search which will ultimately lead to a costly marriage followed sooner or later by division of the family property. Faced with the prospect of considerable expense and the loss of a hardworking adult member of the household, prospective arrangers naturally prefer to

FIGURE 7–9 The brides are absent, but their brothers are present. A bridegroom should be strong and a willing worker. Gopalpur, South India. (PHOTO BY ALAN R. BEALS)

delay a young man's wedding as long as possible, preferably until the bridegroom become increasingly rowdy and bumptious. His work suffers and he spends his nights womanizing, drinking, and/or gambling. Normally this sort of behavior indicates to the arranger that the groom is ready for marriage, and the arranger commences to search for a suitable bride. Where the arranger has decided that there will be no marriage or that the marriage must be delayed, he may try to control the groom's behavior by force, by reason, or by getting rid of him altogether. Both the arranger and the groom may speak to friends and neighbors thereby setting in motion a process of negotiation and arbitration which may ultimately reconcile their differences. Where a lack of cash and other resources makes immediate marriage impracticable, the groom may go to the city or elsewhere to seek a job or he may indenture himself to a wealthy landlord in order to obtain the cash needed for his marriage. Sometimes, not shown in Figure 7.11, the interest and other charges due the landlord are so high that the groom or his family never receive any cash and the groom works the rest of his life to pay off his debts. In most cases the bride-search ultimately begins and the bridegroom ultimately obtains a bride.

The bride-search is influenced by the fact that the ideal bride, in addition to being beautiful, hardworking, and astrologically correct, should be related to the groom as a mother's brother's daughter, father's sister's daughter, or sister's daughter. Because landed property is handed down within a joint family consisting of the male descendants and younger brothers of the family head, residence after marriage is generally within the groom's joint family. Further, in any small caste or jati all of the households in the village are likely to belong to the same exogamous lineage. Very often all of the women in the village in the groom's jati are considered to be his "sisters." Except where two or more lineages within a village exchange daughters, marriages tend to involve bringing in a woman from another village.

Granted that the groom's mother would like to see her brother's daughter brought into the family, it stands to reason that she would argue in favor of mother's brother's daughter marriage. Now, and here we return to the subject of this chapter, if both the mother and the son's wife come from Village A to Village B, a one-way flow of women from A to B is established. Cash, the "brideprice," flows in the reverse direction from B to A. If we assume that the groom's father wishes to continue and maintain relationships with his sister, and brothers and sisters are considered very close, then the father's sister goes from A to B and the groom's wife goes from B to A. In other words, there is an exchange of women between the two villages, and also an exchange of cash. A similar condition of equal exchange exists when the groom marries his sister's daughter.

Let us go a little further and assume that Village B is a wealthy village where some families have more land than they know what to do with and

FIGURE 7–10   South Indian marriage.

that Village A is a poor village where some families have no land at all. Because a wife from a poor family will work harder and be less critical of her husband's house, the wealthy families from Village B will naturally wish to acquire women from Village A, while the poor families in Village A will shun women from Village B. Mother's brother's daughter marriage now becomes the favored form of marriage between the two villages. Being wealthy and faced with a shortage of labor, some of the fathers in Village B are likely to decide to obtain their sons-in-law as well as their daughters-in-law from Village A. Now, both mother's brother's daughters and mother's brother's sons are being brought into Village B and the population of Village A is declining. Ultimately, this movement of population would tend to wipe out the economic differential between the two villages and a pattern of sister's daughter or father's sister's daughter marriage might develop as a means of maintaining the restored economic and population equilibrium.

Although in real life, the patterns of marriage in South India are more complicated than the above description suggests, the system as a whole functions as a means of maintaining a good fit between the resources available to a village and the numbers of men and women living in it. In

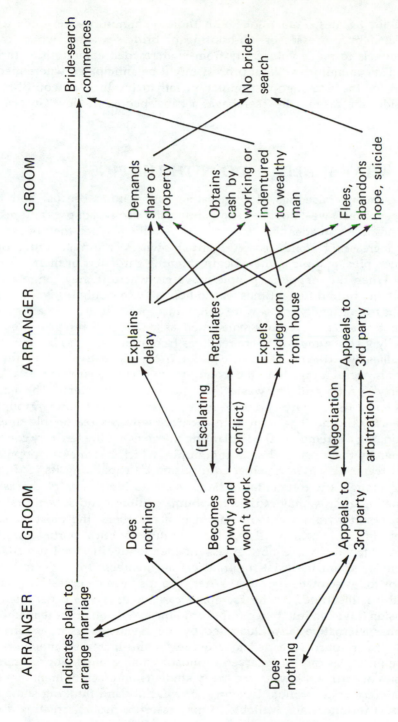

FIGURE 7-11 A fragment of a process: Initiating the search for a bride.

the United States, France, or South India, community size tends to be regulated by processes of job-hunting or bride-searching which cause individuals to move voluntarily from overcrowded communities to less crowded communities. What process might be anticipated where mechanisms for the exchange of population fail to produce an equilibrium? Consider the case of the Tsembaga, a tribal people in New Guinea.

WHAT SHALL WE DO WITH THE PIGS?

The Tsembaga raise pigs, sweet potatoes, and manioc. Because both pigs and people eat sweet potatoes and manioc, the survival of pigs and people depends upon an adequate balance between them. When the pig population increases beyond reason, garden owners begin shooting other people's pigs, and pig owners begin shooting gardeners or their wives or pigs. When this happens, people move elsewhere if they can. Another possibility in traditional times was to hold a *Kaiko* or pig festival wherein groups from friendly tribes were entertained periodically over a period of about a year and everyone consumed as much pork as possible. The friendly visitors, most of them relatives from other groups, became military allies by virtue of their participation in the pig festival. When the pig festivals were completed, the community was prepared to attack an "enemy" group and lay waste their houses and gardens. The enemy abandoned its territory and took up residence among friendly groups. If the enemy did not lay claim to its territory within a reasonable time by performing a ceremony called "planting the *rumbin*," the territory could be claimed by the victors. Thus, a community which became overpopulated could regain its environmental equilibrium by expanding its territory.

Although environmental hazards, such as high rates of disease or competing groups, may cause a few human cultural and subcultural systems to suffer from a chronic shortage of members, the most common pattern is one in which tribes, villages, clubs, political parties, or other groups fluctuate in size more or less independently. In a well-run cultural system, mechanisms exist for transferring members from overcrowded groups to less crowded groups. Where groups become excessively large, and this is illustrated by the Tsembaga case, conflict may occur resulting in fission (division into two groups) or in the expulsion of some members. Another alternative, also illustrated by the Tsembaga, is to acquire the additional resources needed to provide for the increased membership. These processes can be observed in most human groups. For example, a physics department having too many students and faculty members may introduce tougher standards, firing some faculty and flunking some students. If resources are available, it may resort to fission, creating a new department of biophysics. It may also grow by taking over the resources of some other department which has been unsuccessful in recruiting students. The specific processes used in the regulation of the population of physics departments are different from those used in Peyrane, South India, or among the Tsembaga. One of the key questions for anthropology, then, is to consider the range of possible ways of regulating group size and the kinds of impact they have on the people who use them.

SUMMARY

Cultural systems exist by virtue of the fact that their cultural messages appeal to people in sufficient numbers to staff the various statuses required for the operation of the cultural system. A complete cultural system or society has the capacity of producing its own membership as well as obtaining members from other cultural systems. Human reproduction is the fundamental requirement before any other systems of population regulation can be brought into play.

In 1798, Malthus made appropriate calculations and recognized the tremendous potentialities for the rapid increase of human populations. In recent centuries and decades, the growth of world population has approached Malthusian rapidity. Only in the last decade or two has the increase of the human population perceptibly slowed. This is due to increasing recognition of the dangers of limitless population increase and may represent a universal human tendency to develop means of regulating population short of the famine, pestilence and mass killing feared by Malthus.

Traditional human societies such as those of Tikopia, Ireland, and South India practiced effective but not always perfect means of population regulation. Such regulation does not prevent famine, pestilence or mass killing, but it reduces their frequency. Such traditional means of regulating population operate before marriage takes place by maintaining a high cost of marriage, institutionalizing various forms of spinsterhood or abstention from marriage, or subjecting some individuals to poor medical care, malnutrition, or drug abuse. Once married, the high cost of children or the presence of numerous other children may lead to abstention from sex, interrupted sexual intercourse, or the use of contraceptive techniques. When these fail, abortion, infanticide, or child neglect are employed. Surplus adults or older children may be starved or driven away, or a pattern of migration may be established. If population continues to grow, the inevitable results are famine, pestilence, or mass killing.

Even when birth and death rates maintain a stable population, problems remain. An example from South India illustrates the difficulties involved in maintaining households of appropriate size. The cultural tradition offers a number of processes that can be employed in order to remedy lack of husband, wife, male child or daughter. The Nunivak Eskimo and the Alorese freely exchange children between families. Processes of adoption, marriage, visiting, and employment are required to maintain functioning household units. The inability of a family household to maintain a consistent population structure helps to explain why even the smallest human societies involve a number of cooperating households.

In addition to systematic exchange between households, there is a constant movement of people from one social unit to another. Examples from Gopalpur in South India, ancient India and Greece, and the United States illustrate the general process of migration and return from rural areas to places where there is a shortage of labor. Examples from Peyrane and South India explore the manner in which complex systems of bride-search and marriage may act as a means of adjusting community populations to their resources.

Where the absence of an overarching political and social system places difficulties in the way of exchanges of population between communities, warfare between neighboring communities, illustrated by the case of the Tsembaga, may serve as a means of enlarging the territories of overpopulated communities. In sum, where mechanisms for the regulation of population fail to operate through the exchange of population between groups, groups that become excessively large may either undergo processes of fission or processes for enlarging the resources available to them.

For Further Reading

The growth and decline of world population is a frequent topic of discussion in such journals as *Science* and *Scientific American. Population, Resources, Environment* (Ehrlich and Ehrlich 1972) is a useful recent summary of the issues in this field. *Culture and Human Fertility* (Lorimer 1954) remains the principal source for anthropological discussions of population regulation.

Man, the Hunter (Lee and DeVore 1969) provides discussion of population regulation among hunter-collectors. Lee has also edited a volume dealing with *Population Patterns in the Past* (1977). Other materials include Polgar's *Culture and Population* (1971) and Spooner's *Population Growth, Anthropological Implications* (1972).

Relevant Case Studies include Beals' *Gopalpur* (1962), von Fürer-Haimendorf's *The Konyak Nagas* (1969), Messenger's *Inis Beag: Isle of Ireland* (1969), Deng's *The Dinka* (1972), Horwitz's *Morne-Paysan*, and the Halperns' *A Serbian Village in Historical Perspective* (1972).

Problems and Questions

1. Collect some evidence concerning premarital search procedures in your own tribe or group. What sort of impact do these procedures have in determining who shall be married or in influencing the frequency of marriage?

2. Examine census figures for any nation or set of nations. What are some factors that seem to affect fertility and mortality?
3. Examine several ethnographies and compare the methods used to regulate household membership. To what extent does the maintenance of household membership involve the exchange of members among households, communities, and other groupings?
4. Obtain some figures concerning household composition in a neighborhood or other grouping of people. What are the mechanisms that regulate household size and composition?
5. For any organization or group in your own society, what are some of the ways in which resources, jobs, and opportunities are allocated? Can you think of a better way?

SYMBOLIC MESSAGES
AND RITUAL PROCESSES

What shall we ask about such things?

Maintaining satisfactory relationships with an environment and recruiting or producing a sufficient number of members are so essential that there is little need to wonder why women dig up arrowroot or why fathers, if they aren't busy hunting or plowing, take care of children while the women work. There are a great many activities in society which are not so obviously necessary. Why, for example, must one pray before eating? Why, in parts of the rural United States, is it necessary to "pass the time of day" before obtaining gasoline or groceries? Why must a substantial part of the gross national product of the United States be used in the celebration of Christmas?

The basic argument of this chapter is that as hens cluck and meadowlarks sing, so humans conduct simple, ordinary, and lavish rituals. We consider Raymond and Stewart climbing trees. What part of their behavior has to do with climbing trees? What part of it consists of interaction rituals that define and maintain relationships among Raymond, Stewart, and the not-to-be-forgotten graduate student in psychology lurking in the background? We attend next to the ritual desecration of Dr. Pouissant and to the questions of ritual deference and demeanor. Subtle choice of words and tiny gestures constitute the unnoticed rituals that accompany every moment of human life.

But to what extent are words, gestures, and symbols to be considered

220

automatic and innate? How universal is the subtle language of body movements, symbolic gestures, and ceremonial enactments. In the United States, the rituals of Christmas are numerous and infinitely symbolic. The example of Christmas illustrates that people are unable to say what their own symbols mean to them. Discovering the hidden meanings of ritual symbols is a difficult task. What, for example, are the meanings that people in the United States attach to varying degrees of distance between self and other?

Rituals redefine relationships and so create changes in the things people do and in the way they think about the things they do. The Hopi Powamu ceremony introduces questions about why rituals are performed and what their effects upon the individual might possibly be. Can we think of rituals, especially initiation ceremonies and other rites of passage, as the traditional equivalent of brainwashing and/or education? If so, what are some of the techniques likely to be used?

One of the common opinions about rituals is that they promote social integration. Because almost any activity carried out in accordance with the cultural message is likely to strengthen social integration. This may not be particularly exciting. The example of marriage ceremonies in South India provides a means of thinking about if and whether a set of marriage rituals contribute to the strengthening of the marriage.

But many rituals do not seem useful. Some are expensive, time consuming, and apparently without practical effect. The possible value of Saora marriage to tutelary spirits is considered. Are healing rituals part of the cure or are they a disease in themselves? A final question, illustrated by an examination of wedding ceremonies in Tenejapa, concerns the extent to which rituals can be expected to vary from the ideal. Are rituals, especially religious rituals, a matter of rigid conformity, a time when individualism runs rampant, or both? This chapter has to do with those clucks, songs, speeches, and rituals that seem so superfluous, but may not be.

WHAT GOOD IS THE SONG OF THE MEADOWLARK?

In the morning chickens feed in the village street, scratching in the dirt and clucking. At a hint of movement in the sky above, the rooster puffs up to twice his normal size and dashes through the flock screaming, "hawk, hawk." Silently the hens scuttle to safety. This trivial incident demonstrates the value of social life and its essence. Although there may be an adaptive value in clustering large numbers of plants or animals of the same species in one place, the central adaptive strategy of most social animals revolves around communication and cooperation. The rooster keeps watch and gives warning. The hens obey, and the hawk looks elsewhere for its dinner.

It is not hard to assign meaning to the rooster's cry of warning. Other animal sounds, like the song of the meadowlark, have a less obvious meaning. If the meadowlark merely wishes to establish his identity and location—his status if you like—why doesn't he, for it is he that does the singing, cluck like a chicken? For that matter, does the chicken's cluck say, "I am here and all's well," or is it done merely in aid of digestion. Perhaps, if we could talk to chickens, they would have an answer. If they are at all like human beings, they probably do not know why they do what they do. If they did they might not tell an anthropologist.

In this book, much of what human beings do is discussed from a utilitarian perspective. Working through their cultural systems, human beings carry out a variety of useful activities or processes. "Hunting a wallaby," "planting corn," or even "arranging a marriage," can be conceived in utilitarian terms as means of obtaining food or regulating population. In the practical business of planting corn, we observe people interrupting their activity with horseplay, idle gossip, bursts of song, or even elaborate rituals and prayers claimed essential for the germination of the seeds or the bringing of rain. One of the most challenging problems in anthropology is the search for explanations of human activities that seem meaningless or impractical and that the ordinary person usually cannot explain. Why do

FIGURE 8–1   In honor of the god, Shiva, bullocks are decorated and taken in procession through the village. The ritual confirms the status of the bullock as sacred animal and partner in agriculture. Namhalli, South India. (PHOTO BY ALAN R. BEALS)

you sing excerpts from *La Traviata* in the shower? Why do you celebrate Christmas?

Although a great deal of human activity can be explained by the hypothesis that human beings, like chickens, are foolish creatures, most anthropologists cling to the idea that there must be method in such madness. Many human performances which seem necessary, yet seem to have little relevance to such practical matters as earning a living or reproducing the species, may have to do with the regulation of relationships within and between groups of people. If processes for the regulation of membership have the practical effect of ensuring the presence of the warm bodies needed for the various groups and task forces required for the operation of a cultural system, then another class of processes seems to be required to inform individuals concerning their membership status, the nature of the ongoing activity, and the presence and status of other members or groups. Some of these processes, like the prayer for rain which initiates the corn planting process, are parts of other processes, but others, like a high school graduation, seem almost entirely devoted to announcing and confirming status. The prayer for rain, while it could be regarded as a means of symbolizing the beginning of the corn planting process, might also be regarded as a morale boosting device that promises future status as successful corn planters to the supplicants.

Because singing in the shower or praying for rain has no easily identified practical purpose and because people are nevertheless inclined to feel that such activities are necessary, they come under the general heading of ritual. A *ritual* is an oft-repeated action lacking any obvious practical consequence yet stimulating discomfort or anxiety when it is not performed. A complicated and highly formalized ritual is often referred to as a *ceremony*, but anthropologists are not in general agreement concerning these definitions. A ritual, such as a prayer for rain, which takes cognizance of awesome or supernatural forces can be defined as a *religious* rather than a *secular* ritual. Here some anthropologists would define religion as having to do with a state of mind that regards some things as sacred or awesome, while others would rest their definition on a Western and presumably scientific distinction between the natural or "real" world and the supernatural world.

Rituals can be further defined in terms of the people they involve: personal, interpersonal, familial, community, tribal, intertribal, and so on; or they may be defined in terms of the kinds of events that cause them to take place. Thus, *rites of passage* mark stages in the life cycle of the individual such as birth, puberty, marriage, and death; *calendrical ceremonies* mark stages in the annual cycle of activities; and *crisis rituals* mark periods of illness, famine, or catastrophe. The simplest, most common, and least understood kinds of rituals are those interpersonal rituals that mark the day-to-day interaction of human individuals. What is the nature of such rituals? Can they be detected in an ordinary description of behavior such as the following?

WHO'S WHO AND WHAT'S GOING ON?

Suddenly Raymond ran *eagerly* to another tree.
He started climbing the tree with great energy.
He remarked *in an offhand way*, but with slight emphasis on the second word, "I hope I can climb this tree." *He seemed to say this to himself as a form of encouragement.*
In a high pitched, soft sing-song he said, "I hope, I hope, I hope."
Raymond continued climbing the tree, *cautiously* grasping one branch and then another, and fixing his feet firmly.
He called out to Stewart in a *playfully boastful manner*, "Stewart, this tree is harder to climb than the other one."
Stewart called back *very firmly and definitely*, "No, it isn't."
When Raymond was as high as it seemed safe to climb, he settled in a crotch of the tree with his hands gripped tightly around the branches.
Exuberantly he sang out, "Owww, owww, whee. Do you see me?" (Barker and Wright 1955:207).

In the above episode, the performances of Raymond and Stewart can easily be interpreted as representative of one of the processes characteristic of a particular cultural system. It can be given the label, "tree climbing process" and classified under the general heading of "children's play." In utilitarian or practical terms, the tree climbing process can be interpreted as a means of developing physical skills which will be useful in adult life. Because the observer has tended to ignore the problem of communication between Stewart and Raymond and, in particular, has only summarized their nonverbal communications, it is more difficult to understand and to "see" the interaction rituals that form a part of the tree climbing process. When Raymond runs "eagerly" to the tree and says, "I hope I can climb this tree," he seems to be performing a ritual which changes his status from that of a person watching Stewart climb a tree to that of a tree climbing person. When he says his tree is harder to climb, he seems to be establishing status as Stewart's competitor.

Raymond's assertions of his status with regard to Stewart are necessary if the tree climbing process is to be a social act. What is missing from this example, as it must be from most examples of human behavior, is the presence of the anxiety that would exist if the rituals were improperly performed. The more subtle rituals, especially those performed every day, tend to be invisible both to performers and observers simply because they are performed constantly. Is it really fair to classify Raymond's eagerness as a ritual and to give it the same significance as a prayer for rain? One approach to this problem is to consider what happens when two individuals meet and both perform inappropriate rituals.

AM I NOT SACRED, TOO?

Once last year as I was leaving my office in Jackson, Miss., with my Negro secretary, a White policeman yelled, "Hey, boy! Come here." Somewhat bothered, I retorted: "I'm no boy!" He then rushed at me, inflamed, and stood towering over me, snorting "What dija say, boy?" Quickly he frisked me and demanded, "What's your name, boy?" Frightened, I replied, "Dr. Pouissant. I'm a physician." He angrily chuckled and hissed, "What's your first name, boy?" When I hesitated he assumed a threatening stance and clenched his fists. As my heart palpitated, I muttered in profound humiliation "Alvin."

He continued his psychological brutality, bellowing, "Alvin, the next time I call you, you come right away, you hear?" I hesitated. "You hear me, boy?" My voice trembling with helplessness, but following my instincts of self-preservation, I murmured, "Yes sir." Now fully satisfied that I had performed and acquiesced to my "boy" status, he dismissed me with, "Now, boy, go on and get out of here or next time we'll take you for a little ride down to the station house!" (Kochman 1971:67–68).

Here, the incident was almost certainly triggered by some improper aspect of Dr. Pouissant's demeanor. *Demeanor* is a term used by Erving Goffman (1967:56–84) to describe the manner in which one individual

presents himself to another. Dr. Pouissant's demeanor involved his physical appearance as a "Negro" combined with costume and gestures which may have reflected his status as a physician or a middle-class person. Dr. Pouissant's demeanor may have involved a breach of ritual etiquette which demanded that Negroes dress and act poor. Dr. Pouissant's demeanor, then, was a profanation or defilement of the policeman's sacred values comparable to that which might occur if a minister preached a sermon in his undershorts.

Goffman defines the proper exchange or rituals indicative of regard for the status of other individuals as *deference*. In this case, Dr. Pouissant further profaned the policeman's sacred values by claiming, first, an equal status as an adult, and, second, a superior status as a physician. This is what Goffman defines as *ceremonial profanation*. In response, the policemen brutally invaded Dr. Pouissant's personal space and destroyed his ritual status by touching (frisking) him. The normal and ceremonious conduct of everyday life depends upon deference, the tender and ritual regard which each person exhibits toward all other persons. Because interaction rituals are performed automatically without thought ("Good morning, how are you?" "I'm fine."), people are generally unaware of their ritual nature, the fact that they are performing them, or their precise meaning. In linguistic terms, "How are you?" seems to call for a medical report, but, in fact, its real meaning is closer to "I know and recognize you; do you know and recognize me?" Regardless of medical circumstances, the proper answer is "Fine." All rituals, including interaction rituals, involve the use of symbolic actions, gestures, objects, and words that seem to be meaningful but whose meaning is often unknown to the performer. How are such symbolic codes to be interpreted and understood?

What Does an Eyebrow Flash Mean?

The accompanying drawings illustrate a widely distributed human gesture known as an "eyebrow flash." According to Eibl-Eibesfeldt (1970:420), the eyebrow flash occurs in a variety of widely distributed

cultures as a part of the ritual of greeting expressing the fact that the greeter is in an especially good mood. How is the widespread distribution of the eyebrow flash to be explained? Eibl-Eibesfeldt feels that the eyebrow flash and various other gestures such as nodding, bowing, or smiling may derive in whole or part from a biologically rather than culturally inherited system of communication. Such gestures might be viewed as representing aspects of a prehuman or prelinguistic system of communication which, since it is biologically inherited, could be expected to be universally present among human beings. Because particular cultural systems might train their members to avoid smiles or eyebrow flashes or to use such gestures in highly restricted ways, Eibl-Eibesfeldt does not expect that the same gestures would have the same meanings in all human groups: "We know that innate behavior patterns can be suppressed by training" (1970:424). The facts of the case seem to be that interaction rituals tend to involve gestures and body movements many of which seem to have similar meanings in widely separated human cultures.

Some authors believe that widely distributed similarities of meaning are common to other rituals as well. Initiation rituals seem often to involve death and rebirth and there is an accompanying symbolism of doors and arches through which the novices must pass in order to be reborn as members after they have been ritually slain. Bruno Bettelheim (1954) suspects that operations upon the male or female genitals practiced during initiation rituals reflect universal envy (see Foster 1972) of members of the opposite sex. Others have argued that such operations are likely to cause sterility or death and are therefore a clever means of controlling population. The opposite point, that the operations, usually performed at puberty or a few years before, are designed to increase sexual awareness and potency has also been made. Some small but statistically significant correlations seem to indicate a relationship between permissive child rearing and the need to assert adult dominance by severely chastizing young initiates.

Whenever a human characteristic is widely distributed about the world, there are always some individuals who insist that it must therefore be biological in origin. Puberty and sex, even though deeply affected by such cultural factors as nutrition and training, are unquestionably biological. Initiation rituals held at the time of puberty, many are held long before or after, certainly are triggered by the human biological clock. We understand the biological basis of puberty. Much less is known about the basis of rituals of circumcision, and they are not nearly as common as puberty itself. There may be some universal symbolism to genital operations or they may simply represent an idea that is very old and therefore very widespread. All human beings make use of fire; one or two groups of humans have been reported unable to make it. Is there a connection between human biology and the ability to use fire? It certainly helps to have fingers. Fires symbolize warmth and togetherness in many cultures and play an important part in many rituals. Because fires have the universal property of creating sensations of warmth, we can predict a universal symbolism in which fires represent warmth, not cold. But what about all of the other things that fires mean? How can we relate the arbitrariness of human language to the fact that so many symbols seem "natural" or inevitable. What does a snake symbolize or a pot?

IS THE SYMBOL CULTURAL OR BIOLOGICAL?

Because of their common biology and the universal possession of languages and cultural systems, human beings share a great many experiences so that there are widespread similarities in the meanings attached to different things and particularly to the symbols in rituals. It is hardly startling to discover that arrows are masculine or that pots are feminine. Feces, blood, and dead things often symbolize danger and pollution. If you ask someone to indicate the direction from which the sun rises, it is obvious that he is going to have to point with his finger, or his lips, or his

FIGURE 8–4 "Basavanna is our mother." The great god Shiva first came to earth as a wild buffalo, then as a bullock, and finally as a man. The image of Basavanna symbolizes the divine concern that provided human beings with the sacred cattle that pull the plow, give milk, provide fertilizer, offer leather for sandals, and, finally, meat for the poor. (PHOTO BY ALAN R. BEALS)

chin or in one of the limited number of ways in which direction may be indicated. The shape of the human body and the distribution of human muscles place restraints on the manner in which pointing may be conveniently carried out and even if our man points awkwardly from our viewpoint with his shoulder or with his elbow, we are likely to get the message. Is the message, therefore, biological or is it cultural?

The United States' Christmas ritual involves eggnog, Christmas trees, ornaments, Yule logs, the Virgin and Child, and the colors red and green. Do these things have a universal symbolic meaning? Could we say that eggnog symbolizes mother's milk, that the evergreen tree symbolizes life everlasting, that the ornaments symbolize fruitfulness, that the Yule log symbolizes the eternal flame of life, that the Virgin and Child symbolize fruitfulness, that red symbolizes menstrual blood, and the green symbolizes life and vegetation? If so, we could interpret the symbols of Christmas as having to do with fertility or with life and death in some way. The point is, we are just guessing. Perhaps the color red symbolizes death and red and green together symbolize death and rebirth.

How Do We Know What the Symbols Mean?

One of the best ways of finding out what things mean is to ask people. Imagine, then, walking up to a United States citizen and saying: "What is the meaning of eggnog?" or "What does an eyebrow flash mean?" The hidden significance of eggnog, if it has a hidden significance, can only be understood in the context of the whole system of meanings that the members of a cultural system use in the communication of ideas and feelings. One way to begin to understand eggnog, for example, would be to examine the various ritual contexts within which the consumption of various drinks occurs. Or, since eggnog is more or less white, we might consider the various ritual contexts in which whiteness is important. Might we connect the fact that white symbolizes virginity in certain contexts with the fact that Christmas has to do with the Virgin Mary? Does the whiteness of the eggnog symbolize snow or does it symbolize nothing at all?

Does eggnog derive its meaning from some prelinguistic, biologically inherited system of communication or is its meaning culturally assigned? The answer to such questions depends upon what eggnog means or, more importantly, from whence its meaning comes. If the meaning of eggnog comes solely from the fact that it is a whitish fluid and if all whitish fluids signify mother's milk for all human beings, then we would have to say that at one level at least it can be interpreted as a universal and biologically based symbol. But a ritual drink like eggnog is freighted with all kinds of meanings and psychological associations. To the extent that these meanings are cultural; that is, to the extent that they are shared by a set of

FIGURE 8–5   "Thou shalt make no graven images." These are Muslim religious symbols used in processions in Gopalpur, South India. (PHOTO BY ALAN R. BEALS)

members of a cultural system, the meaning of eggnog is cultural. To say that something is cultural is to say that it arises in a complicated way out of interactions among human biological factors, environmental factors, and the various experiences that the successive sets of members of the cultural system have undergone.

Any kind of thing or action to which meaning can be assigned is likely to derive some part of its meaning from universal human characteristics. Such universal characteristics are likely to represent common human biology, common human experiences, or very ancient and widespread ideas. The proper question to ask about eyebrow flashes, eggnogs, and other such things is not whether they are of biological or cultural origin, but to what extent and in what way various different factors have affected their meaning.

An important point about rituals and ceremonies is that they involve things and actions that have meaning but whose meaning is not clear. The messages inherent in the casual rituals of daily interaction, as well as the messages inherent in more formal and complex rituals, are often unconsciously transmitted and received. We are cheered by cheery greetings, but, as informants, it is not clear to us precisely how the message was delivered or exactly how it triggered our own cheeriness.

How Close Are You?

For example, the psychological state of a given individual and his relationships to other individuals are deeply influenced by how close to other persons the individual is standing. But what does it mean when individuals stand close together or when they stand far apart? Is there a hidden message in the rituals of nearness and farness? For the United States, Hall (1959:163–164) gives the following partial interpretation of the meaning of distance:

1.	Very close (3–6″)	Soft whisper; top secret
2.	Close (8–12″)	Audible whisper; very confidential
3.	Near (12–20″)	Indoors, soft voice; outdoors, full voice; confidential
4.	Neutral (20–36″)	Soft voice, low volume; personal subject matter
5.	Neutral (4.5–5′)	Full voice; information of non-personal nature
6.	Public Distance (5.5–8′)	Full voice with slight overloudness; public information for others to hear
7.	Across the room (8–20′)	Loud voice; talking to a group
8.	Stretching the limits of distance (20–24′ indoors; up to 100′ outdoors)	Hailing distance, departures.

Granted a certain amount of local variation, it is plain that citizens of the United States could not manage themselves or their social lives unless they knew in some way how to maintain proper distance. Of course, they manipulate and influence each other through their management of distance. People use interaction rituals in subtle ways to influence each other and establish their status. Does this sort of thing also take place in those more formal and complicated rituals for which the term ceremony is appropriate? Do Hopi Indian ceremonies change individual behavior and, if so, how?

RITUAL IMPACT: HOW DID YOU FEEL?

Among the Hopi Indians of the southwestern part of the United States, the infant in traditionally oriented groups is bound to a cradleboard soon after birth. He is taken off the cradleboard only for the changing of soiled diapers or for bathing. Eating, sleeping, and traveling all take place on the board. After he is three months old, the child is released for progressively longer periods. Children are usually nursed on demand or whenever they cry or whimper. As soon as the child begins to demand solid food, adults give him part of whatever they are eating. As the child approaches one year of age, he is encouraged to walk and to speak his first words. A child is weaned when the mother becomes pregnant with a second child, few babies nursing for more than two years. When the child can walk and understand, an effort is made to toilet-train him. The child comes home to eat when he pleases (but not when adults are eating), eats whatever he wants, and sleeps when he feels like it. Girls may spend the night in friends' houses while boys frequently sleep in a group at some distance from the family house. The child may touch everything he sees, but must stay away from the cliff, the stove, and the ladder leading down into the ceremonial house (*kiva*). He is told not to fight, tease, or injure anyone, but not really prevented from doing so. Until he is six, the male child has no duties. After six, he may be asked to accompany his father to the fields where he guards the cornfields against prairie dogs, runs errands, chops wood, picks fruit, and helps with the harvesting (Dennis 1940).

Hopi parents are not completely permissive. If children misbehave, a bugaboo katcina* may appear, masked and carrying a basket in which to stuff naughty children. Parents may have great difficulty in defending children from these monsters. Fathers tend to punish children only when they are annoyed, but the mother may call upon one of her brothers to punish all the children for the offense of any one. Good children, and of course there are no strong precedents for badness, receive gifts: "You have helped your father in the fields so the katcinas have brought you a nice bow and arrow" (Dennis 1940:47).

In the Hopi system of thought, thinking about good or appropriate things has a positive effect upon this world and the world of the katcinas. The good thoughts and action of the katcinas affect this world. Katcinas bring gifts to children and rain. Trouble in the world comes from those who think "mean" thoughts, the "two-hearts." A great many Hopi, sometimes members of one's own family, are, often unknowingly, two-hearts who must bring illness and disaster upon their relatives or die of a kind of supernatural starvation. Hopi rituals, which maintain a relationship between the Hopi and the katcinas, preserve what little good there is in the world.

All of this is soon recognized by the child. He knows that if he pretends to be sick, he may cause illness in others. He knows that a dream may spell danger to his friends and relatives. In a moment of rudeness a child may offend someone who turns out to be a two-heart, and the child

---

* Katcinas or kachinas are supernatural figures sometimes impersonated by masked men. Their meaning and role in Hopi life are explained in the following examples.

may sicken and die. For protection in this unsafe world, the child may rely upon the katcinas. No matter what happens, the katcinas will be there to enjoin correct behavior and prevent disaster.

Between the ages of six and ten, the child must prepare himself to undertake adult responsibilities. The child's passage from the permissive world of childhood to the harsher world of adult work and responsibility is marked by his initiation into either the Powamu or the Katcina society. Parents decide which of these societies is to be selected. The Powamu society has a relatively mild initiation rite which takes place on the fifth day of the Powamu ceremony. Initiation into the Katcina society is considered more difficult and also takes place on the fifth day of the Powamu ceremony, or, if there is a Powamu initiation, on the day following. The initiates to both societies are present through ten days of intense ceremonial activity.

What Is the Ceremony Like?

At the climax of the sixth day of the Powamu ceremony the Katcina initiation takes place as follows: The chief priest of the Powamu society (dressed in white, holding in his left hand a gourd, four corn ears, and a knife-shaped wooden implement, and in his right a crook to which the corn ear and the cornmeal packets are fastened) takes a position to the right of the ladder leading down into the underground ceremonial room. He is Muyingwa, the god of fertility and growth. An old man asks: "Taa, hakah um pito?" (Well, where did you come from?) The katcina replies that he came from below. The old man says, "Tell us why you wander about?" The katcina explains how those below made a ladder with turquoise strands holding it together:

> Eastward we came, traveling on a road marked with yellow corn seed (shelled corn). We beheld the house of the Akush Katcina chief. In a beautiful yellow mist was the house enveloped. So we went in. The Akush Katcina chief was there. He has beautiful yellow corn seed, beans, watermelons, muskmelons, and that way he lives. Here these Oraibi children, little girls, little boys, of different sizes, here at the *sipapu* shall they know our ceremonies; yes they shall know them. Beautiful ladder beam, beautiful ladder rungs, tied to the beam with turquoise strands. Thus, we came out.
>
> Westward we came. On a road marked with beautiful blue corn seed we traveled. We beheld the house of the Nakachok Katcina chief. Beautiful white mist enveloped the house. Thus we went in. The Nakachok Katcina chief was there. Having beautiful blue corn seed, beans, watermelons, muskmelons, he dwells there. These Oraibi children here, little girls, little boys, of different sizes, here at the *sipapu* shall they know our ceremonies. Yes, they shall know them! Beautiful ladder beam, beautiful ladder rungs, with turquoise strands are they tied to the ladder. Thus we came out (Voth 1901:99).

And so it goes, westward again to the Hototo Katcina enveloped in red mist, southward to the Mastop Katcina enveloped in white mist, northward, westward, southward, eastward, southward, and northward. The deity continues:

> And now you gather your people, your children, all of them, into your lap and hold them all very fast (protect them). But now this time open your hands to these people that this yucca may enlighten their hearts, and when their hearts have been enlightened here their heads will be bathed with roots of this yucca and then they will be done.
>
> And thus then follow to the white rising and to the yellow rising this road marked with nice corn pollen and on which these four old age marks (crooks) are standing. On them you will support (or rest) yourselves, and over yonder, where the shortest one stands, may you fall asleep as old women and as old men. But I am not wandering alone. Here at the corner they have already

arrived (referring to the four Koyemsi Katcinas behind the curtain in the corner of the kiva); come in, be welcome (Voth 1901:100–101).

The deity sprinkles the candidates with water and leaves the kiva. The Koyemsi katcinas, who seem little more than boys, touch every candidate with a corn ear and a stone axe. They stand aside and there is silence. All know that soon other katcinas will come to flog the initiates. There is a loud grunting noise; rattles and bells are heard. There are poundings on the roof and the word u'huhuhu is howled repeatedly. The two Ho katcinas enter the kiva and stand on either side of a large sand painting, grunting, howling, rattling, trampling, and brandishing the yucca leaves to be used as whips. The Hahai-i katcina stands at the southeast corner of the sand painting holding a supply of whips.

A sponsor seizes a nude candidate and drags him onto the sand mosaic holding both of his hands. The boy attempts to protect his sexual organs from the pointed tips of the yucca leaves as he is beaten on the legs and hips. Mothers and fathers shout encouragement at their children or accuse the katcinas of hitting too hard. Some children endure the flogging without flinching, others jump away and scream. Sometimes a frightened child micturates or defecates. When it is over the Hahai-i katcina is severely beaten by both Ho katcinas who then begin scourging each other while the initiates cheer. The katcinas leave and the initiates may now know ceremonial secrets. On following days the community is filled with katcinas and there are dances and ceremonies. On the tenth day, more recently on the ninth day, the katcinas appear in the village and order all people into their houses. Later, there is a procession in which the people accompany the katcinas. At the conclusion of the ceremonies, all parents are ordered to cover up or otherwise hide their children. As soon as this is done, the katcinas remove their masks. They are men, not gods (Voth 1901:101).

What Was the Effect?

Years later Don Talayesva described his experiences to the anthropologist, Simmons:

I recognized nearly every one of them, and felt very unhappy, because I had been told all my life that the Kachinas were gods. I was especially shocked and angry when I saw all my uncles, fathers, and clan brothers dancing as Kachinas. I felt worst when I saw my own father and whenever he glanced at me I turned my face away.
    I kept thinking . . . about the Kachinas whom I had loved (Aberle 1950:83–84).

The above description of the Powamu ceremony and the katcina society initiation is fragmentary and incomplete. It is difficult for an

FIGURE 8–7 Hopi kachinas visiting the Pueblo during the Powamu or "beanplanting" initiation ceremony. The photograph was taken by James Mooney, whose study of the ghost dance is reported in Chapter 11 at Walpi Pueblo in 1893. (COURTESY OF THE SMITHSONIAN INSTITUTION NATIONAL ANTHROPOLIGICAL ARCHIVES)

outsider to grasp all the complexities or to understand why the process of initiation should take precisely the form that it takes among the Hopi. Anthropologists disagree about the extent to which the dramatic discovery that the gods are men is surprising or shocking to the children. The situation may be like that in the United States where some children believe in Santa Claus and others never take him seriously. Because most children only undergo the relatively mild Powamu initiation, they are not whipped, but they do see their friends whipped. The child learns that years ago, the katcinas did actually visit the earth. Now, the two-hearts have frightened them away and they appear as spirits inhabiting the masks worn by human beings. Such information must never be revealed to the uninitiated.

Anthropological understandings of such a complicated ceremony can be reached at many different levels. Historically, the Powamu ceremony can be compared with ceremonies held by neighboring groups and tribes and certain elements in the ceremony can be shown to have been borrowed and to have diffused or spread from group to group. Such a ceremony may also be understood as a complicated system of symbols, a kind of hidden message which is not fully understood even by the participants. Symbolic representations of fertility, for example, might be sought in the equipment, drawings, and decorations used. By comparing the Powamu ceremony with all other Hopi ceremonies or other processes that make up Hopi life, it might be possible to arrive at a picture of the basic organization of the cultural system.

Because the obvious intent of the Powamu ceremony is that of converting boys into men, we are inclined to wonder if it really does so and, if so, how it accomplishes its ends. Don Talayesva remembers:

> I thought of the flogging and the initiation as an important turning point in my life, and I felt ready at last to listen to my elders and to live right. Whenever my father talked to me I kept my ears open, looked straight into his eyes, and said, "Owi (Yes)" (Aberle 1950:84).

Why did the ceremony affect Don Talayesva in this way? One explanation is that the ceremony offers the initiate a clear choice. He may conclude that the katcinas are not real and accept the consequence that he can no longer be a Hopi, or he can accept the spiritual nature of the katcinas in which case all of the benefits of membership accrue. On its face, the whole ceremony involves trickery and meaningless cruelty ("when I saw my own father . . . I turned my face away") on the part of the very same people who have treated the child so indulgently in the past. Logically and emotionally, the child's only escape is the recognition that his parents and relatives behaved as they did as a means of countering the machinations of the two-hearts.

In general, where rituals are designed to produce striking changes in the daily behavior of individuals, a variety of psychological devices appear to be employed: drug taking, pain, fatigue, isolation, starvation, repetition, music, propaganda, dramatic performances, feasts, confessions, and processions. The combination of a number of such techniques to form an elaborate ceremonial process mobilizing all of the symbolic and behavior controlling apparatus of the cultural system almost certainly results in deep and irreversible changes in the personalities of many who are subjected to them. The cynical young child who does not believe in Santa Claus or who has never been deceived by the katcinas may not be so deeply affected by earnest endeavors to change his personality. Such individuals, and they exist in many if not in all parts of the world, may yet respond to ceremonies by dramatically changing their behavior. Whatever else it may do or signify, an elaborate initiation ceremony indicates that the adults mean business. The initiate must "grow up" or else.

Many rituals and ceremonies have importance, not so much for their role in changing individuals as for their role in changing relationships among individuals or in affirming the solidarity of particular groups. How is it possible for rituals to strengthen social bonds?

HAVE YOU COME TO EAT THE HOLIGI?

One day during the slack period after harvest, a group of well-dressed men and women arrive in Gopalpur in procession accompanied by musicians. These men and women are relatives of Siddanna who, along with several elders of their village, have come to discuss a possible marriage of one of their sons to Siddanna's daughter. After resting for a decent interval in the courtyard of the village temple, they march in procession to the open space in front of Siddanna's house. Men from Siddanna's house go through the village, stopping at every house and announcing, *"Biigaru* have come to our house, so come." Gradually, one or two persons from each house in the village, along with all of the children in the village, go to Siddanna's house and sit.

When all have gathered, someone says, "Is there anyone here from the Stoneworker's colony?" A man stands up and says, "Yes, we were invited." A messenger arrives from the Police Headman of the village, "I am not feeling well, but pretend I am there and talk." The Village Crier addresses the biigaru: "What is your village; why have you come?" The biigaru reply, "We have come because there is *holigi** in Siddanna's house. We have come to eat the holigi." The Crier turns to Siddanna: "Have you

---

* Holigi, a party treat, something like a pancake.

got holigi in your house? They have come to eat the holigi." Siddanna answers, "Yes there are holigi in my house. If they have come to eat the holigi, let them eat." The Crier asks the biigaru, "What is the *oli* on your side?" They reply, "It is 75 rupees; what is it on your side? How many saris do we have to give you?" Siddanna answers, "Here the oli is 110 rupees and two saris. One sari must cost 15 rupees, one must cost 20 rupees if the people are poor. The mother's sari and the full stomach sari are included in the oli. Are you ready to give this much oli or not?" The biigaru reply, "Yes." Siddanna's people say, "We must also be given an anklet weighing two seers, a leg chain weighing one half seer, a silver girdle weighing one seer, a bracelet of ten tolas, an upper arm bracelet of one seer, a gold earring weighing one tola, a nose star, a marriage necklace and one or two *masi*." (Usually the nose star and marriage necklace are not mentioned at this time.) The biigaru reply, "Yes."

The biigaru have brought a sari for the bride, flowers, and two blouses. The sari is placed on a plate and given to the bride along with the two blouses, rice, dried dates, betel leaf and nut, and a half coconut. A lamp is lit and placed before the bride. A diagram is drawn with rice. The bride and "the girl-who-sits-beside-her" sit on the diagram and put on the sari and the blouses. A blouse and one rupee are given to the girl-who-sits-beside-her. Turmeric powder is rubbed on the girls' foreheads and on everyone sitting nearby. Two half coconuts are filled with rice, areca nut, and other materials and poured into the bride's sari. This is called

FIGURE 8–8 A few men from Gopalpur obtain permanent jobs in factories. Here, the prodigal son returns for a two-week vacation bringing the first radio ever seen in the village of Gopalpur, South India. (PHOTO BY ALAN R. BEALS)

the *stomach filling,* and it gives the bride a somewhat pregnant look. Brown sugar is now given to the biigaru and other portions distributed to the Village Headman, the Police Headman, the Accountant, the Crier, the Blacksmith, the Priest, the Carpenter, "People from Other Villages," and to everyone present. All except the biigaru and the family leave. Siddanna's family prepares food and feeds the biigaru. Invited guests from the village then come and eat. All sleep. The next morning, the biigaru and other guests are given holigi and they return to their village.

People in South India do not rush hastily into marriage. The eating of the holigi is just one of a series of steps leading to a climactic marriage ceremony. Although either party can withdraw from the marriage at any point, the cost of the separate ceremonies along the way must have the effect of increasing commitment and reducing the chances of a withdrawal just before the final ceremony is to take place. Another easily seen characteristic of the ceremony is that it ensures the presence of a large number of witnesses to the unwritten marriage contract.

But why is it necessary that everyone in the village be invited, that anyone who can't come present his excuses, and that everyone receive and eat brown sugar? Villagewide participation in the ritual argues that: (1) no one in the village is sufficiently angry with Siddanna to refuse to attend; and (2) all know about and approve of the wedding. It is not so much a matter of the ceremony promoting or establishing social ties or social integration within Gopalpur as it is a demonstration of the preexistence of such ties. In fact, all public and community ceremonies in Gopalpur *must* be properly conducted, yet they cannot be conducted if there is open conflict in the village. Outstanding conflicts between the bride's village and the groom's village would also rule out the possibility of marriage. Because the enactment of a large ceremony, no less than the enactment of a minor interpersonal ritual, requires a process of cooperation and of recognition of status, it is possible to interpret rituals of all kinds as being enforcers and regulators of human relationships.

The Powamu ceremony and the various South Indian marriage ceremonies illustrate varieties of ritual which can, at least from some viewpoints, be interpreted in utilitarian or practical terms. Both varieties of ceremony appear to affect human behavior and to develop a broad acceptance of and commitment to specific changes in status and role behavior. The processes of becoming a man or a married couple seem to be directly facilitated by the ritual. In the same way, Rappaport's description of the Kaiko ritual in New Guinea attributes to it the practical effect or function of regulating populations of pigs and people. Although almost any ceremony can be explained in terms of the fact that it provides insurance by encouraging the accumulation of goods or that it gives everyone a good high protein meal or that it is good for business, many rituals and ceremonies are hard to explain in practical terms. What are the following rituals good for?

HOW DID YOU OVERCOME YOUR PROBLEM

I was born in Jaltal, an ailing child with a great head that caused my mother much pain. While I was still in the womb, my father mistook a snake for a bit of wood and struck it with his axe. This snake was really the God Ajorasum, and when I was born he made me very ill. But my father called a shaman, who sacrificed a fowl to the angry god and dedicated a pot with many promises and I recovered. Later, when I was old enough to play with other children and take the cattle out to graze, my father sacrificed a buffalo to Ajorasum on the bank of a stream (Elwin 1955:135).

Here, the purpose of these healing rituals is evidently that of restoring and maintaining health, but, if it works, it is not clear why it works. The following more complicated series of events is even harder to explain:

When I was about twelve years old, a tutelary girl called Jangmai came to me in a dream and said, "I am pleased with you; I love you; I love you so much that you must marry me." But I refused and for a whole year she used to come making love to me and trying to win me. But I always rejected her until at last she got angry and sent her dog (a tiger) to bite me. That frightened me and I agreed to marry her. But almost at once another tutelary came and begged me to marry her instead. When the first girl heard about it she said, "I was first to love you, and I look on you as my husband. Now your heart is on another woman, but I'll not allow it." So I said "No" to the second girl. But the first in her rage and jealousy made me mad and drove me out into the jungle and robbed me of my memory. For a whole year she drove me.

Then my parents called a shaman from another village and in his trance my tutelary came upon him and spoke through his mouth. She said to my parents, "Don't be afraid, I am going to marry him. There is nothing in all this; don't worry, I will help the boy in all his troubles." My father was pleased and bought a she-goat, and two cloths, bangles, a ring and a comb and arranged the wedding. The shaman sat down in the house, put the gifts and a new pot in front of him; tethered the goat near by and, singing, singing, fell into a trance. My tutelary's mother, father and sisters brought her to me and I fell to the ground unconscious. Jangmai asked for her cloth and the shaman dressed me in it. Then she demanded the other things, gift by gift, and they put the ring on my finger and gave me the bangles and necklace, and did my hair with the comb (Elwin 1955:135–137).

A tutelary is a spirit from a high ranking jati who falls in love with and "marries" a male or female of the Saora tribe in India. After a "wedding" has taken place, the afflicted (or favored) individual becomes a shaman who can be possessed by spirits and so diagnose and cure illness. The position of shaman is one of great responsibility and importance. It is tempting, then, to think of Saora healing rituals as a means of providing a place for those Saora who seek some greater importance in life than the daily round of farming, eating, and sleeping which is the lot of the ordinary person. In effect, ritual marriage to a tutelary spirit might be regarded as a means of preventing or treating mental illness. It is equally possible that Saora mythology concerning illness and tutelary spirits is itself responsible for the creation of the mental illness which it cures.

Why Healing Rituals?

The most obvious fact about magical or supernatural healing rituals in most cultures is that they operate in areas where practical cures are unavailable. In the United States, if there were a quick and easy cure for arthritis, people would hardly feel a need to cure it by wearing copper bracelets. Because the course of any illness is affected in some degree by the patient's state of mind, it can be argued that any authoritative treatment will be beneficial. Even where psychological assistance is of no conceivable value, the absence of any other effective treatment combined with the fact that psychological treatments often are effective would encourage people to attempt rituals that depend upon magic or supernatural agencies for their effectiveness.

Illness, especially severe illness, is a threat to the status of the individual as a member of his cultural system and also to the status of the family or work group of which the individual may be an important part. Healing rituals can be interpreted as a means of coping with the resulting anxiety. Because rituals in general tend to occur during those anxious moments when the individual or the group is undergoing a change in status, it is possible to argue that the fundamental source of human ritual activity is human anxiety and uncertainty.

In Saora healing rituals, the shaman identifies the precise cause of the illness and, while he is possessed by the spirit or deity responsible, reveals the exact steps required for treatment and cure. Fine if it works, but what if it doesn't work? How does that allay anxiety? The Saora tend to explain the failure of their healing rituals by appealing to the willful nature of supernaturals. Spirits and deities are easily offended and it is always easy to identify some failure or inadequacy in the performance of ritual which has offended the supernaturals. That rituals have to be performed in just the right way offers an escape clause which explains why some performances are ineffective. The same kind of error occurs in all processes carried out within cultural systems. Psychologically a ritual error may be no different from planting the seeds too deep or not planting them deep enough. It is a predictable sort of human error which does not challenge fundamental certainties.

One of the important characteristics of rituals, and of other cultural processes as well, is the element of repetition. Magical rituals in particular depend upon the correct performance of every detail of the ritual process. In everyday life, the omission of morning coffee or bedtime toothbrushing may create considerable anxiety. In most places, the use of inappropriate dress or of taboo or obscene language may provoke violent and even

murderous reactions. The fact that rituals of all kinds may be spoiled by profane or sacrilegious acts has often led to the conclusion that there is one and only one right or normative way of carrying out the characteristic behaviors appropriate to any particular cultural system. Especially in the performance of magical or religious ceremonies there is an inclination to conceive of the individual member as a slave to his cultural tradition. The difficulties inherent in observing and describing large numbers of different activities lead anthropologists to speak of typical or normative ways of doing things rather than to attempt any systematic exploration of the range of variation which may actually occur. What, then, are the kinds of variation that can properly occur in the conduct of a ceremony?

VARIATION: HOW MANY CHAMBELANES?

In an attempt to understand some aspects of variation in the conduct of wedding ceremonies in Tenejapa in Mexico, Duane Metzger and Gerald Williams (1963:1076–1101) began by collecting a series of phrases and sentences that people actually used in discussing wedding ceremonies. One such phrase was "Vamos a nombrar nueve chambelanes" (Let us appoint nine male attendants). One of the things you can do in planning a wedding, then, is to appoint different numbers of attendants. One way of interviewing people about the number of male attendants there might legitimately be would be to strike out the word "nine" in order to create the *substitution frame*: "Let us appoint ———— male attendants." Metzger and Williams discovered that any number of male attendants between zero and nine was acceptable. Another substitution frame, "Let us appoint _____ _____," led to the discovery that you could appoint *chambelanes, damas, padrinos, madrinas, madrinas de arras,* and *pajes.* There are, then, several types of attendants that can be appointed and different numbers of each type (see Table 8–1).

TABLE 8–1   Variables in Choice of Participants in Tenejapa Wedding Ceremony

No.	Chambelan	Dama	Padrino	Madrina	Madrina de Arras	Pajes
0	X	X			X	X
1	X	X	X	X		
2	X	X	X	X	X	X
3	X	X	X	X		
4	X	X				
5	X	X				
6	X	X				
7	X	X				
8	X	X				
9	X	X				

Some additional rules apply, however. We must name the same numbers of *chambelanes* and *damas*, of *padrinos* and *madrinas*, and of *madrinas de arras* and *pajes*. If we name large numbers of *chambelanes* we must name the largest possible number of *padrinos* and *madrinas de arras*. If we name zero or a small number of *chambelanes*, then we can name zero *padrinos* and only one *madrina de arras*.

Decisions about the number of attendants to be appointed at a wedding are obviously based upon a weighing of expenses against the desirability of an elegant ceremony. Certain minimum performances are required if the ceremony is to be regarded as a wedding ceremony, but beyond that the holding of the ceremony offers a rich texture of alternatives that allow for the expression of individual style or the wealth and social position of the families concerned. Although "Hiya, buddy" and "How are you, sir?" represent the same ritual of greeting, their messages concerning status are expressive of very different personalities or situations.

SUMMARY

Praying for rain probably does not cause it to rain, but it probably makes people feel better about the fact that it is not raining. People in many different cultural systems would be upset if nobody prayed for rain. Ritual behavior is behavior that is not clearly or directly connected to any positive effects in the real world but is still considered necessary or desirable. The argument of this chapter has been that rituals ranging in scale from minor rituals of interaction to major ceremonial activities such as weddings and funerals share the common property that they inform people about the statuses of other individuals, about the status of society, or about the status of the environment. A prayer for rain is a demand that changes take place in the environment. Rituals can be defined in terms of the people involved: personal, interpersonal, family, community, tribal, and intertribal. Other rituals are triggered by specific events and seasons. Rites of passage include birth, puberty, marriage, and death. Calendrical ceremonies depend upon the times of the year, and crisis ceremonials are held at times of illness, famine, and catastrophe.

The fact that every human being lives in a cultural world thick with ritual activities and symbolic gestures is illustrated by the tree-climbing activities of Raymond and Stewart. The invisible rituals of every day permeate every activity. They are a broadcast of intention and status: "Here I am; watch me; here is what I'm doing; admire."

The human person is sacred. It is protected within the temple of the body by a screen of ritual courtesies. We recognize the importance of "ordinary courtesy" and the fact of its existence only when the screen is rudely torn apart. Dr. Pouissant and a policeman threaten each others' worlds. The rituals of deference and demeanor are illustrated through an act of ceremonial profanation.

One of the problems in interpreting ritual behavior at all levels has to do with the extent to which the language of ritual activity is universal or widespread. Because such symbolic gestures as eyebrow flashes or circumcisions are common, it is tempting to some to explain their frequency on the grounds that they share some sort of basis in common human biology or in common human experiences. The human body and brain certainly provide some limits to human activity. On the other hand, very old ideas, such as the use of fire, may be widespread simply because they are old and have had many years in which to spread.

For example, how might the symbolism of the Christmas ritual in the United States be interpreted? Do the ornaments on the tree symbolize fruitfulness; does the eggnog suggest virginity; and do red and green suggest death and rebirth? Maybe so, but on the whole, a concept of universal symbolism does not take us very far towards an explanation of the meaning of Christmas. What is needed is careful study of the symbol systems of the various groups of people who celebrate Christmas. Until then, one guess is as good as another. The work of Hall on the importance of spatial distance in defining the meaning of interpersonal ritual in the United States provides a further indication of the superiority of research over guesswork.

An extended discussion of the Hopi initiation ritual introduces some of the problems involved in determining the effects of ritual activity upon individuals. Without doubt the ritual produces dramatic change in the behavior of at least some Hopi. Is this the result of subtle psychological pressures equivalent to brainwashing or does it merely involve a recognition that the adults mean business?

Another problem has to do with the impact of ritual upon social relationships. Since marriage ceremonies almost invariably precede marriage, it is an easy guess that they make the marriage work better. It is difficult, however, to enumerate concrete effects. About the best argument is that, since people have to be well enough adapted to get by, they can't afford to spend too much time in activities that are useless or wasteful. The case of healing rituals, which certainly don't heal people in any direct way is investigated through a description of Saora shamanism. Again, there are probably important psychological benefits to the healer and the person being treated. Saora rituals may play a vital role in maintaining Saora society and stabilizing its relationships to the outside world. Then, again, it may not.

Finally, the example of Tenejapa wedding rituals permits consideration of the role of variation in ritual performances. Rituals, almost by definition, are stereotyped and repetitious, yet all rituals permit subtle communications expressed as individual variation.

For Further Reading

Most of the works of Erving Goffman, especially *Interaction Ritual* (1967), deal with the rituals of everyday life. Lessa and Vogt's *Reader in Comparative Religion* (1965) provides a good summary of various approaches to rituals, ceremonies, and "religious" acts. Young's *Initiation Ceremonies* (1965) and Van Gennep's *The Rites of Passage* (1961, first published in French in 1908) discuss one variety of ritual.

Case Studies emphasizing ritual include Hoebel's *The Cheyennes* (1960), Vogt's *The Zinacantecos of Mexico* (1970), Deng's *The Dinka* (1972), Leis' *Enculturation and Socialization in an Ijaw Society* (1972), Buechler and Buechler's *The Bolivian Aymara* (1971), and Pospisil's *The Kapauku Papuans* (1963).

Problems and Questions

1. Observe some rituals of greeting. Are there any differences in situation or social status that would explain variation in such rituals?
2. Compare marriages or other ceremonies from several different societies. Suggest some possible explanations for any similarities or differences.
3. Do graduation ceremonies, farewell parties, or other rites of passage make any difference in the behavior of individuals in modern society? What messages do such ceremonies convey?
4. What might be some functions of a ritual such as Christmas or Easter? What

sort of data would you need to demonstrate that the ritual actually fulfills the functions you suggest?

5. Examine any kind of public or private ritual behavior. Does it involve symbolic acts? Do the symbols seem to have universal meanings? Can you suggest the meanings of any of the symbols?

6. Examine a film or television program that displays human interaction. What sorts of interpersonal rituals do you observe?

9 CULTURAL TRANSMISSION

How is culture transmitted?

As members are recruited to cultural systems and participate in the complex ritual processes which guide them in movement from one status or situation to another, it is important that they conform to the expectations of fellow members. Such conformity is the result of cultural transmission, the process of learning the relevant parts of the cultural message. People raised in a single culture sometimes have difficulty grasping the full impact of learning upon their speech, perceptions, and behavior.

This chapter begins with a quotation from a Navajo Indian. The things that he has to say are different from the sorts of things that persons raised in other communities in the United States might have to say. Equally important the way he says these things is different. Other statements made respectively by Navajo and Hopi Indian children are presented. What are the differences that exist among the Navajo, the Hopi, and other representatives of the United States? These people are different because different cultures and subcultures have been transmitted to them. We consider, then, the nature of cultural transmission, and the nature of the human life cycle. Culture continues to be transmitted up to the moment of death. Apparently small things, like the shapes of rooms, may well have important influences upon the individual. Even within the same cultural system such factors as status, birth order, sex, and age are important in accounting for differences in individual perception of cultural messages.

The earliest indications of how the individual is to be treated during the process of cultural transmission occurs at childbirth. Iroquois, Ngoni, and Malitbog childbirth scenes are described. What sorts of expectations are set up in these different cultures? How do they differ from ours? Later, when it comes time for weaning, the child has direct experience of the nature of its new world. Ngoni, Malitbog, and Modoc treatments of the young child are contrasted. What are the effects of such practices upon the growing child? To what extent do resulting differences in personality lead to different ways of coping with similar problems?

249

The example of Modoc childhood leads to questions about the extent to which culture has to be taught or otherwise forcibly transmitted. Is cultural transmission something that is done to children and new members by adults and old members? Or might it be a largely unconscious flow from one person to another?

The Blackfish school provides an example of the forcible transmission of one culture to the members of another. What happens when systems of formal education drift away from the real-life needs and knowledge required by the membership of a local cultural system? Is there a humane way to create a nation state and a national culture? Some of the Menomini Indians, like the Kwakiutl exposed to the constant pressure of an alien way of life, have attempted to find a new cultural message. What sorts of things do happen when the traditional culture disappears, yet the new culture offers little but poverty, drugs, and despair?

When a new cultural message is offered, the individual may change dramatically. Initiation rituals at Daytop House and among the Ngoni make use of some of the same techniques to secure such radical change in personality. What is the impact of such a wrenching and violent change in personality?

HOW DO THEY GET TO BE LIKE NAVAJO?

The quotation below is a translation of a statement made by a Navajo of the American Southwest. The statement tells us something of what the Navajo are like. Is there, for example, a characteristic way in which the Navajo report happenings and present information?

One day, as we were herding at the edge of the woods, a man came riding out in the flat on the trail going to the northeast and southwest. When he'd almost passed by he looked up and saw us, so he turned his horse and started riding towards us. My father said, "Who's that fellow? Do you know him?" I said, "No, I don't know him." He rode up, and it was a fellow named No Neck. They called him No Neck because he had a big, round, short neck. He was an Along the Stream. His father's name was Little Wife Beater; he was a Reed People. My father recognized him and got up and shook hands with him, saying, "Where are you from? I haven't seen you for a long time, my cousin. I'm very glad to see you again." He said, "I'm from below Oraibi." "Where are you heading for?" my father asked him. "I'm going to my older brother's place. They say he lives around here somewhere, and I'd like to visit my relatives who live here. That's where I'm going." My father said, "When did you start?" "Yesterday morning I started from my place." Then my father said to him, "Tell me how the places are towards your home. Tell me how the weather is and what the land is like, the grazing, the water, the feed for the stock. Get down off your horse and tell me all about those things." As he got off his horse he said, "I've got nothing to tell." But when he sat down beside my father he said, "There's nothing from here on all the way down to Popping

Rock Point. A little beyond there is good feed; that's where the feed begins. From there on this way there's nothing, but from there on over towards Cedar Standing, down in that flat, there's plenty of grazing and water'' (Dyk 1967:133).

If you have formed any ideas concerning the nature of the Navajo from the above quotation, then you may be able to distinguish Navajo responses from those of their neighbors, the Hopi. The statements below are responses made by Navajo and Hopi children to a set of ambiguous pictures (Thematic Apperception Test). The children were shown the pictures and asked to make up a story about each one. Which of the stories are Navajo and which are Hopi?

1. He is mad. His mother must have scolded him because he refused to do it. He is going to do it.
2. I don't know what this boy is saying, maybe he is crying. When they get a scolding, they cry.

1. It is an Indian man. He was working in his field. He is tired. He will go back home.
2. He has a stick with him. I don't know what he is doing.

1. He is crying. His parents spanked him because he did not want to do what he was told. He will do it now.
2. This boy is laying on a bundle and going to sleep (Henry 1947:7).

In each case the first reply was that of a Hopi and the second reply was that of a Navajo. What sort of rules or generalizations would have per-

mitted us to make the distinction accurately? Evidently, from this limited sample, Navajo prefer not to speculate about motives or about past and future events. Like ideal scientists, they report exactly what they see and hear without interpretation or editorial comment. The Hopi, at least in these examples, despite the fact that they are close neighbors of the Navajo, always tell what they think might have happened in the past and what they expect will happen in the future. They always seem to explain why people are doing the things that they are doing—"The boy cried; his mother spanked him."

Why do these differences exist?

The Navajo children may simply be more fearful (with good reason) of outsiders than the Hopi. The traditional Navajo way of life is one of hunting and gathering. It may be that a sense of the past and the future is less important for some hunter-gatherers than it is for agricultural peoples like the Hopi who must plan their activities at least a year in advance. Perhaps, too, there are differences in the Navajo and Hopi languages that encourage a different approach to things. All of these "explanations" point to a single cause. The Navajo approach things differently than the Hopi because the Navajo are brought up differently. The differences between the members of different cultural systems are largely due to the fact that different cultural traditions are transmitted to them. The process of cultural transmission begins at the onset of life when the unborn fetus is affected by the diet, patterns of activity, health, and psychological state of its mother. It continues throughout all of the problems and stages of life as the individual learns how to survive and adapt, how to walk and talk, how to satisfy sexual urges, how to raise children, how to be a grandparent and, finally, how to grow old and die.

In all cultures, the process of cultural transmission must come to terms with the regularities of the biological processes of growth and decay. The helpless newborn remains in close contact with its mother. A little later, a brother, sister, or other caretaker may begin to carry it about during its waking hours. The Klamath Indians of southern Oregon had cradle boards with sharpened ends so that the baby could be stuck upright in the ground where it could watch its mother cook or grub up tubers. At the end of two years or so, when the next baby is on the way, the child ceases to nurse and begins to eat solid food. By the age of three, the new baby dominates the home, and the three-year-old is sent outside to be disciplined and raised by siblings and peers.

Between ten and sixteen, depending upon a variety of cultural and nutritional factors, the child begins to attain physical and sexual maturity. At eighteen or so, when full growth is attained, the young person is expected to perform the work of an adult. Later, sometimes at the same time, the young person becomes a parent and assumes a major role in the transmission of culture to an infant. As the children grow, the parents' activities gradually shift from the world of productive labor to the world of political and economic management. Finally, there comes grandparenthood, reduced activity, and eventually some form of retirement.

Depending upon situations and cultural traditions, the transition from the infant, "mewling and puking in its mother's arms," to the "lean

FIGURE 9–1 South Indian children are carried around a great deal and learn to walk rather late. Perhaps that is why they are not tied in to their walkers. Namhalli, South India. (PHOTO BY ALAN R. BEALS)

and slippered" grandfather presses against biological realities in different ways. In one culture children may be put to work almost as soon as they are capable of walking. In another culture, even the thought of asking an unmarried person to work might be considered abhorrent. Similarly, old age can be a long season of honor and contentment or a short episode of despair.

Cultural systems differ greatly in the content of the messages that are transmitted to their members. Consider, for example, the Euro-American baby lying on a rectangular sheet on a rectangular mattress in a rectangular crib in a rectangular room staring at a rectangular ceiling. How different to be born in the shade of a tree, to be carried about in one's mother's arms and to see on every side a desert plain ornamented sparsely with free-form rocks and plants. We do not know what this difference does to the infant brain, but we do know that people raised in different cultures may perceive lines and circles and rectangles in remarkably different ways.

Early childhood experience of particular environments and settings is only part of the incredibly complicated process that transforms the infant into the adult. As the infant begins to learn a language, it is exposed to grammatical arrangements of different sorts of words. Does the language emphasize the stable, unchanging properties of things or does it emphasize the potential for change inherent in all things? Benjamin Lee Whorf studied the grammar of the Hopi language and concluded that it permitted the Hopi to see the world in a manner compatible with Einstein's theory of relativity. Speakers of English, on the other hand, have difficulty expressing the concepts of the theory. Most linguists believe that "you can say anything in any language." Even so, it may be easier to say some things in one language than in another. There is a need for continued exploration of the relationships among language, perception, thought, and behavior.

Within any particular cultural systems certain kinds of information are made available to all members. Thus, all babies born in the United States are likely to experience the rectangular room and the English language. Out of such common experience and common information arise the more stable and consistent elements of the cultural tradition. Students of psychological anthropology have long considered the possibility that such common experiences lead to the formation of a basic personality type that is characteristic of each cultural system. We might predict, for example, that Hopi and Navajo people would behave in rather different ways in certain situations.

But just as there are differences between cultures, so also must there be differences between individuals raised in the same culture. Relative wealth, position in a class or status hierarchy, birth order, sex, age of parents, genetic inheritance, and a host of other factors ensure that each individual possesses a unique personality and a unique conception of the

cultural message. Variation around a basic personality or around a basic set of themes and experiences is essential if the members of a cultural system are to retain a capacity for flexibility and change. Even beyond this, life in the social group would be appallingly dull if the group did not contain a planner, an athlete, a clown, a helper, a leader, a rebel, and all the other sorts of persons who make things interesting or do the work. It takes all kinds to make a cultural system. Although a cultural system contains different sorts of people who understand the cultural message in rather different ways, all but a few are aware that achievement of their own, perhaps rather peculiar, goals is dependent upon the goodwill of their fellow members. Individuals, then, are game players. They conceal or reveal different aspects of their personalities to different people. They perform as they know they are expected to perform. Through it all, they constantly add to their store of knowledge concerning their fellows and their cultural tradition. It is this mastery of the game that in most cultures moves the middle-aged human being into domination of the social life of the family and the group.

The following sections provide examples of the various kinds and stages of cultural transmission. They offer suggestions about the answers to such questions as, what do we learn, and how and when do we learn it.

WHAT DOES BIRTH SIGNIFY?

The Iroquois Indians of the eastern United States held the traditional belief that individuals should be strong, independent, and free. Accord-

FIGURE 9–2 A Cree Indian woman and her children in a government constructed housing development. Here again, a sharp decrease in infant mortality leads to rapidly increasing population. (PHOTO BY PAUL CONKLIN, COURTESY OF NORMAN CHANCE)

ingly, when the mother felt that the time had come for her delivery, she went into the woods, sometimes alone, sometimes accompanied by an older woman, and gave birth to the child. She prepared for delivery by eating sparingly and exercising frequently. The newborn infant was washed with cold water or snow, wrapped in a skin, and tied into a cradle board. Carrying the baby on her back, the mother returned to her work.

The Ngoni of Malawi in Africa attach importance to correct behavior and courtesy in relationships between people. Upper-class people are expected to set an example to others and to avoid disgracing their families. Accordingly, the Ngoni wife said nothing to her husband or her mother-in-law concerning her pregnancy. She carried on her work as if nothing was happening, fearful lest her parents be blamed for any weakness she might show.

When the signs of childbirth became unmistakable, the young mother informed a friend of her condition and the friend brought the senior women in the family. To prevent its pollution, the senior women removed all of the husband's property and all good and useful household utensils from the house. The young mother sat on a mat leaning against the knees of another woman. The older women remained in front to receive the baby. The mother was not expected to cry out or to groan. When the baby

FIGURE 9–3 Cultural expectations about children are expressed during such processes as childbirth and weaning. They are also expressed in terms of gestures and appearances. A Fanti mother and children from Ghana in Africa. (PHOTO BY DAVID KRONENFELD)

was delivered it was washed by a senior woman and rubbed with castor oil.

The mother, the baby, and the house were now ritually unclean. The mother, therefore, could not cook or do housework for a number of days. Other women cleaned and purified the hut, making it "safe for the husband to sleep in" (Read 1968 p. 22). After the baby's umbilical cord had dried and fallen off, the baby and the mother were dressed up and asked to sit on a mat outside the house. The husband and his brothers were then introduced to the baby. Later, other people in the village greeted the baby and offered small presents. Children were told that the mother had found the baby on the river bank.

In Malitbog, an agricultural and more or less Roman Catholic community on the island of Panang in the Philippines, children are regarded as gifts of God. They are the joy of the home and the support of their parents in their old age. The birth of a healthy child is a demonstration that the parents have led a blameless life. When the day of delivery approaches, the woman is watched carefully. If she goes out, she is always accompanied by a child or some other person who can help her if necessary. Friends constantly inquire if the birth has taken place. The women in the house prepare clothing, diapers, and special objects to protect the mother from environmental spirits that might cause trouble. The father obtains coconut oil, firewood, containers, and other materials required at the time of delivery. The woman's father prepares a delivery bed.

As soon as there are hard and frequent contractions, the husband, carefully observing a variety of rituals and taboos, fetches the midwife. The woman is now considered to be at "the portal of death." When contractions become steady and the woman feels cramps around her waistline, she leans against a pile of pillows supported by a trunk. Her legs are separated and a foot brace provided. The husband kneels behind the wife. He holds her shoulders for comfort and encouragement. Elaborate rituals conducted by the midwife ensure that both mother and child are safe after the delivery. The baby is washed in lukewarm water and oiled. For nine days, the mother and child are protected from the open air. Windows are closed, and the mother is forbidden to work. If the baby frets or cries, the men of the house are expected to say awake, for the child is conversing with a spirit that will determine its future life expectancy.

The birth of a child generates expectations. The circumstances surrounding the birth help to determine the child's attitude toward the world and the people in it. It helps to determine the attitude of the parents toward the child. Because the Malitbog father is intimately involved in the birth of his child, one might expect that he would continue to assume responsibility later on. In fact, fathers rock children to sleep at night, stop work to mend their toys, and play happily with children who interrupt their midday nap. "Children of their fathers" though they might be, the traditionally raised Ngoni child rarely received much care or attention from the father. The Iroquois hesitated to punish their children or interfere with them in any way.It was believed that, rather than sacrifice their freedom and independence, the children would commit suicide.

The childbirth scene, by itself, probably has little effect upon the child. But what would one think of a childbirth scene in which the birth of the child is so painful to the mother that she must be anesthetized, while the baby must be brutally slapped and removed from the mother's presence? Such scenes are the means by which messages concerning the future treatment of the child are conveyed to the parents and the significant others who will have an impact upon the child's development. The Iroquois scene informs us of the importance of self-reliance and independence. The Ngoni assert the importance of the painful and rigid conformity that is the price of aristocratic superiority. In Malitbog, there is a message of love and mutual support. What does the birth scene in the United States say about the mother and child, and about the society in which *they* are to live? What might be concluded about recent changes in the United States birth scene, especially the introduction of prepared and natural childbirth?

WHAT SORT OF PERSON?

This section explores the process of childrearing and its relationship to cultural transmission. The Ngoni child was traditionally the property of its father's family. If the father's family was well disposed, they would permit it to be visited by its mother's family a suitable interval after birth and under suitable circumstances. As the mother was an aristocrat, she was not expected to take primary responsibility for the care of the infant. Rather, a teenage baby-sitter was selected who cared for the baby during the daylight hours. The mother could play with the baby if she wanted to, but most babies were attached to the baby-sitters and saw their mothers only when suckled.

The moment for weaning was chosen by the mother's mother-in-law and by other senior women in the father's family. These women came to the house one morning and announced, "We want to wean this child." (Read p. 27). The senior women placed a hot paste of ground chillies on the mother's breast and held the baby near it, and told the baby that the breast was now bad. At this point, the child was taken away to spend its nights with the father's mother or another kinswoman.

In Malitbog, in the Philippines, the newborn child must be protected from dangerous "airs" and from supernatural spirits. Later, the child must make a transition from center stage, where it is protected and admired by all, to the status of a yard child required to play and live outside the house for much of the day.

Hearing an unfamiliar voice, the boy stopped crying for a while and then resumed crying, rolling, kicking, and tearing his clothes. Still no one came to pick him up. Finally, he bumped his head against the door until it bled. Thereupon, the adult members of the family, including the mother, came running to him. His older sibling held him, as the mother bandaged the wound. He stopped crying, but continued to gulp sobs and tears rolled down his cheeks. The mother went out to the kitchen and returned with a ripe banana. She took the boy and danced around. Jumari reached for her breast. She suckled the child until he was fast asleep. (Jocano p. 29)

If this, rather inconsistent, behavior fails to lead to weaning, the mother eventually rubs bitter tasting substances on her breast. She tells

FIGURE 9–4 Processes of personality formation and cultural transmission are deeply affected by the kinds of relationships that children establish with the adults around them. Here, a father from Malitbog in the Philippines cares for his children. (PHOTO COURTESY OF F. LANDA JOCANO)

the child that the *aswang* will come and get it if it doesn't stop suckling. Because the milk of a pregnant woman is bad for the child, efforts at weaning gradually become more and more drastic. Eventually the child will be left with its grandmother, aunts, or other kinsmen for two to four months. Once the child is weaned it spends more and more of its time in the yard outside the house. It must be toilet trained, and it will be slapped or beaten if it cries or refuses to eat.

As in Malitbog, the Modoc regarded infants as requiring considerable care and attention. Babies were carefully bathed and massaged so that they would grow up to be attractive. The father and mother abstained from meat during the first five days after birth so that they would not become sick. Normally, mothers expected the child to nurse for about two years at which time the child's cradle was outgrown and disposed of. If the child wished to nurse for a longer period, it was quite acceptable although the child would be teased by other children. Children were given the breast whenever they seemed hungry and mothers often nursed older and younger children at the same time.

Parents, especially fathers who had more unscheduled time, often sat up through the night to care for infants or sick children. Fathers were also active in holding, hugging, and amusing children. Fathers and mothers often lectured young children concerning respect and obedience, but training was generally postponed until the child was older and much of it was done by older siblings or by playmates. On the whole, Modoc children learned by watching and doing. They were not made to learn or made to do.

What does all this mean? Anthropologists have searched for easy answers to questions about the nature of different systems of childcare and their effects upon children and adults. Some have felt that particular patterns of weaning, wrapping, or toilet training have produced particular and permanent effects upon the individuals who have experienced them. It is more likely that the basic messages of love and hate, fear and self-confidence, independence and dependence, and so on are built up through years of repeated incidents that reinforce the central values of each culture.

We react strongly to other systems of child rearing. Are the Modoc too permissive? Shouldn't they take a stronger hand in their children's care? Aren't the Ngoni too Spartan and too strict? Won't their children become spoiled and spiritless? Is it *our* system of child rearing that causes drug addiction, violence in the streets, or other problems? As far as training goes, it must be argued that all systems of child training practiced by established cultures are successful. The children do grow up to be like their parents. It is only in the obvious cases where children are made sick or insane, unable to function in their cultures and their settings, that a claim can be made that some particular pattern of child rearing is unsuccessful.

The child that is beaten or battered will usually grow up thinking that it is a good idea to beat and batter his or her own children. Whether such a person will be generally sadistic or not depends very much upon larger contexts. So long as human beings understand each other and maintain reasonably accurate perceptions of reality, the behavior of any single individual will depend heavily upon context. The desire to beat and batter children can be suppressed if the situation demands it. If a cultural tradition, represented by parents, playmates and other teachers, emphasizes violence or any other kind of behavior, there is a likelihood that violence generally produces the desired result. If it fails to do so, sane individuals will generally attempt some other behavior.

Characteristic patterns of child rearing generally produce the desired result—the more or less accurate transmission of culture across the generations. Because they do this, it cannot be said that one method is inherently better than another. We cannot say that Modoc permissiveness or Ngoni strictness is wrong. If the Modoc and the Ngoni were not the way they were, perhaps neither would have survived under the particular conditions they experienced. While the style used in the transmission of culture tends to create personalities of a particular kind, it must be emphasized that a personality is expressed only as a set of preferences selected from a range of alternatives. Some people prefer violence, some affection, some flight, some conversation, and so on. People tend to do what they prefer. Their preferences permit us to identify their personalities. Most people in most cultures have personalities that encourage them to attack their problems quite directly. This does not mean that they would attack the hot lava pouring down the sides of the volcano. Hot lava makes cowards of us all. Thus, the expression of personality depends upon the circumstances as much as it depends upon the content of the cultural message.

The Ngoni, the people of Malitbog, and the Modoc have quite different child-rearing practices. In many situations, they behave quite differently. For all, there are situations in which they love, kill, run, attack, hurt, heal, and otherwise behave like human beings. Their approach to particular situations, their style of attack, their character may be different, but their solutions to similar problems are quite often the same.

HOW DO YOU GET THE MESSAGE?

A Modoc Indian of northern California tells us, "When I was a child the first thing I did in the morning was to go out and play" (Ray 1963:107). In the tall reeds and grass lining the shores of Tule Lake, young Modoc boys ceaselessly played hide and seek under the warm summer sun. When the lake water got warm, they swam and raced in the lake. Every boy had a miniature bow and arrow made for him by his father. They shot fish in the marshes, and frogs, watersnakes, and chipmunks.

> "After a while I played with rye-grass arrows. We used strips of bark as feathers. A big boy would sharpen the stalk to make a point. We played at dodging these rye-grass arrows. If you were hit by one it broke the skin. When you saw an arrow coming, you turned aside. If two or more arrows came you twisted around and jumped sideways."

After this, there was always dodge ball, which only hurt when the ball made of reeds hit you behind the ear. Older boys, about ten, tied a ball of mud and reeds to a stick and dodged that. At other times a kind of gun that would fire eight or ten feet was made with a piece of hollow willow and a ramrod. Small boys made peashooters using juniper berries for peas.

There were also slingshots, similar to the one used by David to kill Goliath. These were used to kill small animals including rabbits and ducks. Boys used to stand far apart and play at dodging slingshots. Boys also hunted rabbits with bows and arrows or with rocks always hoping to obtain enough rabbit skins to make a blanket. At the end of the day,

FIGURE 9–5 Menomini Indian children of Wisconsin practice dance steps. The opportunity to participate with adults in a common enterprise is a powerful incentive. (PHOTO COURTESY OF GEORGE SPINDLER)

having fed and cared for themselves all day, "I used to hear my father's mother tell stories of the mythological times" (Ray 1963:109).

Girls rarely played warlike games, but they nevertheless competed vigorously to see who could jump farthest on one leg, to see who could climb a mountain fastest, to see who was quickest at making little baskets. When parents had stockpiles of beads they used to organize competitions for the collection of eggs. The first girl to bring back a basket of eggs received a bead wristlet or a necklace.

Children were never asked to come to meals; they would come if they were hungry. Such formal training in hunting or carrying out domestic chores as might be required did not begin until adolescence, but children were free to accompany their parents and to watch them at work. When children made small bows or baskets, abundant parental praise followed: "My parents were proud of me; and the prouder they were of me the more I wanted to work hard and the better I felt. So I was never lazy" (Ray 1963:106).

Children were expected to be courteous and obedient to all adults. If they were not; they were whipped. Incorrigible children might be severely whipped, locked in the sweathouse, or even sent away. Mostly, though, children were told: "These mountains, these rivers hear what you say and if you are mean they will punish you."

We tend to think of cultural transmission and of systems of education as things that adults do to children or that members do to prospective members. We think of children as being trained. Families are considered to raise children just as if they were agricultural crops and the parents the possessors of the harvest. Although the Modoc parents were quite capable of using force for self-protection or as a last resort when all else failed, they appeared to feel that child rearing was a gross assault upon the rights of children. Children might be advised if they wished to listen. They might be praised if they did something good. Culture was transmitted by example, by experience, by the fact that certain activities were supported. It might almost be said that Modoc culture was not transmitted but received.

A culture is transmitted best when the things that people are urged to do are the things that people naturally want to do. It is not too much to ask that when someone shows us how to paddle a canoe, hunt a deer, or operate a typewriter, we are shown the easy and efficient way. When parents must argue with children, punish them, bribe them, or frighten them to make them keep quiet, go to bed on time, do their homework, gather firewood, or otherwise perform cultural acts, then it is evident that the acts themselves are not presented in a way that makes them desirable to perform. In some way, the cultural system has been distorted so that the tradition, instead of being a tool for enhancing life and making it easier, has become something that causes people to do things they would not otherwise do.

If the Modoc can transmit their culture without even trying, we may wonder why people in other cultures find it so difficult to arrange for cultural transmission. Consider the extreme case of an alien school teaching an alien culture. What is the purpose of what happens? What is the effect of what happens? What is the message that gets delivered?

WHAT DO THEY LEARN IN SCHOOL?

One teacher remarked:

I wanted to stay here several years, and I decided that I would do it with love. But they were so impertinent. If we were going to stay, we had to be tough. Discipline is based on fear and not on love. They respect me because they are afraid. So I strapped it out. It worked (Wolcott 1967:87).

Another teacher wrote:

The village, on arrival from a boat trip presents the most desolate picture. Neglected shacks in a generally filthy state smell profusely when the warm weather breaks through. The children, always filthy, came to respect us. . . . (Wolcott 1967:88).

Other teachers said things like the following:

I have just finished giving all the grades II–VIII I.Q. tests—WOW!—now I know why I usually had the feeling of beating my head against the proverbial brick wall! I have out of 8 students tested, only one I.Q. over 76! They're all of near idiot caliber—God! I was bowled over. Then I figured out their respective M.A.'s (mental ages) and this was just another shock wave!! Even my 13–15-year-olds have M.A.'s of 10!! How can you stop from lowering your own bloody standards after reading results like this? (Wolcott 1967:91).

This was the worst group I ever taught in my life, white or Indian. (Wolcott 1967:91).

No student has ever graduated from the Blackfish school and gone on to the eighth or ninth grade at Alert Bay. Most students remain, repeating grade after grade, until they are sixteen and can leave the school. Some of the students wrote:

Today is Friday. It is the last day of school for the week. I'm anxious for three o'clock. I'm sick and tired of school. (Wolcott 1967:96).

The first day of school he rang the bell about ten o'clock. He said his watch stopped. And he kept ringing it at ten o'clock. We hardly worked. We just draw when we get in a class. When I used to ask him to help me. He used to give me a wrong answer. He isn't a schoolteacher. He's a piano teacher. He used to make excuses on school days. He used to say he's got a cold or a bad headache. (Wolcott 1967:97).

Blackfish Island is about six miles long and two miles across. The village consists of about eighteen frame houses, five of which are unoccupied. Villagers see themselves as part of a social network consisting of twelve interrelated villages. The village and the surrounding related villages are occupied by Kwakiutl Indians who speak the Kwakwala language and who maintain many of the economic and social activities characteristic of the Kwakiutl tradition. The Kwakiutl live on the coast of British Columbia on both sides of the straits and estuaries that separate the northern part of Vancouver Island from the coast.

For centuries, the Kwakiutl have lived upon the salmon and other seafoods abundantly available in the region. Today, many rely upon commercial salmon fishing in order to obtain money for food, clothing, and the various necessities of modern life such as sugar, flour, canned milk, tea, peanut butter, and jelly. Families are reluctant to leave the island for the town of Alert Bay because they cannot count on living off the land.

In the traditional pattern of subsistence activity, young children are expected to assist their parents. Boys especially are needed to help out at home when the adult males are out in the boats. Often the boys go with their fathers on the boats:

I am going to go halibut fishing with my father and Raymond. That's why I asked you is there going to be school tomorrow because I want to go with my father. He always has a tough time when he catches halibut. We got one halibut yesterday. (Wolcott 1967:25).

We are going to Gilford Island tomorrow. I'm going to stay there one week. I'm going to dig clams. There is a big tide this week. I'm not coming to school next week. (Wolcott 1967:25).

Families are large and the girls are expected to help out also: My mom is supposed to wash today. I guess she'll be doing it tomorrow instead. I'll have to help her then. Well, I guess it won't be too dull around our house, with the washing machine running all day tomorrow. On Sunday I'll be ironing my clothes. Besides sewing some clothes. (Wolcott 1967:27).

Tomorrow I am planning to clean up our house, it's like a pig house. Because nobody helps my mother when I am in school. (Wolcott 1967:27).

Students can earn good money by not going to school. Even if they are too young to earn money, their services are often vitally needed in the household. Even so, most parents want their children to go to school. Despite the abundant evidence of racial discrimination that confronts the Kwakiutl in all of their dealings with whites, many believe that education can provide an avenue toward a better life. In fact, the education children received was virtually useless and it interfered with the important responsibilities the schoolchildren had. The schoolroom was pervaded with an overwhelming hostility. This hostility was probably not unconnected with the fact that for many years school teachers had been incompetent, discouraged, and convinced that they were dealing with mental defectives.

The Blackfish village school represents an extreme example of a form of cultural transmission imposed by the members of one cultural system upon the members of another. The facts of racism and social discrimination in the rural parts of Canada and the United States mean that the impact of the school is very often the induction of subsistence hunters, fishers, and farmers into the urban lower class. What is imparted is a spirit of angry frustration characterized by a deep sense of failure and incompetence. Few who have endured such teachers and such a curriculum can be expected to place value upon academic pursuits. Especially for students destined for a career of rural or urban unemployment, but for many others as well, school is often a place where the culture that is transmitted is that Johnny can't read, Doris can't spell, Sally can't do math, Joseph can't write, and Robert can't catch.

The formation of the modern nation state composed of a variety of tribal and ethnic groups necessitates the creation of a shared national tradition—an origin myth (e.g., the Pilgrim Fathers) a common language, and a common educational background. Very often establishment of a national culture is an immoral act, the ruthless destruction of one cultural

system by the agents of another. Although they have never lost a war, and never signed a treaty, the Kwakiutl are a conquered people, and the school has been the agency dedicated to the destruction of their way of life.

Less dramatically, wherever there is a formal school system, there is a tendency for conflict to arise between the needs of the formal school bureaucracy and the needs of the local groups upon which it impinges. Contradictions between culture transmitted in the school and culture transmitted by the home and peer group can often be far more damaging to the student than anything that is learned in the school. There seem to be few solutions to the problem of constructing a school system that is responsive to individual and community needs.

For the present, then, the individual in modern society is compelled to make difficult choices among a variety of alternatives. Often, the cultural tradition appears to be not one cultural tradition but several as different life-styles compete for the attention of the urban individual. How much more difficult is the problem of choice when the existing confusion is complicated by the fact that one's parents and close acquaintances have been raised in a quite different Indian or tribal culture. Among the Kwakiutl, drinking, violence, accidental death, and suicide are a frequent response to the fact of being robbed of one culture and denied admission to another. One solution, not yet attempted by the Kwakiutl, is the formation of a new cultural tradition.

The next case considers one of the kinds of things that may happen when individuals are subjected to conflicting cultural messages. They

FIGURE 9–6 Home for the weekend. These young Cree Indian men have found good jobs off the reservation. Their new life-style may well raise questions among their school teachers and parents. (PHOTO BY PAUL CONKLIN, COURTESY OF NORMAN CHANCE)

become confused; they search for answers; suddenly, sometimes over-night, they possess a complete and unified picture of the truth.

CAN YOU FIND THE WAY?

More than a hundred years ago, the Menomini Indians were confined to a tiny reservation in Wisconsin. Like the Kwakiutl, they were pressed to abandon their traditional culture and yet given few opportunities to learn about or move upward within the United States national culture. Despite the handicaps, many Menomini have acquired advanced educations and stable positions within the national culture. Others have not acquired educations and have not found a place in the national culture. Of these, some have tried to preserve traditional Menomini culture; some have followed the Peyote way:

> The next morning the doctor came out, with the hearse just behind. He asked where she was. We told him, "Inside, go see for yourself!" He went in. There she was preparing breakfast. He stopped. He was surprised so much he could not talk. Then he said, "My God! What happened? What medicine did you give her?" We said "Never mind what medicine. That is the work of the Almighty." He went to his car talking to himself.
>
> That was all I needed. I had been looking for something, somehow, somewhere. This Medicine Lodge was nothing for me. I danced, sung, had a good time, that's all. I was in school. I looked over this Catholic religion. It didn't satisfy me. People go to church, they say prayers, they cross themselves. But it wasn't in here. They didn't feel it in the heart. So I go to some more meetings. I learn more. I listen to them songs. I watch the people pray. Finally I see: "This is where we Indians belong. This is our church."
>
> That is the way it is with us. People tell us we are crazy, that we do wrong. We keep right on, worshiping our own way. We pray how we feel, not the way somebody tells us to. We all pray different, from our own heart. (Spindler and Spindler 1971:112).

Another Menomini tells how he found the Peyote road:

> Well, I just happen to . . . how I come across Peyote . . . I was amongst the Winnebago, roaming around after I lost my folks . . . all alone. Of course, I had two sisters, but they in school. I didn't know where to go or what to do, kinda lost like. I come across the people that use that . . . just happened to be traveling through there. Just happened to be a family, very much respected. They invited me to visit them, they asked me how come I roaming around. I told them my bad luck story. I told them I didn't know what to do with myself. Of course, there was other ways I could do . . . drink, carry on like that . . . but I was looking for something good anyway. Of course my Dad didn't know nothing about Peyote. They just told me to watch my step—to follow life in a good way. I remember that, what they told me I had it in my mind.

After attending a prayer meeting, the convert reports:

> That's the first time I use the medicine. I find out about nice people, respectable people. Of course I didn't know nothing about it. I told them about morning, "I think I'm going to follow this, find out for myself, use this medicine . . . follow it up." Then I thanked them. That's all I said. That's how I got started using this medicine, with them people. They used me good. Next morning they was glad to see me . . . they wished me good luck. "Now I have come to something good . . . something . . . very wonderful," I thought. I was glad about it. Until now that's all I have been doing. Now finally they got me to be a chairman and they consider me a very respected man. I never had no trouble of any kind. (Spindler and Spindler 1971:112–113).

In all cultures the membership has certain concrete expectations concerning what children and new members are to become. Interaction between parents and children transmits a part of the cultural message; other

FIGURE 9–7 Menomini Indians representing the Native American Church have sought a middle road remaining Indian yet modifying many traditional priorities. This is the family of a church leader photographed along with anthropologist Louise Spindler. (PHOTO COURTESY OF GEORGE SPINDLER)

parts, sometimes contradictory, are transmitted by playmates, by schools, by experiences outside of the family. In most cultures, the expectations of other people and the design of life and career tend to press the individual along what might be called the official road. In very complicated cultural systems or in cultural systems that are undergoing the stress of changing physical environments or changing relationships to other cultural systems, the official road forks repeatedly, sometimes it appears to disappear altogether.

In the Menomini example, given above, people found it difficult to be either Menomini-Americans or Anglo-Americans. Most of the people who discovered the Peyote Road were people who had been raised to be Menomini Indians. Nevertheless, they went to school where they were told that it was wrong to be a Menomini Indian. When the individual feels that his or her life can be directed competently by other people, there is little chance of deviation from the road pointed out by trusted parents, teachers, or friends. But this sort of trust is often dissolved by experience. Young people in their early teens, and sometimes older people as well, often come to a realization that their trust in parents and others was misplaced. They feel that the traditional road is rocky, boring, or dumb. In the Menomini case, the traditional road must have seemed a road to nowhere. The modern road pointed out by school teachers must have seemed forbidding and inaccessible.

Of the Menomini quoted above, one was dependent upon an aunt who almost died but was cured by peyote. The other had parents that had died. Both were in a position to see that their close relatives could not be relied upon to provide them with lifelong security. The common reaction, typified by the second informant or by the accounts of Saora shamans given earlier (chapter 4), is to wander aimlessly like a lost soul. Such seekers try many different activities. These activities often seem to others to be depraved, dark, unusual. It appears, now, that cultural transmission has failed. What has been produced is a drunk, a nut, a drifter, or an addict.

One day, the light dawns. The worthless and confused individual becomes a shaman, enters a monastery, joins the Peyote cult, or enters the International Society for Krishna Consciousness. There is a sharp and radical alteration in the individual's apparent personality. Shiftlessness is replaced by dedication. Immorality is replaced by conformity—"they got me to be a chairman and they consider me a very respected man."

The explanation of such conversion experiences is difficult. It is hard to get into the frame of mind of the prophet or of the convert. A good guess is that new ways of life and conversion experiences originate in the struggles of the individual to reconcile conflicting cultural messages. These struggles take place in a context within which traditional systems of cultural transmission are breaking down. The new doctrine and its converts reflect the discovery of a philosophical or intellectual means of reconciling the conflict among the messages received. Thus, the Peyote road is neither Christian nor traditional Indian. Jesus and the Bible are the gifts that god made to the Europeans. For the Indians,

> You take that, and the medicine will do the rest. God will talk to you himself. You don't need no bible. (Spindler and Spindler 1971:96).

In the conversion experience, the individual abruptly sees the light and sets about, sometimes with incredible determination, the task of acquiring a new cultural message, a new self, a new way of life. The most dramatic expression of conversion is the sudden acquisition of a new personality virtually overnight. In such a case, what apparently happens is that existing knowledge is gradually and unconsciously shaped into a new personality that becomes dominant through what seems to be a kind of instantaneous crystallization.

The creation of a new cultural message and the teaching of that message to converts is similar but not identical to two other processes that occur in many cultures. These processes are (1) therapeutic change of an existing personality and (2) the conversion of the child into an adult. The next section contains two rather similar examples. The first deals with Daytop, an institution designed to convert young drug addicts into responsible adults. The second example, taken from the Ngoni of Malawi, illustrates one way of changing boys into men.

HOW DO YOU CHANGE THEM INTO ADULTS?

When a prospective member telephones to make an appointment, the prospect is told to phone again at a particular time. Not until the prospect has made a series of fruitless calls, will an appointment be obtained. When the prospect arrives for his interview, he is told to sit on a chair placed in the front part of the house in full view of all the residents. He sits silently for several hours while the residents look him over. Later the prospect is brought into a room and seated at a table with six or eight young adults. They ask questions: "What can we do for you; why are you here; what is the matter with you that you have to shoot dope?" The prospect may say, "I've come to the end of the road . . . I can't stand myself anymore—the way I've been living . . . I'm determined to kick the filthy habit." The interviewers listen for a while and then one interrupts angrily:

> Knock off that shit, will you? Who do you think you are talking to? We ain't no bunch of bleeding heart social workers. The people you see here were dope fiends themselves, see? And at one time we all came in here sniveling just like

you are doing now—"I want to rid myself of the horrors of drug addiction."
(Sugarman 1974:13)

The interview continues. The prospect's weaknesses are exposed and the prospect is expected to admit acting stupidly and like a baby. The prospect must make a commitment. Long hair is cut short, or the prospect is asked to scream, "Help me." The prospect admits to being in an infantile state and begs to be admitted to a group that will deny the prospect almost all rights and privileges. For the duration, the prospect is stripped of all personal property, forbidden to leave, to make phone calls, or to write letters.

The prospect, accepted as a novice, sleeps on a couch in the living room and is given the most menial jobs to perform. Older residents explain the "Concept" and the prospect discovers that he can be treated like a person, perhaps for the first time in his life, if he conforms to the principles embodied in the Concept. During the day, a record is kept of all mistakes and deviations from the Concept. Each morning at a group meeting the culprits are identified and criticized by the membership:

> When are you going to get a grip on yourself, dummy? You've been in here six weeks and all you do is wander about in a daze, leaving dirty paint brushes behind you, dirty coffee cups, leaving lights on, losing your clothes, and I don't know what else. I guess you must sleep in your clothes—otherwise I am sure you'd forget to put them on before you came down in the morning. Get a grip on yourself, stupid. (Sugarman 1974:33).

When a mistake has been made, individuals are encouraged to come forward and confess:

> The question is whether you are man enough to put up your hand and cop to it. Why are people afraid? What makes them hold that guilt in their bellies? What could possibly happen to you for copping to a dirty coffee cup? (Sugarman 1974:34)

In addition to these morning meetings, there are encounter group meetings in which the individual is encouraged to admit deficiencies and to discuss personality weaknesses with others. As the individual learns to be "open" and to conform rigidly to the rules, privileges and affection begin to be received. Ultimately, the "Concept" became a movement as the members of Daytop Village found continued participation in the communal group infinitely more satisfying than the isolation, low status, and demands for initiative that confronted them on the outside.

Violent, radical change in personality is often demanded at the time that boys are transformed into men. Among the Ngoni of Malawi in Africa, the raising of boys by women, many of whom were from other tribes, was looked upon with distrust. Boys of six and a half to seven and a half years of age were typically "impudent, well-fed, self-confident, and spoiled" (Read 1968:49). Ngoni fathers wished their boys to exhibit "toughness, leadership, responsibility, and respect for authority" (Read 1968:50).

Accordingly, as soon as a boy's permanent teeth had erupted, he went to live in the boy's dormitory. In traditional times, it was here that a boy would live until he was fully grown and went to join his regiment. In the dormitory, which was run entirely by the boys without outside interference, the only rules were those determined by age and strength. Younger boys were required to perform menial tasks for the older boys and were beaten frequently. Older boys were expected to share food brought from their parents' houses with the younger boys, but this didn't work too well in practice. Younger children obtained milk while herding cattle and roasted birds in clay. Sometimes they stole maize or peanuts from their mothers' granaries. When not engaged in the herding of cattle or the running of errands, small boys engaged in stick fighting as a means of learning the art of breaking heads and bruising bodies. When life became too difficult, the smaller boys were free to organize and attack a smaller number of older boys. For the most part, the younger boys, as might be expected, idolized and followed the "big ones." The Ngoni were an aristocracy that ruled an empire. The founder of Daytop was quoted as saying:

> . . . our real job ain't got nothing to do with just overcoming drugs. Our real job . . . is confronting a racist community and challenging to live the life we show by example. Our real job is to take those isolated neighborhoods and try to change them into communities. . . . Now that scares a lot of people, but it's time you really understood. (Sugarman 1974:123)

In traditional psychological theory, early childhood experiences were thought to provide the basis of the adult personality. That which is learned well and learned young is sometimes difficult to unlearn. Nevertheless, the perpetuation of the child's personality in the adult is dependent upon a continuity of training and experience. Novice members of Daytop or of the Ngoni tribe are subjected to overwhelming pressures required to transform the personality to the individual.

Rapid personality transformations may also occur as a part of the normal growth of personality. Religious conversions in which the individual rapidly alters his or her behavior in order to conform to a new image as a spirit medium, healer, priest, scientist, or even anthropologist were discussed earlier. Very little is known about the impact of such rapid change upon the individual. At the least it can be suggested that confor-

mity and inflexibility may be the hallmarks of those who have traded or
been forced to trade all or most of one personality for another.

SHALL YOU DIE BESIDE THE RIVER?

In traditional Hindu philosophy a person who has passed the stage of
householder, a person whose children are adults, is free to concern himself
(or even herself) with rebirth into the next life. Freed of earthly responsibility, the individual gradually withdraws from all concern with material
things. Through prayer, meditation, or other means, it becomes possible
to give up all needs and desires. Gradually, the individual acquires control
over the six senses and the nine openings of the body and is able to
separate the soul from the body for longer and longer periods of time. In
the end, freed from all pain and all worldly concerns, the individual
perceives the true reality of God and assumes an appropriate role as a part
of the infinite.

The case that follows represents a part of the author's experiences in
the village of Namhalli in South India. At that time I was attempting to
collect historical materials to serve as a background for a study of cultural
change. I sought old men who might remember how things were in the
old days. Once or twice each week I visited Achary in his garden. Achary
was an old man with a quick intelligence and a long memory. He was
always waiting when I came. Each time, he showed me a place to sit where
mango fruit dislodged by hungry parrots would not hit me on the head.
That was his magic.

In 1952, Achary was old. His flesh hung loosely around his bones and
he remembered events back to the famine of 1877. He remembered his
father and the absolute terror he felt whenever his father looked at him.
When he was a child, his father, a blacksmith, had beaten him with an
iron bar when he made mistakes or broke rules. In the school, the teacher
wielded a bamboo cane with similar painful results.

Achary was raised in the old school and he resented the soft and
irreligious ways that had come to the village. Such evil ways did not
penetrate his own house. His five sons, ranging in age from nine to fifteen
years old, obeyed him without question. They worked hard in the fields
and were exposed to as little of the soft, modern kind of schooling as
possible. The low-class people in the village wore modern clothing made
by machine; not the children of Achary. They went about dressed in rags,
while their father squirreled his money away in a huge iron safe. Although times had changed and young men were marrying while still of
high school age, Achary planned to have the marriages of his sons when
they approached the age of thirty.

Once, Achary was the strongest man in the village. He was an out-

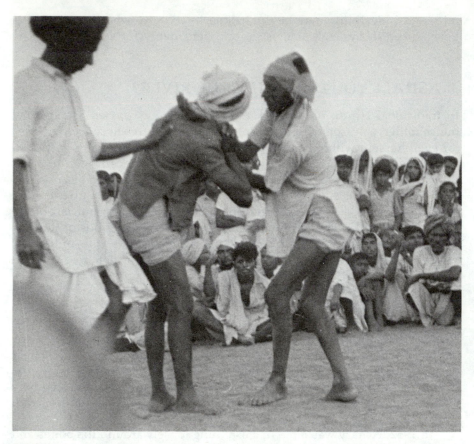

FIGURE 9–8   In most farming communities physical strength is considered a virtue. It was at this kind of performance that Achary excelled. Gopalpur, South India. (PHOTO BY ALAN R. BEALS)

standing wrestler and could bend an iron bar with his bare hands. He ate vast quantities of butter and other health-giving foods. He used his strength to organize wrestling and hymn-singing groups. A few months after I came to the village, his sons locked him out of the house:

> We love our father, but he is crazy. Look at the clothing we are wearing, it does not even cover our behinds. He has not arranged for our marriages. None of us have any education.

Later, when I came to the garden, Achary was digging a hole. It looked very much like a grave, and for a minute I thought he was planning his own burial. After asking a passing boy to climb a tree and fetch us a coconut, he explained that the hole was for meditation. He would sit cross-legged in the hole and cover the top of the hole with a stone. He would sit there. Already his soul had left his body for brief periods. He was now free of responsibility for his sons and could concern himself with his own spiritual welfare. He had, he said, many disciples, one of them a policeman, another a high governmental official. He advised them how to conduct their lives and how to achieve a meritorious existence.

After our interview, he said he was going over to the next garden. There, he and another old man were going to prepare a special tonic having many remarkable and curative properties. He told me now about his youth when he was a wrestler, when he performed prodigious feats of strength, when he ate incredible quantities of food.

Achary had learned to be an old man. It is true, he learned his lesson

FIGURE 9–9 Where there has been rapid cultural change old people may find their knowledge obsolete or they may find themselves to be valued repositories of tradition. This man, Nahpone Perrote, was one of the four men who knew the details of the Mitawin ritual of the Menomini Indians in Wisconsin. (PHOTO COURTESY OF GEORGE SPINDLER)

the hard way. Most old men in the village simply retired to their gardens, where they could usefully employ themselves in the pursuit of small boys and monkeys intent upon stealing fruit. Surrounded by coconut and banana trees, the gardens were tropical islands in the midst of the barren farmlands of the village. In Namhalli, at that time, learning to be old had a special challenge. Being old in 1952, in a village coming under the influence of a nearby city, had unprecedented aspects, for the old had become progressively less useful and less powerful. In the old days, the old man had a pot of gold hidden in the mud walls of the house. If he became angry at his descendants, he would not tell them where it was. Now, there was little gold to hide.

Even so, the pathway to old age was clearly marked. There were gardens that needed watching. Above all, there was the opportunity to commence a period of spiritual development—to become truly free, to achieve eternal bliss. As I left the garden, I passed Achary's new daughter-in-law carrying an elaborate midday meal. In 1966, Achary was older but still strong and healthy. In a short time, during 1952, he had learned perhaps as much as he had learned at any other period in his life. In less than an hour he had changed from a powerful head of a household into a foolish and powerless old man. Fortunately, he had available a cultural message that informed him concerning the correct ways of growing old and transcending mortality.

SUMMARY

The concept of cultural transmission implies that the members of different cultures behave in rather different ways. The chapter begins with a quotation from a Navajo Indian and a puzzle. What are the characteristically Navajo properties of the quotation? Does the quotation provide evidence that is helpful in separating the Navajo and Hopi stories that are given? In fact, Navajo and Hopi responses to the same pictures are remarkably different. The differences are accounted for by the fact that different cultures are transmitted to the Hopi and to the Navajo.

The process of cultural transmission operates, literally, from womb to tomb. There are different things to learn in each stage of life. There are different teachers and different modes of transmission. In addition to the obvious verbal messages, culture is transmitted by such things as the rectangular sheets, beds, and rooms that confront the Euro-American child. Even the grammar of the language that is spoken may have subtle effects upon the manner in which the individual conceptualizes nature.

All of these things taken together tend to produce personality characteristics that are widely shared among the members of any particular cultural system. On the other hand, the cultural message is not transmitted in quite the same way to all individuals. Wealth, birth order, sex, age of parents, and a host of other factors have an impact upon the personality of the developing individual. Later, demands for the performance of a variety of different roles cause personalities to adjust and change. As they grow, people learn how to play the cultural game with increasing skill and success.

The examples of childbirth among the Iroquois, Ngoni, and Malitbog people illustrate how the approach to birth and the rituals surrounding birth convey a host of cultural intentions toward the child and its mother. Iroquois ideals of self-reliance are summed up in a process of motherhood that takes place virtually without assistance. Ngoni stress upon proper behavior is marked at each stage of the reproductive process. In Malitbog, in marked contrast to these two heroic cases, the arrival of "a gift of God" is greeted with appropriate concern and ceremony. The future treatment of the child is signified by the reception it receives at birth. Although the cultural message may or may not reach the infant, the mother, father, and all onlookers are informed of the child's relative importance and of their future roles with regard to the child.

By contrast, the process of weaning communicates directly to the child. The Ngoni and Malitbog cases indicate the continuity between the weaning process and the childbirth process. The Ngoni child is subjected to the same strict regime that earlier affected its mother. In Malitbog, concern for the child makes the weaning process inconsistent. Modoc reluctance to engage in deliberate training or unnecessary discipline meant that children were not weaned at all. They quit nursing when they were ready to do so or when other children teased them.

The wide range of variation in patterns of child rearing suggests that the cultural message can be satisfactorily transmitted in an enormous number of ways. Most people turn out to be sufficiently similar to their parents and peers to permit their functioning as proper members of their cultural system. Thus, all cultural systems have satisfactory methods of cultural transmission. Although contrasts between different systems of cultural transmission are noteworthy; it is also noteworthy that people from quite different cultural systems are likely to approach similar problems in quite similar ways.

The case of the Modoc Indians suggests that cultural tradition need not involve very much direct instruction or even very much deliberate influence of parents upon children. The Modoc cultural system provided a setting within which children learned how to behave as Modoc without being weaned, disciplined, punished, manipulated, or consciously taught. Because the Modoc do not find it necessary to wean their children or otherwise control and discipline them, it is possible to wonder why weaning and other forms of direct control are essential in other cultural systems.

The case of the Blackfish school illustrates a conflict between cultural messages embodied in a conflict between teachers and students. Although the Blackfish school is an extreme example, it illustrates the problems encountered in complex societies where different parts or segments of the cultural system possess quite different cultural messages. Conflicting cultural messages are sometimes resolved, as in the case of some Menomini Indians, through the emergence of a new cultural message such as the Peyote cult, which manages to reconcile the conflict for some individuals. The process of conversion to the Peyote cult illustrates how adult personalities can be dramatically changed.

Examples drawn from Daytop and from the Ngoni illustrate how rapid personality transformations are sometimes achieved by transferring the individual to a radically different and stressful situation. In both cases, overwhelming pressures result in what appears to be the abandonment of an old personality and the assumption of a new one. It is possible that such rapid personality change leads to conformity and inflexibility, but there is little concrete evidence of its effects.

Cultural transmission continues throughout the lifetime of the individual. An example from India indicates how an established cultural pattern for behavior during old age can be activated by the individual once the onset of old age is recognized. In this example, Achary's behavior and life-style change rapidly in a very short period of time, and a variety of new ways of doing things must be learned.

This chapter has not attempted to exhaust all that is to be known about cultural transmission. There is much to be learned. There are many conflicting theories. There are few certainties. Culture is transmitted and received at many levels and through many different media. Thus, it is always difficult to say what has been transmitted or how. Perhaps an awareness of these complexities is the most important thing to be transmitted at this point. The many modes of cultural transmission are a further testimony to the variety of human adaptive strategies made possible by the cultural message.

For Further Reading

Descriptions of the transmission of culture to children include Margaret Mead's *Growing up in New Guinea* (1930) and *Coming of Age in Samoa* (1928), Spiro's *Children of the Kibbutz* (1958), Whiting's *Child Rearing in Six Cultures* (1963) and Deng's *The Dinka of the Sudan* (1972).

Case Studies in Education and Culture, listed on the last page of this book, offer a convenient way of surveying the field. A classic, and never surpassed study of cultural transmission characterized by stunning photographs is Bateson and Mead's *Balinese Character* (1942). Also of interest are Ogbu's *Minority Education and Caste* (1978) and Kimball and Burnett's *Learning and Culture* (1973).

A useful survey of education and anthropology is Spindler's *Education and Cultural Process* (1974). A recent addition to the case studies in cultural anthropology is Dougherty's *Becoming a Woman in Rural Black Society* (1978). This and Aschenhenner's *Lifelines: Black Families in Chicago* (1975) are important descriptions of cultural transmission in the United States.

Problems and Questions

1. Examine the life history of an individual. What does it say about processes of cultural transmission?
2. Consider a group consisting of people of about the same age. What sorts of behavioral standards are there, and how are they transmitted?
3. From an ethnography, what are the main ways that the cultural message is transmitted?
4. Examine a TV program or other similar material. What is the cultural message?
5. Compare children's books from different cultures or time periods. How do the messages differ? Why?
6. In theory, inconsistent or contradictory cultural messages are expected to occur in all cultures. Are there major contradictions in your own culture? How are they resolved or dealt with?

10 CONTROL OF BEHAVIOR

What are the key questions?

Processes of cultural transmission prepare the members for the parts they are to play in the operation of the cultural system. But the cultural message is diverse and moves through many channels. Different individuals receive different aspects of the message. There is another problem too, one that is quite marked in the culture of the United States: that which we are taught to do sometimes turns out to be quite different from that which we ought to do or have to do. What happens when the expectations aroused in individuals through transmission of cultural messages simply are not met?

Related to this is the problem of writing rules and laws that take account of the kinds of things that actually happen. The opening section deals with an imaginary case similar to the famous gedanken (thought) experiments performed by Albert Einstein in justification of the Theory of Relativity. What sorts of problems are posed by the existence of unpredictable events? What happens when things happen that are not covered by the rules? Can you really make rules that no one will feel a need to break?

The next section, "What is the solution?" is concerned with the ways in which people do the right things but get into trouble anyway. Are there culturally approved ways of opting out of difficult situations, or can you manipulate the rules in such a way that you come out smelling like a rose? The cases of Miguel and Sulli illustrate ways that individuals can use artful manipulations to advantage. In the case of Biboi, and in the earlier cases of the Makah and the Lugbara, the inherent conflict in a troubled situation could not be resolved.

Because individuals can bend the rules or evade them, cultural systems offer a variety of devices designed to discourage potential rule breakers. Cases from Dutch Guiana and South India raise questions about religion and social control. Other examples from Spain, South Africa, and the United States raise questions about the opinions of others and their impact upon Ego's behavior.

Cases from the United States and Nigeria explore ways in which the expected presence of "foul-ups," witches, and perhaps other kinds of subversives can be used as a means of social control. Next, what is the value of confession and is "virtue its own reward?" Eskimo and Ngoju examples explore these matters.

But sometimes there is disagreement concerning whether a rule has been broken or not. How are conflicts between individuals to be resolved? A case from Nigeria leads to consideration of the effects of unending and expensive judicial procedure. The problem of contradictory rules is raised in terms of examples from South India and Bulgaria. What do you do in a "no win" situation?

Conflicts, expecially those between husband and wife, often seem disorderly. Are they really? To what extent may conflicts involve ritual and symbolic gestures? A husband and wife dispute from Alor suggests some answers. An analysis from South India raises questions about the extent to which there is an underlying order in human conflict.

WHAT ARE THE RULES AND CAN YOU FOLLOW THEM?

If cultural systems exist in perfectly predictable environments where members have succeeded in developing a cultural tradition which predicts all that will happen, they reflect a utopian state where meals are always served on time, where cross-cousins are always available for marriage, where brides are always beautiful and grooms always handsome, where enemies are always defeated after just the right amount of conflict, where children never cry, where criminals do not exist, and where nothing ever happens except what already happened. In Utopia, all families contain precisely the same number of children, and all children have precisely the same number of playmates, siblings, mother's brothers, and father's sisters. Every 104 years, one of the young men suggests an expedition to the faraway hills, but each time he does so, an official known as the Expedition-quasher says, "Let's go another day." There is no real change in Utopia; all is as it was when the state of perfect predictability and environmental equilibrium was first achieved.

On the other side of the faraway hills lies the equally imaginary community of Hillside. For years Hillsiders have been attempting to study themselves and nature with a view toward establishing the same degree of predictability enjoyed by their neighbors, the Utopians. At present, the only predictable thing in their lives is that on November 23, when they make their traditional attack on the Utopians, they get defeated. Some years ago, a brilliant Hillsider scientist, R. B. Branaslaski, concluded that predictability should start in the home. If, he reasoned, rules were written governing the behavior of each relative toward every other relative, there would be at least one area of life that was perfectly predictable. Branaslaski proposed two simple rules for the control of family interaction: (1) men have authority over women; and (2) older people have authority over younger people. Branaslaski felt that this would prevent quarrels within the family and, since everybody would obey the oldest male, help to make family behavior predictable.

As soon as Branaslaski's rule had been passed, a series of violent quarrels developed between mothers and sons. Mothers claimed that since they were older they had authority over their sons; sons claimed that since they were male they had authority over their mothers. Branaslaski solved this problem by decreeing that the older men should hold an initiation ceremony for the younger men and that, after the initiation ceremony, the young men would be permitted to give orders to their mothers instead of the other way around. A number of young men were promply initiated. As soon as the initiation had taken place, these young men entered into conflict with their fathers because the young men and their fathers both wanted to give orders to their mothers at the same time. Bruised and battered youths and parents appealed to Branaslaski for relief. Branaslaski decreed that all young men, immediately after their initiation ceremonies, should leave home and live in a young adult residence on the outskirts of the village. This solution worked well for several weeks before complaints began coming in from neighboring villages. The young men were stealing women and cattle, misbehaving, picketing, rioting, and making noises in the night. Again the problem was brought before Branaslaski, but by this time he had achieved true wisdom and merely remarked, "Think how dull things would be if everything were predictable."

Although men have authority over women in most cultures, most men spend their early years under the domination of their mothers. Branaslaski's use of an initiation ceremony to create an abrupt transition between boyhood and adulthood disregards the knowledge that boys mature gradually over several years and at different rates. In every culture, different sets of rules must govern the behavior of children and adults, yet there are long periods during which individuals are neither children nor adults. The contrast between Utopia and Hillside is a contrast between what people expect from their cultural traditions and what they get. In effect, a cultural tradition is a set of earnest policies designed (insofar as it is designed at all) to control and render predictable the forces of nature and the vagaries of human behavior. If the forces of nature are predictable, they do not seem *easily* predictable and the same can be said for human behavior. Despite a universal human diligence in the conscious and unconscious formulation of written and unwritten rules to cover every conceivable situation, cases often arise in which human beings do not do what other human beings expect them to do. Every cultural system, then, must contain processes designed to cope with the unexpected perversities, contrariness, and unpredictability of the human animal.

Young men have a tendency to emulate their fathers, but, as the following example taken from the Makah Indians of the northwest coast of the United States indicates, the prospects of immediate gratification may delay this process.

> This happened in Ozette. This chief fixed up his son to catch a whale. He built a canoe for him, make harpoon, and blow up the hair seal for floater. About dozen of them. So when he got everything, he told his son, "You must bathe every night. You must bathe every night if you want to be clean, if you want to catch a whale. Go in the salt water and bathe every night and pray. Ask for a whale." So this young man went off every night. And he didn't bathe at all. He went round look for sweetheart. Well, about a month, pretty soon this young man brought his sweetheart home to his father's house. Well, this old man got up. They used to have a flat roof, all flat roof, loose cedar timber on top. So this old man shoved that board one side. "You always sleep late in the morning!" And he goes with the light in the house to his son's bed. And two heads laying there. One woman head and one man. He went to his wife and said, "That young man! After I had hard time making things, he spoil the things. He got a woman now instead of a whale." He go around, go around. They used to have five, six family in the house, big house. He went around there pouring out all the slops, put them in his square bucket made of cedar. He open his son's face and throw that on his son's head. He said, "I didn't want you to catch woman! I want you to catch whale, not woman. You spoil yourself!" (Colson 1953:183–184).

Although the inexplicable failure of human plans can often be attributed to the fact, noted even in ancient Babylon, that each successive generation of human beings is markedly inferior to the one before, trouble in this world and unpredictability cannot be blamed entirely upon the generation gap. Consider the Lugbara of Uganda in Africa:

> When the bride becomes pregnant the marriage becomes more settled, and when she is a mother of a son it is complete. If she does not become pregnant it is said that the blessing which her father gave her on her marriage day, by spitting on her forehead, was not given with a good heart, and visits are made

to persuade him to bless her properly. If she does not conceive within six months or so there is usually quarreling and the wife is sent home and the bride-wealth demanded back, or a sister may be sent in her place. Although her own lineage will try to blame the matter on the husband's lineage, usually by accusing them of witchcraft, it is generally accepted that barrenness of the wife is the cause (Middleton 1965:56).

Here, again, all human efforts, all the careful marriage arrangements, are unavailing. Among the Hillsiders, the Makah, the Lugbara, among all of the peoples of the world, the perversities of nature and humanity result in rule breaking and in the defeat of expectations. Even the good man who does all the "right" things may find himself in difficulties. The following section deals with good intentions and difficult problems.

What Is the Solution?

He (Miguel) had boasted to his age mates that he would "conquer" Margarita at a forthcoming dance. It was important for him to carry out his plan to prove his *machismo*. Retreat from his open declaration of intent would have "reduced" Miguel in the eyes of his friends. A few days later, he was stunned to discover that his elder brother had become interested in the same girl. For Miguel to proceed with his plan of seduction would be a serious affront to his brother. Caught in this dilemma, Miguel brooded. He could see no out from the hopeless situation. When illness struck him, it seemed like a blessing rather than a misfortune. The day before the dance, Miguel noticed stiffness and pain in his left leg. As the pain increased, he mentioned it to his parents. His mother examined Miguel and announced that he had *aire*. He was ordered to bed for twenty-four hours with a poultice of ground tomatoes and herbs over the stiff leg. Before the dance, his elder brother came to Miguel's bedside to wish him a rapid recovery (Madsen 1964:98).

Here, in an example from South Texas, the young man avoids conflict and loss of face by consciously or unconsciously making use of a culturally sanctioned process which permits graceful withdrawal from an impossible situation.

In most of the cultures and communities of the modern world, processes of rapid cultural change multiply the unpredictabilities of human life creating problems only gifted innovators can solve.

Before he had finished the first year at the mission school, he had to do something about his steady girl. She was now of an age when suitors were clustering around her and she could hardly avoid marriage to someone else if Sulli delayed any longer. Not that she would be forced by her parents, but rather that she would very likely become pregnant—given the usual proclivities of a young Kota woman—and then she would have to get a father for the child. Many a man would be only too eager to get an attractive young wife, with a child on the way to boot.

She came to Sulli and clasped his feet, he tells, in the gesture of entreaty. "She was 16 and her breasts were so big and she was very beautiful. But the teacher had told me that the boys who get married leave their studies, they don't care for the lessons. . . . So that night I thought hard which was best. If I married, I would have a few days happy and then all the rest of my life I would have to dig the earth and sweat. If I worked hard for about four years, then all the rest of the time I would be a teacher or a government servant."

He put her off temporarily with an excuse and disposed of her entreaties permanently with a stratagem. Among her suitors was a gay youth who sang very well and had a persuasive way with the girls. Sulli arranged with this lad to stay the night in a house where the unmarried young men and women of the village often came to sing and then to sleep. Sulli and his girl were there that night. He acted coldly toward her. When the lamp was put out and she came to sleep at his side, he did not cover her with his cloth as usual but straightaway turned his back to her and pretended to fall asleep.

Rebuffed and angered, she made little resistance to the singer when he crept over and induced her to move to the other side of the room to lie intimately with him. Then the singer coughed, a signal prearranged; Sulli struck a match and saw her there in the singer's arms. At once she came over to beg his forgiveness but he was adamant and would have nothing more to do with her (Mandelbaum 1960:291–292).

Where men are less wise in the manipulation of the rules of their traditional cultures, the cleavage between culturally induced expectations and the realities of life may widen dangerously. Consider the case of Biboi, a member of a Brazilian Indian tribe.

Biboi was the son of a Mundurucú chief who had been educated by a Brazilian trader and thus felt himself to be superior to his fellows. He was installed as the chieftain of Cabitutú by his trader patron in the expectation that he would relay to the group information about the trader's needs for wild rubber. Biboi had no kinsmen in Cabitutú and was younger and less prestigious than many of the men of the village. In an attempt to strengthen his position, Biboi contracted a marriage with a widow several years older than himself. Finding the older woman unattractive, he brought home a second wife. The first wife expressed her displeasure violently and her brothers ordered Biboi to remove his second wife from the village. Biboi sent her to his father's village of Cabruá.

Having left his pretty bride in the safe confines of his father's house, Biboi returned to Cabitutú to set matters right and quiet the discontent. But he continued in his arrogant and demanding ways and the sentiments of the villagers became further inflamed, with no small assistance from his first wife and her family. There grew among them a firm determination to kill him. . . .

In the meantime, the person of the young wife was not as secure as Biboi thought it would be. Her husband was away and she was a rather wayward girl; whatever rectitude she possessed was certainly no match for the insistent attempts upon her body by the men of Cabruá. Soon, all of the men of the village except those prohibited by incest regulations—and there were some exceptions even to this—were enjoying the favors of Biboi's young wife in the underbrush surrounding the village, at the stream, in the forest, in the gardens, or whenever they might find her alone. . . .

The balance of power and of moral correctness lay with Biboi's opponents, and the task of his supporters was made most difficult by virtue of the fact that Biboi had almost ceased to be a social person—the rules no longer applied to him. We left the field before the curtain fell on our little drama, but one could already predict the conclusion. This was seen most clearly when, shortly before our departure, Caetono fell from a palm tree and lay seriously injured for several days. Knowing that the people of Cabitutú would kill him as soon as they were assured of his father's death, Biboi came immediately to Cabruá and remained there until the old man's recovery was certain. During this period, Biboi approached me and said, "You know, if my father dies, I will leave this land and go to live on the banks of the Tapajós River." I asked why, and, in fine Biboi style, he answered, "Because it is so beautiful there." Biboi knew that his life as a Mundurucú was finished (Murphy 1961:60).

In the Kota example, Sulli approximated what Malcom McFee calls a 150 percent man—a man who knows his own culture and a newly introduced culture as well and can therefore manipulate both to his advantage. Biboi, by contrast, was a 75 percent man—at home in no culture. He did not know the rules for getting along in Mundurucú society and was far too superior to consider them worth learning. Even if he had been more sophisticated in coping with the realities of his two different cultural situations, he would probably have encountered difficulties. As it was he found himself forced to choose between death and exile.

In the above cases, Miguel and Sulli extricated themselves from difficult situations by manipulating available cultural resources in such a way that their behavior appeared to be above reproach. In the other cases, among the Makah, the Lugbara, and the Mundurucú, conflict arose over the question of the appropriateness of the behavior of the different individuals involved. Because individuals may always choose to break rules or to do things in improper ways, processes of social control are often designed to attach punishments or disadvantages to rulebreaking behavior. How do the Bush Negroes of Dutch Guiana encourage conformity to the rules?

WHAT HAPPENS WHEN YOU BREAK THE RULES?

Why is it, Bayo, that Sadefo lost his food in the still water? Was it because he felt safe and didn't take care in such small rapids?

"No," he said promptly, "that's how kunu works. A man travels on the river all his life. He goes over small rapids and large rapids. He carries loads and returns to his own village. But then something happens. His boat is good. He walks *koni*—carefully—but he loses his food, or his entire load, or his boat, or even his life. Something is working against him. It might be *wisi*—bad magic, it might be kunu. If you have kunu then your enemies can make their bad magic work against you. So it is" (Herskovits 1934:65–66).

When men break rules, they are afflicted with *kunu*, a kind of weakness which renders the individual powerless against the attacks of his ever-present enemies. If a man breaks numerous or important rules, ancestors or gods can be counted upon to bring death to one member after another of the rulebreaker's family.

Such automatic punishments may also afflict the evildoer after his death. South Indian evildoers receive the following punishments in the afterworld:

1. A man who always sees the young and beautiful girls and describes her dress and her shape, that fellow will be nailed to the wall with sharp nails and then thrown into melting limestone and limewater poured into his eyes.
2. The man who loves another man's wife and makes false to his own teacher will be beaten with a hammer to reduce his pride and asked to walk on a stick. His teeth will be removed and he will be cut into pieces and cooked on the fire and branded with hot iron bars.
3. A man who abuses others will have dirty things poured into his mouth.
4. The man who loves his friend's wife or his brothers' wives of if he loves others often will be asked to embrace a heated steel pillar.

5. The man who wishes to love a woman of good character has a mixture of sand and lime poured into his eyes.
6. The man who puts up cases and quarrels for the property of others will be asked to put his hands in the fire.
7. The man who causes others to be sinful and jealous is put into a stone mill and ground up.
8. The man who kills sheep, goats, and buffaloes will have his head cut off and played with like a ball.
9. People who cheat their own brothers or steal property will be cut to pieces and thrown to the crows.

The concept of automatic punishment implies that something or someone, ordinarily a supernatural figure or mechanism, keeps track of the individual's sins and follows up with inevitable retribution. Such a device is likely to be effective only when the individual has a direct experience of swift and effective punishment and so experiences fear and guilt whenever he commits a misdemeanor. Another process of social control is illustrated in the following, taken from an ethnography of a Spanish village:

"*Verguenza* is the regard for the moral values of society, for the rules whereby social intercourse takes place, for the opinion which others have of one. But this, not purely out of calculation. True verguenza is a mode of feeling which makes one sensitive to one's reputation and thereby causes one to accept the sanctions of public opinion."

Thus a *sin verguenza* is a person who either does not accept or who abuses those rules. And this may be either through a lack of understanding or through a lack of sensitivity. One can perceive these two aspects of it.

First as the result of understanding, upbringing, education. "Lack of education" is a polite way of saying "lack of verguenza." It is admitted that if the child is not taught how to behave it cannot have verguenza. It is sometimes necessary to beat a child "to give him verguenza," and it is the only justifiable excuse for doing so. Failure to inculcate verguenza into one's children brings doubt to bear upon one's own verguenza.

But in its second aspect of sensitivity, it is truly hereditary. A person of bad heredity cannot have it since he has not been endowed with it. He can only behave out of calculation as though he had it, simulating what to others comes naturally. A normal child has it in the form of shyness, before education has developed it. When a two-year-old hides its face from a visitor it is because of its verguenza. Girls who refuse to dance in front of an assembled company do so because of their verguenza. Verguenza takes into consideration the personalities present. It is verguenza which forbids a boy to smoke in the presence of his father. In olden times people had much more verguenza than today, it is said (Pitt-Rivers 1961:113–114).

A contrast from South Africa:

> The all-embracing virtue to the Nyakyusa is wisdom (*amahala*). It includes the enjoyment of company and the practice of hospitality, for no man is wise who is surly, or aloof, or stingy; it includes neighborly behavior, dignity, respect for law and convention, but it does not include display. The wise may dance, but they do not need to dance in order to be wise, and those who commit adultery, or are boastful, or quarrelsome, show foolishness (*ubukonyofu*) and sinful pride (*amatingo*), the opposite of wisdom. Wisdom is expressed in all relationships, not only in village relationships, but it is *learned* in the village; pagan Nyakyusa insist that "it is by conversing with our friends that we gain wisdom" (Wilson 1963:89–90).

And again, in the United States:

> Gangs and clubs. This is the age for the blossoming of clubs and gangs. A number of kids who are already friends decide to form a secret club. They work like beavers making membership buttons, fixing up a meeting place (preferably hidden), drawing up a list of rules. They may never figure out what the secret is. But the secrecy idea probably represents the need to prove they can govern themselves, unmolested by grownups, unhampered by other more dependent children.
>
> It seems to help the child, when he's trying to be grownup, to get together with others who feel the same way. Then the group tries to bring outsiders into line by making them feel left out or by picking on them (Spock 1957:389–390).

In many human cultures those who lack verguenza or amahala, or those who are labeled "dumb guys," are brought into line through gossip, ridicule, and other forms of verbal attack. The fear of losing "face," of losing the regard of valued others, is a major device for the control of behavior which operates in every known culture. The phenomena labeled ridicule, shame, teasing, gossip, and so on involve a real or threatened withdrawal of psychological support on the part of the other members of the cultural system. With the withdrawal of affection and approval, there is often a suggestion that the individual really belongs in some other group: In Spain, gypsies and (playfully) infants are sin verguenza; in Plainville (West 1945), there are "the people who live like animals." Such "untouchable" groups are also found in India and Japan. Sometimes the implication that the rulebreaker is not a proper member of the group is carried even further.

Who Is Responsible for This?

The B-29 crew members were distributed throughout the airplane in the following manner:

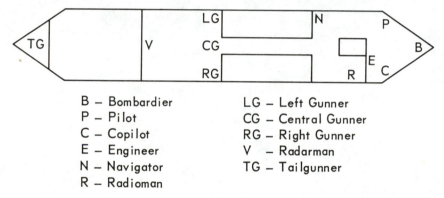

B — Bombardier
P — Pilot
C — Copilot
E — Engineer
N — Navigator
R — Radioman

LG — Left Gunner
CG — Central Gunner
RG — Right Gunner
V — Radarman
TG — Tailgunner

FIGURE 10–1   Position of B-29 crew members.

Studies conducted during the 1950s of the behavior and attitudes of the members of such crews indicated that almost every crew possessed a *foul-up*. A foul-up is a person who through stupidity and sometimes malign intent is responsible for practically everything that goes wrong on the airplane. The person most often named as a foul-up was the tailgunner, with the radioman a close second. Although the tailgunner was the lowest ranking member of the crew, this did not ordinarily apply to the radioman. Thus it cannot be argued that the lowest ranking or least trained member of the crew was automatically assigned the status of foul-up. The tasks assigned to the radioman and to the tailgunner were not vital to the actual flying of the airplane, and thus the status of foul-up cannot be attributed to anxiety over the performance of important tasks. Similarly, there are other men who have equally unimportant roles in the flying of the airplane, so it is not a matter of picking out the least important members of the crew as targets of hostility.

The selection of tailgunners and radiomen as foul-ups seems to be connected to their degree of interaction with members of the plane crew when it is in flight. The tailgunner sits alone in a small compartment. He has few duties beyond looking out of the window. He can't move around much. If he smokes, he is likely to start a small fire and suffocate. Deprived of stimulation, the tailgunner has a tendency to fall asleep. Because of the fire hazard, the pilot is required to communicate with the tailgunner periodically to see if he is still conscious. Because the tailgunner is usually asleep, the crew spends many anxious moments buzzing him on the intercommunications system and hoping that he will respond.

Although the radioman is located in the front compartment of the plane, he is visually accessible only to the navigator. Even here, the navigator must turn around in order to see him and can only see the radioman's back. Because the radioman must maintain communication with ground stations, he is also inaccessible through the intercommunication system. The duties assigned to the tailgunner and the radioman are such that they cannot participate freely in crew patterns of communication and their activities are consequently somewhat mysterious. One of the consequences of the relative isolation of the tailgunner and the radioman is that, should the crew parachute from the airplane, there is always a chance that they will do so without informing anyone. Thus, the tailgunner and the radioman can inflict a kind of ultimate disgrace upon the crew and its pilot. We can hypothesize, then, that a foul-up is a person about whom other members of the crew are anxious because he tends to violate notions of proper behavior, can inflict a grave loss of status upon the crew, and cannot be subjected to continuous observation or control.

Is It the Same in Africa?

A somewhat similar situation exists among the Nupe, a tribe in Nigeria. Nupe territory consists of strips of forest alternating with park land. In 1931, 300,000 Nupe lived in cities and villages, most earning their living through agriculture. Traditionally, men perform all of the agricultural work, while the women refine the harvested crops and sell them in the marketplace. Because the Nupe environment is hot and humid, there is a relatively high incidence of disease, and illness is one of the central problems of life. Illness is quite frequently caused by witchcraft, and witches are always women. In particular, they are believed to be women who do not laugh, never play or joke, get angry easily, and have no friendly words for others. The witch is an enemy of male authority who attempts to dominate family relationships through malignant attacks upon her husband and his relatives.

In fact, Nupe women are often away from home for long periods. While the husband is slaving away in the fields, the wife may set up a business empire, perhaps in modern times acquiring a fleet of motor-buses. Women have been known to place their husbands in debt and to take over the father's role of providing financial assistance to male children. The real power and actual dominance of the Nupe woman is countered by the possibility that she will be accused of witchcraft (Nadel 1954).

For the B-29 crew and the Nupe, those whose behaviors are hard to control and whose activities are mysterious are likely to be made into scapegoats when misfortune strikes. Among both groups, fear of being identified as a foul-up or a witch provides a powerful incentive toward correct behavior. In both cases, the normal fear of gossip and ridicule is powerfully supported by the danger of direct accusation and subsequent punishment. A foul-up may be beaten or transferred, while a witch may be killed. A scapegoat or witch spoils things for others mainly by means of a malevolent and/or inexplicable desire to do the wrong things. The logic of scapegoating is "I am good or my people are good, and therefore this trouble is being caused by somebody bad." Such logic leads to conflict, violence, and mistrust, and anthropologists often wonder whether the price of this kind of social control is not too high. If you can't blame others for your misfortunes, then you are left with no recourse but to blame yourself. Consider the following.

What Did You Do That Was Wrong?

Among the Iglulik Eskimo a village may be haunted by evil spirits that cause all game to vanish from the district. When this happens, shamans instruct community members to gather together in a single overcrowded room where they can be suitably purified. The shamans themselves go outside, returning shortly to report that numbers of angry spirits have appeared in the village. People in the room now begin to reflect upon their misdeeds and especially upon the various *tabus* or rules of life that they have violated. People confess their sins to the assembled community and ask forgiveness. As they confess more and more spirits appear outside. The people are terrified and beg the shamans to help them. The shamans leave the room and do battle with the spirits, returning covered with blood and with their clothing in rags.

The next day there is no hunting. All gather before breakfast and once again confess to their various breaches of the rules. The shamans finish purifying the community and go outside. The men follow them and return with one of the shamans attached to a dog's harness. He acts like a madman, lashing out on every side. When the harness is removed, the shaman returns to his normal manner. He sings a spirit song and there is a grand feast composed of the best food available. After the meal each person lays out objects of value he possesses and these are exchanged without regard for their actual worth. All are happy and there is no more fear (Rasmussen 1929:120ff).

The guilty man is punished by the anxious fear, often a certainty, that he will be caught and punished. For him, confession and punishment or forgiveness is a relief. The Eskimo exploit this psychological principle by creating a host of "rules of life," rules which often seem to make no sense and are therefore often broken. The process of confession and forgiveness creates solidarity at times when solidarity is most needed. The process is akin to those forms of psychotherapy in which the individual may cure himself by reporting his transgressions and innermost thoughts to a forgiving outsider. These examples of automatic punishment, scapegoating, and guilt and confession all emphasize the consequences of misbehavior. Social control may also be achieved in more positive ways. From the Ngoju of South Borneo:

> Use your hard bones, stiffen your soft muscles. Cultivate the large field, work the wide clearing.
>
> So that you can show each other the heaps of golden cloud-flowers (rice) and measure the quantity of golden blossoms of the dew-clouds (rice).
>
> Use part of the abundance of the golden cloud-flowers, employ the rest of the blossoms of the dew-clouds for the purpose of the wrought gold-work, the acquisition of the golden scales of the Watersnake (gold or gold ornaments).
>
> From the remainder of the gold-work buy roots from the trunk of the tree; with the balance of the golden scales of the Watersnake cut through the chains of the gongs. (The roots of the Tree of Life, which are referred to here, consist of gongs. Gongs are thus to be bought with the gold.)
>
> If you act so, your renown will gradually increase and will spread to the surrounding villages and people will begin to speak about you on neighboring rivers.
>
> Keep in mind that large stones are worked with a small knife (Schärer 1963:127–128).

In effect, do the right thing and you will be richly rewarded. But all of the subtle and not so subtle systems of reward and punishment and of the giving and withdrawing of social approval involve the existence of rules that may be easily understood and followed. In the course of everyday life, human beings in all cultures encounter situations in which, regardless of the possible consequences, they find it necessary to break the rules or to behave in ways which others interpret as violations of the rules. Conflict then arises and the problem becomes one of restoring the social fabric torn by disagreement. How do the Ibo of Nigeria cool such conflicts?

CONFLICT: WHO WAS RIGHT?

In the course of a quarrel about the cutting of some palm nuts a man, K., . . . and the widow, G., of his dead father, fell to abusing one another. She said that he and the other sons of his father were talking against her to the family of the girl she was trying to marry to her son and were telling them that she had not enough money to pay the bride price. The man, K., retorted by asking if that was why she was trying to kill them by supernatural means, by magic that is to say, or by making sacrifices to a spirit to kill them. The widow then made the provocative remark . . . "Why don't you die and let us mourn for you?" (Green 1964:116).

Later G. went to one of her kinsmen and asked him to interview K.; K. admitted accusing G.; and G. paid a fee to a member of the court, who held an informal inquiry and judged the case in her favor. K. appealed by taking a drum and beating it in various parts of the village. The elders convened and decided that both G. and K. should furnish funds to buy a goat for a feast. At the feast, the dispute would be settled. There were further discussions, but the ethnographer concludes:

When I returned to the village a year later the case had not been retried nor had the decision been carried out. Also G.'s opponents had tried to make her refund the money they spent on the case but she had refused (Green:124).

Particularly in larger and more complicated cultural systems, when two individuals or subgroups disagree, there is often some outside source of moral authority to which the dispute may be appealed. At times the moral authority, in this case a court and a council of elders, may settle the dispute by providing authoritative decisions concerning who did wrong. In this case, where both parties appear to have knowingly committed breaches of proper behavior, legal procedures had the effect of drawing out and delaying any settlement and at the same time increasing the cost of settlement. Ultimately the contending parties have no choice but to forget the whole thing.

Because legal procedures involving recourse to third parties are often costly, difficult, and time consuming, it can be argued that those who appeal to third parties generally have in mind some rule that their opponents have violated. Very commonly, in the spirit of "if you can break a rule, I can break a rule," both parties to the dispute have broken a rule and both parties feel entitled to a judgment in their favor. Particularly in small groups, the third party, faced with the necessity of continuing to live with both disputants, cannot bear the risk of a decision in favor of either party and therefore tends to delay decision while gradually increasing the cost of arbitration. In other cases, the opposed parties are genuinely confused about the nature of the rules that apply to their situation or the rules themselves are inconsistent or inapplicable.

How Big a Share?

For example, South Indian rules concerning the inheritance of land seem crystal clear. When a group of brothers live together in the same household, each is entitled to an equal share of the family property when the household is divided. When two brothers live together, each is entitled to half of the family property. Suppose, however, that one of the brothers dies before claiming his share and the surviving brother undertakes the responsibility of raising his brother's children to maturity. Suppose that the surviving brother has one son and the deceased brother has two sons. Inevitably when the two adopted children reach maturity, they will tend to claim two-thirds of the family property. The surviving brother will tend to claim that they are only entitled to a 50 percent share; namely, the share which would have been claimed by their father had he survived. Because the rules do not spell out what should be done in a case of this kind, such cases almost always involve bitter conflict and end up as legal cases to be settled by the village elders. Such cases arise frequently enough to cause a great deal of trouble, but not frequently enough to merit the formulation of a more precise rule of inheritance. A cultural tradition, viewed as a body of law, cannot be sufficiently specific to cover every conceivable source of disagreement. This is one of the reasons why conflict can be assumed to be universal in human society and why processes for the resolution and settlement of conflict must be present.

FIGURE 10–2 Men of importance gather to discuss the division of a dead man's property. How much should go to the wife? How much to each male child? Gopalpur, South India. (PHOTO BY ALAN R. BEALS)

Can You Win?

Consider, now, the following case from Bulgaria. Here two definite rules are listed in order of importance: (1) peasants should defer to the power and prestige of urban men; and (2) business contracts must be honored. In this case it seems likely that both men knew the rules, and it is fair to argue that Trayko Danev was well aware that he would lose his case. Why, then, did he bring the case?

After these two men went out, Trayko Danev, whom the reader knows by now as one of the richest peasants in the village, brought charges against a Sofia merchant for breach of contract in a financial transaction involving hay. Trayko apparently had justice on his side and was ready to prove his case by the use of two witnesses, one of whom was to testify regarding the agreement made and a second to testify regarding the partial fulfillment of the agreement. The first witness testified:

"As I recall the incident, I was at the table with this merchant and Trayko Danev and heard them make an agreement whereby Trayko said he would give 780 leva for hay. He went away and that is all I remember."

Trayko then asked for the testimony of the second witness, whose name had been written on the brief as Nikola.

The Judge (Mayor): "Nikola. Nikola. But the last name is not written."

The Merchant (Defendant): "Your Honor, I object. This man has not indicated the last name of his second witness and God knows how many Nikolas there are in Bulgaria. Furthermore, the second witness was present in the courtroom while the first witness was testifying. Therefore, the second witness, according to law, cannot testify, no matter what his last name is."

Trayko: "I didn't tell him to come in here. It's not my fault."

Judge: "The defendant's objection sustained. We cannot accept the testimony of the second witness unless the defendant agrees."

Defendant: "I do not agree."

Judge: "In that case, the plaintiff loses, since he cannot use the second witness and cannot prove his charge" (Sanders 1949:164–165).

One possible interpretation is that Trayko Danev thought that a rich peasant enjoyed the same privileges as a rich merchant. If so, he was rudely disabused of his misinterpretation of the rules. More probably, because a man does not become a rich peasant by being an idiot, Trayko Danev saw this as a situation in which he might get his money back, but in which, win or lose, the cupidity of the merchant would be exposed to public view. After the public trial, it seems unlikely that the Sophia merchant would have many more opportunities to violate his agreements. From this case, it can be suggested that one reason that people break rules, such as the rule that peasants should stay away from law courts, is that they wish to call attention to intolerable situations. To make a dispute public is to expose both parties to the threat of ridicule and punishment and to call into being all of those subtle forces by means of which the members of a group compel their fellows to conform to the cultural tradition.

The above point is made again in the following case, but, here, conflict can also be seen as an exchange of ritualistic and symbolic actions which carry a clear and definite meaning. The case of Fantan the Interpreter, from the island of Alor in Indonesia, also opens the question of universal characteristics of husband/wife conflict.

FIGURE 10–3 Each member of the adjudicating committee must satisfy himself concerning the exact measurements of the land in question. Gopalpur, South India. (PHOTO BY ALAN R. BEALS)

Can This Marriage Be Saved?

About a month ago Fantan's wife gambled and lost her dance necklace and anklets. Fantan said he gave her money to try to win them back, but she only lost that too. He was angry, and in telling me about it he put his anger on the moral basis that women should not play cards though it was all right for men. . . .

On Friday (November 18) Fantan was wandering about and joined a game in a remote garden house where some unmarried girls were gambling. . . .

Early Sunday morning (November 20) while he was away two of the girls present at the gambling told his wife about the episode. When he returned from an early market where he had been with me, his wife berated him for returning the jewelry to Fungata when she herself had none, and for not winning hers back for her. She asked if Fungata were his sister or maybe his wife and implied that he had had intercourse with her. She boxed his ears, and he picked up a rattan switch and hit her twice across the thigh. She took her field knife and hit his shoulder with the flat of the blade. He was terrorized and told me he had a large wound. This was patently untrue; he had not even a scratch. . . .

His wife then ran off to Karieta and fought with Fungata. They came to blows, and in ripping off Fungata's necklace, Tilamau broke it. She then came back to the house, but Fantan had meanwhile hidden himself in the servants' quarters behind my house. . . .

Meanwhile Fungata had already made a litigation with the chief of Dikimpe because of her broken necklace. The chief said Tilamau would have to pay a fine; but neither Tilamau, her parents, nor Fantan would pay. So the chief of Dikimpe was angry and brought the oath stone (*namoling*) from Karieta and swore an oath, saying that they could not come to him any more to try cases. . . .

So early Monday morning (November 21) Fungata brought her case to the tumukum. Involved at first were only Fantan, Fungata, and Tilamau. The older and more responsible people did not appear. Fantan, meanwhile, was avoiding his wife. . . . He returned to his own house in the early morning to discover that his wife had burned his rattan switch with a leprosy curse. . . .

When Fantan ran to me in the morning after discovering that his wife had cursed him, he said that this morning at the litigation he was going to divorce his wife and then marry Fungata. . . .

Both Fantan and Tilamau insisted, when asked by the tumukum, that they wanted to separate. The tumukum then had Tilamau's parents called. This she didn't want. Her excuse was that they would talk loudly and vulgarly.
. . .

November 23, 1938

Fantan still insisted that his own divorce proceedings must go through and that if he didn't separate from his wife he would surely die of leprosy. . . .

November 24 1938

There was still no indication that Fantan's divorce proceedings would be continued. . . .

November 25, 1938

At about seven-thirty in the morning I was told that Fantan's parents-in-law had instituted litigation in Karieta.

Tilamau's backers kept insisting on a divorce. Fantan told me before the litigation began that he was angry at its being called, that it was his right to litigate. (This was not true, since either side could sue for divorce.)

Then the tumukum spoke to Fantan's sister and her husband, who had come after being summoned, and told them if Fantan and Tilamau fought again to take them next door to the mandur of Dikimpe and see that they each got a lashing. . . .

December 3, 1938

On November 30 Fantan went to Kalabahi. He traveled with his father-in-law, with whom he was now on perfectly good terms. He had still not spoken to his mother-in-law. "She is still making a sour face at me." Then he told with evident self-satisfaction that he had slept at home the night of December 1, after his return from Kalabahi. He said that he and his wife were happy together again (DuBois 1961:372–380).

Despite the violence of this dispute and the apparently irrevocable actions by both parties, Fantan and Tilamau refused to exhibit actions which would have symbolized a desire for divorce. Tilamau continued to cultivate her husband's garden and resisted the suggestion that her parents be involved in the dispute. Fantan on his side refused to take steps that might have led to the return of the bride-price that he had paid at the time of his marriage. Through his violent actions, Fantan loudly and publicly exclaimed, "See how my wife is extravagantly wasting family resources." Tilamau for her part was exclaiming, "See how my husband overreacts every time I make a small mistake." Although both acted angrily and "without thinking," neither went so far as to commit breaches which would have led to punishment. By the time the tumukum reached his verdict, "Settle down or you will both get a lashing," pressures from relatives and friends had apparently brought both parties to a state of mind where they were prepared to make concessions.

In terms of cultural universals, it seems probable that a husband and wife who are unable to agree concerning each other's proper conduct will inevitably seek to involve relatives and third-party arbitrators in the dispute. In the United States, a husband whose wife repeatedly lost large sums of money at the bridge table might also have vengefully sought a Fungata, thus exposing his wife to a very real threat of divorce. Although the general tactic of solving "irreconcilable" disputes by involving additional persons in the dispute can be regarded as universal, a comparison of the United States and Alor shows that most of the specific actions whereby the dispute is widened and brought to the attention of the authorities are quite different. Leprosy curses and rattan switches have fairly precise symbolic meanings on Alor even though the use of physical aggression by men and verbal aggression by women may have to do with fairly widespread biological differences in the size, weight, and physical strength of men and women.

Social control, getting people to do the right thing, inevitably involves conflict and dispute and formal and public means for resolving such conflicts and disputes. Very often, the breaking of a rule is a symbolic gesture which is met by other symbolic gestures. A poet or lunatic may break rules in a meaningless or unintelligible way, but such people are often unpredictable, unresponsive to punishment and reward, and beyond understanding in terms of cultural regularities. The ordinary person involved in ordinary conflicts plays a cultural game, a kind of ritual in which the individual exhibits behaviors which are grammatical and meaningful as performances of processes of conflict and resolution.

Because, even more than in the case of ritual, the proper conduct of a dispute involves great freedom in the choice of individual actions, the study of conflict and social control involves the study of a great many cases before the rules of the game or the meaning of the various behaviors involved can be established.

Where Have You Been?

In the South Indian village of Namhalli, husbands and wives appear to define the initiation of severe marital conflict as any behavior which can be construed as a denial of the marital relationship. About half the time such a denial is concretely expressed in the form of a direct rumor or visible evidence that the wife has committed adultery. More rarely, it is evidence that the husband has done so. In addition to direct rumors or messages on the order of "what was your wife doing with so and so," the wife may reveal her adulterous nature by gazing boldly at strange men, by stealing from the family grain supply, or by the possession of candy or other goods. The commencement of a marital dispute may also be signaled by chronic illness, sexual impotence, or improper performance of household duties.

Once the existence of a marital dispute is established, couples may move quickly or slowly toward divorce or reconciliation; they may involve few or many outsiders; or they may use much or little physical violence and verbal aggression. The endpoint of a marital conflict is, of course, either divorce or reconciliation. Completed conflicts tend to move through five stages: beginning, physical violence, flight, arbitration or third party intervention, and divorce or reconciliation.

The movement from beginning to physical violence may involve warnings, demands for explanations, mild or salutary beatings, or scolding. At this stage, both husband and wife may express dissatisfaction by means of little misdeeds and noncompliances which are of great symbolic significance. The wife may serve cold food, forget salt or chilies, slight important relatives, or address fellow villagers as "potential spouse." The husband is likely to deliver a mild or salutary beating, but he may also fail to purchase new clothing at festival time, spend his earnings on the cinema, patronize prostitutes, or leave town. The spouse's response to these signals of dissatisfaction is of great importance to the outcome of the dispute. If the husband contents himself with demanding an explanation or giving a warning, divorce is almost inevitable. If the husband delivers a salutary beating, divorce practically never occurs. If the spouses scold each other in public, people intervene and divorce is avoided.

In roughly two-thirds of recorded marital conflicts, the conflict escalates to the stage of physical violence. Here, the most common happening is that the husband beats the wife with a stick or in some other violent way. At this stage, he has "eyes like a tiger." Although, as indicated in Figure 10–3, the wife may beat a third party or attempt to injure herself, the wife's strategy is evidently to provoke an outburst of violence. In a few cases, not represented in Figure 10–3, the wife's tears and recriminations may have the effect of physical violence. In any case, the home situation is now unbearable and the victim, almost always the wife, flees or is driven out. Here, the further the wife flees, the lower the likelihood of reconciliation. If she flees starving into the fields surrounding the village or runs weeping down the village streets, she is sure to be discovered by neighbors or officials and returned to her husband. If she flees to her natal village, her mother and father are likely to support her against her husband and divorce is inevitable.

Where the wife flees in an appropriate manner it symbolizes a plea for intervention and arbitration. Sometimes a single distinguished elder will take the wife back to the house and urge the husband to mend his ways; at other times a formal council of elders intervenes until divorce or reconciliation has taken place. Figure 10–3 presents the network of alternatives used in a number of actual cases of conflict. The headings, 1A, 1B, and so on, represent the stage of the conflict and the different major alternatives available at each stage. The lines connecting the different stages represent the patterns followed by actual cases of conflict. Such a diagram is a means of arriving at the set of rules that govern participation in marital conflict.

Although Figure 10–3 is only a first attempt at an explanation of marital conflict, it serves to illustrate the general nature of cultural processes. Traditionally, anthropologists and sociologists have described human behavior in terms of usual or customary practices. Those who break rules have been described as "abnormal," "deviant," or "nonconformist." Such a "normative" view of human behavior is useful for certain purposes, but it does not provide a fair view of the complexity of human life. Human beings conform in a variety of ways. Thus, even though Figure 10–3 represents only the essential parts of the conflict process, it still provides each husband and wife with a variety of ways of conforming to the proper method of carrying out a domestic conflict. There is no single proper way of fighting with one's spouse; there are a variety of ways.

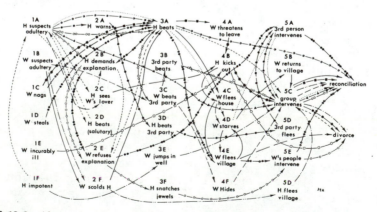

FIGURE 10–3 Alternatives in marital conflict, South India.

In a sense, it is abnormal and forbidden to enter into a marital dispute. Husbands and wives should treat each other properly, listen to each other's complaints, solve their own problems. Individuals who become involved in public marital conflict enter forbidden territory, but it is forbidden territory for which the cultural tradition provides a map. In other words, marital conflict, although disapproved, is a well-known fact of life and for this reason cultural traditions tend to provide individuals with rules and guidelines which will enable them to settle their differences, to seek third-party arbitration, or in other ways to return to a normal and appropriate status.

All of the cases in Figure 10–3 deal with married couples who entered into conflict concerning the rules of appropriate behavior and who carried out their inappropriate conflict appropriately. There are rules which govern rulebreaking. When a husband, instead of merely beating his wife or his wife's lover, ends up killing or permanently injuring one or both of them, his behavior falls outside of "behavior appropriate to husband/wife conflict." In such a case, it is likely that the husband has, in fact, followed the norm for murder in Namhalli; that is, he has assaulted his wife with the heavy knife used for chopping wood. By his actions, however, he has fallen outside of the norms of marital conflict and now falls under those cultural processes which have to do with murder and its punishment.

Here, too, as in all other cases of rulebreaking, processes of social control are brought to bear against the offender. Although gossip, ridicule, formal trials, and other mechanisms of social control always involve costs to the individual, the principal thrust of such processes involves not the punishment of the individual but repair of the breach that has been created by the misbehavior and the return of individuals to their proper roles as functioning members of the group. When the balance of rewards and punishments that ensures that most individuals behave properly most of the time is disrupted by the pressure of external events, the membership of the cultural system must react by redrawing the maps of appropriate behavior in such a way as to include new alternatives or to restore the preexisting balance of reward and punishment. Cultural systems must contain processes for the rewriting of cultural traditions so that they take account of stresses or new problems produced by changing relationships between the cultural system and its environment. The following chapter deals with the problem of cultural change.

SUMMARY

A cultural tradition can be regarded as a set of policies whereby human beings attempt to render predictable the forces of nature and the vagaries of human behavior. Where, as in Utopia, success has been achieved, there is no problem of misbehavior and no need for mechanisms designed to cope with improper and unexpected human behaviors. In Hillside, which serves as the prototype for all nonimaginary human communities, it turns out that it is impossible to write rules which deal precisely with reality or which cover every conceivable situation.

Although the case of the Makah shows that rule breaking and conflict can sometimes be attributed to the faulty transmission of culture known as the "generation gap," the case of the Lugbara illustrates the fact that trouble can also be traced to the failure to predict such "minor" events as a woman's barrenness. From south Texas, the case of Miguel provides evidence that even when a human being scrupulously obeys the rules, he may still encounter difficulties and conflicting situations. The problems of behaving appropriately are magnified when new and changing circumstances produce situations unforeseen within the cultural tradition. Thus, Sulli confronts the problem of delaying his marriage by means of brilliant improvisation upon the rules of his culture. Biboi, unfamiliar with his own cultural tradition, is trapped in the chasm between new and old.

When rules are broken, processes of social control act to return the rulebreaker to social conformity. In Dutch Guiana and South India, the conscious rulebreaker is threatened with automatic and supernatural punishment. In other cultures, gossip and ridicule confront the individual with the loss of his "face" or social identity, and the individual acts to avoid being labeled a sucker, a dumb guy, or a sin verguenza. Complex societies often contain untouchable groups and social control may then capitalize on the individual's fear of being labeled, as in Plainville, one of the "people who live like animals." Scapegoating is the practice of attributing the misfortunes of the many to the misdeeds of a few. The examples of the B-29 crew and the Nupe are evidence of the manner in which the individual's fear of being labeled a foul-up or witch may be used to enforce conformity. Processes of confession, in which the individual confesses his mistakes and receives appropriate punishment or forgiveness, are illustrated by the case of the Eskimo.

When individuals disagree concerning whether rules have been broken or not, the task of healing the breach and applying processes of social control tends to fall to a third party who possesses the moral authority required for convincing arbitration or judgment. Because even a properly endowed moral authority such as a court or council often finds it difficult to rule in favor of either party, some courts, such as those of the Ibo, may act by prolonging the dispute and increasing its cost to the participants. An example from South India shows why convincing resolution of disputes is often impossible and therefore why processes of arbitration and adjudication are necessary. The case of Trayko Danev suggests that, even where rules are clear and definite, they may still be broken as a means of calling public attention to intolerable situations.

The use of rule breaking, conflict, and public litigation to call attention to insolvable interpersonal problems is also illustrated by the case of Fantan and Tilamau. This dispute raises questions concerning the meaning of the various behaviors interchanged in the course of a dispute. Thus, although there might be some universal attributes of husband/wife disputes, marital disputes as well as other kinds of conflict can be interpreted as exchanges of culturally meaningful behaviors. The problem of establishing the nature of the rules governing marital disputes and interpreting the meaning of the behaviors exchanged is discussed in terms of an analysis of South Indian marital disputes. Processes of conflict, like many other cultural processes, are seen as involving not so much conformity to a norm as selection from a variety of acceptable alternatives.

For Further Reading

A variety of works deals with aspects of politics, law conflict, and government. These include *Political Anthropology* (Swartz, Tuden, and Turner 1966), *Law and Warfare* (Bohannan 1967), *Political Anthropology* (Balandier 1970), *Divisiveness and Social Conflict* (Beals and Siegel 1966), *Law in Culture and Society* (Nader 1969), *Two-dimensional Man* (Cohen 1974), *Friends of Friends* (Boissevain 1974), and *Stratagems and Spoils* (Bailey 1970). Some recent works include Moore's *Law as Process* (1978), Hamnett's *Chieftainship and Legitimacy* (1975), and Edelman's *Political Language, Words that Succeed and Policies that Fail* (1977).

Most of the Case Studies deal with problems of social control, especially Lessa's *Ulithi* (1966), Hudson's *Pudju Epat* (1972), Beals' *Gopalpur* (1962), the Spindlers' *Dreamers without Power* (1971), Jones' *Sanapian* (1972), and Bascom's *The Yoruba* (1969).

Problems and Questions

1. Examine some portrayals of conflict situations on television or elsewhere. What sorts of behavior are presented as being likely to trigger violent responses?

2. Consider a familiar cultural system, large or small. What are some of the more important techniques of social control that are utilized?

3. For any cultural system, what are some alternative ways of behaving? How do people make decisions about which alternative is most proper or most suitable? What do people think about when making decisions?

4. What are some of the methods of social control used in a particular cultural system? How do they differ from the standard methods characteristic of your own cultural system?

5. From television, history books, or other sources collect some case histories of disputes or conflicts. Is there any pattern in the way such disputes are carried out or resolved?

6. Can you discover any human settings in which violence is absent or comparatively rare? What are the factors that seem to lead to such a reduction in violence?

11 CULTURAL CHANGE

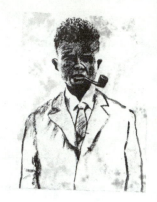

Why are things done differently?

In discussing social control a number of things that might cause individuals to break rules or to carry out activities disapproved of by their relatives and neighbors were discussed. At the root, change in culture is simply what happens when individuals do things in a different way, somehow manage to overcome any objections their neighbors might have, and, in fact, convince their neighbors that the new way is the right way. A new idea is an innovation. Innovations come about through invention or diffusion (borrowing). Thus, the key processes of cultural change are invention and diffusion.

Because ideas change as they spread or diffuse from one cultural system to another, it follows that a clear distinction cannot always be maintained between invention and diffusion. What is important is that the members of a cultural system accept a new idea. Here, it is important to remember that not all change is adaptive. New ideas may be accepted simply because they are interesting or simply because they appear to offer advantages that, in fact, they do not offer. If an innovation proves to be costly, painful, or maladaptive people are likely to give it up and try something else. Just as is true in the case of genes, some innovations may have relatively little adaptive significance and so be little affected by the various forces of selection. Imagination, borrowing, and reaction to threats to survival lead to cultural change, a process that is complicated and not yet fully understood.

This chapter opens with a case taken from the history of Pitcairn's Island. The case illustrates the growth and development of a new cultural system brought into existence when a group of British men and Tahitian men and women founded a new colony on an isolated island. What follows is complex. Did they develop an economic system and a social and religious system adapted to the island environment? Why did they almost exterminate each other? Could a book, a mere message, have had an impact on their lives?

FIGURE 11–1   The Indians of Mexico invented the wheel, but used it only for the construction of what are apparently toys. Rugged terrain and the absence of appropriate draft animals may explain why discovery of the principle of the wheel failed to stimulate additional inventions. (PHOTO BY ALAN R. BEALS FROM THE MUSEUM OF ANTHROPOLOGY, MEXICO)

The story of Pitcairn illustrates the problems involved in developing comprehensive theories of cultural change. A second case, dealing with the Hopi and Tewa Indians of the American southwest, considers the kinds of things that might account for the persistence of a particular way of life in the face of major obstacles. How did the Hopi and Tewa escape the fate of less fortunate American Indian groups? Why have they refused to accept Christianity? How have they maintained their leadership and their pride of membership?

A third example, taken from South India, considers a situation where rapid cultural change brought about conflict within the village and a submergence of ordinary morality and cooperation. Is conflict a way of coping with crises? Or is conflict likely to be triggered and intensified by certain kinds of stress? What is the role of moral authority in change?

A final case, the case of the Dakota Sioux, considers the kinds of things that happen when ordinary problem-solving techniques fail. Why do people create and adopt new religions? In what way is the restructuring of the supernatural world to be considered adaptive? Does it help to create new gods?

WHAT CAUSED THESE CHANGES?

The following is a brief summary of some of the things that are known to have happened when two separate cultural systems came together briefly and gave rise to a third. The example illustrates the processes of invention and diffusion mentioned above. It introduces the yet unsolved problems of explaining and predicting the course of development that any particular culture might follow.

The account begins with the well-known mutiny on the *Bounty*. After the mutiny, the mutineers, led by Fletcher Christian, sailed to Tahiti. Later, in the fall of 1789, afraid that the British navy would find them and hang them, eight mutineers set sail in search of a safe hiding place. They were accompanied by twelve or thirteen Tahitian women and six Tahitian men. The mutineers had become friendly with the Tahitian men and women during a long stay at Tahiti. The attractive contrast between the easy life at Tahiti and the hard life aboard the *Bounty* is thought to have been one of the causes of the mutiny. In 1790, a settlement was established on Pitcairn's Island, and the *Bounty* was run ashore and burned. Years later, in 1934, Pitcairn's Island was visited by the anthropologist Harry L. Shapiro. The following derives from his account (Shapiro 1936, 1962).

After this, a village site was selected and the island divided up amongst the mutineers, the Tahitians being given nothing. Despite this and other evidence of discrimination, the Tahitian men and women worked willingly beside the mutineers. After two years, Williams, one of the mutineers, lost his Tahitian wife, who fell from a precipice while collecting birds' eggs. Williams demanded another wife. After considerable discussion, the mutineers gave him the wife of one of the Tahitians. The Tahitians now resolved to murder the mutineers. The Tahitian wives of the mutineers informed their husbands of the planned attack. The ringleaders fled into the woods where they were later killed by the remaining Tahitians who had been promised forgiveness if they carried out this execution.

For two years all was quiet. Two of the whites, Quintal and M'Coy, became increasingly brutal in their treatment of the Tahitians, who had now become little more than slaves. The Tahitians once again planned to execute the mutineers. In a few hours, all but four of the nine mutineers were dead. M'Coy and Quintal escaped to the mountains. A man named Adams who was friendly to the Tahitians was severely wounded but permitted to survive. He was joined by Young who had been hidden by the Tahitian women.

After a week, the Tahitian men began to quarrel concerning their rights to the wives of the dead men. Menalee shot Timoa and would have shot Tetaheite also had not the women prevented it. Menalee ran off to the mountains to join Quintal and M'Coy. Thus strengthened, Quintal and M'Coy appeared in sight of the village and fired a volley of shots. The others sent Adams to negotiate. It was agreed that if Quintal and M'Coy killed Menalee they would be permitted to return. They did so but were still afraid to come back.

The women insisted that the remaining Tahitian men be put to death as a punishment for the murder of their mutineer husbands. A woman who had been renamed Susan killed Tetaheite with an axe. The other Tahitian was shot by Young. After seeing the hands and heads of the dead men, M'Coy and Quintal returned to the village. Relationships among the men, women, and children on the island continued to be poor. The women demanded permission to leave and insisted that a boat be constructed for them. The boat was built and launched, but it promptly capsized. The women were deeply dissatisfied by this turn of events. M'Coy and Quintal, for their part, made a point of beating the "girls" frequently and planned to subject them to the silent treatment.

The women now decided to kill the mutineers in their sleep. The plot was discovered, the women promised to reform, and the mutineers threatened to kill the first woman who stepped out of line in the future. A second plot also failed, but again no punishments were administered. Whenever displeased, the women now withdrew to uninhabited parts of the island where they lurked with their muskets. This was the situation in 1795. During 1796, circumstances gradually improved. The men became increasingly sociable; dinner invitations were regularly given and received; and there was constant exchange of provisions based upon a regular accounting.

On April 20, 1798, M'Coy successfully fermented the ti plant. Not to be outdone, Quintal constructed a still. An abundant supply of strong drink was now available. M'Coy soon began to suffer from delirium, and finally threw himself off a cliff. The remaining citizens resolved never again to touch spirits. In 1799, Quintal's wife fell from a cliff while hunting birds' eggs. Although there were several single women on the island, Quintal wanted the wife of either Adams or Young. Quintal sought to murder both, but failed in his first attempt. Adams and Young killed him with an axe.

Adams and Young, the meek and the guilty, had now inherited Pitcairn's Island. They decided to bring up the children in a Christian manner. Morning and evening family prayers were offered. Sunday services were extended throughout the day. Young began to teach the children, but his health was poor and he died, apparently of an asthmatic attack, within the year. The semiliterate Adams was the sole survivor of the mutineers of the *Bounty*. He sought to expiate his offenses by instructing the children in the proper way of living. He slowly deciphered the Bible and interpreted it for the children.

What Kind of Culture?

For eighteen years, Pitcairn was completely isolated. Even after its rediscovery, there were few visitors. For the Tahitian men and women, Pitcairn was familiar ground. They knew how to construct and use all of the equipment required for fishing, farming, and hunting on the island. Coming from a more specialized and urbanized culture located half the world away, the British mutineers had little to contribute beyond their superior weapons and their violent contempt for "Blacks," "Indians," and Tahitian culture.

The original houses built on the island were constructed with a view toward making them resemble British cottages. The builders lacked nails, glass, cut stone, mortar, and tools for cabinet work. It was impossible to dig a cellar or even a foundation. The resulting house was unique. Rough logs were laid across boulders and square posts were stuck (mortised) into the logs. Crosspieces were placed across the posts and the posts grooved so that planks could be fitted to form a wall. The roofs were covered with thatch made in Tahitian style.

For furniture, the British disdained Tahitian mats and constructed crude beds, chairs, and tables. Sea chests were used for storage. "Candlenuts" arranged on a string and ignited were used for lighting in the Tahitian fashion. Nobody on Pitcairn knew how to weave and there was no fiber suitable for making cloth. The Tahitian women made cloth out of the bark of the breadfruit and paper mulberry trees and dressed their husbands in it. The men wore a *maro*, a long strip of bark cloth wrapped around the waist with one end passed between the legs and tucked in. The women simply wrapped a piece of bark cloth around their waists. A mantle of bark cloth, which could be thrown over the shoulders to keep off drafts, completed the costume. Women on Pitcairn, unlike women on Tahiti, took care to conceal their breasts. Hats were made in Tahitian style.

Cooking by the women was done in underground ovens on red-hot stones. Meals were served twice a day as in Tahiti and consisted of yams, taro, sweet potatoes, and other largely Tahitian food. Almost all foods were cooked separately; only one dish consisting of a mixture of ingredients was known. Raw fish, a delicacy on Tahiti, was not consumed.

Farming was carried out more or less in the Tahitian manner. For fishing, the English hook and line was used as well as the Tahitian fishing spear. Use of a torch to attract fish at night was borrowed from Tahiti. Swimming and surfboard riding (the children used to swim the seven-mile circuit of the island) were borrowed from Tahiti.

In Tahiti, women were comparatively free and often occupied positions of authority. Normally, Tahitian women prepared the food, serving it first to the men and then eating by themselves later. This custom was accepted by the mutineers. At Pitcairn, women were expected to work in the fields along with the men until the time of their marriage. During the time of Adams, and before, there is no question but that the ten mothers exerted a powerful influence. The children were all raised together, making few distinctions between "my" mother and "your" mother. Adams was regarded as the father of all of the children even though they maintained the last names of their actual fathers. He ruled the colony as a patriarch until the day of his death.

Pitcairn became a large family of extraordinarily devout Christian fundamentalists whose means of subsistence and techniques of child rearing were essentially Tahitian. During the nineteenth century as vessel after vessel visited the island, the reports flowed in of a Christian paradise where scantily clad natives practiced literal Christianity, where there was no fighting, no swearing, and no hatred. Gossiping was literally forbidden, because Adams required all of his children to think well of each other. Property was borrowed freely and returned with no need to ask permission as was the custom on Tahiti. The land, however, was inherited by both male and female descendants of the original mutineers. This meant that over the years, depending on the number of heirs, sharp discrepancies in wealth developed. Some young people lacked sufficient land to support a family. Those who experienced poverty, however, could draw from a community reserve supply of food established by Adams. Such loans could be repaid later, perhaps after a long voyage aboard a passing whaler. From 1800, long before it was so in most other places, education was free and compulsory for children between the ages of six and sixteen.

When Adams died in 1829, he left behind him a utopian community. Pitcairn was free of violence and dissension. The equality of women, at least by the standards of the day, was an established fact. There was no crime, no serious poverty, and, despite an intense religiosity, little repression of one human being by another. After his death, Adams had wanted the islanders to establish a governing council that would retain his patriarchal authority. The islanders managed their affairs without the aid of government for about three years. In 1832, a gentleman arrived from London with letters (forged) showing him to be governor of the island. A reign of terror followed. It was 1837 before the dictator was exposed and another year before he was removed.

At the same time, formal government came to Pitcairn. The new constitution provided for the annual election of a chief magistrate by all residents of the island, both male and female, over the age of eighteen. The magistrate was assisted by a council consisting of one elected member and one member appointed by the magistrate. The magistrate's oath of office was as follows:

> I solemnly swear, that I will execute the duties of magistrate and chief ruler of Pitcairn's Island, to which I am this day called on the election of the inhabitants, by dispensing justice and settling any differences that may arise, zealously, fearlessly, and impartially; and that I will keep a register of my proceedings, and hold myself accountable for the due exercise of my office to Her Majesty the Queen of Great Britain, or her Representative. So help me God. (Shapiro 1962:177).

By 1850, Pitcairn had a regular code of laws stating the duties of the Chief Magistrate, placing limitations upon his power, and instituting trial by jury. There were also laws concerning dogs, whose owners were to be fined if they chased goats. Children who killed cats were to be whipped, teenagers who did so were fined twenty-five dollars, and adults fifty dollars. Other laws were dedicated to efficient use of resources, to the preservation and conservation of trees and other aspects of the environment, and to the regulation of relationships with visiting ships.

Despite the heavy borrowing from both parent cultures, the history of Pitcairn is an extraordinary testament to the creative ability of quite ordinary human beings. In constructing houses, boats, and furniture, the mutineers created a whole string of innovations. Adams' creative interpretations of the Bible and his emphasis on the New Testament permitted him to invent a way of life characterized by love and nonviolence. A strikingly original social invention, for example, was Adams' successful abolition of gossip. The earlier development of a common fund for the purpose of making loans to those in need also appears to have been an original invention.

Could This Have Been Predicted?

Pitcairn culture represents an unusual case in which men and women from island countries located half a world apart voluntarily combined for the purpose of constructing a new way of life. Reconciliation of the vast differences between the two parent cultures was a bloody process that was finally resolved through the death of all but one of the adult males on the island. Later, the people of Pitcairn had to adapt to the problems of increasing population and to the unusual threats and/or advantages brought by visiting ships. Some visiting ships brought school teachers, missionaries, new technology, opportunities to migrate, and fresh ideas about how the social and political life of the island should be conducted. Other ships, sometimes the same ships, brought epidemic diseases, bullies, and dictators.

Many theories that emphasize adaptation as the main source for cultural change place a heavy emphasis upon the primacy of environment and technology in determining the course of events. Other theories stress the primacy of ideas as instruments that cause human beings to alter environments to suit their needs. The technological and economic systems of Pitcairn were plainly of Tahitian origin. One would expect that social relationships and world view would therefore closely approximate the situation on Tahiti. Considering that the children on the island were raised almost exclusively by Tahitian mothers, it seems almost inevitable that British influence would die out completely. Certainly theories relating child-rearing practices to customs and world view would lead to an expectation that children reared in Tahitian fashion would adopt Tahitian ways of looking upon the world and upon each other.

Pitcairn social relationships and world view are partly British in origin, a fact which supports the theory that great ideas are impervious to environmental influences. They are also, in considerable degree, the invention of one man, Adams, who bolstered his utopian ideals with interpretations from a Bible that he could read only with great difficulty. Although some of Adams' ideas almost certainly derived from Christian and Young, both educated members of the officer class, Adams' role as the surviving male on the island gave him an almost unlimited power to mold the developing Pitcairn culture as he saw fit. Here, although the Tahitian women were the de facto rulers of the island, their power was readily conceded to Adams in what could hardly be considered a victory for the equality of the sexes.

Against all expectations, Adams was successful in designing and perpetuating what might be called a synthetic cultural tradition. Like the prophets of old, he literally created a new heaven on earth. An interesting theoretical problem arises when consideration is given to the fact that a single extraordinary individual can radically change a culture. This "great man theory" does not entirely square with the view that cultural systems develop in response to environmental pressures. On the other hand, many of Adams' ideas did not stand the test of time. Ultimately, Pitcairn affiliated in a formal way with the British government and with the Seventh Day Adventist Church. Some, but not all, of Adams' social and religious ideas may, then, have been maladaptive to the extent that they had to be changed, but even this is not certain.

Overall, the Pitcairn evidence seems to suggest that any determining role played by selection and adaptation is played rather vaguely. A basically Tahitian system of production seems able to accommodate Christianity in its various forms just as well as it can accommodate the traditional Tahitian world view. A Pitcairn house may be slightly less suited to the environment than a Tahitian house, but that slight difference does not seem to have bothered anybody or threatened anybody's survival.

The case of Pitcairn's Island leads to the following conclusions: (1) a variety of different cultural systems can generally adapt quite well to any particular set of environmental conditions; (2) although some degree of consistency must be maintained within cultural traditions and between cultural traditions and processes, a sufficiently adapted cultural system can be constructed out of disparate and unrelated elements. The events on Pitcairn's Island need not cause the rejection of theories about adaptation, great men, great ideas, or the unitary quality of cultural systems, so long as we agree that adaptation is very often an indulgent master, great men have limitations, great ideas must ultimately confront reality, and cultural systems can operate effectively even when they possess a substantial number of internal contradictions or unrelated parts.

On Pitcairn's Island a new cultural system was formed and underwent a process of developmental change and growth. This process involved the diffusion of ideas from outside and a substantial amount of assimilation into the wider cultures of the English-speaking world and the Seventh Day Adventist Church. On the whole, although handicapped by their isolation, the people of Pitcairn have eagerly sought an identification with the spreading and increasingly homogeneous culture of the urban centers of the modern world. Like most of us, the Pitcairners desire to be "modern." The next case deals with a group of people who for three centuries have resisted programs of forced assimilation into Spanish, Mexican, and United States' culture.

The Tewa and the Hopi, the people with whom this example deals, have always accepted new ideas that they thought were good. Their members have attended great universities and obtained Ph.D.s in anthropology and other subjects. Despite this they have successfully maintained the basic outlines of a way of life that has existed in the southwestern deserts of the United States for more than a thousand years. What accounts for resistance to change or, more correctly, selective change? Can we reconcile a conservative stance with theories that interpret constant adaptive cultural change as the major mechanism for human survival? The following case is based upon the work of Edward P. Dozier, who was born in the Tewa pueblo of Santa Clara.

CAN WE CHANGE AND STILL BE THE SAME?

The Spanish first came to the region surrounding what is now Sante Fe, New Mexico, in 1540—long before the first British colony had been established in North America. The Spanish created a government and, in 1634, only a few hundred years after the Normans terrified England with their Doomsday Book, took a census. The region contained approximately 10,000 Tewa-speaking Indians. These Indians lived in established pueblos or villages. The pueblos of Tesuque, Nambe, San Ildefonso, Santa Clara, and San Juan still exist and still carry on many of the traditional practices of the Tewa.

Beginning with the arrival of Coronado in 1540, the Spanish made incessant demands upon the pueblos for food and other supplies. In one village, several hundred Indians were ruthlessly exterminated. Another, smaller expedition consisting of a few Spanish friars disappeared. By 1610, the Spanish-Mexican Indian capital was established at Santa Fe and the work of "civilizing" the Indians was proceeding rapidly. By 1630, it was reported that 60,000 Pueblo Indians had been converted to Catholicism and churches built in ninety villages.

The building of elaborate governmental buildings, churches, and dwellings for the Spanish and their Mexican Indian allies led to intense needs for Pueblo Indian labor. Indians who failed to attend church were whipped. Indian religious practices were forbidden. Masks and prayer sticks were burned. Religious leaders were hanged as witches. Civil officials sought to extract large amounts of tribute from the Indians under their control as well as employing them constantly as forced labor. All of this might have been endured if Christianity had been more effective in securing good harvests than the traditional religion. It was not.

In 1675, forty-seven Pueblo religious leaders were publicly whipped in Santa Fe. Revenge came in 1689 when, after three weeks of fighting, 2,000 settlers were forced to flee, while 21 missionaries and 375 colonists were killed. Churches and public buildings were torn down. The leaders of the rebellion sought to wipe out every vestige of Spanish influence. After several unsuccessful attempts at reoccupation, the Spanish returned in 1693. Three years later, after an unsuccessful revolt, many of the residents of the Tewa pueblos fled westward into Arizona and the country of the Hopi Indians.

Although the Tewa had been "Catholics" for nearly one hundred years, they brought nothing of Christianity westward with them. They were reluctantly accepted as neighbors by the Hopi who required man-

power in order to repel the attacks of nomadic Indians and of the Spanish. Although the Tewa and the Hopi shared the same general culture, they spoke totally unrelated languages. It is noteworthy that since the coming of the Tewa to Hopiland, armed attacks upon the Hopi have come to a complete halt. Thus, the Tewa, if only by accident, have fulfilled the promise made when they settled in Hopi country.

The central goals of the Hopi have to do with leading a good life, thinking good thoughts, and so appealing to the kachinas who bring rain. Anger, killing, and warfare are inimical to this goal. Open competition for wealth or high position, and contact with unclean foreigners are equally despised. The Tewa, traditionally, were less concerned about rain—their forefathers practiced irrigated agriculture based on perennial streams— and more concerned about curing. The Tewa had no technology for food production or for appeasing the supernatural that was felt to be worthwhile by the Hopi. In time, a division of labor developed. The Hopi maintained the necessary prayers for rain; the Tewa dealt with the Navaho, missionaries, government officials, law and order, tourists, and employers.

The Tewa have been a marginal community living between the Hopi and their impure neighbors. As warriors and mercenaries, the Tewa value aggressive and individualistic behavior. Government officials and whites generally find the Tewa to be progressive and friendly. Similarly, relationships between the Tewa and the Navaho are much more friendly than are those between the Hopi and the Navaho. The Tewa invite Navaho singers and curers to their pueblo and have adopted some Navaho ceremonial practices. Hopi bitterly resent Christian missionaries and ignore them to the extent possible. Unfortunately, there is little that they can do since overt expressions of hostility would be improper and unHopi. The Tewa, similarly, have no use for missionaries but their attitude is one of live and let live:

> It is best to be polite to missionaries, let them come in and preach. We will go on with what we are doing. It is not good to drive anyone away; we must be nice to people no matter who they are. But we feel that no one should disturb what we want to do. If they urge us to listen, we say nothing. Sometimes they talk a long time telling us that our dances are evil and that we must stop them. They say unless we go the "Christian Road" we will not be saved. But we just keep quiet and they get tired after a while and leave us alone (Dozier 1966:34).

Tewa and Hopi relationships with the United States Bureau of Indian Affairs have varied through time. Toward the beginning of this century, Indian children were kidnapped and taken by force to boarding schools in the east. In these schools use of Indian languages was forbidden and brutal physical punishments were administered to children who acted like Indians. Investigators searched for and found immoral and anti-Christian practices in Tewa and Hopi ceremonies. The "Religious Crimes Code" permitted Indian service officials to stop any ceremonial practices that were considered un-Christian (Dozier 1966:33).

In the 1920s the United States began to allow the Indians to practice their traditional religion. Programs designed to separate adults and children, thus preventing the transmission of Indian culture, gradually tapered off. As of 1966, a generation of school-trained Tewa and Hopi have developed resistance toward traditional culture. They are critical of the religious life and reluctant to undertake ceremonial and ritual obligations. Some loiter about trading posts and drink liquor. One factor tending to inhibit such flirtations with Anglo culture is the fact that the place in Anglo culture prepared for Indians is a place of poverty, destitution, and unemployment. For many, perhaps most, it is better to collect the unemployment check on the reservation than off the reservation in a reeking and dangerous urban ghetto.

Despite all of this, the Tewa have been far more friendly to whites than either the Hopi or the Rio Grande Tewa. In fact, the Tewa appear to have played a major role in facilitating the accommodation of the Hopi to the rapidly changing circumstances in which they have found themselves. It is significant that neither the Hopi nor the Tewa have yielded their basic identity. After four hundred years of forced cultural change, the culture of the Tewa still exists. As in the case of Pitcairn, the culture of the Tewa contains items borrowed from other cultures—the Rio Grande Tewa, the Hopi, the Spanish, and the Anglo (English-speaking). It also contains numerous items that are plainly the result of independent invention. Many of these items stem from the Tewa role as protectors of the Hopi.

In thinking about the Hopi and the Tewa and most of the other Pueblo peoples as well, the most critical question that comes to mind concerns the manner in which these peoples have maintained important aspects of their traditional cultures in the face of overwhelming pressures from outside. On the northwest coast, religious rituals were ruthlessly suppressed. In the east and in the plains, American Indians were massacred, made to endure death marches, robbed of their lands, deprived of their livelihoods, subjected to starvation, and deprived of education, medical care, and other forms of governmental assistance. During the boarding-school period, children of many American Indian groups were stolen from their parents and subjected to intensive indoctrination.

Through it all, Pueblo Indian culture managed to function. It managed to change and adapt without losing its essential character. It has been suggested by B. J. Siegel that some cultures tend to persist because their status system is oriented around religious matters which tend not to be modified by external pressures. The Hopi, in particular, have sacred responsibilities which make them considerably more important to the world than are the various unclean and polluted outsiders who visit them from time to time. The Hopi, and after them, their Tewa protectors, rest serene in the knowledge of their own superiority, a superiority that arises, not in military might or technological know-how but in deeper understandings of religion and humanity. To a considerable degree, the pueblos are religious communes and like many other religious communes are able to survive and maintain a unique culture even in the face of military might and political persecution.

Another factor in the preservation of Hopi and Tewa culture is that people, especially young people, who have come to disagree with the policies of traditional leaders, have been persuaded to move out into less traditional pueblos at the foot of the mesa and more accessible to visits from outside. It is only recently with the formation of a tribal government that a progressive majority has begun to exert pressures upon the more conservative villages. Until recently, then, the impact of modernization has been to create a buffer zone of "progressive" villages which serve to isolate and protect the conservative interior villages. In some cases, historically, individuals have had one house in a progressive village at the foot of the mesa and one house in a conservative village on the top of the mesa. In a similar way, wealthy individuals in India have been able to maintain a consistent identity with two cultures simultaneously by having two living rooms, one furnished in European style with chairs and tables and one with mats and carpets in Indian style.

Traditional pueblo religious leaders are strong, confident, and impressive. Hopi and Tewa children exposed to other cultures experience no feelings of inferiority, neither do their parents. Because the moral authority of traditional leaders and traditional culture has remained unquestioned, the Tewa are able to borrow from Hopi, Navajo, and Anglo cultures in a selective and relatively nondisruptive way.

Another equally important factor in the preservation of many Indian groups in the American Southwest is that representatives of Spain, Mexico, and the United States did not control a technology that could make use of the arid wastelands which supported such groups as the Apache, Navajo, or Pueblo Indians. The industrialization of Arizona and New Mexico in recent years has created increasing pressures upon all

FIGURE 11–2 Over the years the more progressive Hopi have moved into new communities at the foot of the Mesa. Changing house styles reflect individual adaptations to the United States national culture as well as increases in cash income. (PHOTO COURTESY OF ROBERT LAIDLAW)

existing groups of Indians. In many cases, individuals capable of earning good money through wage work find it difficult and unrewarding to continue to contribute to traditional patterns of religious and social activity. The autocratic rule of Pueblo religious leaders is not always acceptable to those who have a strong and viable alternative life-style in Albuquerque or Phoenix. At the same time, strong movements toward the preservation of the best of traditional cultures, often enthusiastically supported by the tourist dollar, encourage the possibility that the old ways may continue to survive as the Tewa, Hopi, and other Pueblo groups adapt to their own special situation within a broader and more tolerant society.

What If They Don't Agree?

The Tewa and Hopi changed and accommodated to take their place as part of the culture of the United States Southwest. Despite constant changes, their culture remains intact. Part of their success lay in the fact that individuals who disagreed with official policies as set forth by community elders were free to move elsewhere. In some of the pueblos, especially those along the Rio Grande River, it was not so easy to move. At times, in various pueblos, disagreements festered and the needed unity in the face of the stresses of modernization and "Americanization" was permanently or temporarily lost. Bernard Siegel has described how the pueblo of Picuris was disrupted by conflict (Beals and Siegel 1966).

Over and over again in human history, communities that need to take arms against a thousand perils are seen to fall literally to pieces because their inhabitants were unable to agree concerning the appropriate actions to be taken. Recall, for example, the Athenians debating what to do about the Spartans or the Macedonians. Namhalli in South India, which is described with Picuris Pueblo in Beals and Siegel's *Divisiveness and Social Conflict* is another case in point.

During World War II from about 1940 to 1946, Bangalore City was a way station and training place for British and American troops being sent to fight the Japanese in Burma and points east. Namhalli, a tiny village just outside of Bangalore and just outside the barbed wire that separated the soldiers from the villagers, was in a position to sell milk, vegetables, and other goods and services at enormous profit. Villagers built new houses, purchased consumer goods, invested in education, and encouraged sons and daughters to marry and have children. People in Namhalli couldn't get enough of the good modern things that were offered in the city—the motion pictures, the radio, fancy cookery, movie magazines, bleached and pressed clothing, bicycles, and so on.

But the war ended and the troops went away. India became independent. Agricultural prices were controlled through the importation of grain from the United States. There were no jobs and it was almost impossible to

FIGURE 11–3 Women quarreling in Gopalpur, South India. Quarrels often start in the house and move out into the street and the village. Men claim that disputes between brothers are caused by their wives. (PHOTO BY ALAN R. BEALS)

sell what was grown in the fields. By 1952 the children born during the war were old enough to help out on the family farms, but all of the land in the village was in use. There were more people than the land could support and there was no place to go. In 1952, there was crop failure, and the last resources left over from the prosperous war days were exhausted. Village pasture lands were stripped bare of vegetation. Avenue and orchard trees—practically anything that was alive—were cut down to feed the village goats.

There was an air of despondency in the village. When great men visited, people said, "Sahib, what am I going to do? I have five sons and only five acres of land." Later they would warn the visitor about the other people in the village: "The people in that house," they would say, "have killed a man; so and so stole his brother's land; you can't trust anyone in this village; sin is up; we will get no rain."

The vegetarian castes held a special firewalking ceremony to which they invited none of the other villagers. You people are too sinful, they said. Only the pure can walk on fire. The other castes met and decided to hold an exceptionally large celebration in honor of the village god. When the village god went in procession, his "chariot" could not pass under a tamarind tree belonging to a member of the vegetarian castes: "You can't pass under this tree. It is a sin to cut a branch of a fruit-bearing tree." To which the nonvegetarians replied, "It is a sin to attempt to stop a religious procession." A sword was drawn. Harsh words were exchanged. Finally, the offending branch was raised with a rope and the procession passed.

There was much that needed to be done in the village. There was land to be reclaimed. There were drainage ditches to be dug. Help should have been sought from the government. Cooperation was desperately needed but for the next five years there was none. A thief stole the image of the village god from the temple and sold it. Religious celebrations ceased to be

FIGURE 11–4   The priest measures off the 108-foot bed of coals needed for the fire-walking ceremony in Namhalli, South India. (PHOTO BY ALAN R. BEALS)

held. The village seemed caught in an endless cycle of misery, anger, and despair. Population seemed to be increasing without limit while food supplies and resources steadily declined.

What Happened Next?

By 1960, the situation in Namhalli had changed dramatically. The barren, windswept lands surrounding the village sprouted forests of casaurina trees destined for the cooking stoves of Bangalore. A new stone bus stop marked the entrance to the village. Carefully leveled roads lined with stone gutters led to and through the village. There were street lights, bicycles, electric irrigation pumps, and sleek, well-fed people dressed in the latest urban style. In about five years, between 1955 and 1960, Namhalli had changed from a downbeat and despairing place into a modern and prosperous suburban village.

In 1953, there was one high school graduate in the village; now there were many and every child in the village was planning to attend high school. Construction of a telephone factory a few miles away had created a labor shortage. Educated people, especially high school graduates, obtained jobs as skilled and well-paid workers at the factory. There was one factory worker in the village in 1952, a man who worked at a military vehicle depot. In 1960, there were more than thirty factory workers and by 1966 there were more than a hundred.

As cash flowed into the village from the pockets of factory workers, village agriculture was transformed. Unproductive fields devoted to grain crops that could not be sold at a profit due to price control were replaced with casaurina plantations for firewood. Cash was used on the lower fields to construct irrigation wells. Such wells provided water that could be used to raise profitable fruit and vegetable crops that were not affected by price control. Working a few hours a day, a man who owned a half-acre of irrigated land could make as much money as a factory worker.

A nice-looking house, plenty of good food, modern clothing, access to good medical care, including shoes with socks, and the price of a ticket to the latest English film are bound to create a sense of well-being. But the prosperity of the village came from more than money. It came, as to some extent did the money itself, from a revolutionary change in the social organization of the village. In 1952, the village worked, like the United Nations, by means of universal agreement. If any action was proposed, it had to be approved by the head of every house. After 1952, nobody cared very much what happened in the village. The old form of social organization was lost, but there was no new form to take its place. The revolutionary change in social organization was the importation of a device called a "chit fund" from the factory. A chit fund or rotating credit association involves a group of members who pool their cash—for example, ten rupees from each member—to form a common fund. If there were twenty members, the fund would involve two hundred rupees. The resulting fund is then auctioned to the highest bidder who may or may not be a member of the association. Thus, a man might borrow two hundred rupees and

FIGURE 11–5   In Namhalli, South India, a few years ago this growing family depended upon a limited amount of land for their subsistence. Now, the two older brothers are factory workers and the younger brother has quit his teaching job to manage the family grape garden. (PHOTO BY ALAN R. BEALS)

then, usuallly at the end of the month, return two hundred and twenty or even two hundred and fifty rupees to the fund.

There are no defaulters under the chit-fund system because the members of the fund are numerous and inclined to respond to the threat of default with unrestrained violence. Chit funds were set aside to take the school children on bus trips, to refurbish the village temple, and to serve a variety of religious and public-service functions. The chit-fund system enabled farmers in the village to borrow money that could be invested in the improvement of their fields. In the words of the economists, the chit fund was one device that provided the investment capital required for modernization. Accordingly the village modernized.

There is more. The factory workers provided a model for a totally new way of life. On the other hand, neither the factory workers nor the other members of the village were in any sense required to accept the factory-worker model. The village has maintained its traditional religion, but it has softened and in some places erased the traditional habits of discrimination between castes. Preferred marriage to a mother's brother's daughter or other close relative has continued to be practiced. Western-style clothing is worn in some contexts, but comfortable and traditional wrap-around clothing is preferred at home in the village. A few people have been spoiled by modernity embracing a hedonistic life-style and spending

FIGURE 11–6 Money earned by a factory worker provided the investment capital required for a half-acre grape garden. The family's annual income has now increased tenfold. Namhalli, South India. (PHOTO BY ALAN R. BEALS)

their scarce funds on alcohol, sex, and other extravagances. For most people the factory-worker model has been a model of self-improvement, hard work, and wise investment.

Where the Pueblo Indians have preserved their traditional culture and maintained a sharp distinction between modern and traditional, the people of Namhalli have erased the distinction completely. The Pueblo Indians must maintain constant vigilance to preserve their way of life against constant threat from the outside. The people of Namhalli have grasped the modern world and turned it to their purposes. They are aware of the possible consequences of Arab control of oil prices. They are worried about the possibility of war between the United States and Russia. When they need help from the government, they know the person to talk to. They know if a bribe must be paid and if so how much. In a word, the people of Namhalli have ceased to be the victims of modernity. They are now among its perpetrators. As they help to manufacture the telephones, radios, airplanes, and machine tools that are helping to transform India, they have become the willing agents of rapid and overwhelming technological change.

Why Did These Things Happen?

They have a saying in Namhalli, perhaps borrowed from some colonial English schoolmaster; it is "Money makes many things." In traditional times, essentially before 1940, people in Namhalli had little money, but they obtained most of their needs and wants through subsistence agriculture and the sale of small amounts of grain and cattle. As the population of the village expanded and desires for urban manufactures and consumer goods steadily increased, there was a proportional increase both in poverty and in the feeling of being poor and disadvantaged.

During World War II, the village embarked on a course of modernization. After the war, lack of money made further modernization impossible. As soon as money became available during the late 1950s, modernization took place at an accelerated pace. At first glance, the theoretical explanation of Namhalli's history of change appears perfectly simple. World War II created desires. Poverty after World War II created frustration leading to conflict. Access to money in the late 1950s ended conflict and created a climate for modernization.

With regard to the purchase of cinema tickets, aluminum cookware, bicycles, manufactured clothing, and improved farm equipment, it is money that makes modernization possible. Across the world, though, there are many people who have money and do not spend it upon technological innovations. Even in India, there are many villages that have failed to adapt to the presence of a nearby city. Men from Namhalli were able to move into factory employment because they possessed better English and greater literacy than villagers from other parts of South India. Education, not just education but knowledge, is a prerequisite for any kind of human adaptation. People in Namhalli perceived that they needed cash, and they used their intelligence to discover a way of obtaining cash.

But what caused the conflict in Namhalli? One explanation is that some level of conflict and potential conflict or strain is characteristic of all human groups. When outside forces or stresses act upon groups in such a way as to intensify existing conflicts, the presence of unprecedented conflict creates difficulties in coping with the various problems the group or community faces. In other words, Namhalli fell apart because certain kinds of outside forces triggered increasing conflict which grew beyond the capacity of the community to halt it. The ultimate result was a radical change in the social order of the village.

In the nineteenth century, Bangalore City was little more than a small town. As the city grew, the villages around it were increasingly subjected to new ideas. Although some of these new ideas might be characterized as urban Hindu, British, Western, or simply urban, they might best be described as involving an emerging world culture that exists every place but originated no place: in a word, modern. Because modern culture contains the remnants and fragments of many other cultures, because it is endlessly complex, it fails to present any unified set of ideas to those exposed to it. People in Namhalli were suddenly and overwhelmingly subjected to a modern school system stemming from John Dewey, to a military subculture devoted to sex and alcohol, to modern forms of Krishna cults, to fundamentalist Christianity, and to a host of other new and confusing ideas. The result of such a buzzing, blooming confusion of contradictory messages is what is called *value conflict*.

Values, of course, are the ideas that people have about good and bad, right and wrong, proper and improper. If the values in question deal with how you should treat your father, your wife, your boss, your servant, your friend, your brothers and sisters, or other individuals with whom you have daily contact, then the sharing of the same values by both parties is of the utmost importance if everyone is to get through the day peaceably. When there is extensive value conflict, people naturally choose the values that suit them best. The boss accepts the notion that his employee owes him unswerving obedience; the employee for his part accepts the idea of cooperative decision making. Because the two people have different expectations about the relationship, both soon become angry and conflict begins.

That a village like Namhalli receives different values from different sources does not necessarily mean that the resulting value conflicts will be imported into the village. Disagreement and disruption are possible only where village leadership is weak or divided. A key element in the development of conflict in Namhalli appears to have been the loss of any mechanism for ensuring agreement among its members concerning values and plans for action.

Traditionally, the management of village affairs was of little concern to government so long as the taxes got collected. Under British influence, government took an ever-increasing interest in the day-to-day management of village affairs. The village headman and council, which ran the traditional village, were gradually reduced in power and importance. The headman became a minor government servant. The role of the village council was so sharply defined by government regulation that virtually all of its powers were lost. The stage was set for the village to be managed in western style by police and law courts. The only problem was that there were no police and the law courts were too expensive and inaccessible.

Very briefly, then, Namhalli suffered from extensive conflict because it lost its leadership, because it was subjected to value conflict, and because it encountered economic difficulties. Had these and other related things not happened, the conflict would have taken a different course. Quite possibly Namhalli's movement toward modernization would have followed a different pattern. Namhalli's recovery from its period of disastrous conflict involved new leadership, new values, and more money.

The three cases presented so far are all histories of a fairly reasonable or realistic adaptation or adjustment to rapidly changing conditions. Pitcairn Islanders, Pueblo Indians, and South Indian villagers started with different cultural traditions and encountered rather different circumstances as they struggled to come to terms with the modern world. Perhaps the people of these three places did not always make the best possible decisions about what to do next, but on the whole, given their particular goals and objectives, the decisions made probably do not seem shocking or unreasonable to most of us. What they wanted is pretty much what they got.

Most people are fortunate. They have plenty of time to make decisions. about what to do, and they have many choices open to them. For some cultural systems, the time of decision is short and the opportunities to decide are few. Consider what happened to the Dakota Sioux when their land was taken, their buffalo killed, and their people penned up and starving.

WHERE WILL ALL THE WHITE MEN GO?

Toward the end of the last century on the plains of North America, there was an ecological disaster. The great herds of buffalo, which stretched from horizon to horizon and provided an abundance of meat and hides to a variety of Indians, mountain men, and roughnecks of miscellaneous origin, were gradually disappearing. The wild and free pattern of life where men lived by the horse and the gun and by killing the buffalo and each other was coming to an end.

A "squaw man," a white married to an Indian, describes the year he killed his last buffalo. He speaks to an Indian named Red Bird's Tail:

> I told him of the conditions south and east of us, that there were no buffalo anywhere, except the few between us and the Yellowstone, and even there, no herds of more than a hundred or so. "Are you sure," he said, "sure that the white men have seen all the land which they say lies between the two salt waters? Haven't they overlooked some big part of the country where our buffalo may have congregated and from whence they may return?
>
> There is no place in the whole land, I replied, north, south, east, or west, that the white men have not traveled, are not traveling right now, and none of them can find buffalo. White men are just as anxious to kill buffalo for their hides and meat as you are.
>
> On our way homeward the next morning, I saw a lone buffalo calf—almost a yearling—standing forlornly in a clump of rye grass near the river. I killed it, and took off the hide, horns, hoofs and all. The Crow woman tanned it for me later and decorated the flesh side with gaudy porcupine quill work. That was my last buffalo. Along in the afternoon we started something like seventy-five head which had come to the frozen stream in search of water. They scampered wildly across the bottom and up the slope of the valley to the plains. That was the last herd of them that Nat-ak-ki and I ever saw. (Schultz 1956).

By 1883, the last of the buffalo were gone.

During this period, the largest and strongest Indian tribe in the United States were the Sioux Indians. The 26,000 Sioux were awarded the present state of South Dakota by treaty. When gold was discovered in the Black Hills, the Sioux reservation was decreased by one-third in size. In 1888, the cattle raised by the Sioux were decimated by disease. Next year, in 1889, crops failed and an additional half of the reservation was taken away. Food and other supplies promised by treaty never appeared. The Sioux were being squeezed and starved out of existence.

That same year, 1889, word came to the Sioux through the Shoshoni and Arapaho of a new Messiah who had appeared in the west. In the fall, the tribal council sent a delegation by railroad to visit him. The delegation mailed letters back confirming the fact that a redeemer had appeared. When the delegation returned, they testified that there was a man at the base of the Sierras. He was the son of God and he bore upon his body the scars of the time when the whites had crucified him. The Messiah had come to punish the whites for their wickedness. In the spring of 1891, he would wipe the whites from the face of the earth, resurrect all the dead Indians, bring back the buffalo, and restore the supremacy of the Indians.

Receiving word of this movement from an educated Indian who

served as postmaster, the Indian agent promptly made arrests and prevented a council meeting from taking place. There were reports that the Indians of the west planned a general uprising in spring 1891. Meanwhile, Kicking Bear returned from a visit to the Arapaho and confirmed that they were involved with the movement. Attempts to suppress the movement ended in failure and the Sioux quickly became active participants.

Alarmed, the government in Washington sent anthropologist James Mooney to investigate matters. This was 1890. Mooney traveled to Mason Valley at the base of the Sierra Nevada Mountains. There, he encountered a man named Wovoka or Jack Wilson who had talked with God. As a youth, Wovoka was an orphan raised by a rancher named David Wilson who taught him some English and some Christianity. Wovoka was a "good Indian" with a reputation for industry and reliability. When Wovoka was fourteen years old, there was an eclipse of the sun and he fell asleep in the daytime and was taken to the other world. God told him to go back to his people, to tell them to be good and to love one another, to stop quarreling and to live in peace with the whites. People should work hard; they should not lie, cheat, steal, or kill. Those who followed God's instructions would be reunited with their friends and relatives in a world free of sickness, old age, or death. God taught Wovoka a dance that would hasten this process. (Mooney 1896).

In Wovoka's words:

> Grandfather says, when your friends die you must not cry. You must not hurt anybody or do harm to anyone. You must not fight. Do right always. It will give you satisfaction in life. Do not tell the white people about this. Jesus is now upon the earth. He appears like a cloud. The dead are all alive again. I do not know when they will be here; maybe this fall or in the spring. When the time comes there will be no more sickness and everyone will be young again. Do not refuse to work for the whites and do not make any trouble with them until you leave them. When the earth shakes do not be afraid. It will not hurt you. I want you to dance every six weeks. Make a feast at the dance and have food that everybody may eat. Then bathe in the water. That is all. You will receive good words again from me some time. Do not tell lies. (Mooney 1896).

Later, the Sioux came to believe that the whites had been sent to punish them for their sins. Their sins were not expiated and the day of deliverance at hand. Soon, all the Indians that had ever died would come driving immense herds of buffalo and fine ponies before them. Whiteman gunpowder would be powerless. The whites would be overwhelmed and smothered by a deep landslide held down by sod and timber. The few whites who escaped destruction would become small fishes in the rivers. The earth would tremble, there would be a flood of water, which would wash into the mouths of the whites and choke them with mud. There would be storms and whirlwinds. When the time came, everyone would assemble at certain sacred places and prepare for the abandonment of the present world by stripping off their clothing and discarding all metal and weapons.

At Pine Ridge on the Sioux reservation, the agent was a man named Royer, called by the Sioux, "Young-man-afraid-of-the-Indians." As the Indians danced and prayed, he sent daily telegrams to the War Department demanding that troops be sent. On November 19, 1890, the first troops arrived and a few of the Indians fled into the badlands. By December, everything was quiet and the government decided to arrest the "ringleaders." On December 12, the Indian police were sent to arrest Sitting Bull. Sitting Bull and his followers refused to come. The military was called in and the green recruits promptly opened fire on both Sitting Bull and the Indian police. Sitting Bull, six of his men, and six policemen were killed by the soldiers.

Outside of Sitting Bull's refusal to accept arrest, none of the Sioux leaders showed any desire to fight. Big Foot voluntarily turned himself in and was then sent to recall some of his followers who were still in hiding. He found some of them and was bringing them back to the Pine Ridge agency when he met (December 28) Major Whiteside of the Seventh Cavalry. The major demanded unconditional surrender and the Indians surrendered. The Indians were moved to Wounded Knee creek and told to camp. There were 470 soldiers and 106 Sioux warriors. All other Indians had been caught and returned to the agencies.

The Indians were camped on an open plain surrounded by soldiers. Four machine guns were aimed point blank at the encampment. At eight o'clock in the morning of December 29, the Indians were asked to come out of their tipis and surrender their guns. Soldiers searched the tipis, frightening the women and children, and recovered some forty old and ineffective rifles. Yellow Bird, a medicine man, walked among the warriors blowing upon his eagle-bone whistle and urging resistance. The soldiers' bullets would be useless against the ghost shirts the Indians were wearing.

Yellow Bird stooped down and threw a handful of dust into the air. Black Fox is reported to have drawn a rifle from under his blanket and fired at a soldier. The soldiers fired a volley that probably killed half of the Sioux warriors. The machine guns opened fire upon the women and children. In the next few minutes, two hundred Indians were killed and sixty soldiers. Bodies, including those of women with children, were found scattered up to two miles from the scene of the disaster. Three days later, a four-month-old baby girl was found alive beside her mother. She was wrapped in a shawl and wore a cap embroidered in beadwork with the American flag.

What Else Was There to Do?

Mooney had little difficulty in explaining why the Indians did as they did. He wrote:

> The wise men tell us that the world is growing happier—that we live longer than did our fathers, have more of comfort and less of toil, fewer wars and discords, and higher hopes and aspirations. So say the wise men but deep in our own hearts we know they are wrong. For were not we, too, born in Arcadia, and have we not—each one of us—in that May of life when the world was young, started out lightly and airily along the path that led through green meadows to the blue mountains on the distant horizon beyond which lay the great world we were to conquer? And though others dropped behind, have we not gone on through morning brightness and noonday heat, with eyes always steadily forward, until the fresh grass began to be parched and withered, and the way grew hard and stony, and the blue mountains resolved into gray rocks and thorny cliffs? And when at last we reached the toilsome summits, we found the glory that had lured us onward was only the sunset glow that fades into darkness while we look, and leaves us at the very goal to sink down, tired in body and sick at heart, with strength and courage gone, to close our eyes and dream again, not of the fame and fortune that were to be ours, but only of the old-time happiness we have left so far behind.
>
> As with men, so it is with nations. The lost paradise is the world's dreamland of youth. What tribe or people has not had its golden age, before Pandora's box was loosed, when women were nymphs and dryads and men were gods and heroes? And when the race lies crushed and groaning beneath an alien yoke, how natural is the dream of a redeemer, an Arthur, who shall return from exile or awake from some long sleep to drive out the usurper and win back for his people what they have lost. The hope becomes a faith and the faith becomes the creed of priests and prophets, until the hero is a god and the dream a religion, looking to some great miracle of nature for its culmination and accomplishment. The doctrines of the Hindu avatar, the Hebrew Messiah, the Christian millennium, and the Hesunanin of the Indian ghost dance are essentially the same, and have their origin in a hope and longing common to all humanity. (Mooney 1896:657)

People living in groups and societies have ways of coping with their outstanding problems. These ways of coping, which constitute their technology, their how-to-do-it manuals, are derived from experience. When traditional ways of coping fail to produce expected results, people search about for more effective ways of handling their problems. The Sioux tried fighting; they tried cattle raising; they tried farming. They tried signing treaties with the United States. Their problems and those of most other American Indian groups continued insolvable. Traditional ways of coping continued to be ineffective and nothing that was tried worked. The Tewa and Hopi, by contrast, found a solution that worked. They changed and adapted without touching the stable religious core of their culture. People in Namhalli might have adopted a new religion, but to do that they required leadership and their leadership had been destroyed. In time a new leadership might have been created and a religious cult might have succeeded, but before this could happen an economic rather than a religious solution to their problems became available.

More than the others the Sioux faced genocide and ethnocide, the death of their people, the death of their way of life. They embarked upon one final collective enterprise. They danced and prayed and waited for the

FIGURE 11–7 Change does not always create problems nor need one culture be swept away by another. Here, chiefs of the Blood Indian tribe in Canada attend a modern performance of the traditional Sun Dance. They are fluent in the English and Blood (Kainai) languages, and all successful ranchers (PHOTO COURTESY OF GEORGE SPINDLER)

whites to disappear. What else could they have done? What else was there to do? Strangely, the Sioux may not have danced in vain. The shadow of the massacre at Wounded Knee stretches across the years. It was one of the last great killings of American Indians. It contributed to the end of the more brutal policies of extermination. By the 1930s even ethnocide, the systematic destruction of Indian cultures and traditions, was being called into question.

Another American effect of the ghost dance was that it aided the development of an American Indian national culture. The Sioux Indians did not dance alone. The ghost dance triggered friendship among individuals in different and formerly hostile tribes. The spread of the ghost dance was made possible by the railroad and the postal service. The ghost dance, itself, by providing a sense of Indian nationhood, laid the foundation for future cooperation represented by the religious and political movements that work toward Indian rights at the present time.

Across the world, religious movements anticipating the creation of a new heaven and a new earth or, at the very least the complete reformation of society, have been a frequent feature of cultural change. Many of these movements have invited ridicule or surprise. When people throw their money in the ocean or sell their property and await the arrival of a flying saucer that will carry them to the planet Clarion, bystanders are likely to question the sanity or practicality of their decisions. But for a few quirks of history, Gautama Buddha, Jesus Christ, and Karl Marx and the movements that they founded would have been regarded the same way.

The people who form movements generally have nothing to lose. They are rarely confronted with *any* desirable alternatives. By joining a movement, they recover the community that may previously have been lost to apathy or factionalist dispute. A moral order is created; leadership is established. People become capable of acting in concert to solve their problems. Very often, as was the case in the ghost dance, those in authority react to the formation of a new cult or a new movement by arresting its leaders and by persecuting its true believers. Such repression may strengthen a movement, driving more and more individuals into its embrace. More often, as was the case of the ghost dance, the violence of repression creates a counter-reaction even as it successfully destroys the movement. The ghost dance led to changes in government policy, so that Indians may now legally develop and maintain their own forms of religious worship.

But Is It Rational?

Because the creature or culture that is best adapted to any particular environment is most likely to survive within it, it has been argued that existing cultures stand at some sort of pinnacle of adaptation. To reach the adaptive perfection that supposedly characterizes all existing cultures, it is necessary that a cultural system be free of inefficiencies or inconsistencies. It is necessary that its members be faultlessly rational and that they invariably choose the best of all possible solutions for whatever problems may arise. This all seems logical and certainly leads us to consider that much of what people do has to make pretty good sense. When people choose to maintain their traditional culture as did the Tewa, choose to enter into conflict as did the people of Namhalli, or choose to don bullet-proof shirts and await the millenium as did the Sioux Indians, it is reasonable to explore the possibility that there is method in their apparent madness.

At the very least, every cloud has a silver lining. If we want to explain cultural change it is good to look at any positive effects that that cultural change might be thought to have. Ghastly and life-threatening mistakes are likely to be soon remedied by extinction either of the mistakes themselves or of those who have made them. Looking closely at their own cultural system, or at any other, most people can detect a variety of dubious practices, immoralities, inefficiences, and bad things. A common-sense view of such impressions is that, indeed, most people are not perfect. Most cultural systems are expedient arrangements of "shreds and patches"* that have come together in part by accident, in part by conscious design, and in part by virtue of a desperate desire to get by.

Lacking competition of any serious kind and free of any serious environmental threats to their survival, the Pitcairn Islanders were able to assemble a cultural system that not only worked but that was universally admired. Like most cultural systems it had its flaws. It lacked any pattern for dealing with foreigners and it lacked any means of controlling its population. Rather, like their British and Tahitian ancestors, the Pitcairn Islanders' version of population control was simply to get on the next boat and sail toward the west or, in the case of the Tahitians, the east. Perhaps today, the Tewa and Hopi are living in a fool's paradise. The next wave of fanatical Christianity that sweeps the United States may destroy their religious life entirely. Their pueblos may yet be the site of strip mines or power plants. Right now, though, they are getting by. They are adapted. The Indians are still having troubles at Wounded Knee Creek where there have been shoot-outs between Indians and FBI agents. Namhalli's apparently successful adaptation to urbanization may prove to have been faulty if the village can find no way to protect its land from urban factories and suburban developments.

* In Gilbert and Sullivan's *Mikado*, a wandering minstrel is described as "a thing of shreds and patches." When Robert Lowie applied this concept to culture, he was soundly abused by functionalist theoreticians who evidently believed that "everything is for the best in this best of all possible worlds." Today most anthropologists would agree that cultures are integrated, but not very well.

In the process of cultural change, people make decisions. They attempt to solve problems. If the problem is visible and seems important, they take considerable care with their decisions. They try to make the best possible choices. Even so they make mistakes. Some cultural systems are overwhelmed by others. Some survive long enough to face the next environmental catastrophe and embark upon a further course of change. Decisions are never made totally at random. The possibilities inherent in any situation are generally limited and quite visible. Knowing how the environment is changing, the kind of problem that people face, and the kinds of problems they possess, the observer can generally predict the broad outlines of change. But the pressure of events rarely permits the study of alternatives, and so most decisions to change are made on the basis of incomplete knowledge. They permit us to get by, but they prevent us from reaching perfection.

SUMMARY

After the mutiny on the *Bounty*, a few of the mutineers and their Tahitian companions established a colony on Pitcairn's Island. In a series of increasingly brutal encounters all but one of the men on the island was killed. Adams, who survived not because he was strong but because the women protected him, then became a patriarch who created a new, nonviolent cultural system based upon his limited understanding of the Bible.

The culture created by Adams, the Tahitian women, and the children of the Tahitian women was a complex mixture of Tahitian, British, and newly invented elements. Because Tahitian culture was adapted to islands in the South Pacific not too far from Pitcairn, it could be predicted that Tahitian agricultural practices would be adopted. This was indeed the case. However, the adoption of an essentially Tahitian economic system had virtually no impact upon other aspects of the culture. Pitcairn was a utopian Christian commune grafted onto a Tahitian economic system. Even this is an oversimplification. The people of Pitcairn invented a range of economic, social, and religious devices that is a testimony to the creative ability of the ordinary human being. The case of Pitcairn's Island illustrates how the processes of diffusion, invention, and adaptation are twined together in complex patterns as people go about the business of making decisions and solving problems.

Another set of decisions led a group of Tewa Indians to flee across the desert and join with the Hopi Indians in a program of resistance to dangerous outside influences. For nearly four hundred years, although the Hopi and Tewa have changed and adapted, the essential outlines of their traditional religious culture have remained intact. One possible explanation for this is that emphasis on religion, on the other world, enables people to maintain a united front against outside influences. People who did not wish to follow the traditional way were asked to leave, and they did so. Other explanations are that the Anglos could not use the lands or resources of the Hopi and Tewa and that maintenance of a traditional way of life has proven to be a viable way of getting along in modern society. Probably, all of these factors are at work.

Sometimes, whether people seek change or stability, attempts to solve outstanding problems are frustrated by deep and seemingly irremediable conflicts. Faced with drought and overpopulation, the people of Namhalli seemed to turn upon each other. As bitterness and hatred reached new heights, cooperation in the village came to an end. What had seemed a desperate situation now seemed an impossible one.

Within a few years time, there had been further dramatic change. High school graduates from the village had found factory jobs and were investing cash in the improvement of village agriculture. A new form of social organization, the chit fund, was borrowed from the factory. Community religious ceremonies were again held, and the village embarked enthusiastically upon a program of rapid technological change and modernization.

Namhalli's rapid adoption of new technology and new ways of doing things can be attributed, in part, to the opening up of new opportunities to make money. In fact, the overwhelming influence of opportunity upon the modernization of Namhalli suggests that many other peoples would seek education and progress could those things be shown to confer benefits. Conflict in Namhalli appears to have arisen out of contradictory messages constituting value conflict, as well as out of a loss of leadership and a lack of funds.

The cases of Pitcairn, of the Hopi and Tewa, and of Namhalli are all cases where choices and opportunities were available. With the Sioux, the disappearance of the buffalo, the loss of territory, and lack of success at cattle raising and agriculture seem to have created a situation without opportunities or prospects for future survival. Hearing of Wovoka's prophecy of the disappearance of the white men, the Sioux sent a delegation to meet with him. Soon, the Sioux were wearing ghost shirts and participating in dances that would prepare them for the great new day.

Frightened, apparently by the prophecies, the United States government sent troops to the Sioux reservation. Some of the Sioux fled. One group of Sioux surrendered to the soldiers, and the massacre of Wounded Knee took place. Religious movements seem to be an almost worldwide response to situations in which normal coping mechanisms fail to work. Although the ghost dance has to be regarded as a failure—the white man did not disappear—it contributed to the creation of an American Indian national culture and to a gradual easing of genocidal and ethnocidal policies directed toward the American Indian.

Although reason tells us that not all good things are new, it is nevertheless convenient in considering changes in culture to propose justifications for them in terms of function and adaptation. In truth, most people are not perfect and culture is "a thing of shreds and patches." People consider alternatives and they make the best choices they can. Still, they generally lack perfect knowledge and they frequently make mistakes. Cultural change has permitted many human societies to get by, at least for a while, but the changes so far have yet to lead to a perfect society.

For Further Reading

General discussions of change processes include Goodenough's *Cooperation in Change* (1963) and books by Louise Spindler (1977) and by Galt and Smith (1975) dealing with alternative theoretical models of change situations. Works dealing with community development and other forms of assisted or directed cultural change include Brokensha (1969), Clifton (1970), Foster (1969, 1973), and Niehoff (1966).

More descriptive works include Mead's *New Lives for Old* (1956), Wallace's *The Death and Rebirth of the Seneca* (1972), Linton's *Acculturation in Seven American Indian Tribes* (1940), Nash's *Machine Age Maya: The Industrialization of a Guatemalan Community* (1967), Spicer's *Cycles of Conquest: The Impact of Spain, Mexico, and the United States on the Indians of the Southwest, 1533–1960* (1957), Aronson's *The City Is Our Farm* (1977), and Saltman's *The Kipsigis* (1978).

Case studies with useful materials on culture change include *The Eskimo of North Alaska* (Chance 1966); *The Two Worlds of the Washo* (Downs 1966); *Hano: A Tewa Indian Community in Arizona* (Dozier 1966); *Fishermen of South Thailand* (Fraser 1966); *The Qemant, a Pagan-Hebraic Peasantry of Ethiopia* (Gamst 1969); *Modern Blackfeet* (McFee 1972); *Changing Japan* (Norbeck 1965); *Dreamers without Power: The Menomini Indians* (G. and L. Spindler 1971); *Burgbach: Urbanization and Identity in a German Village* (G. Spindler 1973); *The Zinacantecos of Mexico: A Modern Maya Way of Life* (Vogt 1970). The *Case Studies in Education and Culture* (Wolcott 1967; Warren 1967; Singleton 1967; Gay and Cole 1967; Grindal 1972; Modiano 1973; Jocano 1969; Peshkin 1972) all give attention to the role of the school in culture change.

Problems and Questions

1. Examine some advertisements that encourage poeple to accept new products or other innovations. How are innovations made to seem appealing?
2. Gather evidence concerning an individual inventor or innovator. Why was that person the innovator and not someone else?
3. Attend a public council meeting or committee meeting. Are any innovations proposed? Are the innovations proposed in response to problems or for some other reason?
4. Read an ethnographic description of cultural change. What sorts of things cause change? Is there any pattern?
5. For any group or society familiar to you, is change taking place? What sorts of changes can be expected in the future?

12 QUESTIONS AND PROCESSES

What are the most important questions?

In this, the final chapter, it is appropriate to begin to ask questions about our questions. What is the value of all this? Are we simply amused by the Hopi or the Nyoro, or is there some lesson to be drawn from their cultures and their fate? The first questions have to do with whether or not anthropology has accomplished anything. Anthropologists, like most social scientists and most laymen, have more than a suspicion that their efforts are wasted. Can it be that all our enterprise is a waste of time? Do we not have ethnocentric biases and imperialist motives that we can never overcome? Perhaps, rather than being a mere plaything of the socially useless, anthropology is a positive evil in the world. Has anything been accomplished?

The answer depends upon how much is expected to have been accomplished in less than a hundred years. Many cultures and archaeological sites that might have disappeared without a trace have been described in some fashion. A great many important questions about our own ways of life have been found. There are even a few answers to such questions as, do all human beings perceive things in the same way, is the Oedipus conflict real, or is adolescence a time of troubles?

What more should anthropologists do? Would we find some new questions? Would we ask some of the old questions in a better way? Are we doing an adequate job of describing cultural systems. Can we do more? What strategies should be pursued in order to find general answers to our questions? A final section asks questions about the future of the subject matter of anthropology, the human species. Where are we headed? What are our chances? Does anthropology have anything to say about the modern world or the future of humanity? What will the next civilization be like? But perhaps we are not so different from all those other people. Manyamei Limut Garing pops the question and receives an unexpected but not so unusual answer.

WHAT HAS BEEN ACCOMPLISHED?

In Utopia the successful young person is captain of his team, hotly pursued by members of the opposite sex, plays all of the works of Grunebaum on the computerized bazoo, holds a straight A average, prepares a superb almond duck, and manufactures psychedelic drugs in the garage in his spare time. At the age of eighteen or so, those who have failed to accomplish these things look back upon their wasted lives and pronounce themselves failures. In the same vein, anthropologists and their critics, looking back upon the recent progress in their field, incline toward hopelessness and despair. Where are the laws of anthropology? Where is our Newton or our Darwin? Where is our grand theory? What have we done to save the world?

Actually, the first Ph.D. in anthropology was granted less than one hundred years ago. It may be that anthropology has made false starts or involved itself in silly games and infantile diversions, but it is also true that it has been a slum-child of the sciences bereft of manpower and living on the table scraps of the more prosperous disciplines. From the beginning the efforts of anthropology have been scattered across the cultures of the earth and the several million years of human history. Instead of a massive assault on some single human problem, anthropologists have skirmished against a host of questions claiming few victories and accepting few defeats.

The rise of anthropology vaguely corresponds with the colonization and development of the "underdeveloped" nations. It corresponds with the rape and destruction of the archaeological record and the deliberate destruction of countless peoples and their ways of life. At the moment of its founding, anthropology faced the problem of a disappearing subject matter. Early in this century, Franz Boas said to Robert Lowie, "Here is a hundred dollars, go study the Navajo." Lowie set out knowing only that the Navajo lived somewhere to the west of New York. Here was no chance to formulate significant theoretical questions or to develop methodology. Here was only a chance to find some old people and say, "What was it like when you were young?" So it went and so it goes today. Archaeologists snatch their data from the teeth of bulldozers; cultural anthropologists work with remnants of peoples not yet destroyed.

Out of the frantic attempts of these ethnographers have come written records concerning hundreds of cultures that no longer exist or exist in altered form. At this very moment, Brazilian soldiers and frontiersmen are completing the extermination of unstudied Indian Tribes of the Amazon Basin, the mountain peoples of Southeast Asia are perishing in wars they never sought and do not understand, and in California a bulldozer is destroying the last fragile records of a vanished tribe. In a few unthinking moments of history many of the cultures and works of man constructed over centuries have been destroyed. But much has been saved, and the laden bookshelves of almost any library bear testimony to the hero's task the ethnographers performed. So long as there are human beings, so long as they care about others, this monumental contribution of an infant science will remain one of the great treasures of humanity. There are still cultures to be studied and archaeological sites to be excavated, but will we get to them in time?

The ethnographic record, the books and articles written by anthropologists, missionaries, and explorers, contains much information about our own and other people's cultures. Out of the comparison of these materials, out of an awareness of the similarities and differences among the peoples of the world, the concept of culture has gradually emerged. If there is some great discovery in anthropology, some great contribution to human wisdom, then it is the discovery of culture. Of course, human beings have always been aware of culture, but they have often attributed a sacred quality to their own. One's own way of life has always seemed right and proper, perhaps a gift from the creator to be preserved as a sacred trust. Even where men have not been convinced of their superiority to other men, they have seen their own cultures as right for them and other cultures as right for other people.

Brought up in a culture regarded by its members as god-given, biologically inherited, and infinitely superior to all others, the early anthropologists struggled slowly toward the truth: Cultures are invented by ordinary men and passed on to others by means of processes of cultural transmission. Cultures may be sacred because they are beautiful or because they represent sincere, triumphant, human work. Beyond that, they are no more sacred than an eggbeater, a telephone, or any other human work. Historically, anthropologists did not begin to use the term *social heredity* in definitions of culture until the 1920s, and *learning* appeared frequently in definitions of culture in the late thirties and early forties.

In the abstract, the idea that ways of life are simply the product of

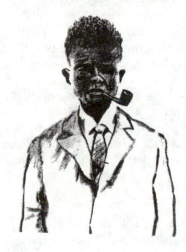

messages handed down across the generations seems innocuous enough. In fact, the view of culture as natural, rather than supernatural, is as revolutionary and as hard to believe as the idea that the earth is round and circles the sun or the idea that human beings evolved by natural processes from other animals. In our daily life we act as though the earth were flat, we speak of sunrise and sunset, and we separate the artificial from the natural. When an ethnographic film shows us Bushmen hunting, warfare in New Guinea, or an Australian aboriginal initiation, we snicker in the back rows. Here are people who do not know how to act properly, crazy people doing crazy things. Do we not recognize that we are equally crazy and that our own customs are equally absurd or, if you like, equally rational? Perhaps we do know it in a way, but we are not prepared to act upon it. The idea that everything we think of as right or wrong was just an idea thought up by some wise man or fool several centuries ago is as repugnant as it is revolutionary and subversive.

Imagine that it is Sunday in Cicero Falls. The minister, a recent convert to anthropology, has decided to express his respect for God in the manner of the ancient Sumerians. He strips off his ornaments and clothing and delivers his sermon in the nude. As anthropologists we are inclined to say, "so what," but as citizens of Cicero Falls we are outraged. Who decided that it was good to wear clothing in a church with the thermostat set at eighty? Who decided that it is wrong to eat dog meat, that cultural transmission can occur in a lecture hall, that "shit" is a dirty word, that only women wear skirts, that you should sleep with the same woman all of your life, or that it is uncomfortable to sit on the floor? Anthropology tells us that these are all arbitrary conventions constructed by men and quite likely to change. Such conventions may, of course, be useful and adaptive in one way or another, but should we not examine them? Perhaps, after all, the Sumerians were right.

We have opened a Pandora's book of questions. Why should a man who collects garbage, surely a difficult and unpleasant job, receive less money than a man who has inherited several hundred shares of stock in the United States Steel Company? Are women properly regarded as inferior to men? Is alcohol really so different from marihuana? Is it really a crime to drive a car that no one else is using? Do prisons reduce crime or do they cause it? Is justice blind or are law courts instruments of oppression? Must children be forced to attend school or might they learn willingly under certain conditions? But suppose our customs are silly, what will we have left if we throw them out?

Why Is It So?

Anthropology, the study of other cultures and the explanation of similarities and differences, leads to the asking of questions that most people, perhaps wisely, prefer not to hear. This is especially true when the only possible answer is "es costombre," it is the custom, we have always done so. A part of the concept of culture is that it is insidious. It affects people in deep ways. It affects the unconscious positioning of their bodies and the sudden flashes of their eyebrows. Much of culture is transmitted and received unconsciously and comes to form a vital but unrecognized part of the individual personality. What does the physicist see when he looks at the tracks made by elementary particles; what does a biologist see when he looks through his microscope? Can it be that he sees what he has unconsciously learned to see? Is science, in fact, a religion or a world view no different in kind from that of the Saora? Anthropologists tend to believe that the world is round, that diseases are often caused by bacteria, that reinforcement contributes to learning, and so on; but at the same time they tend to recognize that most "knowledge" is mythological rather than scientific. People believe what they believe because they want to and because it was passed down from ancestors. In all of the sciences, even the so-called hard sciences, the instrument of observation is a human being brought up in some particular cultural tradition and committed to blind faith in its mythology. Under these circumstances, systematic or even unsystematic exploration in other cultures would seem to be fundamental in separating the truths and myths in any science.

After studying visual perception in a variety of cultures, Segall, Campbell, and Herskovits (1966:213) conclude:

> Perception is an aspect of human behavior, and as such it is subject to many of the same influences that shape other aspects of behavior. In particular, each individual's experiences combine in a complex fashion to determine his reaction to a given stimulus situation. To the extent that certain classes of experiences are more likely to occur in some cultures than in others, differences in behavior across cultures, including differences in perceptual tendencies, can be great enough even to surpass the ever-present individual differences within cultural groupings.

In a way, then, one of the functions of anthropological research has become that of playing a spoiler role in regard to the findings of other sciences. One hears the cry, "The Hopi don't think that way," or "It's not so in my village."

In Freudian psychology the Oedipus complex is conceived as reflecting a *natural* rivalry between a male child and his father. Malinowski (1927) presented evidence that in the Trobriand Islands, where children are disciplined by the mother's brother, the same sort of rivalry develops, not between the child and his father, but between the child and his mother's brother. The locus of the child's rivalries appears to be determined not by biology but by culture. In the same vein, studies of adolescents in the United States have shown the period of adolescence to be a time of great psychological turmoil. Mead (1953) found that adolescents in Samoa did not experience such problems. Far from being of biological origin, adolescent turmoil appears to be no more necessary and inevitable than the Hopi initiation ceremony.

The existence of these small, and not always undisputed, triumphs says more about the promise of anthropology than about its achievements. Cross-cultural research, not by itself but in association with other kinds of research, can contribute to the solution of many of the problems of our society and the human species. If it is accepted that we can "see" our own culture only in the light of contrast with other cultures, then anthropology is vital to the answering of all scientific questions and to the solution of all problems. But if anthropology is to be of use, if it is to pursue the earthshaking implications of the concept of culture, it must put away childish things. It must become a mature science with a well-defined set of questions or body of theory and a well-designed set of research methods or strategies for the discovery of truth. What kinds of questions should anthropologists be asking and how may those questions be discovered?

What Is the Question?

It is a law of nature that silly questions lead to silly answers. Because anthropology is an emergent scientific discipline, anthropologists have often asked the wrong kinds of questions. Sometimes, engaged in frantic efforts to preserve records of a rapidly changing or fast vanishing culture, anthropologists have simply not allowed themselves enough time to think deeply about the nature of culture or the broad theoretical implications of the data they have collected. Even where, as is often necessary in order to obtain funds for fieldwork, anthropologists have worked out careful theories and well-designed research questions and methodologies, they have often discovered that the people they intended to study never did what they thought they did or have stopped doing it or refuse to discuss it.

Very often research in anthropology has been directed by the short-term practical interests of foundations or government agencies. In the United States, studies of acculturation (What happens when one cultural system is strongly influenced by another?) often seemed to be dominated by the question, "How can we make American Indians or Blacks or Mexican-Americans into good American citizens?" In Africa, where the British followed a policy of ruling indirectly through established leadership, anthropological research questions often had to do with the nature and structure of that leadership. In the early years of anthropology, research concerning the historical origins and development of human cultures often seemed to justify a kind of caretaker relationship in which the "advanced" nations "helped" their "backward" brethren along the rocky road to civilization.

Because any realistic understanding of the nature of culture almost requires that an anthropologist have some detailed understanding of a culture different from his own, the early experience of most anthropologists is an ethnographic experience. Thus, the attention of the anthropologist is directed toward the understanding of some particular group of people and the ethnocentrism which might otherwise have been devoted to the supreme and unique virtues of his own culture comes to be focused upon the supreme and unique virtues of the people studied. Confronted with almost any kind of broad explanation of human behavior, the standard response of the anthropologist has often been, "It's not that way in my village." Of course no two things in nature—no two molecules, no two cells, no two individuals—are exactly alike. To the poetic imagination it is precisely the marvelous uniqueness of things that is important. To the scientific imagination what is important are the fundamental uniformities that lie concealed within apparent diversity. Although a good ethnographer must be both poet and scientist, the attempt to be both things at once has often precluded the asking of such questions as, "How is my village like all other villages?"

Of course, the central problem in the understanding of cultural systems lies in the fact that they are wondrously complicated but not too systematically organized. There are may different kinds of cultural sys-

tems and innumerable ways of arranging and classifying them. The parts of different cultural systems are often quite different and they are arranged differently within the system. The complexity of cultural systems makes it impossible to compare entire systems and this means that comparisons must be made in terms of the isolation of some part from the whole. Ideally the comparison of cultural systems should be made in terms of a uniform set of system-defining variables characteristic of all cultural systems. Meteorologists, for example, define storm systems in terms of measurements of wind velocity, wind direction, temperature, and so on. But what are the defining variables for cultural systems and how can they be measured?

Because a cultural system is the result of a relationship among a set of people, a cultural tradition, and a setting, the system variables that would explain a cultural system have to be found in those three things. There is no problem in measuring the number of people of different ages and sexes who form the membership of a cultural system, but what parts of the cultural tradition and the setting should be measured and how may the measurements be carried out? It is easy to think up an almost infinite series of things to be measured and ways of measuring them, but it is not easy to think of measurements that could be applied to any cultural system. Annual rainfall might be extremely important in defining the setting of one cultural system, but it might be totally unimportant in defining the setting of another.

One research strategy for estimating the importance of particular measurements, first suggested by Franz Boas at the turn of the century, is to study groups of cultures so closely related that most of the variables affecting them have the same value. For example, the study of neighboring communities of different population sizes has given indications of the importance of size to the nature of cultural systems. Insights concerning witchcraft have been achieved through the comparison of neighboring groups some of which possess it and some of which do not. The study of villages at increasing distances from urban centers has been used as a means of estimating the effects of urban influence upon villages. Attempts to measure the general influence of environment on culture have been based upon the study of different cultures located within the same general environment or within similar environments. Although most studies that have attempted to control particular variables have produced interesting results, they have rarely been followed up in a systematic way. Thus, we still know very little about the effect of variations in size upon cultural systems even though the question is clearly of great practical significance.

Although there are many ways to skin a cat, most anthropologists suspect that those ways are not infinite. One procedure for the development of research questions involves the investigation of some human attribute that appears to be widespread or universal. Most frequently this approach involves assembling a large number of ethnographies of hopefully unrelated cultures and investigating the factors affecting the nature or the presence of the attribute. The major problem in this sort of investigation centers about the definition and identification of the attribute to be studied. To study witchcraft, for example, it is necessary to know what witchcraft is and then to be able to decide whether it is present or absent. How would one determine, for example, whether witchcraft is present or absent in the modern United States? If it is present, is it really the same thing as witchcraft somewhere else? Unless witchcraft can be very sharply defined, there is always the possibility that superficial resemblances might lead to the lumping together of two quite different things. If something that looks like witchcraft can have different origins or causes in different cultural systems, then it is impossible to find any general explanation of the thing that was labeled witchcraft. Still, the principle of limited possibilities (the ways of skinning a cat are not infinite) would suggest that there would not be too many kinds of things that looked like witchcraft and that they would not have very many different kinds of causes.

On the whole, even though it is not possible to point to any very dramatic discoveries or any undisputed "laws" of anthropology, the field in general has made good progress in developing adequate definitions of cultural systems and perhaps more progress than is readily apparent in identifying important system variables and in working out ways of comparing cultural systems in terms of separated attributes or parts. Although one of the points made in this book is that fruitful comparisons of cultural systems might well be based upon a consideration of fundamental processes necessary to the operation of all cultural systems, other approaches based upon sometimes quite arbitrary definitions of the parts of culture have also proven fruitful. It would appear that the central problem for anthropology at the moment is not so much that of developing new theory or finding new research methods as that of refining old theory and collecting the data necessary to test it. There is still a lag of at least a generation between the development of new research questions and the collection of ethnographic data adequate to provide answers to them. Anthropologists are still engaged in the collection of the data required for the refinement of the urbanization theory first proposed by Park and Burgess in the 1920s and based upon their understandings of urbanization in Chicago.

WHAT HAPPENS NEXT?

The growth of any science is a slow process. At the beginning, time is required for the exploration of possibilities. The field of interest must be defined; appropriate methodologies must be sought. Early research in any field is impressionistic and anecdotal—the bird must be glimpsed before its wingspread can be measured. Simple explanations must be tested and found wanting before more complicated explanations can be attempted. Anthropologists first sought to explain similarities and differences among cultures in terms of single factors such as climate, environment, race, economics, the combination and recombination of a few basic inventions, "divine plan," and techniques of child rearing. The discovery that anthropology, besides being romantic and a lot of fun, involves a lot of hard work is as unappealing to the professional as it is to the beginner. Even when anthropologists accepted the idea that cultural systems represented complex wholes, they were reluctant to throw out the idea of simple causation in favor of the idea of complex interactions among numerous variables each of which exerted complex causal influences upon the others. Anthropologists hoped that their materials could be reduced to a few simple formulas like those of classical mechanics in physics, and only reluctantly accepted the idea that anthropology was much more like meteorology.

The great and meaningful problems in anthropology have to do with the ways in which cultural systems hang together, adapt, and proceed. Questions concerning the manner in which human beings identify and solve the problems that face them remain to be solved. We do not know very much about describing the environment or the environmental stresses that constitute the problems that people in cultural systems must solve if their cultural systems are to adapt. Problems that arise as a result of interaction between cultural systems may be quite different from other sorts of environmental problems, but we have not begun to describe the differences. We know that the members of different cultural systems react to stress in very different ways. Some flee, some fight, some talk, and some pray. We do not know how or why these choices are made or even if they are adaptive or how they are adaptive.

We do not know very much about the relationships between environmental stresses and cultural traditions. Do the ideas that form cultural traditions develop out of reactions to environmental problems or are the environmental problems often created by the kinds of ideas and interpretations that form the cultural tradition? We know that people in all cultural systems, even those regarded as relatively stable, are constantly modifying their cultural traditions and the techniques by means of which they cope with their environments. New ideas develop somehow and are transmitted from person to person, but we are not really sure how such ideas develop or who develops them. Even if we could explain why particular persons become inventors or innovators, we still lack firm explanations of why the innovation was proposed at a particular time or why other persons accepted it. We have many accounts of inventions, of social movements, and of other changes in culture, but we have little systematic or satisfactory theory concerning these matters.

As anthropologists survey the several million years of biological evolution and the several hundred thousand years of cultural evolution that fall within the domain of their investigations, they cannot fail to be aware of the extraordinary and rapid change that has taken place within the last few hundred years. Before our eyes there is an explosive reproduction of people, ideas, artifacts, and weapons. Because Nature, the earth goddess about whom so many anthropologists have written, abhors anything that increases at an increasing rate, the long view of human history tells us that the modern age of change and revolution cannot continue for more than another generation or two. Human populations must stabilize; human consumption of energy and resources must level off; the production of new ideas must slow. There cannot be a situation in which infinite numbers of people consume infinite amounts of energy and resources or produce infinite numbers of new inventions and ideas. As we examine the course of human history and observe that almost everything human is increasing at an increasing rate, we are led to the conclusion that the human species must reach an equilibrium with the environment and with itself or quickly perish from the earth.

In the past, the human species has survived similar periods of explosive cultural change. Ten thousand years ago with the invention of agriculture there was a period of rapidly increasing population, energy consumption, and invention. We can take some comfort in the fact that the agricultural revolution turned out to be self-limiting once the potentials inherent in agriculture and irrigated agriculture were worked out. There is less comfort in the fact that numerous agricultural peoples destroyed their environments and experienced rapid declines in population. If an agricultural civilization like that of Mohenjo Daro could destroy the little world its peoples knew, might not a worldwide civilization destroy the earth?

Whether the current cultural explosion proves to be self-limiting or not, the cultural systems caught up in it must adapt within the next few generations to a totally different and unprecedented set of environmental circumstances. If this adaptation is to be planned and systematic it must make use of the experience and wisdom preserved in the existing variety of human cultural systems. The problem of unlimited population growth can be solved technologically through the development of new techniques of contraception and abortion; but it also needs to be solved culturally through the introduction of new traditions, new forms of marriage, and new social arrangements.

The population explosion itself is merely a reflex of the explosive development of new ideas and ways of doing things. It would hardly have been possible without an explosive increase in the production of food and other requirements for human existence. The explosive development in technology has inevitably led to an explosive increase in man's capacity to exterminate himself or to alter the face of the earth. The threats of atomic warfare, bacteriological warfare, or chemical warfare are obvious and visible. Less visible are the threats posed by the introduction of new chemicals or by slow but massive changes in the seas, land masses, and atmospheres of earth. Does a slight increase in the temperature of the ocean make a difference? As the plastic doodads floating in the Sargasso Sea disintegrate and release the subtle poisons they contain, will the oceans die and will we become extinct? Are we already extinct? Some of these problems of technological explosion are problems for physicists or marine biologists, but the technological explosion also has to do with human cultural traditions and human social arrangements.

The technological explosion is the product of new discoveries and new information. There has been an almost infinite increase in the length and complexity of the cultural message, an information explosion. Because a single human being can "know" only a limited amount, cultural systems have always contained information economies. Some people know some things; others know other things. A cultural system works because the information available to different people is somehow assembled at the proper time and used in the solution of outstanding problems. At the present time we know very little about how information is stored and retrieved in human beings or in cultural systems. Is it possible for a cultural tradition to contain so much information and to become so complicated that it simply fails to function? Are children in the United States or in other complex modern societies learning their cultural traditions through processes of cultural transmission or are they learning uncoordinated bits and pieces of a cultural tradition so large that it cannot be comprehended?

The technological and information explosions have made it possible to transport human beings and ideas from one place to another with great rapidity and in great numbers. Formerly independent cultural systems have been brought into contact with others. Cultural systems which once served a multiplicity of functions have come to serve relatively few functions. Vast increases in population have multiplied the number of existing cultural systems. The cultural differences between New York and Pukapuka are declining while the differences between fishermen and physicists are increasing. It is not known whether this implies a net gain or a net loss in cultural diversity, but the worldwide spread of anything, whether it is DDT or a new idea, should be viewed with alarm. The fact that human beings and human cultural systems are different is the most exciting thing about them, yet the destruction of diversity is implicit in the worldwide spread of rock and roll, communism, capitalism, or anything else. When a song is forgotten or a ceremony ceases to be performed, a part of the human heritage is destroyed forever.

As cultural traditions and cultural systems have become larger and more all encompassing, the little traditions of neighborhood, community,

and tribe have lost their uniqueness and their coherence. One hundred years ago most of the people of the earth lived in small communities in initmate relationship to their neighbors. Because the small community has been so general and pervasive for so many years, anthropologists have often drawn the conclusion that communities are essential to the preservation of human identity and well-being. Looking at the modern world, it almost seems as if the small group and the small community have been declared enemies of the state. It is believed to be more efficient to have one large university with ten thousand students than ten small universities. The same principle holds true for factories and farms and all the other contexts within which people work or play or live.

In many modern societies the life of the individual is governed, not by his neighbors, but by faceless bureaucracies. In modern states and cities such bureaucracies contend against each other for resources and seek to increase their size and influence. Whether seeking to grow or to control their clients, bureaucracies formulate new rules and employ more persons to enforce them. The individual is governed now, not by the cultural tradition of his community, but by the countless and inexplicable rules of the innumerable bureaucracies with which he must deal in order to survive. With the evolution of larger and larger cultural systems and the increasing inclusion of all mankind within a single world order, perhaps all this is necessary, but perhaps it is time to consider what has been sacrificed upon the twin altars of modernity and efficiency.

At any event, the decline of the small community appears to have gone hand in hand with a kind of normlessness and alienation represented in the United States by such code phrases as "the drug problem," "the generation gap," "dropping out," or the "rising crime rate." On an even wider scale most modern nations are witnessing the formation of countercultural groups of people of all ages and degrees of political persuasion. In part these groups appear to represent a conscious effort to revive and perpetuate the lost community of the past in the form of retirement colonies, mobile home parks, or communes. One of the characteristics of such groups is their rejection of all or some aspects of officially endorsed reality. The larger countercultural groups possess their own newspapers, television programs, and trained scientists. In the United States in particular, but in other countries as well, the outstanding problems of society can no longer be approached in terms of established fact or, if you like, establishment fact. Scientists as well as ordinary people disagree concerning the dangers of marihuana, the extent of the Russian menace, the degree of environmental pollution, the causes of poverty, the safety of fluoridation, the effect of capital punishment, the dangers of atomic war, or the consequences of population growth. Although much of the world's population might be brought to agree that humanity faces the greatest crisis in its history, neither scientists nor laymen agree concerning its nature.

If good fiction depends upon the voluntary suspension of disbelief, so do cultural traditions. Modern traditions have been founded upon an information explosion triggered through the use of the scientific method. Although the nineteenth- and early twentieth-century faith in Science as a solver of all problems now seems naive and childish, the alternative to a worldwide scientific establishment enjoying some protection from political and self-serving influences is a return to the more traditional pattern when people made up "truths" to suit themselves. Perhaps it is the case that in times of trouble people tend to return to the mythological truths that comforted them as children.

Perhaps it is time for some Quetzalcoatl, some mythological savior, to appear and lead us to the light. Certainly, in its underdeveloped state the field of anthropology cannot propose itself as an instant source of significant solutions to human problems. The systematic comparison of cultural systems and the achievement of an understanding of ourselves is a formidable task requiring the cooperation of many men, women, and disciplines. The science of stones and bones, the quaint and remote, offers no quick solutions. It offers, instead, two million years of change, conflict, exploration, music, kindness, and cruelty. It offers the first fumbling attempts at an understanding. Above all, it offers an image of humanity—always the same, always different:

My lovely moon, my sister; I feel now that I want to marry you, I should like to unite with you, O my sister, that is the way I feel.

I have no objection, O my brother, and I agree that you shall marry me and that we shall be united, but there is something that I must say to you, O hornbill, O my brother Manyamei Limut Garing Balua Unggom Tingang. Do not be angry in your heart, do not be furious within, O my brother, when you hear my words, when you learn what I have to say to you.

What is your desire, O my sister, and what are the words that you have to speak to me?

Indeed, hornbill, my brother Manyamei Limut Garing, I do not oppose you if you want to marry me, I do not resist your desires if you want to unite your body with mine, I do not refuse you, but you must first carry out my request, you must grant my wish.

My wish is not so wide as the branches of a tree, it is not so big as the boughs of trees. My wish is this, O hornbill, O my brother: seek an island, find a small piece of earth as landing place for our boats, and when you have found it then you may marry the moon, then you can tenderly cling to me, the woman, then I shall permit you to unite with me, the wife.

What you say is too hard, and what you demand is too great, it is more extensive than the branches of a tree, it is bigger than the boughs of trees.

Indeed, Putir Kuhukup Bungking Garing, here now is the land that you desired of me.

Yes, my brother, O my brother, there is some land now and I shall marry you, I shall surrender myself to you—when you have erected a large house, when you have built a tall dwelling.

(Manyamei Limut Garing shakes his head so that his golden ear-rings joggle, he looks hither and thither and he scratches audibly at his face) (Schärer 1963:175–179).

GLOSSARY

Adaptation. The process of altering the cultural or genetic messages in such a way as to ensure the continuing survival of the species, population, or cultural system within a particular environment.

Affinity. In kinship, persons related through marriage rather than descent.

Arbitrariness. The basic property of language is arbitrariness; that is, there is no necessary connection between the sound of a word and its meaning.

Archaeology and prehistory. The study of the nature of human cultural systems through the examination of their physical remains.

Avoidance relationship. A relationship between such relatives as mother-in-law and son-in-law in which direct contact between the relatives is avoided.

Biological anthropology. Study of the relationships among the environment and genetic and cultural messages.

Calendrical ceremonies. Rituals that take place at particular times of the year.

Chromosomes. Large molecules formed by the linking together of genes. In meiosis, the pairs of chromosomes are divided so that each sperm or egg cell contains only half the normal number of chromosomes.

Clan. A large and usually organized group tracing descent from a single ancestor (often more or less fictitious) so that all members are considered brothers or sisters and therefore ineligible for marriage. The most common kinds of clans are those tracing descent through the male line (patrilineal) or through the female line (matrilineal). Smaller, less organized groups are generally called lineages.

Collateral. Close relatives not in the direct line of descent such as father's sister or mother's brother.

Consanguinity. In kinship, persons related through descent rather than marriage.

Conversion experience. An abrupt change in the behavior of an individual in which a completely new world view and way of life appear to be adopted.

Crisis rituals. Rituals that take place in times of crisis.

Cross-cousin. The children of a father's sister or mother's brother.

Cultural anthropology. The comparative study of living and recent human beings. In conjunction with biological anthropology, archaeology, and linguistics, its principle task is the understanding of similarities and differences among cultural systems.

Cultural lag. The situation that obtains when one aspect of a cultural system changes rapidly while other aspects fail to respond. Excessive cultural lag would presumably lead to a situation in which a change in one part of the system would cease to produce changes in the other aspects. At that point, by definition, the system would have ceased to exist.

Cultural message. Information and instructions transmitted among the members of a cultural system through the use of language and other forms of communication. All of the ideas, habits, and other characteristics that are exhibited by the individual as a consequence of membership in a particular cultural system. Expression of the cultural message varies in response to complicated interactions among the cultural message, the environment, and the genetic message.

357

Cultural revolution.   Sweeping and comparatively rapid change in the distribution and density of human populations brought about by new technological and social inventions.

Cultural system.   A human social system composed of a setting, a membership, a cultural tradition, a material culture, and a set of processes, or place, people, plans, paraphernalia, and process. Cultural systems develop as an automatic consequence of conscious and unconscious decision-making activity on the part of human beings in groups.

Cultural transmission.   Training, education, and, in general, the transmission of the cultural message from one individual or group to another.

Cultural universals.   Aspects of culture that are thought to be characteristic of all cultural systems.

Culture.   A general term that may refer to a specific cultural system, to cultural traditions, or to societies.

Decision making.   The conscious and unconscious processes whereby animals select one behavior rather than another. In a less general sense, *decision making* is sometimes used by other authors to refer exclusively to conscious decisions.

Deference.   Displaying ritual behavior exhibiting respect for the status of another.

Demeanor.   The symbolic presentation of one's self to others. The aspects of dress and conduct that indicate status and intention.

Deoxyribonucleic acid (DNA).   The chemical that forms the basis of the genetic message because it is capable of reproducing or replicating itself.

Diffusion.   Borrowing an idea from somebody else.

Displacement.   That aspect of language that permits us to talk about things that are not present but are placed elsewhere or elsewhen.

Domain.   An area, region, or section of reality within which classifications are to be made. In a popular game, the expression "animal, mineral, or vegetable" suggests three major domains.

Dominant allele.   A gene that is fully expressed even when it is paired with a "recessive" gene containing different instructions.

Drift.   The process whereby chance happenings, rather than adaptive advantages, lead to the selection of some characteristics rather than others.

Ecology.   The study of relationships among the various species constituting an ecosystem. Cultural ecology is the study of the understandings of ecology held by members of a cultural system, while anthropological ecology emphasizes the role of human cultural systems in the ecology.

Ecosystem.   The system formed by interrelationships among the various species, including human beings, occupying an environment.

Ego.   The speaker, the person being interviewed.

Environment.   All of the interrelated physical, chemical, biological, and social factors located outside the boundaries of a cultural system.

Ethnocentrism.   The belief that one's own cultural tradition and people are more important than and superior to any other.

Ethnocide.   The destruction of another culture, with or without the destruction of its members.

Ethnographer.   A person who studies and describes a cultural system.

Ethnographic case.   A single observation or interview. One of the facts underlying an ethnographic hypothesis.

Ethnographic hypothesis.   A best guess concerning a particular process or cultural system. Ideally, it is verified by reference to a series of ethnographic cases.

Ethnography.   A set of systematically derived hypotheses concerning the nature of a cultural system and the content of its tradition. In its ideal form, never to be achieved, ethnography would contain all of the information required to behave both properly and improperly in a way consistent with the expectations of the members of the cultural system.

Ethnoscience.   The study of systems of labeling and classification applied in different cultural systems to the things believed to exist.

Evolution.   Any process of change; more specifically, the processes whereby cultural and genetic messages are changed. Over a period of time, evolutionary change can lead to the development of new species and new cultural systems.

Factionalist dispute.   Disputes that divide a community and interfere with cooperative attempts at problem solution.

Food producers.   People who produce their own food through reliance upon domesticated plants and animals.

Function.   The role played by a part of a cultural system in maintaining the system. Not the same thing as a mathematical function.

Genealogy.   A directed graph or chart depicting all of the persons believed to be related to each other through common descent or marriage. Note spelling.

Gene pool.   The set of genes present within a particular breeding population.

Genes.   Molecules of DNA (deoxyribonucleic acid) conveying the information constituting the genetic message.

Genetic message.   Information and instructions transmitted by means of genetic inheritance from the parents to the child. Also used to describe all information transmitted by the various mechanisms of biological inheritance. Expression of the genetic message varies in response to interaction between the genetic message and environmental factors including the cultural message.

Genocide.   The killing of all of the members of a cultural system.

Genotype.   The assortment of genes actually possessed by the individual. The genotype interacts with the environment to produce a phenotype. It is analogous to the plans for a house.

Group.   Any cultural system, but more usually a subcultural system, forming a part of a larger system.

Harpoon.   A spear-like weapon with a line attached.

Homo erectus.   The first indisputably human creature characterized by the possession of an elaborate tool kit, a lack of geographical speciation, and, in some places, by the use of fire.

Homo sapiens.   Modern human beings with fully evolved brains permitting the invention and use of languages of the modern form characterized by productivity and displacement.

Homo sapiens neanderthalensis.   Originating about one hundred thousand years ago, *neanderthalensis* possessed a large brain and a habit of burying and decorating the dead.

Homo sapiens sapiens.   The modern form of human being having a smaller brain and a less rugged skeleton than *neanderthalensis*. *Sapiens* is thought to have originated about 50,000 years ago.

Hunter-gatherers.   Human beings who obtain food primarily by gathering plants or hunting animals. Specialized hunter-gatherers who use specialized techniques to exploit a plentiful resource such as salmon, oak acorns, or sea mammals may achieve population densities comparable to those achieved by food producers such as farmers or pastoralists.

Hypothesis.   Usually derived from a more general theory, an hypothesis is the best possible guess about specific events that are likely to be observed in the future. The ideal scientific hypothesis is consistent with all reliable previous observations or "facts."

Ideal culture.   The way things ought to be; in contrast to *real culture*, the way things really are.

Incipient food production.   The early and somewhat ineffective attempts at plant and animal domestication.

Innovation.   A new idea obtained through invention or borrowing.

Intelligence.   Hypothetically, a general ability to solve problems. The evidence suggests that human individuals possess a wide variety of abilities and potentialities rather than a single ability that might be labeled intelligence.

Interaction rituals.   Rituals defining the statuses and relationships among individuals.

Invention.   The creation of a new idea.

Joking relationship.   A relationship between relatives characterized by teasing and practical jokes.

Kinship or kinship system.   All of the relationships that are considered identical to or similar to the relationships between actual relatives. Includes the terms used in refering to relatives.

Kinterms.   Labels given to the different kinds of kin.

Kintype.   A type of relative such as mother's brother, sister's child, or older brother.

Label.   The name assigned to any particular status, such as "chief," "boss," or "slave."

Language.   A specifically human form of communication characterized by the use of combinations of a few basic units or phonemes in order to form complex and meaningful utterances.

Lineage.   A set of individuals tracing descent from a known ancestor. A lineage is usually smaller and less organized than a clan and the people in it are much more closely related.

Linguistic frame.   In interviewing, a linguistic frame is a question that is asked repeatedly with a single word or phrase being changed each time it is asked: "What kinds of *things* exist; what kinds of *plants* exist; what kinds of *conifers* exist; what kinds of *pines* exist; what kinds of *black pines* exist?

Linguistics.   The study of human language and its relationships to culture, including the explanation of similarities and differences among human languages.

Maladaptive.   Any habits or characteristics that increase selection rates and make survival less likely.

Mammals.   Placental mammals, as distinct from marsupials, carry their babies to term within the womb where they receive nourishment by means of the placenta. Mammals are warm blooded and furry. After birth they feed their young by means of mammary glands which produce milk.

Material culture.   Tools, equipment, and other constructed parts of the environment.

Meaning.   The significance of a message both to the sender and to the recipient as determined by examining context or by considering the effect of the message upon behavior.

Moral authority.   An individual or group is regarded as having the ability or power to define proper and improper behavior.

Moral order.   The situation that exists when everyone agrees about the right thing to do.

Mutation.   Change in the genetic message leading to the emergence of new and generally lethal genes. A few mutations are useful or selectively neutral. It is these that may survive to create variation within the species and sometimes new species.

Observation.   The collection of data by directly recording behavior witnessed by the fieldworker.

Oedipus complex.   Psychological problems believed to arise out of a supposed unconscious rivalry between the male child and his father.

Parallel cousin.   The children of a father's brother or mother's sister.

Peasant farmers.   Farmers who practice intensive agriculture and voluntarily or involuntarily contribute a part of their agricultural production to the maintenance of a city and state. In contrast to modernized or industrialized farmers, peasant farmers tend to be economically self-sufficient and to lack manufactured or "modern" tools, tractors, storage bins, or transportation facilities.

Phenotype.   The specific traits exhibited in the developed individual as a result of the interaction of the genotype and the environment. It is analogous to the house that is built more or less according to a set of plans.

Phoneme.   The basic unit of language. All human languages are based upon combination and recombination of a small number of basic sounds.

Plow agriculture.   A form of agriculture in which domesticated animals are used to plow the fields. The use of animal manure or the technique of fallowing (letting the fields rest) often permits continuing or permanent use of the land and the establishment of permanent settlements.

Population.   A set of plants or animals whose members exchange genetic materials with each other more than 50 percent of the time.

Primary kinterms.   Labels given to direct genealogical relatives such as "mother," "brother," "spouse," or "child."

Principles of classification.   Measures or descriptors such as weight, height, sex, direction, age, or number used in assigning particular individuals or cases to the class or pigeonhole in which they belong.

Process.   A series of interlinked events commencing under culturally defined conditions, following a culturally defined plan or pattern, and reaching a culturally defined endpoint. The expression "culturally defined" means that the members of the cultural system agree concerning the meaning, form, and content of the process.

Productivity.   The property of language that enables us to talk about little green men and other things that do not exist or that have not been seen.

Profanation, ceremonial.   The deliberate destruction of sacred values by bringing them into contact with the ordinary, the profane.

Profane.   Having no special significance, ordinary. Profanation takes place when sacred things are brought into contact with the profane.

Punishment, automatic.   The individual who commits misdeeds is automatically punished by a supernatural figure or through some other mystical mechanism.

Race.   Used popularly to refer to ethnic groups, the term race is gradually dropping out of scientific usage. Scientifically, the term falls between *subspecies* and *variety* as representing a step in a progression toward the development of separate species.

Radiation.   In biology, this term refers to population increase and movement into new environments. In the new environments, isolation and increased selection can cause genetic changes leading to the emergence of varieties, races, subspecies, and ultimately new species.

Ramapithecus.   A fossil ape of some 15 million years ago that exhibits characteristics suggesting the beginnings of evolution in the human direction.

Real culture.   The way things really are; in contrast to *ideal culture*, the way things ought to be.

Reality, cultural.   That which the members of any particular cultural system believe to exist.

Reality, scientific.   That which scientists, including anthropologists, believe to exist.

Relation.   The position of one thing or person with respect to another; that is, a chief is higher than a slave, Tom and Richard are friends.

Religion.   Aspects of world view dealing with large issues that cannot be or are not to be examined or tested. Religious ideas often involve uncertainty, supernatural forces, or a sense of awe: There are more things on heaven and earth than are dreamt of in your [natural] philosophy.

Rites of passage.   Rituals that take place at birth, marriage, death, and other stages in the life of the individual.

Ritual.   An often repeated action lacking any obvious practical consequence that stimulates discomfort or anxiety when it is not performed.

Role.   The behavior considered appropriate for members of each status.

Sacred.   Having special significance and needing to be approached with caution and with appropriate ritual behavior.

Secular.   Nonreligious, ordinary, not involving the supernatural.

Selection.   The process whereby some individuals survive and reproduce while others do not. By extension, the process whereby some cultural systems or cultural traditions survive and spread while others do not.

Scapegoating.   The condition in which other persons are accused of causing misfortunes and mix-ups. Fear of such accusations is thought to contribute to social conformity.

Science.   The examination of regular and consistent happenings in the attempt to understand the underlying mechanisms and make the best possible guesses about the nature of observations to be made in the future. The mood of science is practical. It seeks results and is unable to make use of poetry and events that occur only once or that are mysterious.

Social control.   The various processes by means of which individuals are prevailed upon to exhibit culturally appropriate behavior most of the time.

Social structure.   A set of defined positions or statuses each occupied by a group, a set of individuals, or a person.

Society.   Any human cultural system or animal organization within which the processes of birth, reproduction, and death are completed.

Species.   A set of related populations whose members rarely or never exchange genes with populations located outside of the set. Generally members of separate species are adapted to different habitats and species differences are reflected as adaptations to such habitats.

Subspecies.   A comparatively isolated set of populations that appear to be becoming increasingly different from other sets of populations of the species.

Swidden or shifting agriculture.   A form of agriculture in which fields are moved periodically as they become exhausted. Sometimes called slash-burn agriculture in reference to the common pattern of cutting down and then burning trees in order to obtain land for crops.

Symbol.   A word or thing, a sign, that has a meaning that is not self-evident. Something that stands for or represents something else. Thus, red may symbolize blood or flame, or exposure of the teeth may symbolize friendliness.

System.   Parts or aspects related to each other in such a way that change or movement in any one part causes change in all of the other parts. Linear models of causation, cause-effect models, usually are of limited value in explaining the complex interactions that "cause" systems to change.

Taboo, tabu.   A Polynesian word now used to refer to arbitrary restrictions upon behavior such as forbidding certain foods (dog, cat, horse) or certain activities (eating with the left hand, eating peas with a knife, or failing to wear a waist cord).

Taxonomy.   A list of all of the classes or kinds of things within a domain such as the names of all kinds of cooking utensils, the names of all of the conifers, or a list of all of the kinds of kin.

Technology.   That aspect of the cultural tradition which deals with ways of getting things done such as how to plant crops, how to build houses, or how to win friends and influence people.

Translation problem.   The problem of expressing ideas and categories characteristic of one cultural system in the language of another.

Value conflict.   The condition that exists when the cultural tradition contains conflicting messages concerning good and appropriate things to do.

Values.   Ideas about what is good and bad, right and wrong, or proper and improper.

World view.   The view of the world offered by the cultural tradition. A general answer to the question, "What's going on here?"

BIBLIOGRAPHY

Adams, J. Stacy, and A. Kimball Romney, 1959, A functional analysis of authority. *Psychological Review*, 66:234–251.

Agar, Michael, 1973, *Ripping and Running: A Formal Ethnography of Urban Heroin Addicts*. New York and London: Seminar Press.

Alkire, William H., 1978, *Coral Islanders*. Arlington Heights, Ill.: AHM Publishing Corp.

Alland, Alexander, Jr., 1971, *Human Diversity*. New York: Columbia University Press.

———, 1972, *The Human Imperative*. New York: Columbia University Press.

Arensberg, Conrad M., and Solon T. Kimball, 1948, *Family and Community in Ireland*, 2nd ed. Cambridge, Mass.: Harvard University Press.

Aronson, Daniel R., 1977, *The City Is Our Farm: Seven Migrant Ijebu Yoruba Families*. New Brunswick, N.J.: Transaction Books.

Bailey, Fred G., 1970, *Stratagems and Spoils: A Social Anthropology of Politics*. Oxford: Blackwell.

Balandier, Georges, 1970, *Political Anthropology*. Trans. by A. M. Sheridan Smith. New York: Random House (First published in French, 1967.)

Barker, Roger G., and Herbert F. Wright, 1955, *Midwest and Its Children: The Psychological Ecology of an American Town*. New York: Harper & Row.

Barnes, J. A., 1971, *Three Styles in the Study of Kinship*. Berkeley and Los Angeles: University of California Press.

Barnett, Homer G., 1953, *Innovation: The Basis of Cultural Change*. New York: McGraw-Hill.

———, 1960, *Being a Palauan*. New York: Holt, Rinehart and Winston.

———, 1970, *Being a Palauan*. CSCA Fieldwork Edition. New York: Holt, Rinehart and Winston.

Barrow, Sir John, 1846; *Voyages of Discovery and Research within the Arctic Regions from the Year 1818 to the Present Time*. New York: Harper and Brothers.

Bascon, William, 1969, *The Yoruba of Southwestern Nigeria*. New York: Holt, Rinehart and Winston.

Basham, Richard, 1978, *Urban Anthropology*. Palo Alto, Calif.: Mayfield.

Basso, Keith H., 1970, *The Cibecue Apache*. New York: Holt, Rinehart and Winston.

Bates, Marston, 1958, *Gluttons and Libertines: Human Problems of Being Natural*. New York: Vintage Books.

Bateson, Gregory, 1972, *Steps to an Ecology of Mind*. San Francisco: Chandler.

———, and Margaret Mead, 1942, *Balinese Character, a Photographic Analysis*. Special publications of the New York Academy of Sciences, Vol. II. New York: The Academy.

Beals, Alan R., 1962, *Gopalpur, a South Indian Village*. New York: Holt, Rinehart and Winston.

———, 1974, *Village Life in South India: Cultural Design and Environmental Variation*. Chicago: Aldine.

———, and Bernard J. Siegel, 1966, *Divisiveness and Social Conflict, an Anthropological Approach*. Stanford, Calif.: Stanford University Press.

Beals, Ralph L., Harry Hoijer, and Alan R. Beals, 1977, *An Introduction to Anthropology*. 5th ed. New York: Macmillan.

Beattie, John, 1960, *Bunyoro, an African Kingdom*. New York: Holt, Rinehart and Winston.

Beidelman, T. O., 1971, *The Kaguru: a Matrilineal People of East Africa*. New York: Holt, Rinehart and Winston.

Benedict, Ruth, 1934, *Patterns of Culture*. Boston: Houghton Mifflin.

———, 1946, *The Chrysanthemum and the Sword*. Boston: Houghton Mifflin.

Bennett, John W., 1969, *Northern Plainsmen, Adaptive Strategy and Agrarian Life*. Chicago: Aldine.

———, 1976, *The Ecological Transition*. Oxford: Pergamon.

Berlin, Brent, and Paul Kay, 1969, *Basic Color Terms: Their Universality and Evolution*. Berkeley: University of California Press.

Berry, Brewton, 1969, *Almost White*. London: Collier-Macmillan.

Bettelheim, Bruno, 1954, *Symbolic Wounds: Puberty Rites and the Envious Male*. Glencoe, Ill.: Free Press.

Birdsell, Joseph, 1968, Some predictions for the Pleistocene based on equilibrium systems among recent hunter-gatherers, in *Man the Hunter*, Richard B. Lee and Irven DeVore, eds. Chicago: Aldine.

———, 1975, *Human Evolution: an Introduction to the New Physical Anthropology*. Skokie, Ill.: Rand McNally.

Bloomfield, Leonard, 1933, *Language,* New York: Henry Holt and Co.

Boas, Franz, 1948, The limitations of the comparative method of anthropology, in *Race, Language and Culture*. New York: Macmillan (Paper read at meeting of AAAS at Buffalo, first printed in *Science*, N.S. Vol. 4, 1896, 901–908.)

Bodmer, Walter F., and Luigi Luca Cavalli-Sforza, 1970, Intelligence and race, *Scientific American*, October 1970, pp. 19–29.

Bohannan, Paul, 1963, *Social Anthropology*. New York: Holt, Rinehart and Winston.

———, 1967, *Law and Warfare*. Garden City, N.Y.: Natural History Press.

———, and Mark Glazer, 1973, *High Points in Anthropology*. New York: Random House.

Boissevain, Jeremy F., 1969, *Hal-Farrug: A Village in Malta*. New York: Holt, Rinehart and Winston.

———, 1974, *Friends of Friends: Networks, Manipulators and Coalitions*. Oxford: Blackwell.

Bordes, Francois, 1968, *The Old Stone Age*. New York: McGraw-Hill.

Bowen, Elenore Smith, 1954, *Return to Laughter*. New York: Harper & Row.

Brim, John A., and David H. Spain, 1974, *Research Design in Anthropology: Paradigms and Pragmatics in Testing of Hypotheses*. Studies in Anthropological Methods. New York: Holt, Rinehart and Winston.

Brown, Judith K., 1963, A cross-cultural study of female initiation rites. *American Anthropologist* 65:837–853.

Bruner, Edward, 1961, Urbanization and ethnic identity in North Sumatra. *American Anthropologist* 63:508–521.

Buchler, Ira R., and Henry A. Selby, 1968, *Kinship and Social Organization*. New York: Macmillan.

Butzer, Karl W., 1971, *Environment and Archaeology: an Ecological Approach to Prehistory*. Chicago: Aldine-Atherton.

Campbell, Bernard G., 1974, *Human Evolution: An Introduction to Man's Adaptations*, 2nd ed. Chicago: Aldine.

————, 1976, *Humankind Emerging*. Boston: Little, Brown.

Casagrande, Joseph B., ed., 1960, *In the Company of Man: Twenty Portraits of Anthropological Informants*. New York: Harper & Row.

Chagnon, Napolean A., 1968, *Yanomamo: The Fierce People*. New York: Holt, Rinehart and Winston.

————, 1974, *Studying the Yanomamo*. Studies in Anthropological Methods. New York: Holt, Rinehart and Winston.

Chance, Norman A., 1966, *The Eskimo of North Alaska*. New York: Holt, Rinehart and Winston.

Chiñas, Beverly L., 1973, *The Isthmus Zapotecs: Women's Roles in Cultural Context*. New York: Holt, Rinehart and Winston.

Chomsky, Noam, 1966, *Syntactic Structure*, Paris: Mouton.

Clark, J. Desmond, 1970, *The Prehistory of Africa*. New York: Praeger.

Clark, Virginia, Paul A. Escholz, and Alfred A. Rosa, eds., 1972, *Language: Introductory Readings*. New York: St. Martin's Press.

Clifton, James A., ed., 1970, *Applied Anthropology: Readings in the Uses of the Science of Man*. Boston: Houghton Mifflin.

Cohen, Abner P., 1974, *Two-dimensional Man: An Essay on the Anthropology of Power and Symbolism in Complex Societies*. London: Routledge and Kegan Paul.

Cohen, Ronald, and John Middleton, eds., 1967, *Comparative Political Systems*. Garden City, N.Y.: Natural History Press.

Cohen, Yehudi, 1964, *The Transition from Childhood to Adolescence*. Chicago: Aldine.

Collier, John, Jr., 1967, *Visual Anthropology: Photography as a Research Method*. New York: Holt, Rinehart and Winston.

————, 1973, *Alaskan Eskimo Education*. New York: Holt, Rinehart and Winston.

Colson, Elizabeth, 1953, *The Makah Indians: A Study of an Indian Tribe in Modern American Society*. Minneapolis: University of Minnesota Press.

Daner, Francine Jeanne, 1976, *The American Children of Krishna: A Study of the Hare Krisna Movement*. New York: Holt, Rinehart and Winston.

Deng, Francis Mading, 1972, *The Dinka of the Sudan*. New York: Holt, Rinehart and Winston.

Dennis, Wayne, 1940, *The Hopi Child*. New York: Appleton-Century-Crofts (for the Institute for Research in the Social Sciences, University of Virginia, Institute Monograph No. 26).

Dentan, Robert Knox, 1968, *The Semai: A Nonviolent People of Malaya*. New York: Holt, Rinehart and Winston.

————, 1979, *The Semai: A Nonviolent People of Malaya*. CSCA Fieldwork edition. New York: Holt, Rinehart and Winston.

DeVore, Irven, ed., 1965, *Primate Behavior: Field Studies of Monkeys and Apes*. New York: Holt, Rinehart and Winston.

Diamond, Norma, 1969, *K'un Shen: A Taiwan Village*. New York: Holt, Rinehart and Winston.

Dorn, Harold F., 1962, World population growth: an international dilemma. *Science*, 135:283–290.

Dougherty, Molly C., 1978, *Becoming a Woman in Rural Black Society.* New York: Holt, Rinehart and Winston.

Doughty, Charles M., 1937, *Travels in Arabia Deserta*, 2 vols. New York: Random House. (First published 1888; British ed., 1 vol., 1926.)

Downs, James F., 1966, *The Two Worlds of the Washo.* New York: Holt, Rinehart and Winston.

———, 1972, *The Navajo.* New York: Holt, Rinehart and Winston.

Dozier, Edward P., 1966, *Hano: A Tewa Indian Community in Arizona.* New York: Holt, Rinehart and Winston.

Dubois, Abbe J. A., 1947, *Hindu Manners, Customs and Ceremonies*, 3rd ed. by Henry K. Beauchamp. (First published in 1897.) Oxford: Clarendon Press.

DuBois, Cora, 1961, *The People of Alor: A Social-Psychological Study of an East Indian Island.* (First published in 1944 by the University of Minnesota Press.) New York: Harper Torchbooks.

Durkheim, Emile, 1912, *Les Formes Élémentairs de la Vie Religieuse.* Paris: Librairie Felix Alcan.

———, 1961, *The Elementary Forms of the Religious Life.* Trans. by Joseph Ward Swain. New York: Macmillan.

———, and Marcel Mauss, 1963, *Primitive Classification.* Trans. by Rodney Needham. Chicago: University of Chicago Press. (First published in French, 1903.)

Dyk, Walter, 1967, *Son of Old Man Hat: A Navajo Autobiography.* Lincoln: University of Nebraska Press. (First published in 1938.)

Dyson-Hudson, Rada, and Neville Dyson-Hudson, 1969, Subsistence herding in Uganda. *Scientific American*, February 1969, pp. 76–89.

Edelman, Murray, 1971, *Politics as Symbolic Action, Mass Arousal and Quiescence.* New York: Academic Press.

———, 1977 *Political Language: Words That Succeed and Policies That Fail.* New York: Academic Press.

Ehrlich, Paul R., and Anne H. Ehrlich, 1972, *Population Resources, Environment: Issues in Human Ecology*, 2nd ed. San Francisco: W. H. Freeman.

Eibl-Eibesfeldt, Irenäus, 1970, *Ethology: The Biology of Behavior.* Trans. by Erich Klinghammer. New York: Holt, Rinehart and Winston.

Ekvall, Robert B., 1968, *Fields on the Hoof: Nexus of Tibetan Nomadic Pastoralism.* New York: Holt, Rinehart and Winston.

Elwin, Verrier, 1950, *Bondo Highlander: Bombay.* London: Oxford University Press.

———, 1955, *The Religion of an Indian Tribe.* London: Oxford University Press.

Erikson, Erik H., 1950, *Childhood and Society.* New York: Norton.

Fagan, Brian, 1977, *People of the Earth*, 2nd ed. Boston, Mass.: Little, Brown.

Fichter, Joseph H., S.J., 1964, *Parochial School: A Sociological Study.* New York: Anchor Books.

Firth, Raymond, 1963, *We, the Tikopia: A Sociological Study of Kinship in Primitive Polynesia.* Abridged by the author with a new introduction. Boston: Beacon Press. (First published in 1936 by George Allen & Unwin Ltd., 2d ed., 1957.)

Foerster, Heinz von, Patricia M. Mora, and L. W. Amiot, 1960, Doomsday: Friday 13 November, A.D. 2026, *Science*, 132:1291–1295.

Foster, George, 1962, *Traditional Cultures and the Impact of Technological Change.* New York: Harper & Row.

——, 1972, The anatomy of envy: a study in symbolic behavior, *Current Anthropology*, 13(2):165–186.

Fox, Robin, 1967, *Kinship and Marriage.* Baltimore: Penguin Books.

Frake, Charles O., 1964. Notes on queries in ethnography, in *Transcultural Studies in Cognition.* American Anthropological Association special publication, A. Kimball Romney and Roy G. D'Andrade, eds. *American Anthropologist*, 66 (6, Pt. 2):132–145.

Frantz, Charles, 1972, *The Student Anthropologist's Handbook.* Cambridge, Mass.: Schenkman.

Freilich, Morris, 1970, *Marginal Natives: Anthropologists at Work.* New York: Harper & Row.

Friedl, Ernestine, 1962, *Vasilika, a Village in Modern Greece.* New York: Holt, Rinehart and Winston.

——, 1964, Lagging emulation in post-peasant society. *American Anthropologist*, 66:564–586.

——, 1973, *Women and Men: An Anthropologist's View.* New York: Holt, Rinehart and Winston. Basic Anthropology Units.

Fürer-Haimendorf, Christoph von, 1956, *Himalayan Barbary.* New York: Abelard-Schuman.

——, 1969, *The Konyak Nagas: An Indian Frontier Tribe.* New York: Holt, Rinehart and Winston.

Gaeng, Paul A., 1971, *Introduction to the Principles of Language.* New York: Harper & Row.

Galt, Anthony H., and Larry J. Smith, 1976, *Models and the Study of Social Change.* New York: Wiley.

Gamst, Frederick, 1969, *The Qemant: A Pagan-Hebraic Peasantry of Ethiopia.* New York: Holt, Rinehart and Winston.

Garbarino, Merwyn S., 1977, *Sociocultural Theory in Anthropology: a Short History.* New York: Holt, Rinehart and Winston. Basic Anthropology Units.

Gay, John, and Michael Cole, 1967, *The New Mathematics and an Old Culture.* New York: Holt, Rinehart and Winston.

Gleason, Henry Allan, 1961, *An Introduction to Descriptive Linguistics*, rev. ed. New York: Holt, Rinehart and Winston.

Gluckman, Max, 1965, *Politics, Law and Ritual in Tribal Society.* Chicago: Aldine.

Goffman, Erving, 1967, *Interaction Ritual.* Chicago: Aldine.

Golde, Peggy, ed., 1970, *Women in the Field.* Chicago: Aldine.

Goodenough, Ward Hunt, 1963, *Cooperation in Change.* New York: Russell Sage Foundation.

Graburn, Nelson, ed., 1971, *Readings in Kinship and Social Structure.* New York: Harper & Row.

Green, M. M., 1964, *Ibo Village Affairs.* New York: Frederick A. Praeger. (First published in 1947.)

Greenberg, Joseph H., 1968, *Anthropological Linguistics: An Introduction.* New York: Random House.

Grindal, Bruce, 1972, *Growing Up in Two Worlds: Education and Transition among the Sisala of Northern Ghana.* New York: Holt, Rinehart and Winston.

Grinnell, G. B., 1923, *The Cheyenne Indians*. Vol. I. New Haven, Conn.: Yale University Press.

Gudschinsky, Sarah C., 1967, *How to Learn an Unwritten Language*. New York: Holt, Rinehart and Winston.

Gumperz, John J., and Dell Hymes, eds., 1964, *The Ethnography of Communication*. American Anthropological Association special publication. *American Anthropologist* 66 (6, Pt. 2).

Hall, Edward T., 1961, *The Silent Language*. New York: Fawcett.

Hammel, E. A., ed., 1965, *Formal Semantic Analysis*. American Anthropological Association special publication. *American Anthropologist*, 67 (No. 5, Pt. 2).

Hamnett, Ian, 1975, *Chieftainship and Legitimacy: An Anthropological Study of Executive Law in Lesotho*. Boston Mass.: Routledge and Kegan Paul.

Hanks, Lucien M., 1972, *Rice and Man: Agricultural Ecology in Southeast Asia*. Chicago: Aldine.

Hanson, F. Allan, 1975, *Meaning in Culture*: Boston, Mass.: Routledge and Kegan Paul.

Hardesty, D. L., 1978, *Ecological Anthropology*. New York: Wiley.

Harris, Marvin, 1971, *Culture, Man, and Nature*. New York: Thomas Y. Crowell.

Hart, C. W. M., and Arnold R. Pilling, 1960, *The Tiwi of North Australia*. New York: Holt, Rinehart and Winston.

———, 1979, *The Tiwi of North Australia*. New York: Holt, Rinehart and Winston. CSCA Fieldwork Edition.

Hays, H. R., 1964, *From Ape to Angel*. New York: Capricorn Books. (First published, 1958.)

Heider, Karl, G., 1970, *The Dugum Dani: A Papuan Culture in the Highlands of West New Guinea*. New York: Wenner-Gren Foundation for Anthropological Research, Inc.

———, *Dani: Grand Valley Peaceful Warrior*. New York: Holt, Rinehart and Winston, 1979.

Heilbroner, Robert L., 1961, *The Worldly Philosophers*, rev. ed. New York: Simon & Schuster.

Henry, Jules, 1963, *Culture Against Man*. New York: Random House.

Herskovits, Melville J, and Frances S. Herskovits, 1934, *Rebel Destiny among the Bush Negroes af Dutch Guiana*. New York: McGraw-Hill.

Hitchcock, John T., 1965, *The Magars of Banyan Hill*. New York: Holt, Rinehart and Winston.

Hockett, Charles F., 1973, *Man's Place in Nature*. New York: McGraw-Hill.

Hoebel, Edward Adamson, 1960, *The Cheyennes, Indians of the Great Plains*. New York: Holt, Rinehart and Winston.

———, 1978, *The Cheyennes*, 2nd ed. New York: Holt, Rinehart and Winston.

Hogbin, Ian, 1964, *A Guadalcanal Society: The Kaoka Speakers*. New York: Holt, Rinehart and Winston.

Horowitz, Michael M., 1967, *Morne-Paysan: Peasant Village in Martinique*. New York: Holt, Rinehart and Winston.

Hudson, A. B., 1972, *Padju Epat: The Ma'anyan of Indonesian Borneo*. New York: Holt, Rinehart and Winston.

Hunter, Monica (see also Wilson, Monica), 1936, *Reaction to Conquest*. London: International Institute of African Languages and Cultures, Oxford University Press.

Jarvie, Ian C., 1972, *The Story of Social Anthropology; The Quest to Understand Human Society*. New York: McGraw-Hill.

Jay, Phyllis C., ed., 1968, *Primates: Studies in Adaptation and Variability*. New York: Holt, Rinehart and Winston.

Jocano, F. Landa, 1969, *Growing Up in a Philippine Barrio*. New York: Holt, Rinehart and Winston.

Jolly, Allison, 1972, *The Evolution of Primate Behavior*. New York: Macmillan.

Jones, E., 1972, *Sanapia: Comanche Medicine Woman*. New York: Holt, Rinehart and Winston.

Kaplan, David, and Robert A. Manners, 1972, *Cultural Theory*. Englewood Cliffs, N.J.: Prentice-Hall. Foundations of Modern Anthropology Seres.

Kardiner, Abram, and Edward Preble, 1961, *They Studied Man*. New York: World.

Kearney, Michael, 1972, *The Winds of Ixtepeji: World View and Society in a Zapotec Town*. New York: Holt, Rinehart and Winston.

Keiser, R. Lincoln, 1969, *Vice Lords: Warriors of the Streets*. New York: Holt, Rinehart and Winston.

———, 1979, *The Vice Lords: Warriors of the Streets*. New York: Holt, Rinehart and Winston. CSCA Fieldwork Edition.

Kennard, E. A., 1937, Hopi reactions to death. *American Anthropologist*, 39: 491–496.

Kennedy, John G., 1978, *Tarahumara of the Sierra Madre: Beer, Ecology and Social Organization*. Arlington Heights, Ill.: AHM Publishing Corp.

Kimball, Solon T., and Jacquetta Burnett, eds., 1973, *Learning and Culture*. Seattle: University of Washington Press.

King, Al Richard, 1967, *The School of Mopass: A Problem of Identity*. New York: Holt, Rinehart and Winston.

Klima, George J., 1970, *The Barabaig: East African Cattle-Herders*. New York: Holt, Rinehart and Winston.

Kluckhohn, Clyde, 1949, The philosophy of the Navajo Indians, in *Ideological Differences and World Order*, F. S. C. Northrop, ed. New Haven, Conn.: Published for the Viking Fund by Yale University Press.

Kochman, Thomas, 1971, 'Rapping' in the black ghetto, in *Conformity and Conflict*, James P. Spradley and David W. McCurdy, eds. Boston: Little, Brown.

Kramer, Samuel N., 1959, *History Begins at Sumer*. Garden City, N.Y.: Doubleday. (First published in 1956.)

Kroeber, A. L., and Clyde Kluckhohn, 1963, *Culture, A Critical Review of Concepts and Definitions*. New York: Vintage Books. (First published in 1952.)

Kummer, Hans, 1968, *Social Organization of Hamadryas Baboons*. Chicago: University of Chicago Press.

———, 1971, *Primate Societies: Group Techniques of Ecological Adaptation*. Chicago: Aldine-Atherton.

———, 1971, *Bibliography of Primate Studies*.

Kuper, Hilda, 1963, *The Swazi, a South African Kingdom*. New York: Holt, Rinehart and Winston.

Lamb, Sidney M., 1964, The semenic approach to structural semantics, in *Transcultural Studies in Cognition*. American Anthropological Association special publication, A. Kimball Romney and Roy Goodwin D'Andrade, eds. *American Anthropologist*, 66(Pt. 2):57–78.

Lancaster, Jane B., 1975, *Primate Behavior and the Emergence of Human Culture.* New York: Holt, Rinehart and Winston.

Langness, L. L., 1965, *The Life History in Anthropological Science.* New York: Holt, Rinehart and Winston.

Lantis, Margaret, 1960, Eskimo childhood and interpersonal relationships: Nunivak biographies and genealogies. The American Ethnological Society, Verne F. Ray, ed. Seattle: University of Washington Press.

Lee, Richard B., and Irven DeVore, eds., 1969, *Man the Hunter.* Chicago: Aldine.

Leighton, Dorothea, and Clyde Kluckhohn, 1947, *Children of the People.* Cambridge, Mass.: Harvard University Press.

Leis, Philip, 1972, *Enculturation and Socialization in an Ijaw Society.* New York: Holt, Rinehart and Winston.

Lerner, I. Michael, 1968, *Heredity, Evolution and Society.* San Francisco: W. H. Freeman.

Lessa, William, 1966, *Ulithi: A Micronesian Design for Living.* New York: Holt, Rinehart and Winston.

————, and Evon Z. Vogt, 1965, *Reader in Comparative Religion: An Anthropological Approach*, 2nd ed. New York: Harper & Row.

Lewis, Oscar, 1951, *Life in a Mexican Village: Tepoztlán Restudied.* Urbana: University of Illinois Press.

————, 1960, *Tepoztlán: Village in Mexico.* New York: Holt, Rinehart and Winston.

Linton, Ralph, ed., 1940, *Acculturation in Seven American Indian Tribes.* New York: D. Appleton-Century Company.

Loehlin, John C., Gardner Lindzey, and J. N. Spuhler, 1975, *Race Differences in Intelligence.* San Francisco: W. H. Freeman.

Lofland, John, 1975, *Doing Social Life: The Qualitative Study of Human Interaction in Natural Settings.* Somerset, N.J.: Wiley-Interscience.

Lorimer, Frank, 1954, *Cultural and Human Fertility.* (With special contributions by Meyer Fortes, K. A. Busia, Audrey I. Richards, Priscilla Reining, and Giorgio Mortara.) Paris: UNESCO.

Lowie, Robert H., 1956, *The Crow Indians.* New York: Holt, Rinehart and Winston (First Edition published in 1935.)

McFee, Malcolm, 1972, *Modern Blackfeet: Montanans on a Reservation.* New York: Holt, Rinehart and Winston.

MacGregor, Gordon, 1946, *Warriors without Weapons.* Chicago: University of Chicago Press.

Madsen, William, 1964, *The Mexican-Americans of South Texas.* New York: Holt, Rinehart and Winston.

Malinowski, Bronislaw, 1955, *Magic, Science and Religion and Other Essays.* New York: Anchor Books. (First published in 1925.)

————, 1961, *Argonauts of the Western Pacific: An Account of Native Enterprise and Adventure in the Archipelagoes of Melanesian New Guinea.* New York: Dutton. (First published in 1922.)

————, 1967, *A Diary in the Strict Sense of the Term.* New York: Harcourt Brace Jovanovich.

Malthus, Thomas Robert, 1965, *First Essay on Population, 1798.* New York: A. M. Kelley. (First published in 1798.)

Mandelbaum, David G., 1941, Culture change among the Nilgiri tribes. *American Anthropologist*, 43:19–26.

————, 1960, A reformer of his people (South India), in *In the Company of Man: Twenty Portraits of Anthropological Informants.* New York: Harper & Row.

Maranda, Pierre, 1972, *Introduction to Anthropology: A Self-Guide.* Englewood Cliffs, N.J.: Prentice-Hall.

Masters, John, 1958, *Bugles and a Tiger.* New York: Bantam Books. (First published in 1956.)

Mead, Margaret, 1949, *Coming of Age in Samoa: A Psychological Study of Primitive Youth for Western Civilization.* New York: Mentor Books. (First published in 1928.)

————, 1950, *The School in American Culture.* Cambridge, Mass.: Harvard University Press.

————, 1953, *Growing Up in New Guinea.* New York: Mentor Books (First published in 1930.)

————, 1956, *New Lives for Old.* New York: Morrow.

Meggers, Betty J., 1971, *Amazonia: Man and Culture in a Counterfeit Paradise.* Chicago: Aldine-Atherton.

Messenger, John Cowan, 1969, *Inis Beag: Isle of Ireland.* New York: Holt, Rinehart and Winston.

Metzger, Duane, and Gerald E. Williams, 1963, A formal ethnographic analysis of Tenejapa ladino weddings. *American Anthropologist*, 65:1076–1101.

Middleton, John, 1965, *The Lugbara of Uganda.* New York: Holt, Rinehart and Winston.

Modiano, Nancy, 1973, *Indian Education in the Chiapas Highlands.* New York: Holt, Rinehart and Winston.

Montagu, Ashley, ed., 1969, *The Concept of Race.* London: Collier-Macmillan.

Mooney, James, 1896, *The Ghost Dance Religion and the Sioux Outbreak of 1890.* Fourteenth Annual Report, Part 2, Bureau of American Ethnology. Washington, D.C.

Moore, Sally Falk, 1978, *Law as Process: Anthropological Essays.* Boston, Mass.: Routledge and Kegan Paul.

Murphy. Robert, 1961, Deviancy and social control I: What makes Biboi run? *The Kroeber Anthropological Society Papers*, 24:55–61.

————, and Julian Steward, 1956, Tappers and trappers: parallel process in acculturation, in *Economic Development and Culture Change*, Vol. 4, No. 4, 335–355. (Research Center in Economic Development and Culture Change, University of Chicago.)

Myrdal, Gunnar, 1944, *An American Dilemma: The Negro Problem and Modern Democracy.* New York: Harper & Row.

Nadel, Siegried F., 1954, *Nupe Religion.* New York: The Free Press of Glencoe.

Nader, Laura, ed., 1965, *The Ethnography of Law.* American Anthropological Association special publication. *American Anthropologist*, Vol 67, No. 6, Pt. 2.

————, 1968, *Law in Culture and Society.* Chicago: Aldine.

Netting, Robert M., 1968, *Hill Farmers of Nigeria: Cultural Ecology of the Kofyar of the Jos Plateau.* Seattle: University of Washington Press.

————, 1977, *Cultural Ecology.* Menlo Park: Cummings.

Newman, Philip L., 1965, *Knowing the Gururumba.* New York: Holt, Rinehart and Winston.

Niehoff, Arthur H., ed., 1966, *A Casebook of Social Change.* Chicago: Aldine.

Norbeck, Edward, 1976, *Changing Japan*, 2nd ed. New York: Holt, Rinehart and Winston.

Ogbu, John, 1978, *Minority Education and Caste: The American System in Cross-Cultural Perspective*. New York: Academic Press.

Parkman, Francis, 1950, *The Oregon Trail*. New York: New American Library. (First published in 1849.)

Parrington, Vernon Louis, 1927, *Main Currents in American Thought: An Interpretation of American Literature from the Beginnings to 1920*, Vol. I. New York: Harcourt, Brace.

Partridge, William L., 1973, *The Hippie Ghetto: T he Natural History of a Subculture*. New York: Holt, Rinehart and Winston.

Pelto, Pertti J., and Gretel H. Pelto, 1970, *Anthropological Research: The Structure of Inquiry*, 2nd ed. Cambridge: Cambridge University Press.

Peshkin, Alan, 1972, *Kanuri School Children: Education and Social Mobilization in Nigeria*. New York: Holt, Rinehart and Winston.

Pettit, George A., 1946, *Primitive Education in North America*. Publications in American Archeology and Ethnology, Vol. XLIII. Berkeley, Calif.: University of California Press.

Pfeiffer, John E., 1978, *The Emergence of Man*, 2nd ed. New York: Harper & Row.

———, 1977, *The Emergence of Society*. New York: McGraw-Hill.

Pitt-Rivers, J. A., 1961, *The People of the Sierra*. Chicago: Phoenix Books, University of Chicago Press.

Polgar, Steven, 1971, *Culture and Population: A Collection of Current Studies*. Chapel Hill, N.C.: Carolina Population Center.

Pospisil, Leopold J., 1978, *The Kapauku Papuans of West New Guinea*, 2nd ed. New York: Holt, Rinehart and Winston.

Quintana, Bertha B., and Lois Gray Floyd, 1972, *Que Gitano! Gypsies of Southern Spain*. New York: Holt, Rinehart and Winston.

Rappaport, Roy A., 1967, *Pigs for the Ancestors: Ritual in the Ecology of a New Guinea People*. New Haven, Conn.: Yale University Press.

Rasmussen, Knud, 1921, *Greenland by the Polar Sea: The Story of the Thule Expedition from Melville Bay to Cape Morris Jesup*. Trans. by Asta and Rowland Kenney. London: William Heinemann, Ltd.

———, 1929, *The Intellectual Culture of the Iglulik Eskimos*. (Report of the 5th Thule expedition 1921–24, Vol. VII, No. 1, W. Worster, trans.) Copenhagen: Gyldendal.

Read, Margaret, 1968, *Children of Their Fathers: The Ngoni of Malawi*. New York: Holt, Rinehart and Winston.

Redfield, Robert, 1930, *Tepoztlán: A Mexican Village*. Chicago: University of Chicago Press.

———, 1953, *The Primitive World and Its Transformation*. Ithaca, N.Y.: Cornell University Press.

———, 1962, *A Village That Chose Progress: Chan Kom Revisited*. Chicago: Phoenix Books, University of Chicago Press. (First published in 1950.)

Reichenbach, Hans, 1959, *The Rise of Scientific Philosophy*. Berkeley: University of California Press.

Rivière, Peter, 1972, *The Forgotten Frontier: Ranchers of North Brazil*. New York: Holt, Rinehart and Winston.

Rohner, Ronald P, and Evelyn C. Rohner, 1970, *The Kwakiutl Indians of British Columbia*. New York: Holt, Rinehart and Winston.

Romney, A. Kimball, and Roy Goodwin D'Andrade, 1964, Cognitive aspects of English kin terms, in *Transcultural Studies in Cognition*, American Anthropological Association special publication, A. Kimball Romney and Roy G. D'Andrade, eds. *American Anthropologist*, Vol. 66, No. 3, Pt. 2:253.

Rosenfeld, Gerry, 1971, *"Shut Those Thick Lips": A Study in Slum School Failure*. New York: Holt, Rinehart and Winston.

Ross, John, 1819, *A Voyage of Discovery*. London: John Murray.

Sahlins, Marshall D., 1962, *Moala: Culture and Nature on a Fijian Island*. Ann Arbor: University of Michigan Press.

———, 1976, *Culture and Practical Reason*. Chicago: University of Chicago Press.

Salaman, R. N. 1952, The social influence of the potato. *Scientific American*, December 1952.

Sanders, Irwin T., 1949, *Balkan Village*. Lexington: University of Kentucky Press.

Saltman, Michael, 1978, *The Kipsigis, a Case Study in Changing Customary Law*. Edison, N.J.: Transaction Books.

Sapir, Edward, 1921, *Language*. New York: Harcourt, Brace.

Schaller, George B., 1963, *The Mountain Gorilla—Ecology and Behavior*. Chicago: University of Chicago Press.

Schärer, Hans, 1963, *Ngaju Religion: The Conception of God among a South Borneo People*. Trans. by Rodney Needham. The Hague: Martinus Nijhoff.

Schultz, J. W., 1956, *My Life as an Indian*. New York: Fawcett.

Schusky, Ernest L., 1972, *Manual for Kinship Analysis*, 2nd ed. New York: Holt, Rinehart and Winston.

Seeley, J. R., R. A. Sim, and E. W. Loosley, 1963, *Crestwood Heights: A Study of the Culture of Surburban Life*. New York: Wiley.

Service, Elman R., 1971, *Primitive Social Organization*, 2nd ed. New York: Random House.

Shapiro, Harry L., 1962, *The Heritage of the Bounty*, 2nd ed., rev. New York: Natural History Library, Anchor Books.

Simmons, Leo W., ed., 1966, *Sun Chief: The Autobiography of a Hopi Indian*. New Haven: Yale University Press. (First published in 1942.)

Simmons, William S., 1971, *Eyes of the Night: Witchcraft among a Senegalese People*. Boston: Little, Brown.

Singleton, John, 1967, *Nichu: A Japanese School*. New York: Holt, Rinehart and Winston.

Spicer, Edward H., ed., 1962, *Cycles of Conquest: The Impact of Spain, Mexico, and the United States on the Indians of the Southwest, 1533–1960*. Tucson: University of Arizona Press.

Spier, Robert F. G., 1970, *From the Hand of Man: Primitive and Preindustrial Technologies*. Boston: Houghton Mifflin.

Spindler, George D., 1955, Education in a Transforming American Culture, *Harvard Educational Review*, 20(3):144–156.

———, 1958, New trends and applications in anthropology, in *New Viewpoints in the Social Sciences*, Roy A. Price, ed. Washington, D.C.: Twenty-Eighth Yearbook of the National Council for the Social Studies.

———, ed., 1970, *Being an Anthropologist: Fieldwork in Eleven Cultures*. New York: Holt, Rinehart and Winston.

———, 1973, *Burgbach: Urbanization and Identity in a German Village*. New York: Holt, Rinehart and Winston.

———, and Louise Spindler, 1971, *Dreamers without Power: The Menomini Indians*. New York: Holt, Rinehart and Winston.

Spindler, Louise S., 1962, Menomini women and culture change. *American Anthropologist*, Memoir 91, Vol. 64, No. 1, Part 2.

———, 1971, *Culture Change and Modernization: Mini-Models and Case Studies*. New York: Holt, Rinehart and Winston.

Spiro, Melford, 1958, *Children of the Kibbutz*. Cambridge, Mass.: Harvard University Press.

Spock, Benjamin, 1957, *Baby and Child Care*. New York: Pocket Books. (First published in 1946.)

Spooner, Brian, 1972, *Population Growth: Anthropological Implications*. Cambridge, Mass.: MIT Press.

Spradley, James P. and David W. McCurdy, 1972, *The Cultural Experience: Ethnography in Complex Society*. Chicago: Science Research Associates.

Stephens, John L., 1867, *Incidents of Travel in Central America, Chiapas, and Yucatan*. 2 vols. New York: Harper & Row. (First published in 1841.)

Struever, Stuart, ed., 1971, *Prehistoric Agriculture*. Garden City, N.Y.: Natural History Press.

Sturtevant, William C., 1964, Studies in Ethnoscience, in *Transcultural Studies in Cognition*, A. Kimball Romney and Ray Goodwin D'Andrade, eds. American Anthropologist Special Publication 66(3): II, 99–131.

Sugarman, Barry, 1974, *Daytop Village: A Therapeutic Community*. New York: Holt, Rinehart and Winston.

Sutlive, Vinson H., Jr., 1978, *The Iban of Sarawak*. Arlington Heights, Ill.: AHM Publishing Corp.

Swartz, Marc J., Victor W. Turner, and Arthur Tuden, 1966, *Political Anthropology*. Chicago: Aldine.

Tacitus, 1960, Germania, in *Tacitus on Britain and Germany*. Trans. by H. Mattingly. Baltimore: Penguin Books. (First published in 1948.)

Tocqueville, Alexis de, 1960, *Democracy in America*, 2 vols. (The Henry Reeve text as revised by Francis Bowen now further corrected and edited with a historical essay, editorial notes, and bibliographies by Phillips Bradley.) New York: Vintage Books. (First published in France, 2 vols., 1835–1840.)

Tonkinson, Robert, 1978, *The Mardudjara Aborigines: Living the Dream in Australia's Desert*. New York: Holt, Rinehart and Winston. CSCA Fieldwork edition.

Turner, Paul R., 1972, *The Highland Chontal*. New York: Holt, Rinehart and Winston.

Tyler, Stephen A., ed., 1969, *Cognitive Anthropology*. New York: Holt, Rinehart and Winston.

Uchendu, Victor C., 1966, *The Igbo of Southeast Nigeria*. New York: Holt, Rinehart and Winston.

Van Gennep, Arnold, 1960, *The Rites of Passage*. Chicago: University of Chicago Press. (First published in 1909.)

Van Lawick-Goodall, Jane, 1968, The behavior of free-living chimpanzees in the Gombe Stream Reserve, *Animal Behavior Monographs*, 1(3):161–311.

———, 1971, *In the Shadow of Man*. Boston: Houghton-Mifflin.

Vogt, Evon Z., 1970, *The Zinacantecos of Mexico: A Modern Maya Way of Life.* New York: Holt, Rinehart and Winston.

Voth, H. R., 1901, *The Oraibi Powamu Ceremony.* Publication 61, Anthropological Series, III, 2. Chicago: Field Columbian Museum.

Wallace, Anthony F. C., 1956, Revitalization movements. *American Anthropologist*, 58:264–281.

———, 1972, *The Death and Rebirth of the Seneca.* New York: Vintage Books. (First published in 1969.)

Ward, Martha, 1971, *Them Children: A Study in Language Learning.* New York: Holt, Rinehart and Winston.

Warren, Richard, 1967, *Education in Rebhausen: A Gernam Village.* New York: Holt, Rinehart and Winston.

Watson, James D., 1969, *The Double Helix: A Personal Account of the Discovery of the Structure of DNA.* New York: New American Library. (First published in 1968.)

West, James, 1945, *Plainville, U.S.A.* New York: Columbia University Press.

Whiting, Beatrice B., 1963, *Child Rearing in Six Cultures.* New York: Wiley.

Whiting, John R., R. Kluckhohn, and A. Albert, 1958, The function of male initiation ceremonies at puberty, in *Readings in Social Psychology*, E. Maccoby, T. Newcomb, and E. Hartley, eds. New York: Holt, Rinehart and Winston.

Whyte, William Foote, 1955, *Street Corner Society:The Social Structure of an Italian Slum*, 2nd ed. Chicago: University of Chicago Press.

Williams, Mentor L., ed. 1956, *Schoolcraft's Indian Legends.* East Lansing: Michigan State University Press.

Williams, Thomas Rhys, 1965, *The Dusun: A North Borneo Society.* New York: Holt, Rinehart and Winston.

———, 1969, *A Borneo Childhood: Enculturation in Dusun Society.* New York: Holt, Rinehart and Winston.

Wilson, Monica (see also Hunter, Monica), 1963, *Good Company: A Study of Nyakusa Age-Villages.* (First published in 1951 by the Oxford University Press for the International African Institute.) Boston: Beacon Press.

Wiser, William H., and Charlotte Viall Wiser, 1963, *Behind Mud Walls, 1930–1960.* Berkeley: University of California Press.

Wolcott, Harry, 1967, *A Kwakiutl Village and School.* New York: Holt, Rinehart and Winston.

———, 1973, *The Man in the Principal's Office.* New York: Holt, Rinehart and Winston.

Wylie, Laurence, 1964, *Village in the Vaucluse: An Account of Life in a French Village.* New York: Harper & Row.

Young, Frank W., 1965, *Initiation Ceremonies: A Cross-cultural Study of Status Dramatization.* Indianapolis: Bobbs-Merrill.

Zahan, Dominique, 1960, *Sociétés d'initiation Bambara: le n'domo, le Korè.* Paris: Mouton.

INDEX

To make the index a more efficient tool, it has been prepared so that specific information is provided under three headings: one, authors and titles; another, cultures, peoples, and places; and a third, concepts and topics.

Cultures, Peoples, and Places

Concepts and Topics

CASE STUDIES IN EDUCATION AND CULTURE

GENERAL EDITORS

George and Louise Spindler

THE NEW MATHEMATICS AND AN OLD CULTURE:
A Study of Learning among the Kpelle of Liberia
>John Gay, *Cuttington College, Liberia*
>Michael Cole, *University of California, Irvine*

CHILDREN IN AMISH SOCIETY:
Socialization and Community Education
>*John A. Hostetler, Temple University*
>*Gertrude Enders Huntington*

THE SCHOOL AT MOPASS: A Problem of Identity
>*A. Richard King, Teachers College—Columbia*

KANURI SCHOOLCHILDREN:
Education and Social Mobilization in Nigeria
>*Alan Peshkin, University of Illinois*

"SHUT THOSE THICK LIPS!":
A Study of Slum School Failure
>*Gerry Rosenfeld, Hofstra University*

THEM CHILDREN: A Study in Language Learning
>*Martha C. Ward, Louisiana State University, New Orleans*

A KWAKIUTL VILLAGE AND SCHOOL
>*Harry F. Wolcott, University of Oregon*

THE MAN IN THE PRINCIPAL'S OFFICE: An Ethnography
>*Harry F. Wolcott, University of Oregon*

ALASKAN ESKIMO EDUCATION
A Film Analysis of Cultural Confrontation in the Schools
>*John Collier, Jr., California State University*

CASE STUDIES IN CULTURAL ANTHROPOLOGY
GENERAL EDITORS—George and Louise Spindler

* Fieldwork Edition